1968
UNITED STATES OLYMPIC BOOK

U.S. SECTION

© UNITED STATES OLYMPIC COMMITTEE

1969

GAMES OF THE
XIX OLYMPIAD
MEXICO CITY

X OLYMPIC
WINTER GAMES
GRENOBLE

V PAN-AMERICAN
GAMES
WINNIPEG

Prepared for The United States Olympic Committee, New York City.

Editor	Frederick Fliegner, Publisher, Lausanne—Stuttgart
Editing Staff and Translations	Merryl Brown, London Wolfgang Besser, New York Gideon Freud, London Edgar Joubert, Paris
Layout	Siegbert Hugger, Stuttgart
US-Section	Editor: Arthur G. Lentz, Executive Director, U.S. Olympic Committee Layout and Coordination Spencer Advertising Company, New York, N. Y. 10016 Copyright 1969, United States Olympic Committee, 57 Park Avenue, New York, N.Y. 10016

The assistance and cooperation of LIFE Magazine, New York City, in supplying the United States Olympic Committee with many of the photographs appearing in this book is sincerely appreciated.

Reproduction	Graphexpo Establishment, Vaduz (Lichtenstein) Rolf Gunther, Stuttgart (US-Section)
Setting	Belserdruck, Stuttgart (International Section) Maschinensetzerei Karl Lihs, Ludwigsburg (US-Section)
Printing	Offsetdruckerei Ludwig Raiber, Stuttgart
Typography	10/12 point Garamond 10/12 point italic Garamond 9/11 point Garamond 8/12 point Helvetica and Garamond (US-Section)
Paper	Original fine art printing paper, white, subst. 120 grs/sqm. Zanders Company, Bergisch-Gladbach, West Germany
	Unglazed, woodfree, white Offset-Werkdruck. subst. 100 grs/sqm., bulking 1.75 Papierfabrik Salach
Binding	Großbuchbinderei Franz Spiegel, Ulm/Donau

Copyright 1969 by International Olympic Editions Lausanne—Stuttgart, West Germany, P. O. Box 643

Printed in West Germany

CONTENTS TEXT SECTION

Mexico City

CONTENTS TEXT SECTION

CONTENTS TEXT SECTION

CONTENTS PICTURE SECTION

The arena in Grenoble lay bathed in friendly sunshine during the opening ceremony as the United States Olympic Team in attractive red jackets marched in accompanied by the strange and unaccustomed sounds of twelve-tone and electronic music. Terry McDermott, the famous speed skater from the USA, was happy to have the honor of carrying the Star-Spangled Banner in front of his comrades.

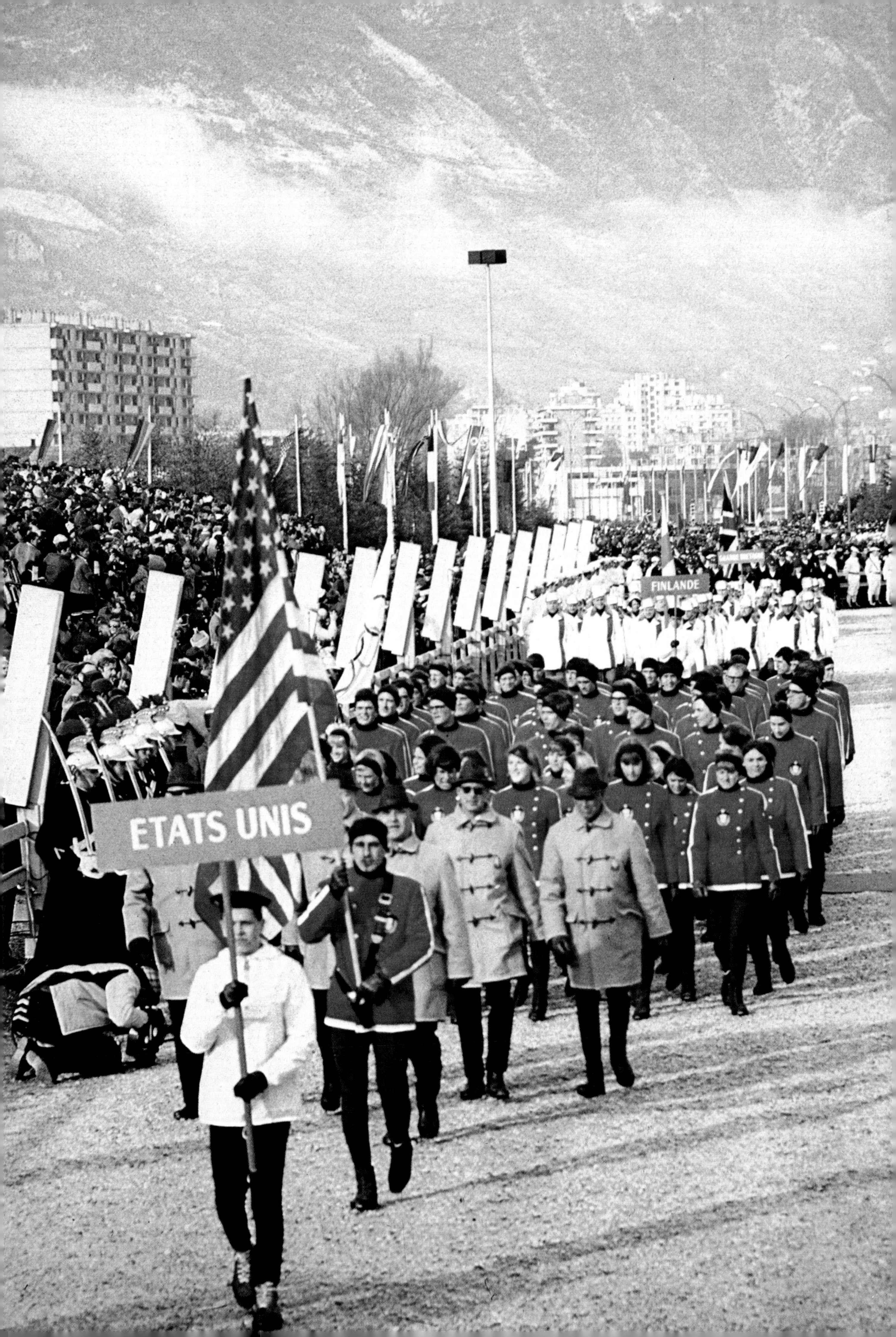
ETATS UNIS
FINLANDE

The United States Olympic Committee is pleased to present the 1968 United States Olympic Book, which reviews the stirring pageantry and athletic performance at the Games of the XIX Olympiad in Mexico City, the X Olympic Winter Games in Grenoble, and the V Pan-American Games in Winnipeg, with particular reference to the successful ventures of the teams which represented our nation in these greatest of international sports festivals.

Produced through special arrangement made with Editions Internationales Olympia, publisher of official books for the International Olympic Committee and other National Olympic Committees, the 1968 United States Olympic Book not only chronicles the respective deeds of our athletes but relates the full story of the Games themselves, along with appropriate reference pictorially and statistically to the achievements of competitors from all nations. Top sports writers from the United States and the best of European writers, each fully experienced in Olympic Games coverage and thoroughly conversant with the sport they describe, have contributed to this volume, thus providing a truly international theme.

For the first time, the inclusion of many action photographs in full color is possible because of the cooperative arrangements.

The United States Olympic Committee is extremely proud of the athletes who demonstrated excellence in the most rigorous of worldwide competition. Their dedication of purpose, their will-to-win, their self-discipline, and their willingness to sacrifice deserved the highest of rewards, and the ample harvest of medals testifies that their efforts were worth while.

The United States Olympic Committee gratefully acknowledges the generous support provided by the sports-loving public, the tremendous contribution by the nation's business and industrial leaders, and the heart-warming response by thousands of voluntary workers from our member organizations to our appeals for funds and manpower to discharge a myriad of responsibilities. Without this assistance, we could not have succeeded. With it, the United States teams reached their goals.

Douglas F. Roby

Douglas F. Roby
President,
United States Olympic Committee

Olympic House
57 Park Avenue
New York, New York 10016
United States Olympic Committee Headquarters

Above: During the imposing parade of the 111 teams, the large and impressive double block from the United States was greeted with admiration and respect by the 80,000 spectators. Self-assured happiness beams from the faces of the young men and women from the USA—they know that they represent the largest sporting nation in the world, as do their deserving leaders.

Right: The Olympic flags in Mexico City wave expectantly, waiting to receive the Olympic Flame on the opening day. These flags gave the Mexicans the certainty that the start of the biggest fiesta they had ever celebrated, was imminent. Flags and fire, choirs and fanfares accompanied the beginning of this wonderful festival.

Janice Romary, six times an Olympic fencer, carries the United States flag, the first USA woman athlete ever selected for this honor. (right)

In the Olympic stadium of Mexico City, colorful representatives of the Family of Man receive a joyous reception. The faces of the young athletes from the Soviet Union, Mexico and the USA mirror this joy. (left)

(Pictures on the following pages) Joy also conquers the many flag bearers, typically the man from Israel (upper right) and Abebe Bikila from Ethiopia, two-time marathon champion, as well as the athletes from Czechoslovakia (lower right) and Japan. Then, Enriqueta Basilio Sotelo, a 20-year-old daughter of a Mexican farmer, climbed like a gazelle the 92 stairs leading to the summit of the gigantic bowl. (picture on right overleaf) These were the last yards of road which Christopher Columbus had also travelled. She closed her eyes and lit the Olympic fire. The cheers of all Mexico engulfed the stadium in this shining hour. The world heard the elated heart-beat of the nation.

Smiling, relaxed and proud, the three men in the box of honor experience the thrills of this hour—from left to right President Ordaz, IOC President Avery Brundage, and Secretary General Pedro Ramirez Vazquez. The six Japanese girls bring with their Olympic flag the strange magic of the Far East into the stadium. The mayor of Tokyo, standing on the cyclamen-colored podium, hands the flag to the representatives of Mexico City, the Olympic city until 1972. Six Mexican girls in Spanish, Indian and Mexican costumes escort the flag from the stadium.

MIRO PROCHAZKA
"Start," Bratislava, Czechoslovakia

Prologue
to the Great
Encounter

For the first time in the history of the Olympics the youth of the world was summoned to the capital of a Latin-American country. It is 72 years since Pierre de Coubertin founded the modern Olympic Games in Europe—but in the meantime the Olympic Flame has been carried to the farthest corners of the earth; in 1956 it blazed in Australia, the island continent; in 1964 it was carried for the first time to Asia for the games in Tokyo; while way back in 1904 St. Louis was already the first North American city to receive the historic flame—Los Angeles followed in 1932.

And now Mexico City—the capital of one of the most progressive and liberal countries in Latin-America—has had the honor of welcoming the Olympic Flame. In the year 2000 this young and go-ahead state will have grown from a 45 million to a 100 million population. Up to 1968, the Olympic Games were never held at a height of more than 658 feet above sea-level—but Mexico City lies at 7,573 feet! The decision of the International Olympic Committee was a courageous step forward into a new and unknown dimension, a decision in favor of this unique people who have developed into a living, pulsating link between the United States and the rest of Latin-America. The youth of the world followed the summons to Mexico with passion and devotion. Never before has a whole nation turned the Olympics into a huge world-wide fiesta with such whole-hearted joy.

Several centuries ago Mexico was invaded by the Conquistadores from Europe; in 1968 came the peaceful invasion by the youth of the whole world. The first invasion changed the complete face of Mexico by force, but this time she was conquered by the peaceful weapons of ancient Greece—by beauty, magnanimity, peaceful contest and the triumphant laurels of sporting victories. And this modern Mexican conquest, the 1968 Olympics, was broadcast into the farthest corner of our divided world by the artificial planet, Telstar. For me, this Olympic festival was an experience of complete joy and unanimity with no consideration of political borders and systems.

I came to Mexico to find the peaceful and friendly youth of the world. And I not only found this genuine and happy youth with their Olympic ideals, I also found the heart of the whole charming Mexican nation. I left my home country after weeks of unrest, and in Mexico City I was conscious of the brotherhood of all the peoples of the world. Here in this "Olympia Mexicana" I could feel the fascination of the Olympic idea; I found my intuition confirmed, why all young people so passionately affirm and defend its free and humane ideal, infecting it again and again with their enthusiasm. In our world filled with force and technical perfection, the Olympic movement gives even the restless and revolutionary youth an answer from Hellas and Coubertin.

I saw the ceremonial under the cloudless skies of the "Holy City," Rome, I experienced the magnificent Alpine panorama at Innsbruck, I followed the mathematical exactness of Tokyo and heard the electronic heartbeats of the great Frenchman Alain Calmat in Grenoble. And I was anxious about the huge, eternally trembling heart of humanity because we Czechs feel we are the heart of Europe, but in the joyful opening ceremony and the splendid Olympic days in Mexico City, I shed my anxiety and became tranquil, thankful and happy.

For me, the Mexican Olympics began with a single quiet word. It was spoken by a small Mexican boy in the outskirts of the city: Olympia—Czechoslovakia! These Mexicans had invited the whole world to be their guests and they greeted us—from Prague, from Bratislava, from Brünn and Pilsen—with so much heart and friendliness that we all felt happy in the peace, the joy and the freedom of Olympia. Perhaps one day the huge strife-ridden world will become a peaceful Olympic village. Perhaps even in the world "Olympic village" all peoples will be able to live together without fear and hate. Frequently when I entered the Mexican Olympic village, filled with all the great Olympic events, I lingered by the statue of Miguel Hidalgo y Costilla, the great Mexican liberator. He fought a lifetime for freedom. I saw the flags and decorations, I heard the fanfares and felt respect during the ceremonies. And at the same time I was conscious in my heart—in unison with millions of others—of the

Flame which Prometheus brought from the gods of Olympia for the first time to the people in all the Olympic arenas. And I experienced here in Mexico the belief in the eternal Olympic fire and was happy.

The glittering procession of the opening ceremony in the Olympic stadium will remain just as unforgettable for me as the wonderful sunny days in the Aztec stadium, where the cultures of the sun and moon worshippers were united with modern architecture.

Between the Mexican spectators, I hourly received the impression that this Olympic festival could be a great mother-country for all peoples. I learned from these spectators that humanity isn't bad and that nobody and no nation in the world is alone and forsaken. I therefore felt grateful to the initiators of this festival, to the organizers, to the wonderful Olympic contestants and the thousands of nameless helpers. And I felt a tender thankfulness to "Queta," the Mexican farmer's daughter, Enriqueta Basilio Sotelo, who was the first woman in the history of the Olympics to ascend the flight of stairs leading to the bowl and light the Olympic fire with the torch which had travelled from the heart of Greece following the same route as Columbus.

JIM MURRAY
Los Angeles Times

Journalists Dish Out Olympic Pewter Medals

We only won one gold medal at Grenoble—or, as Shirley Povich of the Washington Post put it, the National Anthem had a shorter run than a clean play on Broadway—but take heart.

At my instigation, a colleague, John Hanlon, and I have decided to take up the slack and award a whole flock of medals to Olympians who distinguished themselves at the Games.

They won't be gold, they'll be pewter. They won't have the Latin Olympic insignia, "Altius, Citius, Fortius" for "higher, stronger, faster!" but rather the Latin words for "lower, weaker and slower" and, instead of a triumphant runner, they'll show a guy sneezing with a hot water bottle on his head, a frayed robe, thermometer in his mouth and skinny, hairy legs sticking in a tub of hot water. Here they are:

1. The first pewter goes to the journalist who can swear on the head of his mother he saw something of France besides a) the inside of his barracks room; b) the inside of a "lift" (a "lift" is an elevator that takes in floors one hour at a time); c) the inside of a lorry on the way to the mountains; d) the outside of a fog when he got there. Combined points are awarded to anyone who saw as much of Grenoble as from the door of a taxi to the head table at Rostang's Restaurant.

2. Pewter No. 2 goes to anyone who saw the sun before noon or longer than 1 o'clock in the afternoon.

3. A pewter goes to anyone who can show proof he was able to get a steak well done or a chicken he could swear did not die of leukemia. Since this is considered an unfair event—the only way to get a well-done steak in France is to be sure the cow was out in the sun before it was butchered—we will have a second prize, a plastic medal, for anyone who can bring an X-ray showing he does not have trichinosis or a Polaroid showing the center of his steak to be anything but purple.

4. A special pewter with oak leaf clusters goes to the male doctor who stopped the Russian girl from undressing in her male-female test and explained before she got to the half-slip that it was a litmus-paper test not an eye test. This award was hotly disputed by a jury which argued that he should not get a medal and produced a photo of the athlete to prove it. They felt that, since she had a moustache, his performance should be penalized for form and, as in free skating, his feat was not difficult enough for a high enough ordinal for a medal.

5. Avery Brundage gets a pewter for almost detonating the Winter Games and then

touching a torch and throwing gasoline on the already blazing Summer Olympics by a) decreeing the skiers could not show the naked trademarks of their skis, helmets or goggles—and in fact should not give their right name; b) by admitting South Africa. Avery is thus not only victorious in one event but in the combined as well. Avery also takes a commanding lead in the World Cup points for boycotting the Olympics as he has now passed Harry Edwards on the downhill timer in this event.

6. Any journalist who cajoled, stole or was otherwise able to get more than one towel in his two-week stay in the press center gets a pewter and both choruses of his national anthem. Disqualified are those who (a) sneaked down to the super marche with a dictionary and managed to purchase a dish towel big enough to dry oneself if you put it on a radiator after each 4 square inches, or (b) those who used the bedsheet. The form in this event calls for the contestant to stand over the radiator and slap himself vigorously after the bath. The same judges who examine the tracing in the skating compulsory figures examine the contestants in this event for severe chapping. Those who turn blue automatically qualify for the final run-off.

7. A special award goes to the French farmer who sensibly relieved a bladder problem in the center of town in Villard de Lans but nevertheless stood at attention as the French flag went by on a loaded bus. The fact that he smoked his pipe and waved at the same time makes this a combined event.

8. Karl Schranz gets either the Baron Munchausen Award or the Captain Dreyfus Award depending on whether you think he missed a gate or missed his calling—whether you think he should get another run at the hill or a job writing communiques for the Ministry of Truth in Russia.

9. The committee who put the luge run on a part of the Cote d'Azur gets a pewter medal (specially melted in honor of the occasion) as well as two permanently lacquered photos showing the luge run first as a one-mile fondue and later with salmon leaping up it.

10. The journalists and athletes get a special medal for drinking an official 60,000 Cokes a day with the great wines of France all around.

11. The French gendarmerie, 6,705 strong and drafted from all parts of France, get a special award for not arresting a single journalist, athlete or official, not even the combined bobsled teams at Alpe d'Huez who had protested at the firing of a "Bunny" just for falling in love with an Italian sledder. Come to think of it, the bobsled teams ought to get a medal, too, for registering their protest by carrying a Renault car into the lobby of the press center and leaving it there in everybody's way. France gets the Maurice Chevalier Medal because the girl was reinstated.

12. The people of Grenoble get a medal because, with the onslaught of 1,500 freeloading sportswriters, they now know what Parisians felt like when they saw the Germans marching under the Arc de Triomphe. It is to the villagers' credit they did not resort to blowing up lorries full of journalists, re-forming the Maquis or mining the approaches to the slopes. They also showed remarkable restraint in not standing on street corners and sobbing when they saw us marching in and should now be eligible for Marshall Plan funds to rebuild their economy.

13. And finally, the little school kids whose drawings decorated the rooms of the newsmen together with grave and touching bids of welcome and hopes for a pleasant Olympics get a very special salute. Their shining faces at all the events show that not for France was the money wasted. To give kids glowing, permanent memories of a gay two-week's party like that may be worth more than mere francs.

Although no official "audit" has been released by the Organizing Committee for the Games of the XIXth Olympiad, according to the statistics 109 nations of 113 filing official entries competed in the Summer Olympic Games.

Furthermore, entries were filed for 6,082 athletes (Beck and Pesthy of the USA were entered in both the modern pentathlon and fencing and thereby are counted as only two entries). Athletics (track and field) had the largest entry, 1,122—composed of 864 men and 258 women and also the largest number of nations filing entries, 89.

Listed numerically, with the number of men and women athletes for the larger delegations indicated in parentheses immediately after the total number of entries, the nations are:

UNITED STATES OF AMERICA 387 (292–95); USSR 329 (259–70); Mexico 300 (253–47).

West Germany 296 (251–45); East Germany 253 (212–41); Great Britain 237 (186–51); France 210 (178–32); Italy 201 (184–17). Hungary 190 (152–38); Japan 187 (158–29); Poland 186 (148–38); Canada 145 (117–28); Australia 136 (112–24); Spain 129 (127–2); Czechoslovakia 124 (96–28); Cuba 124 (108–16); The Netherlands 123 (96–27); Bulgaria 122 (111–11); Sweden 110 (94–16). Switzerland 93, Argentina 92, Belgium 88, Rumania 86, Brazil 85, Denmark 72, Yugoslavia 71, Finland 70, El Salvador 65, Puerto Rico 62, New Zealand 59, South Korea 58, Guatemala 53, Norway and The Philippines, 50 each.

Also Colombia and Greece, 48 each, Austria 44, Kenya and Taiwan, 43 each, Nigeria and Thailand, 42 each, Ghana 37, Jamaica 35, Ireland 34, Malasia 33, Israel and the United Arab Republic, 31 each, Peru 30, Turkey 29, Uruguay 28, India 28, Venezuela 27, Morocco 26.

And Portugal 24, Chile and the Dominican Republic, 23 each, Senegal 22, Costa Rica and Ethiopia, 21 each, Bahamas, Mongolia, Pakistan, Trinidad Tobago, 20 each, Guinea 19, Panama 17, Ecuador and Ivory Coast 16, Iran 14, Nicaragua and Indonesia, 13 each, Lebanon 12, Uganda 11, Barbados, Congo Kinshasa, and South Vietnam, 10 each.

Then Bermuda and Honduras, 9 each, Iceland and the Virgin Islands, 8 each, British Honduras, Cameroun, Tunisia and Zambia, 7 each, Afghanistan 6, Singapore, Netherlands Antilles, Bolivia, Sudan, Luxembourg and Guiana, 5 each, Burma, Chad, Madagascar, San Marino and Tanzania, 4 each.

Finally, Iraq, Algeria, Ceylon, Sierra Leone, and Syria, 3 each, Mali, Monaco, Liechtenstein and Niger, 2 each, and Central Africa, Fiji Islands, Libya, Paraguay, 1 each.

Note: Gabon, Malta, Surinam and the Congo had entered one athlete each but they did not compete. Among the 19 sports, the number of nations entering athletes are listed below:

Athletics (Track and Field) 89, Shooting 65, Boxing 60, Swimming & Diving 54, Weightlifting 51, Cycling 50, Wrestling 46, Yachting 39, Fencing 34, Canoeing & Kayaking and Rowing, 28 each.

Also, Gymnastics 26, Modern Pentathlon 19, Equestrian Sports 18, Field Hockey, *Soccer, and **Basketball, 16 each, *Water Polo 15, *Volleyball 12.

The sports below are listed in order of total number of athletes entered:

Track and Field 1,122 (864 men, 258 women), Swimming 583 (331 men, 252 women), Rowing 394 (all men), Shooting 377 (374 men, 3 women), Cycling 361 (all men), Boxing 337 (all men), Wrestling 320, Yachting 317 (all men), *Soccer 301 (all men).

*Field Hockey 284 (all men), Fencing 279 (221 men, 58 women), Gymnastics 254 (139 men, 115 women), *Volleyball 214 (120 men, 94 women), Canoeing Kayaking & 208 (171 men, 37 women), *Basketball 191 (all men), Weightlifting 174 (all men), *Water Polo (163 all men), Equestrian Sports 144 (117 men, 27 women), Modern Pentathlon 61 (all men).

(*) Indicates team sports. Number of entries determined by the respective international sports governing bodies.

The small platform of the officials in the Olympic stadium of Mexico City always attracted the glances of the spectators. With infallible precision, these Mexican caballeros and hundreds of nameless helpers performed their prescribed duties. (right)

The line-up at the start from the inside track outwards: Greene (USA), Montes (Cuba), Hines
(USA), Miller (Jamaica), Pender (USA), Bambuck (France), Jerome (Canada).
On this series from left to right and from the inside track outwards: Greene, Montes, Hines,
Miller, Pender.
The 22 year old Hines, a muscular model athlete, 1,84 meter (6'0¹/₂") tall, was the first sprinter
to run the 100 m in 9.9 seconds in the Olympic contest. During the first half of the distance the

4×100 m relay race—the last changeover: Eight sprinters surge out of the curve. For a fleeting
moment they are united with their final runners through the baton and are suddenly sixteen.
Then this dramatic vision passes and eight sprinters hammer along the straight away. On this
series from left to right and from the inside track outwards: Cuba with Montes
and Figuerola, USA with Smith and Hines, Poland with Nowosz and Dudziak, East Germany
with Haase and Eggers, Jamaica with Forbes and Miller, Italy with Squazzero and Berruti,
Germany with Wucherer and Eigenherr, France with Piquemal and Bambuck.
Crackling tension lay over this 4×100 m relay race. Would it be possible to beat the favored
Americans? In both the first heat as well as in the semi-finals the four Cubans, Ramirez,
Morales, Montes and Figuerola had proved themselves against Green, Pender, Smith and

field lay close together with only a few centimeters between them. But then comes Hines, invincible. At the winning-post he has achieved a new world record and a new Olympic record with 9.9 seconds. In 1960 the German, Armin Hary, had broken the American series of sprinting victories. Since then, his world record had been equalled many times, but never beaten. Now the USA sprinters resolved to beat the world record in Mexico and wanted to ensure the predominance of the USA over this distance. And Hines succeeded.

Hines from the USA and had just won. And Jamaica had even run a new world record with 38.3 seconds. In this last changeover, however, it appeared as though there would be a sensational defeat. The Cuban, Montes, pressed the baton into the hand of his comrade, Fiquerola, fractions of a second earlier and Cuba now lies first in the straight away. On the outside track, France's European Champion, Roger Bambuck, flies forwards, sensing his opportunity. But now Hines shows that he is simply stronger. Practically effortlessly he leaves his splendid opponents behind him and goes with a clear lead past the finishing-post. Gold for the USA, silver for the valiant Cubans and a surprising bronze for the French. The boys from Jamaica go away empty-handed and are astonished at how quickly world records can be won and lost in Mexico.

Smith, USA, won the 200 meter dash. The Australian Norman, not in the picture above, was ahead of Carlos, USA, who came in third.

Six meters before the tape Tommie Smith flung up his arms — thus throwing away a new world record (below).

The great winner of the 'quickest 100 meter dash of all times', Jim Hines, USA (gold medal), in front of his teammate, Charley Greene (right) and Lennox Miller, Jamaica.

Above:
4 × 400 meter relay change. Last change. Gold medal for USA team composed of Matthews, Freeman, James and Evans. Silver medal for Kenya, bronze for West Germany.

Left:
Triple triumph for USA in the 400 meter dash: 1st Evans, 2nd James, 3rd Freeman.

Above:
Like a flight of multicolored birds, Mexican spectators cover the Mexican emblem
on the Marathon gate in the Olympic stadium. No one stops them.

Upper left:
Not only in the Olympic stadium, but also in the Olympic village, the American sprinters
were always favored targets of the photographers.

Lower left:
This friendly conversation between Prince Philip and Reginald Alexander, Kenya,
also attracted the immediate interest of the lensmen.

Above:
Like a gazelle, Amos Biwott from
Kenya flew over obstacles and
waterfilled ditches.

Left:
Biwott easily beat his countryman,
Kogo. Against this strong team
from Kenya, the American steeplechase champion, Young, USA,
wrested the bronze medal.

Above right:
At the tape Keino's lead was
almost 20 meters.

Below right:
Again a great win for Kenya.
Keino conquers with ease the USA
favorite Ryun, leaving him only
a silver medal. Bronze medal for
Tummler, West Germany.

*Left and right:
The winner of the
110-meter hurdles was
Davenport, USA. He won
in a new record time,
beating his teammate,
Hall. The sensation was
the third place position
of the Italian runner,
Ottoz, who passed
Coleman, USA.*

*Below:
Davenport's outstretched
arms reveal the joy of
victory.*

Over the middle and long distances, many runners from sea-level nations fell victim to the thin air at the altitude of 2,240 meters (approx. 7,000 feet).

Above:
Start of the 10,000 meter race. Some of the favorites in this field do not yet know
of their defeat. Temu, Kenya, completes the triumph for his home country.
Second was the Ethiopian, Wolde, in front of the Tunisian, Gammoudi. Africa's victory
is complete. The ambitious Mexican, Martinez, was fourth.

Left:
The 50 kilometer walk is the longest distance contest of the games. The group, walking
with the characteristically peculiar rhythm, leaves the stadium through the Marathon gate.
At the end came the lonely winner, Höhne, East Germany. Larry Young, USA.
won the bronze medal.

Above:
During the 800 meter race, Wilson Kilprugut, Kenya, was in the lead until close to the finishing line. Then the Australian, Ralph Doubell, caught up with him and wrested the gold medal from him in world record time. Tom Farrell, the best middle distance runner after Jim Ryun, successfully held off the West German, Walter Adams, for the bronze medal.

Left:
In the 5,000 meter race, the Tunisian Gammoudi, won the gold medal, beating Keino and Temu. Once again, a clear success for Africa. And again, the tenacious Mexican, Martinez, secured fourth place. World record holder Ron Clarke, Australia, finished exhausted in fifth position.

Above:
Since 1960, the Marathon course has been the domain of Ethiopia. Abebe Bikila was the winner in Rome and Tokyo. In Mexico he passed his royal prerogative to his fellow countryman, Mamo Wolde (25) 12 years his junior. Despite his time of 2:20:26, the latter needed 8 minutes more to cover the distance in Mexico than his great predecessor needed in Tokyo. But in the Mexican stadium he received no exceptional acclaim. Hardly anyone noticed him crossing the finishing line. Fewer spectators in the stadium observed the Japanese, Kimihara (silver) and the New Zealander, Ryan (bronze) finish the gruelling race. The efforts of the Marathon runners received more attention in the streets of Mexico City.

Overleaf:
The bells toll from the venerable cathedral on the Zocalo, believed to be the largest square in America. The 72 participants from 44 countries, under the hot sun of this October day, start the 42 km Marathon run through dusty streets and over the 12 km long, straight 'Road of the Insurgent.'

C. ROBERT PAUL JR.

*Publications Editor,
United States
Olympic Committee*

Swifter, Higher, Stronger

In the sixteenth Olympic Games since the inaugural in 1904 more favorites prevailed than at any previous quadrennial gathering of the world's outstanding amateur athletes in track and field.

The men and women, a record entry of 1,459, scoffed at the effects of competing at the 7,400-foot altitude in Mexico and broke or equaled Olympic standards in 18 of the 24 events for men and in nine of the 12 events for women.

Prior to the Games of the XIX Olympiad, the United States was acknowledged to have the strongest team ever sent to the Olympic Games. The well-conditioned athletes from the USA did nothing to belie the pre-Olympic Games prognostications.

The facilities of the *Estadio Olimpico* were magnificent. The all-weather Tartan track and the surfaces for the field events proved ideal for the athletes who encountered miserable weather on two of the eight days of competition.

When the statisticians had completed their reports, the USA continued to reign as the No. 1 nation in track and field, men and women. The most striking development was the emergence of Kenya as a world track power. The Kenyans won their first three gold medals ever in the men's competition, plus four silver and one bronze.

In a competition bringing together the best in the world, with national and area champions in abundance, the performances of several individuals can be spotlighted without discriminating against any gold medalists. Certainly, each of the individual champions demonstrated superiority over his peers in the most exciting competitions ever witnessed by devotees of the Olympic Games.

Any account of the Games of XIX Olympiad failing to mention the accomplishment of discus champion Al Oerter must be considered incomplete and inconsequential. Leading up to the Olympic Games, it was predicted that Silvester, USA, and Danek, Czechoslovakia, would battle for the title won by Oerter in 1956, 1960, and 1964. In fact, Oerter had no more than two throws better than 200 feet in competition prior to Mexico.

In the qualifying round, Silvester broke the Olympic record and Oerter was fifth among the 12 advancing to the final competition. On the third throw (of six) Oerter had the greatest throw of his 13 years in world competition, 212–6½ (64.78 m). It is significant that following Oerter's throw (which proved to be the winning one) no thrower bettered his previous best in the competition. In fact, Silvester fouled three of his last four throws after Oerter *broke up* the competition with his record toss.

Decathlon champion Bill Toomey, USA, climaxed a four-year period of total preparation by winning the most grueling of all track and field competitions. He earned his gold medal in a most convincing manner.

Toomey understood that psychological and mental preparation was equally as important as physical conditioning in the ten-event competition. Consequently, Toomey maintained his physical condition in Mexico with lighter workouts than he was normally accustomed to. To keep himself in psychological and mental readiness he remained away from the *Estadio Olimpico* until the start of his competition.

In setting a new Olympic record in the decathlon, 8,193 points, Toomey had the best performance in three of the individual events—10.4 sec. for 100 meters; 45.6 sec. for 400 meters, and 25–9¾ (7.87 m) for the long jump, all on the first day of the competition.

A comparison of Toomey's winning Olympic effort with those of Rafer Johnson, 1960, and Bob Mathias, 1952, is conclusive. The Johnson and Mathias performances were re-scored under the current scoring tables. Toomey with 8,193 at Mexico is the all-time USA-Olympic best, followed by Johnson 7,988, and Mathias 7,707.

Toomey narrowly escaped elimination in the pole vault where he missed the first two trials at the opening height, before clearing the bar on his final attempt. This was the eighth of the ten events.

How proud the United States can be that Wyomia Tyus, a recent graduate of Tennessee State, became the first woman in Olympic history to retain the 100-meter title and provided the USA with the margin of victory in the 4 × 100 meter relay with a marvelous anchor leg. Miss Tyus and Oerter were the *only* athletes to retain individual Olympic titles.

Few athletes in the 72-year history of the modern Olympic Games captured the fancy of the spectators as did high jumper Dick Fosbury, Oregon State. He had won the NCAA title, finished first in the first Olympic Trials at Los Angeles, and then managed to snare the third and final place on the Olympic team with his best ever jump of 7–1 in the final Olympic Trials.

The world, through the eyes of television, zeroed in on Dick and his now well-known *Fosbury Flop* in which Fosbury goes over the bar "flat on his back." In the final go-round Fosbury was competing for the gold medal against teammate Ed Caruthers and the Soviet champion, Gavrilov. By setting a new Olympic record of 7–4¼, Fosbury edged out Caruthers and Gavrilov who went out at 7–3½.

The most spectacular performance in *any* Olympic Games was the winning long jump of Bob Beamon, USA, a terrifying new world record of 29–2½. This was almost two feet longer than the recognized world mark of Ralph Boston, USA, the bronze medalist at Mexico behind East Germany's Klaus Beer.

The loudest cheers of the 80,000 spectators on the final day were reserved for Kipchoge Keino, Kenya, who made a shambles of the 1,500-meter run by trouncing the American champion and world record-holder Jim Ryun. Keino permitted teammate Jipcho to set a fast 56.0-second pace for the first 400 meters before taking over the lead.

Not that Keino ran like a scared rabbit, but he certainly traveled at a pace for the last 1,100 meters that no other runner in Olympic history had ever attempted. Ryun, in truth, had been affected by a severe attack of mononucleosis in the Spring and most assuredly was sub-par. How well a perfectly trained Ryun would have done in the face of Keino's tactics may be the subject of debate among Olympic Games' devotees for years. It is highly improbable that Ryun, under any circumstances, could have coped with the tempo of the race established by Keino. All Olympic records were smashed in the

eight men's field events and in three of five of the women's events.

Bob Seagren caused multiple "goose pimples" with his strategy in the pole vault. The world record-holder found himself in a veritable dog fight with West Germany's Schiprowski and East Germany's Nordwig. Here is an event that often is won by *gamesmanship*. Of the 12 events won by the USA, Seagren's triumph may be attributed to *gamesmanship*.

Seven men remained in the competition after clearing 17–4¾ (5.30 m) when Seagren (with only one miss up to that time) boldly *passed* the next height. No one else cleared this height 17–6¾ (5.35 m) on the first attempt.

Although Seagren and Schiprowski both cleared 17–8½ (5.40 m) on the second attempt and then both missed all three attempts at 17–10½ (5.45 m), Seagren was determined the victor, on the basis that he had only two misses to three for Schiprowski. The most satisfying triumph for the USA was that of Madeline Manning in the 800 meters. The USA had never been seriously considered in this longest race for women. Yet, Miss Manning, an undergraduate at Tennessee State, finished the metric half-mile at least 15 meters ahead of her nearest competitor.

The "tone" for the Olympic Games was set on the very first day when Naftali Temu, Kenya, knocked off two pre-race favorites, Ethiopia's Mamo Wolde and Tunisia's Mohamed Gammoudi in the 10,000 meters. Temu ran a crafty race and never led during the first 9,000 meters. In the middle of the race the Mexican national champion and favorite of the Mexican fans, Maximo Martinez, enjoyed running in first place before yielding to Great Britain's Hill at 8,000 meters.

Wolde, undaunted by his silver medal in the 10,000 meters, came back on the final day of competition to win the classic marathon race by almost three minutes over Japan's Kimihara.

In the first half of the race, Wolde remained among the first five. His teammate and two-time Olympic champion, Abebe Bikila, (12 years Wolde's senior) ran into difficulties and dropped out at the 15-kilometer mark with leg miseries. The loss of Bikila certainly spurred on Wolde who took command shortly after the half-way mark and on the trip back to the *Estadio Olimpico* remained at the head of the pack as he lengthened his advantage.

For sheer beauty of performance, the victories of Willie Davenport, USA, 110-meter hurdles; Great Britain's Dave Hemery (educated at Boston College), 400-meter hurdles; and Kenya's Amos Biwott, 3,000-meter steeplechase, were appreciated by the knowledgeable fans packing the *Estadio Olimpico* for the daily finals.

Davenport's flawless form and natural speed enabled him to edge out teammate Ervin Hall, Villanova University, and the Italian veteran Eddy Ottoz.

Next to Beamon's performance in the long jump was the finality of Hemery's winning effort in the 400-meter hurdles. In setting a new world record of 48.1 seconds, the blond Hemery sped by Vanderstock and Whitney, USA's entries, in the first half of the race.

The only "sweep" scored by the USA was in the 400 meters as Lee Evans continued his mastery over teammate Larry James with Ron Freeman, third.

Jim Hines was magnificent in the 100 meters, outdistancing Jamaica's Lennox Miller (a student at the University of Southern California) and his constant nemesis, Charlie Greene, also USA. Hines showed the same superiority in this race that Bob Hayes had exhibited four years earlier in Tokyo.

The USA bid for a 1–2 finish in the 200 meters was balked by Australia's Peter Norman. Top favorite, Tommie Smith, suffered a slight leg injury in the semi-final and came back 30 minutes later to run away from the field. Carlos, USA, apparently had second place within his grasp when he slowed down as Smith crossed the finish line. Norman sped by Carlos to win the silver and Carlos had to content himself with a bronze.

The finest performance in the women's events came when West Germany's Ingrid Becker won the pentathlon. She sewed up her triumph at the end of the first day of the two-day competition with a superb performance in the high jump despite a blinding rainshower.

The Soviet coach had privately indicated before the start of the Games that his men and women would win five or six gold medals. The final tally for the USSR was three, all in the men's events. In fact, the Soviets only won a total of 13 medals in track and field.

In addition to the gold medal efforts by the USA, Kenya, Great Britain, Tunisia and Ethiopia mentioned previously, Hungary, East Germany and Australia won single gold medals in the men's competition.

The USA in women's competition led with three gold medals, followed by Rumania with two. Australia, Hungary, East Germany, West Germany, Poland, France and Czechoslovakia won one gold each.

In the USA, relay racing is one of the top attractions at all competitions. Every four years the "spoil sport" experts predict disaster for the hastily-assembled USA teams in these events which were invented in the USA.

The mercurial and raw speed of American sprinters, men and women alike, again prevailed as our teams set world records in all three relay races (two for men and one for women). It's simply a case of speed and desire overcoming the well-trained foreign opposition.

Many of the 27 standards set in Mexico may fall at the Games of the XX Olympiad. But it would be highly speculative to predict that upcoming Games will see such a wholesale onslaught on Olympic standards as was shown in Mexico, or that the pre-meet favorites of the future will run, throw and jump as closely to form again.

Olé, Olympic champions, one and all.

In Ancient Greece, during the Olympic Games a sacred flame burned at the altar of Zeus, in whose honor the Games were held. As the impressive part of the opening ceremony of the modern Olympic Games, the Olympic Flame is lighted. It burns in a conspicuous place in the main stadium throughout the entire Games. The Organizing Committee for the 1936 Games at Berlin conceived the idea of kindling the flame with a torch lit by the sun at Olympia, Greece, site of the ancient Games, and passed from hand to hand all the way to Berlin by a relay of runners.

Starting from Olympia, they ran to Athens, Salonika, Sofia, Belgrade, Budapest, Vienna, Prague, Dresden, and carefully scheduled and managed their race so that the last runner arrived at the Stadium at the exact instant required. The arrival of this torch, carrying the sacred flame, is a most dramatic feature of the first day of the Games. In 1948 the flame was brought by a relay of runners form Olympia to London, and, in 1952, from Olympia to Helsinki. In 1956, from Olympia to Melbourne, the flame was brought by air and by relay. In 1960, it was brought by boat and relay from Olympia to Rome. In 1964, the torch was carried from Olympia to Tokyo by plane and involved visits to the capital cities of 13 Far Eastern nations. In 1968, the flame was brought by boat from Olympia to Italy and thence to Spain. From Spain it followed the route taken by Christopher Columbus, arriving in Veracruz and then by land to Mexico City.

In recent Winter Olympic Games, a similar torch ceremony has been staged, with the Olympic Flame coming from Morgedal, Norway (considered the cradle of winter sports) to the site of the Games.

The Olympic Flame

THE OLYMPIC GAMES, in which amateur athletes of all nations are assembled for fair and equal competition in 18–22 different sports, are held every four years. The Olympic Games celebrate an Olympiad— a period of four successive years and the Games are conducted in the first year of each Olympiad dating from the establishment of the Modern Olympic Games in Athens, Greece, in 1896. Olympiads and Games are numbered consecutively from the date of the first games in Greece, even though it was sometimes impossible to hold the Games.

No discrimination is allowed against any country or person on grounds of race, religion or political affiliation.

The Olympic Games

The words, "Citius, Altius, Fortius," which appear under the circles, were conceived in 1895 by the famous Father Didon, head master of the Arcueil College near Paris, France, while delivering a speech glorifying the athletic achievements of his pupils. The words mean "faster, higher, braver" but the modern version, which has been universally accepted, is "swifter, higher, stronger," indicative of the competing athlete's endeavor to run faster, jump higher, and throw more strongly.

The Olympic Motto

Bob Beamon (6 ft., 4 in., 157 lbs.), completes his first jump in the final competition. He soared from the marker in a wide arc to the end of the long-jump pit. The experts estimated the distance as 8.50 meters. They approached and incredulously shook their heads. They checked the wind. Everything was correct, 8.90 meters (29'2½"). This fantastic world record may last beyond the year 2000.

Beamon's gold medal seems to contain double weight. The former world record holder, Boston (below), surprisingly had to cede the silver medal to the East German, Beer. The previous Olympic record in this event was broken five times in the thin air of Mexico City.

The shot put competition ran according to schedule. Randy Matson, USA (No. 287),
6 ft., 8 inches tall and 270 lbs., secured for himself the gold medal with his first toss
of 20.54 meters (67' 4³/₄") and he exceeded the 20 meter mark four more times. (See also next
page). His teammate Woods (above, center) had beaten him in the Olympic Trials
in the USA. Here, Woods had some difficulty in capturing the silver medal,
beating the Soviet, Gushchin, by only three centimeters.

1

2

The pole vault is one of the jewels of track and field. In Mexico City, in a competition lasting for seven hours, the existing world record was broken three times and the Olympic record set in Tokyo 28 times! Here (and also on the next page) is the winner, Bob Seagren, USA. His new world record jump of 5.40 meters (17′ 8¹/₂″) was duplicated by Schiprowsky, West Germany, and Nordwig, East Germany. Seagren won on fewer misses.

3

4

5

6

A 21-year-old student from Medford, Oregon, Dick Fosbury, with his amazing jumping technique, was the delight of the Olympic stadium. Scoffed at by the experts after his first efforts, he unerringly held to his technique and eventually won the high jump with 2.24 meters (7' 4¹/₄"). He was wildly acclaimed by 80,000 spectators. His countryman, Caruthers (right), scored with 2.22 meters (7' 3⁵/₈") in the traditional style, winning the silver medal for the USA and relegating the Soviet, Gavrilov, to the third position.

Decathlon: 1,500 meter race. In the last event of the decathlon, the leader, Bill Toomey, USA, took no risk. He did not allow his two German competitors, Bendlin and Walde, to pass him and finished this deciding test as a winner, beating Walde and the Soviet Avilov.

Out of 33 participants from 20 nations, only 20 finished the decathlon. But half of the competitors ran the 100 meters in under 11 seconds, and 21 participants long jumped more than 23 feet. In this event, Bill Toomey, USA, competed alone against five outstanding German and two Soviet athletes. Eventually, he emerged the winner. In this two-day long competition, he broke the Olympic record. (See also pages 65, 67, 68 and 69.)

Above left:
After Beamon's superb record long jump, his competitors only fought for the additional places, while Beamon and Boston stood watching in the rain.

Above right:
Toomey as well watches his competitors in the downpour.

Opposite page:
In the highly competitive decathlon, Toomey, USA, gains a distinct advantage with a long jump of 7.87 meters (25' 9³/4"), after running the best 100 meter dash in 10.4 seconds.

Above:
The West German athletes, Bendlin (No. 3) and Walde (No. 53), labor in vain in their attempt to pass their great competitor Bill Toomey, USA, in the first laps of the 1,500 meter run.

Right:
But the award's ceremony unites all three athletes in cheerful and sporting camaraderie.

The 32-year-old discus champion, Al Oerter, is a unique phenomenon in the history of Olympic track and field events. With a new Olympic record of 64.78 meters (212' 6$\frac{1}{2}$") he decisively beat his closest competitors. In 1956, Oerter became Olympic champion with a toss of 56.36 meters (184' 10$\frac{1}{2}$"); 1960 59.18 meters (194' 2"); and in 1964 (his friends thought he would retire after he had won his third gold medal in Tokyo) with a throw of 61.00 meters (200' 1$\frac{1}{2}$").

The dove of peace and the many smiling children were a cheerful Olympic sign in Mexico City. Both mirrored also the peaceful face of this proud nation.

Bob
Beamon

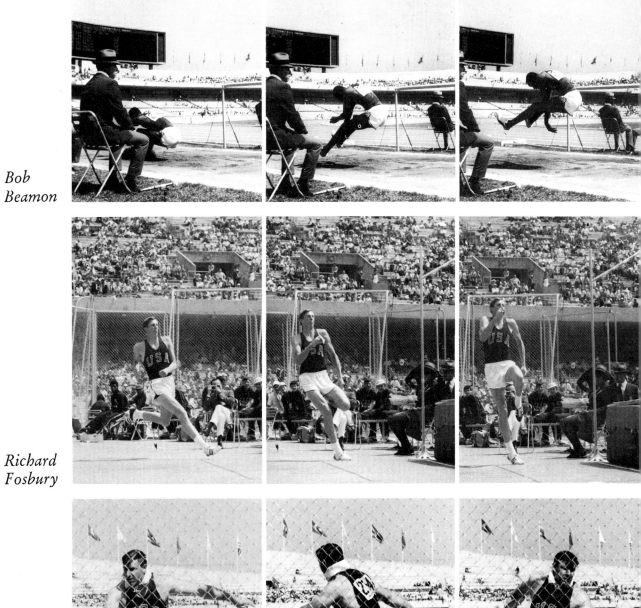

Richard
Fosbury

Al
Oerter

Randy
Matson

Beamon

Because of his tremendous jumping abilities and his glorious series of victories in 1967 and 1968, the 1.89 m. (6' 3") tall and only 73 kg. (160 lbs.) heavy, Bob Beamon was rated as favorite for the Olympic long jump contest. Beamon soon impressed the spectators with his fascinating style. By taking advantage of the extremely favorable atmospheric conditions in Mexico, Beamon leaped with technical perfection into the 21st century by attaining the almost legendary world record distance of 8.90 m. (29' 2¹/₂"). It was his initial jump in the finals. He took only one more, then left his stunned rivals to shoot for second place.

Beamon was born on August 29, 1946, in Jamaica, New York, and lives in El Paso, Texas. Following his success in the Pan-American Games in 1967, where he placed second to Ralph Boston, he won all the contests of any importance in 1968.

Fosbury

When the first pictures of the backwards-high-jumper appeared, the experts were amazed by Richard (Dick) Fosbury. Nobody could quite believe in the 21-year old student from Medford, Oregon. His style was unorthodox. Although previously he had reached the height of 2.20 m. (7' 2¹/₂"), Dick Fosbury's role still was that of the underdog. The first surprise was his victory during the selections for the U.S. Olympic team. Fosbury, who by now excited world-wide admiration with his "Fosbury Flop," came to Mexico and conquered with an assurance which no one would have dared to predict. Only he managed to master 2.24 m. (7' 4"). The experts spoke of him as the "Parry O'Brien of the high jump," because, like the former Olympic champion and world record holder for putting the shot, he may have revolutionized the high jump.

Dick Fosbury was born on March 6, 1947, in Portland, Oregon, and lives in Medford, Oregon. He is 1.94 m. (6' 4") tall and weighs 84 kg. (185 lbs.). His Olympic triumph took place during the arrival of the Marathon medal winners. The Olympic champion Mamo Wolde, Ethiopia, ran his last round practically unheeded, because Fosbury was starting his jump at the winning height.

The 23-year old world record holder, Randy Matson, was among the few track and field favorites in Mexico who understood how to succeed superlatively. As a 19-year old, this young giant of a Texan, 2.00 m. (6' 6¹/₂'') tall and 118 kg. (260 lbs.) forged ahead into world class.

Matson

After placing second in the 1964 Olympics following his countryman and world record holder, Dallas Long, he reached the world's pinnacle for the first time in 1965 with the record shot of 20.70 m. (70' 7''). And in the same year, he was admired in Europe as the champion of the Universiade in Budapest. Randy Matson finally achieved 21.78 m. (71' 5¹/₂'') on April 22, 1967.

Matson, born on March 5, 1945, lives in Pampa, Texas, and was three times USA-Champion and victor in the Pan-American Games. In Mexico he won with 20.54 m. (67' 4³/₄'') beating his countryman George Woods with 20.12 m. (66' ¹/₄'').

The sport journalists respectfully call Al Oerter "the man with the golden arm." Indeed the American discus thrower has yet to meet his equal the world over. He won the Olympic gold medal four times in succession each time improving the Olympic record. In the Games he proves himself to be superior to his compet-

Oerter

itors through his strong nerves. In Melbourne, 1956, he won the Olympic record of 56.36 m. (184' 10¹/₂'') against the world record holder of that time, Fortune Gordien, USA. In Rome, 1960, he conquered again with 59.18 m. (194' 2'') against the world record holder, Rink Babka, USA. In Tokyo, 1964, with exactly 61.00 m. (200' 1¹/₂'') he beat the Czech, Ludvik Danek, who then held the world record. In Mexico he defeated Jay Silvester who prior to the Games threw 68.40 m. (225' 4'') and only reached fifth position in Mexico. Oerter secured his fourth gold medal with the Olympic—and personal—record of 64.78 m. (212' 6¹/₂'').

Oerter was born on September 19, 1936, lives in Astoria, New York, and is 1.93 m. (6' 4'') and weighs 118 kg. (260 lbs.). In Mexico he attracted attention because he arrived with his whole family and practised on a nearby site undisturbed by his children.

*Since the Olympic Games in Rome, 1960, the International Amateur Athletic Federation (IAAF) makes
teaching films from the infield during Olympic track and field events. Toni Nett, a first-
class expert from Stuttgart, West Germany, has filmed all the famous Olympic champions since
1960 with the assistance of his wife. Thousands of up and coming athletes, especially in the younger nations,
have learnt to understand the instructions and ideas of their trainers more fully through these films
which are taken with the slow-motion camera. On this photographic spread, the perfect techniques of the
4 Olympic champions, Beamon (long jump), Fosbury (high jump), Oerter (discus) and Matson
(putting the shot) are shown from the infield of the Olympic stadium in Mexico City in sequences.*

*The 100 meter dash was won by Wyomia Tyus, USA, in the new Olympic and world record
time of 11.0 seconds. She broke the tape before Babara Ferrell, USA (extreme left), and Irena
Kirszenstein, Poland (not shown in picture). Wyomia Tyus did not succeed in making the world forget
Wilma Rudolph in Rome, 1960. But this tenacious and intelligent American girl from Griffin,
Georgia, achieved something so far unattained in the history of Olympic track and field events, either
by a male or female athlete, i. e. to repeat, after four years, an Olympic victory in the 100 meter dash.*

100 meter dash awards' ceremony. It is not tears of emotion Wyomia Tyus wipes from her face. The Mexican heavens bedeck the three fastest female runners of the world—Tyus, Ferrell, Kirszenstein—with pattering showers of rain.

Four days later, she and her teammates received more gold medals, Wyomia's third, in the 400 meter relay which was won in a world record time. (Above right: Last relay change between Mildrette Netter and Tyus. Below right: Wyomia Tyus at the tape, USA in front of Cuba and the Soviet Union.)

Above and opposite Page: One of the toughest races in women's track and field events is the 800 meter run. The English athlete, Ann Packer, set a world record in Tokyo, where she was the darling of the spectators in 1964. 20-year-old, tall Madeline Manning, USA, became her worthy successor in the new world record time of 2:00.9, almost reaching the two minute goal.
Behind Madeline Manning, Ilona Silai (No. 215), Rumania, who broke the tape at 2:02.5, and Maria Francisca Gommers (No. 148), Holland, 2:02.6, won silver and bronze medals.

Although she placed second in the finals, USA's Barbara Ferrell had a moment of triumph. Here, she is winning the sixth preliminary heat of the 100 meters, equalling the then existing Olympic record of 11.2 seconds.

Wyomia Tyus, Barbara Ferrell, and Margaret Bailes, the three finalists representing the USA, recover their breath after crossing the finishing line in the 100 meter dash. Then, Wyomia smiles; she knows why.

Left:
Viorica Viscopoleanu, Rumania, had never succeeded in being placed better than fifth in Tokyo, 1964, in the European championship games, 1968, or in world ranking. She sprang, like Beamon, with tremendous energy in the first long jump attempt and by leaping the fantastic distance of 6.82 meters (22′ 4¹/₂″), she won an Olympic victory and set a new world record.

Below:
Viorica Viscopoleanu, Sheila Sherwood, England (silver), and the Russian, Tatiana Talisheva (bronze) in the unforgettable moment of the award's ceremony.

Right:
Ingrid Becker was the deserving winner of the pentathlon. She secured West Germany's only gold medal in track and field events. When the German favorite and world champion, Heide Rosendahl, withdrew from competition because of an injury, Ingrid Becker outdid herself during the two-day event which was hampered by storm and rain showers. Rome, 1960, and Tokyo, 1964, — where she was not placed — were her steps towards Mexico.

Above:
Ingrid Becker, West Germany, ran the
80 meter hurdles in 10.9 seconds, her best time
for this event, gaining precious points for her
ultimate victory in the pentathlon.

Left:
IOC member Willi Daume hands Ingrid Becker
the first and only gold medal won by a
West German track athlete. Silver for Liesel
Prokop, Austria. Annemarie Toth, Hungary,
received the bronze medal.

Right:
This javelin throw means a gold medal for
Angela Nemeth, Hungary, beating
Mihalla Pene, Rumania, and Eva Maria
Janko, Austria.

JOSEPH M. SHEEHAN
New York Times

Promise...
and
Failure

Rowing at the 1968 Olympics was, paradoxically, an area of achievement and disaster for the USA. In getting all seven of its shells into the finals, the USA accomplished a remarkable feat, not only for itself but for all nations.

But netting only one second-place silver and one third-place bronze medal constituted a nadir. Never before in Olympic rowing had the USA failed to carry off at least one gold medal.

Mexico City's high altitude adversely affected performance. Rowing involves hard, sustained effort, six to eight minutes over the standard course of 2,000 meters. But most of the competing nations also were from low-altitude regions and the US squad probably had more preparatory high-altitude training than most of its adversaries. The inevitable conclusions from the long-range point of view are that the USA lags in the development of world-class intermediate-shell (pairs and fours) oarsmen; should step up its program for developing scullers—single and doubles—and should examine further the matter of organizing a national all-star eight, rather than turning over a job for grown men to a college crew. This despite the fact that varsity eights—except in 1900 and 1964, when Vesper Boat Club of Philadelphia was the successful US standard-bearer—have handled the assignment competently up to 1968. It would be manifestly unfair to label the fine Harvard crew, which beyond all cavil had established itself as the best eight in the nation, as the "goat" of the rowing Olympics. But it's also incontrovertible that the young Cantabs were outrowed and outclassed. They finished a soundly-thrashed

Clinging to her tall and strong father, this little Mexican girl admires, amazed and sceptical at the same time, the efficient foreign girl athletes on the lawn and the red Tartan tracks of the wide stadium.
Thousands of such little Mexican boys and girls dream now of future competitions and Olympic victories.

sixth and last in the final—after making the title race only by way of a second place repechage finish.

The Crimson oarsmen had excuses, legitimate and otherwise. Injuries and illnesses beset them, beginning in preparatory high-altitude training, and coach Harry Parker ultimately was obliged to make boating changes in midstream. Also, some of the socially-conscious "shaggies" (they were so nicknamed because of their general espousal of the younger generation's long hair-plus-facial-hirsute-adornment fad) became possibly over-involved emotionally in the efforts by some black athletes in other sports to use the Olympics as a vehicle for racial demonstrations.

Despite whatever excuses, the conclusion remains that the day of asking a Harvard, a Yale or a Naval Academy crew to face Germany, the Soviet Union, Czechoslovakia, Australia, New Zealand and the other rowing nations who enter mature, long-organized national crews in the Olympics has passed.

Knowledgeable oarsmen and followers of the sport hailed the Mexico City rowing set-up as the "best ever." With no adequate facility available, the Mexicans built a self-contained canal-like ditch some 3,000 meters long overall, 150 meters wide and 2 meters deep in suburban Xochimilco, only a few miles from Olympic Village. Adjacent was a second canal, slightly narrower, which served as a supplementary practice course for the canoeists as well as the oarsmen.

At the finish line of the race course, there was a superb cellularized boat house, providing individual or joint shell storage space and maintenance facilities for the 31 competing nations and an adjoining magnificently-appointed locker, shower and training shed. Stands seating 15,000 to 20,000 spectators lined the last 400 meters of the course, with a roofed clubhouse section, communications center and press cafeteria in the finish area.

A glass-enclosed air-conditioned judging tower that could have doubled for an airport control center was situated on the finish line, equipped with a photo-finish camera and electric timing devices. And on

93

the side of the main canal opposite the stands was a huge electronic scoreboard which flashed the entries and their lanes; the order of crews and their fractional times at 500-meter intervals; and complete final results.

The US left the stake boats fast in the first-round trials on Sunday, Oct. 13, putting its coxless four of Lawrence Terry (bow) and Charles Hamblin (2) of Harvard and Raymond Wright (3) and Peter Raymond (stroke) of Princeton directly into the final and advancing to the semi-finals in the single and double sculls and coxless pairs. Bill Maher of Detroit and John Nunn of Cincinnati in the double sculls and Tony Johnson and Larry Hough of Arlington, Va., in the pairs won their tests.

Harvard's eight, fifth in the trials when a rigging casualty compounded its other miseries; the pairs with coxswain [Bill Hobbs of Harvard, Dick Edmunds of Cornell and Stewart McDonald of Wisconsin (cox)] and the four with coxswain [Bill Purdy, Tony Martin, Gardner Cadwalader, Luther Jones and John Hartigan (cox), all of Penn.] advanced via the repechage. Under the conditions of competition, Har-

vard went directly from the repechage into the final.

In the semi-finals on Thursday, Oct. 17, the other five US entries earned the right to join previously-qualified Harvard and the coxless four in the title round. Maher and Nunn and Hough and Johnson again were impressive victors and, since Harvard had performed well in the repechage, the outlook brightened.

But in the showdown tests of Saturday, the US oarsmen, except for the scullers and coxless pair, found themselves overmatched. In the coxless pairs, Hough and Johnson, out in front from the 300-meter mark, had their race won until the last few strokes, when the East German duo of Jorge Lucke and Heinz-Jurgen Bothe surged past to snatch away the gold medal.

In the double sculls, Maher and Nunn finished strong but started from too far back to seriously threaten the Soviet Union and the Netherlands combinations which placed one-two. In the single sculls, 20-year-old John Van Blom of Los Alamitos, Calif., never really figured in the title contest but was a respectable fourth. The other US crews were completely out of it.

Considering the development of weightlifting on a world-wide level after the Olympic Games of 1920, we can see that it is divided into three periods: During the first period, fighting rules were applied for the first time and it was still unknown how to make the best use of muscle power, from the technical point of view. The movements were slow, hard and lacking in flexibility.

During the second period, more importance was given to technique. The movements became faster and the judges followed the rules strictly. During the third period, though technique continued to be considered of great importance, the use of force became essential. The training of the lifters was more directed towards increase of force than improvement of technique.

At the same time, differences of opinion rose

among the various groups which were trying, in particular, to apply the press movement from another point of view without, however, violating the rules. For this reason, it was proposed at the F.I.H.C. Conferences that the following movements be eliminated from Olympic competition: one-hand clean and jerk, one hand snatch, and two-hand press. If the new lifting system was incorporated into the ideal Central European system, the difference would only be 10%. This would mean that, by using chest, shoulder and thigh muscles, as well as appropriate respiration, the application of the press rules by which the natural hand power is measured, would accelerate the weightlifting movement. However, this advantage did not play an important part in the general development of this sport.

ALI GÜMÜS
"Tercuman," Istanbul

The Sky's The Limit

John Davis (USA) who once asserted that it would never be possible to reach 500 kg (1,102 lbs.) as an Olympic total, and who himself lifted 470 kg (1,036 lbs.), was called the strongest man in the world in 1952. However, this statement was only true for that time; progress could not be stopped and should not be.

The 500 kg limit, which many thought even the heavyweight lifters would never master, is reached today by lifters of less than 90 kg (199 lbs.). And there is no doubt that the 600 kg (1,323 lbs.) mark will be mastered soon. Today's goal is the 600 kg limit, but human ability does not stop here.

During the Olympic Games in Mexico City, which were held at an altitude of 2,000 m (6,562 ft.) and with a much lower oxygen concentration, where long-lasting disciplines showed worse results than usual and older athletes were more successful, age did not enter into account for short-lasting disciplines, such as weight-lifting. In bantamweight, the young Persian athlete Nassiri, and the old Hungarian, Földi, achieved a total of 367.5 kg (810 lbs.). In featherweight,

Miyake, who has been well known for a long time, became Olympic champion with 392.5 kg (865 lbs.), though he missed his own record of 397.5 kg (876 lbs.) by five kg (11 lbs.).

In lightweight, Zielinski (Poland) would have achieved better results than his teammate, Baszanovski, if he had not made such a strong backward movement during pressing, and had spent less time for warming-up. In our opinion, he does not listen to his trainer.

Although we do not know how far Kangasniemi (Finland), Talts (Russia) and Golab (Poland) – who placed first, second and third in Mexico in the 90 kg class (195 lbs.) – can still go, we do know that during the Olympic Games in Munich, Kailajarvi (Finland) and Nemessanyi (Hungary) will fight for the gold medal.

It is immaterial whether in the heavyweight class, Bednarski (USA) or Zhabotinsky will pass the 600 kg (1,323 lbs.) mark. In the future, even more spectacular results will be achieved.

KARL ADOLF SCHERER
*Sport-Informationsdienst
(SID), Düsseldorf*

Swim Splits

The Olympic swimming competitions in Mexico lacked predictability; indeed, they catered to the unexpected. The Americans, not anticipating any problems during the days of the XIX Olympic Games at *Alberca Olympica*, had a few. The Australians, finally deciding to send a strong team, recaptured the number two position in the world. The Russians had to return home without an Olympic champion.

World record holders had little luck in Mexico. Sure gold medal bets could do no better than silver or even bronze. One swimmer who was completely overlooked by the experts hurt the Americans most deeply and painfully: Michael Wenden of Sidney, Australia, who won the 100 meter freestyle in world record time (52.2 seconds) and defeated the most famous swimmer of the post-war period, Don Schollander, in the 200 meter freestyle. Schollander

finished his brilliant swimming career second best!

Only 13 countries—less than in wrestling for example—could place swimmers among the medal winners in Mexico, among them the two German teams, who started separate from each other for the first time. The medal standings below not only show the difference of achievements among the countries, they point out also the absolute superiority of American swimmers.

Country	Gold	Silver	Bronze
1. USA	23	15	20
2. Australia	3	2	3
3. East Germany	2	3	1
4. USSR	—	7	4
5. Canada	—	3	1
6. Mexico	1	1	1
7. Italy	1	1	—
Yugoslavia	1	1	—

9. Netherlands	1	—	—
CSSR	1	—	—
11. Great Britain	—	1	—
12. West Germany	—	—	2
13. France	—	—	1

Only six new world records were listed in Mexico, less than in previous Olympic Games. The extreme altitude did not permit first-rate achievements in the longer distances. Another point should not be overlooked: the new world records in the men's 4×100 meter freestyle (3:31.7 min.) and the women's 4×100 meter medley (4:28.3 min.) both fell short of expectations. In Long Beach or Los Angeles, the same swimmers would have done much better. Mexico did not break the last barriers in swimming at all, even though many results of Tokyo were surpassed.

The tallest swimmer in Mexico was the favorite of the Americans: Roland Matthes from East Germany, measuring 6–2 and weighing 138 pounds, an ascetic type, who opened new dimensions in the backstroke. Matthes was born on November 17, 1951, in a small village in Thuringia, and was almost sent home after his first swimming lesson. He was considered to have no talents. It took a number of years before it was realized what a rare find Roland Matthes was. Former breaststroke champion Marlies Geissler-Grohe built him up systematically and Matthes improved his times by seconds. By 1966 he had not yet made the team for the European championships in Utrecht. But a few months later Matthes set his first European records and finally his first world records.

When he returned home in 1967 from the pre-Olympic Games in Mexico and back to normal altitude, he raised the world record for 200 meters to 2:07.9. The Americans had studied Matthes during the Games in Mexico that year. He became a firm favorite with them. And no one won in a more convincing style at the *Alberca Olympica* in 1968 than Roland Matthes.

The American superiority in swimming—where does it come from? With the invention and organization of the age group program in the late fifties, the top U.S. coaches raised—almost automatically—world record swimmers in great numbers. The motto of George Haines, coach of the world famous Santa Clara Club, is: "Don't think, don't talk, swim!" Children can do this best. Haines knows that children are best equipped to swim world records. "For them it is child's play; they do not ask the purpose of it and they don't think about the demands they are confronted with. Thinking complicates the road to physical perfection." No, there is no secret about the American record babies, who started at the swimming centers aged nine and who have become champions at fifteen.

Swimmers like Debbie Meyer are today just as good as the best Australians were in 1956. Australian *men*, that is. The unforgettable Swede, Arne Borg, who in his lifetime set 31 world records would today be left two lengths behind by Debbie Meyer. Duke Paoa Kahanamoku, the Olympic champion of 1912 and 1920, would have to be at his best if he wanted to place himself today in a 100 meter freestyle final for women. Debbie Meyer is the best example of the American revolution in swimming. Already one of the top swimmers in 1966, she trains six hours daily and, as coach Sherman Chavoor observes: "She still enjoys it."

Start of the 100 meter butterfly which was included in the program of Olympic Games for the first time. Of 47 competitors, the 8 winners in the heats qualified for the final. Three of them were Americans, including Mark Spitz, whose time of 55.6 seconds made him holder of the world record.

*Before trying his strength against America's three swimming stars Zorn, Walsh and Spitz
(above), the slender, 18-year-old student Mike Wenden from Australia had already
established himself a serious competitor for the gold medal as the anchor man in the 4 × 100
meters freestyle relay, finishing in 51.7 seconds. Surprised whispering broke
out among the young swimming athletes from the USA who, thus far, had monopolized all
records and had taken Mike's sixth position in the world champions' list not very
seriously. But Mike Wenden showed no respect for the favorites and in 52.2 seconds swam
to a new world record to get his gold medal. Walsh (52.8 seconds) had to relinquish his old
world record of 52.6 seconds and received in this event as consolation a silver medal. Spitz,
the favorite, had to settle for a bronze medal. Zac Zorn swam the first 50 meters
at high speed and led the field. But, at 80 meters, he was spent and finished last.*

In the 200 meter freestyle, the victory of the Australian Mike Wenden over his American competitors was complete (above). As the anchor man in the 4×200 meters relay, he had already shown that he had come to Mexico City as a perfect favorites' nemesis, and that he was determined to be the "boss" in this field. Don Schollander, the 22-year-old Yale student, was selected to stop Mike Wenden. But he too failed. Mike relied on his 18 years of age and smiled—back in Tokyo, Don had also been 18 years old. Now, Mike left him behind easily in the first 100 meters. At 140 meters, Schollander nearly caught up with him. Then he was thrown back by a bad last turn. But Don Schollander again pulled even with Mike Wenden. However, the 18-year-old was stronger and won! For the first time since 1900, this distance was once again put into competition. The Australian, Lane, held the original (1900) Olympic record of 2:25.2 minutes. Now, in Mexico City, the Australian Mike Wenden beat this record, being clocked at 1:55.2 minutes.

In the 4 × 200 meters freestyle relay (above), a thrilling battle developed between the four Americans, Nelson, Rerych, Spitz, and Schollander, and the Australians, Rogers, White, Windle, and Wenden. The boys from the USA had to struggle with all their might for the gold medal, which originally they had expected as a matter of fact. But Don Schollander had been alerted by his defeat in the 100 meter freestyle. In the last leg, he successfully defended his small lead against his opponent, Mike Wenden, up to the finish. Gold for USA, silver for Australia, bronze for the Soviet Union, which, like Canada, never had a winning chance against the two best swimming nations, the USA and Australia.

Wenden, the Australian, surprised the experts by his clean sweeps. Meanwhile, his competitors regarded the East German world record holder, Roland Matthes (above) with respect. They knew his strength. Nevertheless, he amazed the Mexican viewers with his wins in the 100 and 200 meter backstroke.

The 17-year-old student, Roland Matthes, 1.87 meters (6′ 3″) tall, from the "flower city" of Erfurt, Thuringia, East Germany, proved he was the world's best backstroke swimmer in Mexico City. Was it the captivating regularity of his strokes? Was it his extremely high swimming stance? Was the beauty of his style identical with his ability to almost glide on the water's surface? The American experts were full of admiration for his exceptional talent. His spurts came effortlessly. The reason for not bettering two world marks in addition to setting two new Olympic records was the fact that his opponents did not press him sufficiently. He showed almost no signs of strain when he left the water. Before and during the race he was composed and alert. In his two races, he defeated six outstanding swimmers from the USA, namely Hickcox, Mills, Barbiere, Ivey, Horsley, and Hall.

In the 200 meter breast stroke, the 17-year-old Mexican, Felipe Muñoz, created a sensation. By easily beating the Russian world's record holder, Vladimir Kosinsky from Workuta, he became the Olympic hero of his country. The swimming hall echoed with an inferno of cheers (above). In the 200 meter butterfly, the favorite, Mark Spitz, failed to score. Second in Tokyo, Carl Robie, USA, took the title beating Woodroffe, Great Britain, and Ferris, USA (below).

100 meter butterfly (also see pages 118 and 119). In this event the Americans demonstrated a clear superiority, overshadowing the rest of the field by capturing all three medals. However, the outcome in the finals was a surprise for the 17-year-old Mark Spitz from Santa Clara, California, who came to Mexico as the holder of the world record for the distance, and could do no better than second place. Edging him out for the gold medal was teammate Douglas Russell from Midland, Texas who equalled the existing Olympic standard. In third place was Ross Wales from Princeton University.

Start of the 400 meter individual medley. Here the altitude of Mexico City exacted its price. The existing records were not broken. Charles Hickcox, a student from Phoenix, USA, was dominant (as he also was in the 200 meter event). A backstroke specialist, he had switched over to this competition in 1967. Behind him, Hall, USA, won second place. For the bronze medal, however, a dogged fight was carried on between the West German, Michael Holthaus, 18, and the silver medal winner in the 200 meter race, Greg Buckingham, USA. The result: Holthaus 4:51.386 minutes, Buckingham 4:51.406 minutes. For Holthaus, who at present is a student in the USA, this bronze medal, won against the American world elite, had the relative value of gold.

Overleaf: Lynn McClements, Australia, wins her gold medal in the 100 meter butterfly and offers the photographer a classic moment of joy in victory.

Over the 4×200 meters freestyle, the 14,000 viewers expected a close race between the USA and Australia. But Don Schollander gave his great opponent, Mike Wenden, no chance. Gold for the leading swimming nation, USA. With a silver medal, Australia, however, clinched her second position.

Above:
For the first time in the Olympic Games, a 200 meter butterfly race was included in the women's events. Here the USA girls—who, in general, were more successful than their male colleagues—only managed to take home the silver and bronze for this race and the 100 meter race as well. The 17-year-old Australian typist, Lynn McClements, was the surprising champion for the 100 meters, while the tall and imposing, 6′ 0½″, Dutch girl, Ada Kok, won the 200 event. In the last 10 years she has set 12 world records.

Above left:
Photo-study of the start of the men's 100 meter backstroke.

Below left:
Start of the 1,500 meter freestyle. The 21-year-old student, Mike Burton from California scored a most impressive victory, not only on this, the longest distance in the swimming events, but also in the 400 meter freestyle. Two gold medals for the USA! As a child, Burton had a bad accident and the doctor prescribed swimming lessons as therapy—Mike turned them into world records and gold medals!

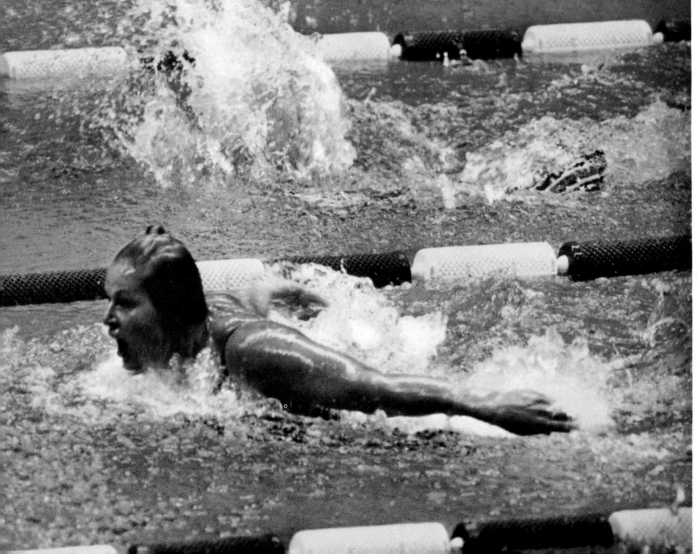

Above:
The lovely Claudia Kolb of U.S.A. mastered the individual 200 and 400 meter medleys—these most difficult and exacting ladies' events—with a superiority similar to that of Debbie Meyer in the freestyle races. Claudia, a gifted member of the Santa Clara University, California, swimming team, won the silver medal for the 200 meter breaststroke in Tokyo, 1964. The U.S.A. coaches make the most of the talents of their girls and boys—and here they reaped the golden fruits of their efforts. In the 200 meters they also managed to gain silver and bronze with Susan Pedersen and Jan Henne. In the 400 meter medley, Lynn Vidali, U.S.A., gained the silver behind Claudia—but 16-year-old Sabine Steinbach, East Germany, fought fiercely and successfully for the bronze against Sue Pedersen.

Above left:
Ada Kok, Netherlands, during her successful attempt to do justice to her rôle as a champion.

Below left:
An excellent motion-study of breaststroke showing the best West German swimmer, Uta Frommater, who was narrowly beaten by Sharon Wichman, U.S.A., in the contest for the bronze medal. Djurdjica Bjedov, Yugoslavia, gained the gold medal in front of the Russian Galina Prozumenshikova. However, Sharon proved herself in the 200 meters and gained the gold defeating the Yugoslav and Russian swimmers.

Debbie Meyer, USA, demonstrating her typical strokes with which she mastered the freestyle races in Mexico ahead of all the other contestants.

American Kaye Hall's excitement bubbled over into tears of joy following her close win over Elaine Tanner of Canada in the 100 meter backstroke. The following two places were occupied by the USA girls Jane Swaggerty and Kendis Moore. In the 200 meter backstroke the USA gained another victory with Pokey Watson—amazing everyone with her demonstration of strong stroking. Again the Canadian, Tanner, was second and Kaye Hall gained the bronze medal.

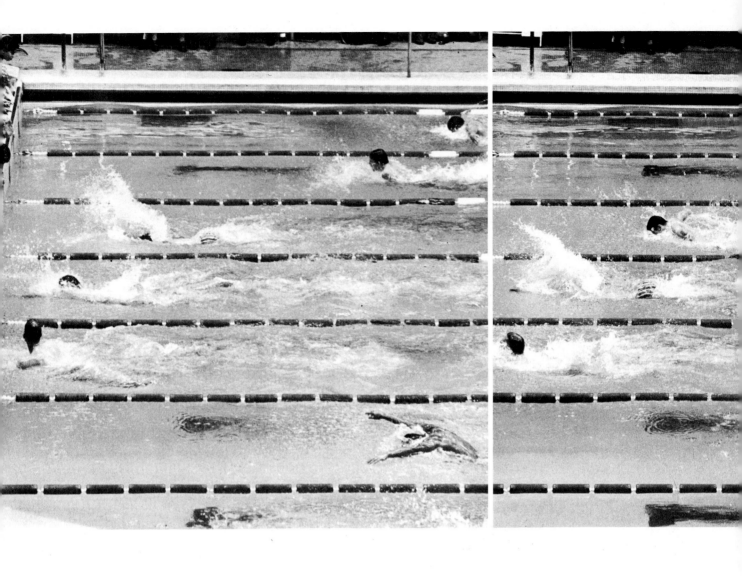

CRONOMETRAJE OMEGA
507 100 MARIPOSA HOMBRES FINAL
RESULTADOS

1	RUSSELL	EUA	0:55.9
2	SPITZ	EUA	0:56.4
3	WALLES	EUA	0:57.2
4	NEMSHILOV	URS	0:58.1
5	MARUYA	JPN	0:58.6
6	SUZDALTSEN	URS	0:58.8
7	STOCKLASA	ALE	0:58.9

0:55.6
0:55.9
TC00559

ELEKTROIMPEX BUDAPEST

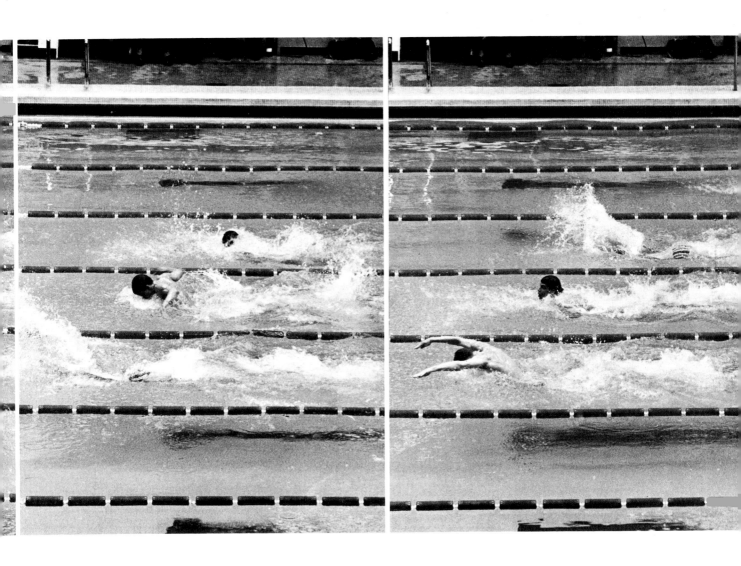

A photo-study of the men's 100 meter butterfly. The three USA boys, Russell, Spitz and Wales, took all three medals home to their country. The Russian, Nemshilov, and the Japanese, Maruya, were well beaten. The Briton, Woodroffe, managed to push himself between Carl Robie and John Ferris, both USA, to gain the silver medal in the 200 meters. At 23, Robie was practically written-off in the USA. He had won the silver medal in Tokyo for the same distance at the age of 19 and Mexico was a golden finale to his career.

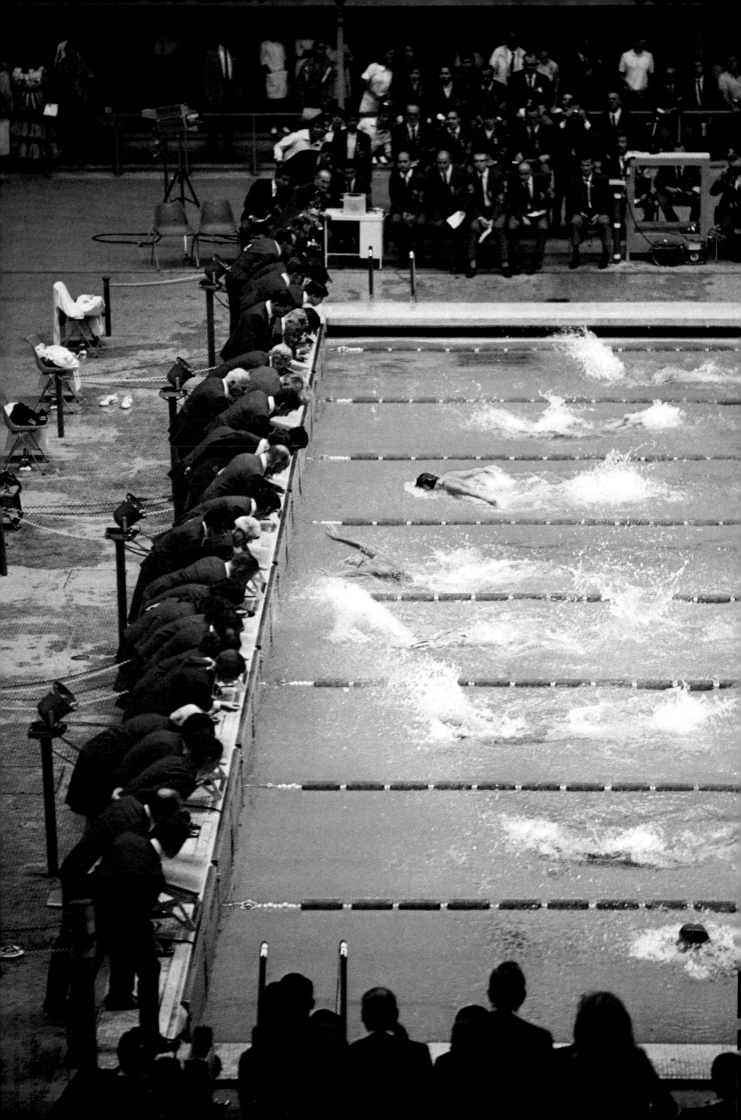

PAUL ZIMMERMANN
Los Angeles Times

*Ah,
to be
Young...*

The greatest array of aquatic talent the world has ever seen left a debris of shattered records in its wake after ten torrid days and nights of competition at beautiful Alberca auditorium in the XIX Olympiad. Half a dozen world marks were washed away and 23 out of 29 events measured by the stop watch were posted as Olympic standards.

In the final analysis it was mostly youngsters in their teens who took command. So spectacular were their performances that not one of the stars at Tokyo four years ago was able to win an individual gold medal.

For example, there was dimpled Debbie Meyer, the 16-year-old lass from the USA who ignored the talk of an "oxygen debt" at the mile and a half altitude to win three individual gold medals, the largest total ever collected by a swimmer.

And then there was 17-year-old Roland Matthes, the East German physical education student, who scored a double in the 100- and 200-meter backstroke tests, then topped this off on the final night with a fantastic 58-seconds-flat first lap in the men's medley relay.

Who will ever forget the night that 17-year-old Felipe Muñoz, fresh out of high school, upset world record holder Vladimir Kosinsky of the Soviet Union to win the 200-meter breaststroke? It was unexpected, of course, and the shouts of "Viva, el Muñoz!" resounded for half an hour after the youth had given Mexico its first gold medal of the Games.

While the almost 14,000 shook the new

Reaching her goal in the 100 meter butterfly! Lynn McClements, the girl from Australia, caused a complete sensation by touching the finish before both of her competitors from the USA, Ellie Daniel and Susan Shields, both of whom finished ahead of world record holder and pre-final favorite, Ada Kok, Netherlands. The public always favors the sensational outsiders. Never before in all her young life was the small and graceful typist from the sixth continent so honored as in this swimming stadium.

Alberca arena with their wild cheers until it seemed the place, like the Walls of Jericho, would surely come tumbling down, Felipe's teammates jammed a huge sombrero, tossed from the stands, down over his ears and paraded him precariously around the pool. Not since Joaquin Capilla accomplished it in the platform diving at Melbourne a dozen years ago, had Mexico scored an Olympic victory and that had occurred thousands of miles away, before anyone in Mexico City ever dared hope the Olympic Games would one day come to them.

Speaking of diving, in the parade of beauty among the feminine stars, it would be difficult to find one in a Miss Universe contest that would out-shine petite Milena Duchkova, the 16-year-old student from Prague. Her grace and charm drew rounds of applause, and high marks from the judges in the women's platform dives as she won over such pretty, and only slightly less proficient, performers as Natalia Lobanova of the Soviet Union and Ann Peterson, the American with the long blond tresses.

Then there was Kaye Hall, tall, blond and blue-eyed. When Catie Ball, her US teammate and world record holder, was forced to return home because of illness, this high school youngster from Washington took over to win the 100-meter backstroke in the time of 1:06.2.

Not entirely unheralded, but certainly overlooked, Kaye rose to the occasion, as she defeated Canada's equally young star, Elaine Tanner, and set one of the world records in so doing.

It was the kind of Olympic competition in which pert 17-year-old Lynette McClements, a secretary from Perth, Australia, mounted the victory podium in the 100-meter butterfly. Then there was the 19-year-old Australian, Michael Wenden, with a 52.2 world record in the classic 100-meter freestyle, and another victory in the 200.

Don Schollander, the Yale student who had made the 100 his first stepping stone to four Olympic gold medals at Tokyo in the freestyle and relays, had to settle for a shared first place on the US 800-meter quartet and second to Wenden in the 200. Thus, Schollander bowed to youth just as his seniors did to him at Tokyo.

That was a classic example of how the new crop of teenagers had taken over.

Yet the youngsters did not run all of the "old folks" out of the pool. Tall, blond Aagje (Ada) Kok of Holland, age 23, came back to win the 200-meter butterfly in the time of 2:24.7. The 100-meter breaststroke turned out to be a race between two of the "oldsters," as Djurdjica Bjedov, 21, a student from Yugoslavia, won by a touch over the world record holder and 1964 Olympic victor in the 200, Galina Prozumenshikova of the Soviet Union. She's now 22.

The "aged," aside from Schollander, fared somewhat better in the men's competition. Carl Robie of the USA, who was denied victory at Tokyo, came back at the age of 23 to emerge victorious, this time in the 200-meter butterfly. And in the place of Schollander, two 21-year-old collegians set the medal-winning pace for the USA. Charles Hickcox won the 200- and 400-meter individual medley tests, and then aided in the world record setting 400-meter medley relay team which was clocked in 3:54.9.

Perhaps the most difficult double of the competition, because of the high-altitude drain, was turned in by Mike Burton, the other US collegian star. The ease with which he won the 400-meter freestyle in 4:09.0, and then came back to far outdistance his world opponents by taking the 1,500 meters in 16:38.9, both Olympic marks, was little short of remarkable.

In the longer race, Burton was expected to have serious competition from altitude-seasoned Guilliermo Echevarria of Mexico, who had broken the world record last summer; and Greg Brough of Australia. The way it turned out, teammate John Kinsella, a powerful 17-year-old, was Mike's only opposition. The high-school youth was a distant second, but well ahead of Brough. As for Echevarria, he was a length of the pool back, in sixth. In Mexico the men and women natators from the USA gleaned 23 gold medals out of the 33 at stake, and piled up a total of 58 places out of a possible 99 gold, silver and bronze awards. They contributed 3 of the 6 world records, and 19 of the 23 Olympic marks posted or tied. These are the world records established:

Men
100-meter freestyle—Michael Wenden, Australia, 52.2.
100-meter backstroke—Roland Matthes, East Germany, 58.0.
400-meter freestyle relay—USA (Mark Spitz, Zac Zorn, Steve Rerych, Ben Walsh), 3:31.7.
400-meter medley relay—USA (Charles Hickcox, Don McKenzie, Douglas Russell, Ken Walsh), 3:54.9.

Women
100-meter backstroke—Kaye Hall, USA, 1:06.2.
400-meter medley relay—USA (Kaye Hall, Catie Ball, Ellie Daniel, Sue Pedersen), 4:28.3.

The Olympic records posted were so numerous, it would be easier to list the handful of events which survived the assault of this greatest array of swimmers ever to compete in the international games. Despite the amazing performances at Mexico City, it would be foolhardy to predict anything but an even more remarkable display at Munich four years hence.

The ceremony honoring the victors in the Alberca Olimpica found the Mexicans repeatedly savouring this colorful spectacle with a joyful devotion of which only they are capable. The grace of the gloriously costumed Mexican girls with the medals on red velvet cushions, the dignity of the officials and, behind, the laughing and reflective satisfaction of the champions all make a lasting impression on the spectators. Olympic history would be poorer without Mexico City. Thirty-three times the Olympic fanfares rang out for the champions and 23 times the gold medal winners of the USA saw their Star Spangled Banner in the middle of the flags, and sometimes to their great joy, it was on the left and right as well! But then, only exceptional athletes stand on top of the victory dais, and the goddess of victory, the 'hic et nunc' (the here and now) decorates the unknown with the laurel wreath of Olympic victory.

◁ 200 METER MEDLEY

1. Claudia Kolb USA (Gold)
2. Sue Pedersen USA (Silver)
3. Jan Henne USA (Bronze)

SPRINGBOARD DIVING ▷

1. Bernie Wrightson USA (Gold)
2. Klaus Dibiasi Italy (Silver)
3. Jim Henry USA (Bronze)

◁ 200 METER BREASTSTROKE

1. Sharon Wichman USA (Gold)
2. Djurdjica Bjedov Yugoslavia (Silver)
3. Galina Prozumenshikova USSR (Bronze)

PLATFORM DIVING ▷

1. Milena Duchkova Czechoslovakia (Gold)
2. Natalia Lobanova USSR (Silver)
3. Ann Peterson USA (Bronze)

◁ 100 METER FREESTYLE

1. *Michael Wenden Australia (Gold)*
2. *Ken Walsh USA (Silver)*
3. *Mark Spitz USA (Bronze)*

4 × 100 METER FREESTYLE RELAY ▷

1. *USA (Gold)*
Jane Barkman, Linda Gustavson,
Sue Pedersen, Jan Henne
2. *EAST GERMANY (Silver)*
Gabriele Wetzko, Roswitha Krause,
Uta Schmuck, Gabriele Perthes
3. *CANADA (Bronze)*
Angela Coughlaw, Marilyn Corson,
Elaine Tanner, Marion Lay

◁ 200 METER BREASTSTROKE

1. *Felipe Muñoz Mexico (Gold)*
2. *Vladimir Kosinsky USSR (Silver)*
3. *Brian Job USA (Bronze)*

100 METER FREESTYLE ▷

1. *Jan Henne USA (Gold)*
2. *Sue Pedersen USA (Silver)*
3. *Linda Gustavson USA (Bronze)*

Alberca Olimpica in Mexico City seats 14,000 spectators, and is one of the world's most striking swimming pools. Sensible and technical, it compares with the National Gymnasium in Tokyo, which IOC President Brundage called the most beautiful swimming pool in the world.
What will happen in Munich 1972? Will the Japanese and Russians recover from their precipitous downfall in the Alberca Olimpica? Will the Australians manage to retain their second place behind the USA? Will the East Germans bring still further new talent into the limelight?

Above: A thrilling waterpolo game played in the Alberca Olimpica comes as a welcome interlude between swimming contests.

NEIL ALLEN

The Times, London

The Men and Women of the Games

For most visiting pressmen the Games of the XIXth Olympiad were a strain and a trial beyond the normal call of duty. Communications to Europe and transportation round the vast Mexican capital daily presented problems which tended to take the edge off one's appreciation of the international triumphs as 112 countries met in the greatest of all sports competitions.

There was an unusual background of tension to these Games after the students and police of Mexico had been involved in a bloody confrontation. Even for those who chose to ignore this political back-drop and concentrate simply on sport, there was the problem of altitude and the effect lack of oxygen could have upon so many competitors in the continuous endurance events and sports.

But it is the human factor, rather than records or physiology, which makes sport come alive. And the men and women of Mexico, in their varied, intriguing ways, lived up to the casts of heroes and heroines we had seen at previous Olympics. Time and again an Olympic victory came alive not when the result went up on the giant illuminated score-board, or when the fanfares sounded but when the champion, sometimes the runner-up, gave a brief insight into his or her psychological interior. We can take, as a starting point, the remark of that wise old French writer, Michel de Montaigne: "We are all affected by the imagination. Some of us are knocked over by it." And take the case of Al Oerter who has been called the champion of champions of Mexico. I have a special link with Al, for he has won the discus throwing gold medal at all the four Olympics I have reported. At Melbourne, Rome, Tokyo he had been first and when he won again at Mexico there were even those ready to think of him as a superman. Yet the story behind Oerter's success is not of magical powers but of a great competitor who used his imagination to the full. This is how he told it to me:

"I didn't think I had a chance of beating Jay Silvester, the world record holder, until the day of the final. Then I suddenly became convinced that my 13 month plan of lifting weights, practice throws and mental preparation was going to work. The most important of these three proved to be mental. Over the years I've learned to imagine every possible circumstance in a competition.

I can lie in my bed and say 'Right. I'm in ninth place in the qualifying competition and it's raining. What do I have to do? Where do I have to move?' Or, I'm lying fourth in the Olympic final and there's just one throw left. What do you have to remember? I don't put myself into some dream world where I explode the discus out of sight. I simulate a competition as realistically as I can and I concentrate on the basic movements across the circle depending upon the weather.

If you do it often enough, with plenty of variations, then nothing in the Olympic final can come as an unpleasant surprise. When I came through in the third round in Mexico, the others didn't seem to have the same kind of mental reserve to fall back on. I got the impression that Silvester and Milde of Germany were tightening up as they said to themselves 'Jeeze, we're losing to Oerter. Who'd have thought of that?'"

Competitiveness is surely one of the most valued qualities in modern American society. But though Oerter lives up to the image by his comment, in 1964, "these are the Olympics—you die for them," he has another side to his interest in sports. Though he guesses he has thrown the discus some 33,000 times in the last 16 years, he insists "the discus is only important to me nowadays because it guarantees my presence at the Games. Throwing the discus a long way gives me the right to be there. And to be at the Games as a competitor is something I value very much.

Throwing a discus is just part of my family's belief in recreation like skiing and sailing. But it has an aesthetic pleasure of its own. Watch a small boy throw a stone across a pond. Sure it's good to see it go a long way. But it's the flight, when it skims across the water, which can please him most. It's fun."

David Hemery, winner for Great Britain of the gold medal in the 400 meter hurdles, is another one of Mexico's champions with a rare personality. After he had streaked over the 10 barriers in a world record time of

48.1 sec. and came up for press interview, an American reporter remarked to me: "He's the kind of British guy you only see in the movies." By this remark I think he meant that Hemery has charm, politeness and a diffident public manner—all of which mask an analytical mind which is brought to bear with great success upon his racing. Hemery, a little nearsighted, soft voiced and seeming more of an introvert than he really is, has always been ready to discuss the Olympic challenge that faced him from America's top hurdlers. That he does so fluently, dispassionately and realistically, had sometimes caught off balance reporters more accustomed to the "I can eat him for breakfast" kind of bravado from a potential champion.

Hemery owes much to the USA for, though he was first taught to hurdle in England by Freddie Housden, it was while he was studying at Boston University that coach Billy Smith showed him invaluable ways of building up his strength between the years 1964 and 1968. Hemery must remain one of the most modest, honest and intelligent champions I have met, but in case this may seem bias from a British reporter, I quote what his American coach said when the Olympic tumult and shouting had died away:

"I got the impression there was nothing else I could teach him, but he was so eager, so polite and so cooperative he finally convinced me I was doing a good job—in fact I felt he was doing me a favour. We were a great team and a happy one. Nothing was too much for David. He never shirked a task and I never once heard him moan, although at times I knew he felt like hurling his training gear into the nearest lake. I have known many great athletes but none so naturally gifted, so well behaved and so grateful."

Hemery's father is a successful accountant in Massachusetts.

For Madeleine Manning, who won the women's 800 meter gold medal for the USA in Mexico, the early years in Cleveland were not easy at all. When we met once, in Tokyo in 1967, she told me how much she owed to her coach, Alex Ferenczy. "He started me really. I'm a little slow to believe in myself, perhaps because I was brought up a little hard and I hold back from true self-belief. You wouldn't believe how hard he worked in order to convince me that I had what it takes to be a winner."

Madeline's heroine was Wilma Rudolph, who won three gold medals in 1960. She admired "Skeeter" Rudolph's dress sense, poise and charm even before she realized she was a great athlete. Yet Madeline has the same feminine qualities for all the demands of the 800 meters. She also gave the sport "humanity." By which I mean that I have forgotten already what her winning time was at Mexico, but I shall not forget, what she once told me about the pleasure of running at night:

"I was quite alone, running through the trees, and it was so quiet I could hear the birds and insects. My breathing was so steady, it was a kind of music and my long stride, pattering alone, gave just the right backing. It was like you were in a Utopia. I love to run at night."

There were so many others who, when they talked, made medals and records and chauvinism seem unimportant compared with the stimulating vitality of young minds and young bodies. I remember the beaten ones too . . . prideful sprinter Charlie Greene . . . sadly disappointed featherweight boxer Albert Robinson . . . and the great miler Jim Ryun who said to me before the 1,500 meters "You can be a world record holder but you're still human."

Who will deny that Debbie Meyer is proud of her three gold medals? Many of the nations represented in Mexico were not able to take home even one medal, let alone a gold!
The great swimming nations Russia and Japan did not succeed in obtaining one single gold medal.
This happy girl from the USA poses with her medals for the photographers almost as though it was really the most normal thing in the world. Perhaps here is the secret of the American coaches.

Start of the 100 meter butterfly. This interesting photo-study shows the exact moment of the start of this race. Like her countryman Wenden, 17-year-old Lynn McClements of Australia won a surprising victory just ahead of the favorites from the USA, Ellie Daniel (silver) and Susie Shields (bronze). Ada Kok, the world record holder from the Netherlands, only gained fourth place.

Away from the heat of the contest and its nerve-consuming atmosphere of competing,
winning and losing, the participants from all nations meet in friendship and often with great
amusement in the Olympic Village. Here the Australian Alan Rigby dumps the British
weightlifter Gerry Perrin into the Olympic Village swimming pool.

The 20-year-old Californian, Sue Gossick, rated fourth place in springboard diving in Tokyo.
In Mexico, however, her talents had fully developed for an Olympic victory and despite
the strong international competition, she secured an important gold for the USA.
The Russian, Tamara Pogozheva, slipped into second place ahead of Keala O'Sullivan and
Micki King, both from the USA.
In platform diving the scene was unmistakably dominated by the 16-year-old Czech from
Prague, Milena Duchkova. She came to Mexico as the favorite and collected the gold
quite ingenuously ahead of the Russian, Natalia Lobandova and Ann Peterson, USA.

The Italian, Klaus Dibiasi, (here shown from right to left in one of his artistic dives)
only succeeded in gaining silver in the springboard diving, taking second place to the champion
USA-diver, Bernard Wrightson. However, in platform diving not even the enthusiasm
of the Mexican spectators, who only wanted their own 31-year-old Alvaro Gaxiola to win,
could deprive Dibiasi of his victory. The passion of the public was rewarded when Alvaro
received silver, thus relegating Win Young, USA, to third place. Keith Russell, USA,
placed fourth and he was followed immediately by yet another Mexican, Robinson.

NEIL ALLEN
The Times, London

Some Surprises in Swimming

Several days before we left for Mexico I predicted that the Americans could win as many as 62 of the individual swimming medals and take the three men's and two women's relays. In fact they won 47 individual medals and all five relays. Thus the USA won 23 out of 34 Olympic acquatic titles.

I think this breakdown is worth giving to explain that the Olympic swimming was certain, in my eyes, to be dominated by the USA. But I must add that though the results showed that the famous American age-group national program is continuing to produce champions—and will do so again at Munich in 1972—the rest of the world is still fighting back.

How else can we explain that—for all the number of great freestyle sprinters in the USA—it was Australia who still provided the winner of the men's 100 and 200 meters in Mike Wenden. And that East Germany's willow-slim Roland Matthes won both 100 and 200 meters backstroke gold medals and also set a world 100 meters backstroke record on the first leg of the medley relay.

This British observer felt that the American swim team was unluckier than most in suffering from the notorious stomach ailment known as "Montezuma's revenge." One of these, and perhaps my favorite for the way he epitomizes determination, was Mike Burton. He was stricken by the illness and when he turned out for the 400 meters heats, he had lost about eight pounds in body weight. He had fallen sick at the beginning of the week and, after treatment in the Olympic village hospital, he fainted when he was in the elevator.

Fortunately, the doctor was passing by at the time and Burton was treated carefully, being given a tremendous amount of liquid to make up for the amount of weight he had lost. Mike recalled "It was just a question of wait and see. I felt so weak

that the question of swimming 400 meters seemed ridiculous. I turned out for my heat and I handled myself very carefully. All the time I could feel, or at least I hoped I was feeling, the strength coming back into my body."

Yet Burton survived his heat ("handling myself very carefully"), won the 400 meters final from the Canadian world record holder Ralph Hutton and then took his second gold medal by winning the 1,500 meters in 16 min. 38.9 sec., when many of us had believed that only someone living permanently at high altitude—like Mexico's Guillermo Echevarria—could possibly beat 16 min. 40 sec. at these Olympic Games. When people ask me about American swimming I usually mention "age group programs." But I prefer to take as an example Mike Burton—of whom the former Olympic champion Murray Rose has said, "He has more guts than any swimmer I know." Debbie Meyer also had her share of illness but you would never have thought so to see her flow through the pool on her way to victories in the 200, 400 and 800 meter freestyle. Claudia Kolb was deceptive too, for she was so far out on her own in the 200 and 400 meter individual medley races that it was easy to overlook her remarkable versatility.

What was not easy to forget was one title which did not go to the USA—that for the 200 meter breaststroke. It went to Pepe Muñoz and thus gave the hosts, Mexico, not only their first gold medal of these Games but also only their fourth in the history of the modern Olympics. They call Muñoz "Tibio" or luke-warm because his father comes from Aguascalientes ('hot water') and his mother from the village of Rio Frio ('cold river'). He was a 17-year-old schoolboy and he had red eyes after his victory because the emotional pleasure of a whole nation had moved him to tears during the playing of the national anthem. I have never seen any swimming arena in such a tumult and never have so many bewildered international reporters received so many kisses from so many beautiful interpreters.

When Mike Wenden won the 200 meters for Australia, one American murmured "I

Bernard Wrightson (left) was the dominating Olympic champion in the springboard diving event. The Italian Dibiasi was next, placing ahead of James Henry of USA.

guess we missed the Big Apple." Wenden closed down the career of the great Don Schollander, and Don, who had been the hero of Tokyo four years ago, bowed out with a few well chosen words and a self deprecating smile.

Afterwards an American housewife, who flitted around the press interview room poking her camera into the faces of champions, descended upon Wenden and asked him to hang his medal round Schollander's neck. Wenden looked at her and grinned. "Well," he drawled, "in the British Commonwealth Games I understand they were offering £ 50 for a medal. I'll loan this one at five pesos an hour." "You will get a copy of the photo," promised the determined lady. "Okay," said the man who had just dethroned Don Schollander, "make it three pesos."

BODO HARFENBERG
"Sport Office," West Germany

The Mysterious Men from the Ivory Coast

The canoeists were scheduled late in the Olympic programm in Mexico. Therefore, they were able to absorb the physiological impact of how the African athletes had virtually demolished their rivals in the gruelling long distance running events. Biwott's victory in the steeplechase, the one-two-three finishes of Gammoudi, Keino and Temu in the 5,000 and of Temu, Wolde and Gammoudi in the 10,000 meters, as well as Keino's triumph over Jim Ryun in the 1,500 meters: all this had impressed the canoeists very much. Although nobody from the established canoe countries ever had any dealings with their competitors from Africa, there was quite some excitement in the camp when it became known that the canoeists from the Ivory Coast were to train on the course.

The reasons given by trainers and athletes why they showed up at the course at precisely that time were slightly ridiculous: they claimed to be studying the flow of the waves or they simply strolled along the shores of the course without any apparent reason. Nobody wanted to admit that they really wanted to watch the men from the Ivory Coast.

The performance they witnessed should have calmed their anxieties. The same night, however, rumors were spreading around rapidly: the gentlemen from the Ivory Coast obviously had only put on a tactical act. In reality, they were just as fearsome as their fellow-African runners, Temu, Wolde and Keino, with tremendous ambitions and unbelievable durability in the thin air of Mexico. The day came closer, when the men from the Ivory Coast had to show their true colors. The trainers of the crews who were to meet the unknown athletes in the preliminaries, acted nonchalantly and minimized the danger, but many of them had fear written all over their faces when they cautioned against the Africans.

Well, as it turned out, all caution was unnecessary. Hardly had the starting signal been given when the mystery collapsed. The Africans began acting as if their boats had sprung a sudden leak. Their paddle motions were extremely unorthodox and their body movements were those of contortionists. Needless to say, they all failed to make the next heats. But they did not feel sorry for themselves at all and cheerfully told everybody they felt excellent and had no need for oxygen masks which were administered to many other competitors. They even ran over to their opponents, shook their hands and wished them well.

They did more than that, however. They unpacked their photographic equipment and became busy studying the techniques of their more experienced opponents. The objects of those studies had barely left the course when the gentlemen from the Ivory Coast again took to their boats to practise, and, indeed, do much better already.

In Munich, one can safely assume, the trainers will really have reason to heed the warnings, which were premature in Mexico: watch out for the men from the Ivory Coast!

HY GOLDBERG
Newark News

The International Gladiators

The art of self-defense, as exemplified by well-trained athletes wearing eight-ounce gloves on their fists, has spread around the world. As a sport, boxing once was confined largely to Europe and the Americas, but after two weeks of thunderous competition in the Arena Mexico, encompassing 300 bouts, Olympic medals were scattered to the far corners of the globe.

In the 11 weight divisions, the gold medals were spread among 7 nations, but the total of 44 medals (a bronze is awarded to each losing semi-finalist) went to the gloved warriors from 21 nations. They came from the length and breadth of Europe; from North, Central and South America; from Uganda and Cameroun in Africa; from Korea and Japan in the Far East.

Scrappers from the Soviet Union, who returned home from Tokyo with three championships in 1964, matched that achievement in Mexico City, and one of their victories was scored by Boris Lagutin, a veteran Olympian in the light middleweight (71 kgs) division. The 30-year-old Lagutin had been a bronze medalist in Rome in 1960 and had captured the gold in Tokyo.

The USA and Mexico were joint runners-up, each with two gold medalists. The USA originally was the dominant power in Olympic ring warfare. When boxing was added to the program in 1904, with seven basic divisions, the Americans swept the boards. By 1964, they were reduced to one gold medal, won by heavyweight Joe Frazier.

In 1968 George Foreman, a 19-year-old 218-pounder, retained the heavyweight crown for the USA and he was joined on the winner's podium by Ronnie Harris in the lightweight division (60 kgs).

To the delight of a roaring crowd of 15,000 Mexicans who witnessed the finals, the host country emerged with its first two champions in Olympic boxing history. Ricardo Delgado captured the gold medal among the flyweights (51 kgs) and Antonio Roldan was the featherweight (57 kgs) winner.

Poland, with three gold medalists in Tokyo, had one this time, Jerzy Kulej, who repeated his 1964 triumph in the light welterweight (63.5 kgs) class. The other winners were Francisco Rodriguez, Venezuela, light flyweight (48 kgs); Manfred Wolke, East Germany, welterweight (67 kgs); and Christopher Finnegan, Great Britain, middleweight (75 kgs).

Seven fighters from the USA reached the semi-finals, compared with six from the Soviet Union and five from Poland. The survivors of those battles included five from the Soviet Union, and three each from the USA and Poland. After Rodriguez of Venezuela had beaten Yong-Ju Jee of Korea for the light flyweight title, the first of the Polish finalists, Artur Olech, bowed to the Mexican flyweight, Delgado.

Olech, a 29-year-old Polish policeman, was making his second bid for a gold medal. In 1964, he was beaten by Fernando Atzori of Italy. This time, he was confronted by a hometown favorite, who countered his wild swings with an effective straight left. Delgado's jab, and an occasional right cross, bloodied Olech's nose and held him at arm's length through most of the three rounds. As the first Mexican ever to capture an Olympic boxing championship, Delgado was given a rousing reception.

In the next bout the Soviet bantamweight, Sokolov, gained a second round technical knockout over Bridari Mukwanga of Uganda. The tall, slender Sokolov, backing away from Mukwanga's rushes, hammered the African steadily with a strong left hand, and the Soviet scored a knockdown just before the end of the first round. He continued to land damaging blows in the second round and after two minutes, the referee stepped in and declared Sokolov the winner.

In the featherweight final, Robinson, USA, circling and jabbing, kept the Mexican Roldan at bay during most of the first round, staggering him with a right to the body just before the bell. Robinson delivered three hard blows to the head at the start of the second session, and one minute had elapsed when a huge gash was opened over Roldan's left eye. The bout was interrupted while a doctor examined the eye, and when he advised against a continuance of the contest, the referee disqualified Robinson for butting. The American also was denied the silver medal, but he was absolved after an examination of the films the following day and was awarded the medal, although there was no reversal of the disqualification. In the lightweight division, Harris, a 20-year-old US college student, dethroned Josef Grudzien, Poland's 1964 gold medal winner. Both men had scored impressive victories en route to the final. Harris drew a bye at the start, then captured four straight decisions, with the loss of only one judge's vote. In five winning contests, the 29-year-old Grudzien, also gained the unanimous nod of the five officials in four of his bouts. In the final, all five ballots were cast for Harris, who puzzled the Pole with his left-handed style, and employed a straight right effectively throughout the contest.

Kulej, another Polish gold medalist in Tokyo, enjoyed a better fate than his compatriot, gaining a 3–2 decision over a Cuban light welterweight, Enrique Regueiferos. Kulej was a wild swinger, compared to the straight, hard punching Regueiferos, but the veteran Polish scrapper landed often enough, usually in toe-to-toe exchanges, to finish with a slight margin.

Wolke, a soldier from East Germany, used caution and a good left hand to hold off Joseph Bessala of Cameroun in the battle for the welterweight crown. In a contest that was devoid of any serious blows, Wolke jabbed his way to a 4–1 decision, the straight left discouraging Bessala's attempts to move in and fight at close quarters.

Soviet Union's veteran light middleweight, Lagutin, a tall, skilled scrapper who punches straight from the shoulder, gained his second successive Olympic gold medal with a unanimous decision over Rolando Garbey, a 20-year-old Cuban soldier. Garbey, who had scored three knockouts in his four preliminary contests, was no match for the skilful, experienced Soviet battler, who floored him with a short right to the jaw in the opening round, and maintained his superiority through the second round with a variety of blows.

The Cuban rallied in the final session, and had the crowd in an uproar when he staggered Lagutin with a left and a right early in the round, but the Russian quickly steadied, and hammered Garbey into a corner before the final bell sounded. Lagutin had the rare distinction of winning a boxing medal in a third consecutive Olympiad. He had captured a bronze in Rome in 1960 prior to the gold in Tokyo. Only Laszlo Papp of Hungary has won three Olympic gold medals in boxing. He was the middleweight champion in 1948 and the light middleweight titleholder in 1952 and 1956.

In the middleweight final, the judges voted 3–2 for Finnegan, a blond southpaw bricklayer, over Alexei Kiselev of the Soviet Union. As a light heavyweight, Kiselev also had won the silver medal in Tokyo, and this time he was beaten by a narrow margin in a battle of left-handers. It was the first Olympic victory for a British boxer since 1956, and Finnegan achieved it largely through a powerful finish. They fought evenly through the first two rounds, but Finnegan began using his right hand with better effect in the final session, and during the last minute of scuffling, he rocked the Soviet with a quick left and a right that he swung from the floor.

The third gold medal of the evening for a Soviet scrapper was acquired by Pozdniak on a default when his light heavyweight foe, Ion Monea of Rumania, was unable to box because of an injured nose. But a fourth gold for the Soviets was out of the question once Foreman began landing his sledge-hammer blows on the slow moving Soviet heavyweight, Iones Cepulis.

Cepulis' nose turned crimson during the opening minute from the American's straight left, and the first time Foreman crossed his right, he staggered Cepulis. Another right before the end of the round buckled the Russian's knees, and at the start of the second round, Foreman staggered him when he switched his attack to the body. Cepulis took a count of eight on a "standing knockdown" after one minute, and at 2:30 of the second round, the referee to called a halt and declared Foreman the winner on a technical knockout. It was the fourth heavyweight victory for the USA in the last five Olympic Games.

The Russian gymnast, Olga Kharlova while soaring during a horse vault presents the photographer with a graceful and impressive motif.

*Vera Caslavska from Czechoslovakia reached the peak of her ability in Mexico City and her
highest level of near perfection. Her excellent condition showed in all her efforts. In the
all-round, she captured the most coveted gold medal, beating the Russian, Voronina.
She achieved further Olympic victories on the uneven parallel bars (picture above), in the floor
exercises (right side), and at the horse vault. On the beam, however, she had to content
herself with the silver medal, yielding the gold to the young Russian, Natalia Kuchinskaya.
Vera Caslavska's ability was at its best in Mexico. She had arrived with grief, sorrow
and a lack of training. Now she was happy to have achieved such a victory for her homeland.
But now, the queen of gymnastics, 26 years old, stepped down, ceding her throne to youth.
The nineteen-year-old student Natalia Kuchinskaya, from Leningrad, and many others,
are on the road to their first victories. No previous female athlete could pride herself on such
a long and successful career.*

Opposite: Erika Zuchold, East Germany, dismounts from the uneven parallel bars, with championship grace.

Vera Caslavska performs on the balance beam with perfect precision.

In the all-around individual awards, a second Czechoslovakian, Rimnacova, scored far behind the winner, Caslavska, reaching only the seventh position. In between, were three Russians and two East Germans.

In their first Olympic trial, the East German women gymnasts gained third position
in the ranking, falling behind the Soviet Union and Czechoslovakia. In their first Olympics,
they beat the Japanese. After Vera Caslavska's retirement, the young gymnasts from
East Germany will try to reach second position and lay siege to the leading position of the
Soviet Union. The picture shows 16-year-old Karin Janz on the uneven bars scoring a precious silver medal for East Germany. On this apparatus, she was second only to the great Vera.

Right page: Natalia Kuchinskaya, the young Russian favorite from Leningrad,
tries to compensate for her bad luck on the uneven parallel bars by magnificent performances
on the other apparatus. Here she completes an excellent vault on the horse.
She achieved the gold medal on the beam and the bronze in the individual awards combined.

j&f
HOLLAND

Cathy Rigby was the best woman gymnast of the young US team. In the team competition, the American girls were sixth, falling behind Japan and Hungary. The pictures show Cathy Rigby on the uneven bars and, below, surrounded by her teammates. Impressed and astonished, they watch the efficiency of the Russians, and Czechs ...!

Right: The Russian, Voronina, gained the second highest total score on all apparatus, behind Vera Caslavska, after the Russian Kuchinskaya surrendered her chances by faulting on the uneven bars.

Since 1952, Japan's and Russia's male gymnasts have been staging a relentless
battle, eagerly observed by the more experienced nations participating
in these events, Switzerland, Finland and Germany. The precision of the Russians,
aided by the power of their muscles, and the catlike smoothness and lissomeness
of the Japanese, have caused these two great competitors to leave the others
in the lurch, again and again.

Left: The Japanese, Endo, the great Olympic winner of the combined
individual awards in Tokyo, could reach only eighth place in Mexico City.
He won only one medal—for the horse vault.

Above: One of the young, talented newcomers in Gymnastic sports—the
Japanese, Tsukahara.

Following pages: The great Japanese winner of the Olympic combined
individual awards, Sawao Kato.

Russian gymnasts on the rings. They were as perfect and self-assured as everybody expected them to be; but the Japanese were simply better and more elegant.

The Russian Klimenko performs on the rings. However he didn't succeed in beating his Japanese opponents with this exercise. He only managed to gain a bronze medal on the parallel bars.

REX BELLAMY
The London Times

Gymnastics– Miss Caslavska and Others

Vera Caslavska (Czechoslovakia), the entire Russian women's team, Mikhail Voronin (Russia), and Sawao Kato and Akinori Nakayama (Japan) ... these were the gymnasts whose skill and character glittered most brightly amid the soaring tiers of the *Auditorio Municipal* in Mexico City. As the names roll off the typewriter, the pictures roll back before the mind's eye. It was a gloriously exciting and highly accomplished competition in which craft and art were magically blended. For all that, the bare facts of international gymnastics remained basically unchanged. The Japanese men increased the gap between themselves and the Russians. The Russians increased the gap between themselves and the Germans. In the women's event the Soviet Union's advantage over Czechoslovakia was slightly but temporarily reduced. But the precocious Russians (average age 18) did well to win at all—and will doubtless go booming ahead as they gain experience. They no longer have to worry about Miss Caslavska, now Mrs. Josef Odlozil, who has retired. The East German men's and women's teams both earned bronze medals. The men and women of four countries—the Soviet Union, Japan, East Germany, and Czechoslovakia—have the strength in depth to dominate the sport for years.

In Mexico, as in Tokyo, gymnastics was one of the great attractions of the Games. Since the Mexicans themselves are not experts (their teams both finished 14th), this was superficially surprising. But only superficially. Mexicans like throwing themselves about. Even the children's playgrounds dotted about the city are equipped with parallel bars. And the circuses around the world are mostly equipped with Mexican tumblers and acrobats. But the dedicated discipline demanded by the Olympic routines does not suit their nature.

Opposite page: The Russian favorite Voronin achieved the silver medal with this exercise on the horizontal bar. He was beaten by the Japanese Nakayama both in this event and also in the individual awards combined.

Besides their enthusiasm for the sport itself, the Mexicans had other incentives. They have a flair for—and appreciation of—the beautiful and the artistic, which attracted them to the *Auditorio Municipal*. Also Czechoslovakia's finest Olympic athlete in any sport, was the blonde and attractive pocket dynamo, Miss Caslavska, who had the engaging good taste to select the "Mexican Hat Dance" for her floor exercises. Small wonder that the crowds were queueing for tickets long before the competition began.

Inevitably, this vast and enthusiastic Mexican crowd did not so much watch the gymnastic's competition as take part in it. When Miss Caslavska was given only 9.6 for her optional exercises on the beam, there was a roar of protest—and its volume steadily increased. Berthe Villancher, president of the women's technical committee, hustled over to the judge-referee concerned. After five minutes of bedlam, the mark was changed to 9.8 (an astonishing sign of weakness). The crowd then permitted the gymnasts to carry on with the show.

Another case of overmarking occurred in the floor exercises. This time Natalie Kuchinskaya of Russia was the lucky gymnast. Miss Caslavska's luck was irrelevant to the final placings. But Miss Kuchinskaya's flattering mark clinched her a bronze medal in the free exercises. This was tough on Larissa Petrik (Russia) and Erika Zuchold (East Germany).

Though slightly exaggerated by the final statistics, the gap between Miss Caslavska and the rest was indisputable. Her closest rival was expected to be the 19-year-old Miss Kuchinskaya. But an early fall from the uneven parallel bars ruined the Russian's chances. Miss Caslavska knew how it felt; in Tokyo she had trouble with the same piece of apparatus. In Mexico her mastery was such that it was an astonishing 9.9 on the uneven bars that made her title secure. She stepped down to an echoing ovation and a series of hugs from her team-mates. Perhaps the greatest single example of Miss Caslavska's greatness was her floor work in the apparatus finals. She was already overall champion. She had already tucked away one medal after another.

But on the floor in the free exercises, those slim and lovely young Russians were marvellous. Their work was a dazzling marriage of gymnastics and ballet, with every movement beautifully coordinatd. Miss Caslavska had to follow them—and it quickly became apparent that, merely to share the gold medal, she had to do the best floor work of her life. The pressure on her was immense. When she stepped up to face the challenge, you could have heard a pin drop. Crowd and competitors alike watched with bated breath. Then, suddenly, there was the jolly little "Mexican Hat Dance" and she swung gaily through a routine as close to perfection as you could get. It was Miss Caslavska's last challenge—and she rose to it like the peerless competitor she is. On the final count, she made Olympic history, with four gold medals (including the all-round award) to add to the three she won in Tokyo. She was beaten only on the beam—by Miss Kuchinskaya, who is her likeliest successor.

But the 26-year-old champion was the only Czechoslovak to win an individual medal. The Russians showed us the depth of their resources. Zinaida Voronina, at 20 the "old lady" of the Russian team, collected a gold, a silver, and two bronze medals (her husband did even better with seven medals). Miss Kuchinskaya won four medals, Miss Petrik three. These four—and Miss Zuchold and 16-year-old Karin Janz, the East Germans—were the stars of the show. But make a note of the fact that the gymnastics "Establishment" came under fire from America. Linda Metheny, 21, was only 0.025 of a point away from a bronze medal on the beam. Cathy Rigby, only 15 and a diminutive 4′10″ (she looked like an animated blonde doll), finished 16th overall, 1.8 points behind bronze. The American women finished sixth, the men seventh.

The men's event was less satisfactory than the women's in that Voronin and Nakayama could arguably be assessed as just as good as Kato, if not better. After the compulsory exercises Voronin led from Nakayama and Kato. At the end, they finished with a quarter of a point between them—a ridiculously small percentage of Kato's winning 115.90. Individually, Voronin won two gold, three silver, and one bronze, Nakayama three gold, one silver, one bronze, and Kato two gold and one bronze. That the 22-year-old Kato should come out on top was something of an arithmetical curiosity. But he was at his best when he needed to be, finishing his work with a 9.9 in the free exercises. In the free exercises Japan had an impressive clean sweep of the medals and in fact filled the first four places. Voronin was out of luck, because it was here that he was suddenly handicapped by an old injury he had almost forgotten about.

Japan placed four men in the first five overall, which meant that Voronin's team-mates could not give him the support he needed in the team event. East Germany achieved third place in spite of the fact that only Klaus Köste, on the horizontal bar, came anywhere near an individual medal. The haul of individual medals was 11 to Japan (five gold, two silver, four bronze), eight to Russia (two gold, three silver, three bronze), and one each to Finland and Yugoslavia. The pommelled (side) horse was the only event in which Japan was unplaced. The free exercises was the only event in which Voronin was unplaced. Sadly, we can only guess what effect Franco Menichelli of Italy might have had on the overall scene. He won three medals in Tokyo. In Mexico he looked to be in the best form of his career. But he broke an Achilles tendon when making his last landing in the free exercises. They carried him from the arena in tears—and for Menichelli and Italy, that was that. The tragedy is that he was 27; for all practical purposes, it was his last chance.

As I say, the bare facts of international gymnastics remained basically unchanged. But Kato will obviously have a lot of trouble confirming his new authority, and a new queen must be found for the throne vacated by Miss Caslavska. But if Mexico is any guide, we have not seen the last of her. As the medals were handed out, I looked round at the judges who stood silently watching. Boris Shakhlin was there. Larissa Latynina, too. Doubtless the memories of greatness were crowding back on them. Perhaps Mrs. Odlozil will join them at Munich—and the golden memories of Tokyo and Mexico will come crowding back on all of us.

158

ALMON LOCKABEY
Los Angeles Times

Men Against the Elements

If the 1968 Olympic Yachting Games at Acapulco, Mexico, proved nothing else they proved that you can't prognosticate the weather—a year, a month, a week, or sometimes not a day in advance. For two years in advance of the big show at Acapulco, sailors throughout the world were making dire predictions that there wouldn't be enough wind during October to finish most of the races. As a result many sailors arrived with light weather boats that were rigged and tuned for the expected zephyrs.

And what happened? There was wind every day. Sometimes more than some of the skippers could handle. In any event, it called for some hurried re-tuning. In another respect the weatherman dished up what everyone expected but not everyone could cope with. It was hot. Humid, muggy hot. The kind of heat that enervates and saps strength and energy. Several skippers ended the series with badly burned faces that not even healthy doses of anti-sunburn lotions could protect.

Added to the hot breezes was a sea generated by an offshore storm that often had waves and swells running counter to the wind direction, resulting in some confused, sloppy conditions that obviously took their toll of skippers and crews who were accustomed to more normal conditions.

Paul Elvstrom, the current world champion Star Class skipper from Denmark—who could do no better than fourth in the final standings—summed it up pretty accurately when he commented after his only win in the sixth race: "We decided what was the proper thing to do, then did the opposite." "Under conditions like these you can't predict a windshift," commented a frustrated New Zealand skipper plagued by swells running counter to the wind condition. "Most of us are going home and learn how to sail all over again."

But the adverse conditions—such as they were—failed to daunt the gold medal winners. US gold medalists Lowell North in the Stars and Buddy Friedrichs in the Dragons were both used to sailing in semitropical conditions. Even so, North sailed the first three races suffering from a fever brought on by a combination of heat and the customary Mexican abdominal ailment.

But how about such brilliant performers as Rodney Pattisson of England in the Flying Dutchman Class, Valentin Mankin of Russia in the Finns and the Sundelin brothers, Ulf, Jorgen and Peter in the 5.5s? All came from considerably cooler climes but never seemed to be bothered by the heat. In all three cases their gold medals could be attributed to a determination to win.

Pattisson and his crew, Ian McDonald-Smith, who came the closest to a perfect score in the Flying Dutchman Class, attributed their victory to three years of dedicated sailing with the 1968 Olympics as their ultimate goal. Attention to such details as minute shifting of weight to compensate for constantly changing wind and sea conditions and an intimate knowledge of the boat's performance under all conditions were just a couple of things that paid off for the British sailors. The only thing that robbed Pattisson of a perfect score was a disqualification in the opening race in which he collided with another boat. Most skippers in the class agree that this unfortunate situation was due to a poor starting line which could not be crossed on starboard tack, resulting in a jam at the port end of the line. Pattisson went on to win the race by the same large margin as the following five, but the DSQ turned into his throwout race. His second place in the final race turned out to be his worst performance.

The Sundelin brothers in the 5.5s expected their toughest competition from the USA, England and Germany. But when the final scores were toted it was the 66-year-old Swiss, Louis Noverraz, who had given them the most trouble. Noverraz will be remembered as the gold medal winner in 1936, only to be disqualified later for alleged professionalism. It wasn't until three years ago that the International Yacht Racing Union rescinded the ruling and declared that he had never been a pro. His silver medal at Acapulco was a reward long overdue.

Again, the victory of Sundelin and his two younger brothers was a result of the finest kind of teamwork in which every member of the crew knows his job and performs it to perfection. Ulf said he and his two brothers work on the theory that each man should know the other's job equally well.

They even traded off on the helm under the belief that no one man can concentrate on handling the tiller more than 15 minutes at a time in competition as demanding as the Olympics.

Buddy Friedrichs admitted that the Acapulco heat was not as troublesome to him and his crew, Barton Jahncke and Gerald Schreck, since it was not too different from that to which they were accustomed on Lake Pontchartrain. The long Pacific swell caused them some difficulty in the early stages of the series but, here again, several years of sailing together had welded a team capable of solving such minor difficulties. The worst race of the US team was a sixth in the second race in which they were over the starting line early because of gear difficulties, forcing them to restart behind the fleet.

Mankin's victory in the Finn Class was somewhat of a surprise, though a popular one. The 30-year-old Russian, a 15-year veteran in the Finn Class, made many friends among to the competitors, race officials and spectators. Skipper superiority in this class was particularly important as all of the Finns were of one mold—built in Mexico—and all of the sails, from the loft of Lowell North in San Diego, were as nearly identical as possible. Skippers who found things such as masts and rudders not exactly to their liking had time before the series started to make minor changes within the measurement tolerances. Despite Mankin's experience and skill in these one-man machines, many observers before the series picked 1964 gold medalist Willi Kuhweide, West Germany; European champion and Gold Cup winner Henning Wind from Denmark; and Pan American Games winner Joerg Bruder of Brazil as the skippers to beat. The big surprise came in that Mankin is known as a heavy-weather sailor. Although the winds at Acapulco were not as light as expected, they never got to the heavy-weather stage with possibly one exception when the breeze whistled up 14–16 knots.

The remarkable thing about the 1968 Olympic yachting was that in every class except one, the gold medal was cinched in the next to the last race. The exception was Rodney Pattisson in the Flying Dutchman, who had to sail the final race to assure his victory because of the first race DSQ. In the other four classes, skippers could have remained on the dock for the last race and still collected their gold medals. To their credit, none did. And to their further credit, they all won their final races. In many a previous Olympics the gold medals have not been won until the final and often frantic race.

The job done by the various Mexican committees was virtually flawless from opening to closing ceremonies. Skippers and crews who had sailed in the 1964 Olympics at Enoshimo, Japan, proclaimed the Mexican planning and facilities just as efficient.

The only serious mishap occurred on shore when early one morning a Mexican Navy craft patrolling the mooring area went out of control and slammed into several 5.5s moored at the seawall. Most seriously damaged was the Australian boat Barrenjoey, which had a large hole stove in her port side and several broken frames. The accident happened about 7 o'clock in the morning and the boat was repaired and on the starting line by noon of the same day, testifying to the speed and skill of Mexican shipwrights and a Canadian boat builder who joined forces to put the boat back in shape for the start.

Opposite page: The Olympic yachting events were held miles away in the Pacific outside the Bay of Acapulco. As the average wind force varied between 4 and 5, the expert yachtsmen found themselves facing unexpected problems. They were accompanied by both heat and wind. In the Dragon class the European favorites were beaten by the sailmaker 'Buddy' Friedrichs from the USA with his two friends Jahnke and Schreck. He had already managed to beat the international élite in 1966 on the Öresund outside Copenhagen. The Dane, Aage Birch, was only able to gain the silver medal in Mexico.

Above: The superb scientifically planned rowing course of Xochimilco will long be remembered by the rowers from 13 countries who took part in the Mexican Olympics. The high altitude made this course the most difficult in the world. The New Zealanders are shown here winning the coxed fours ahead of East Germany and Switzerland.

Left above: The Olympic Flame which burned in the yachting harbor of Acupulco against a background of white luxury hotels stimulated the victors or consoled the losers during the hard-fought yachting events.

Left below: The yachtsmen from the USA were the most successful in Acapulco with their victories in the Dragon and the Star classes. The USA gained the gold medal in the Star class with Lowell and North. North took his revenge on the Dane, Paul Elvström, who had beaten him in the previous two world championships.

The German rowing-eight wins a precious gold medal with Meyer, Schreyer, Henning, Ulbricht, Hottenrott, Hirschfelder, Siebert, Ott, coxswain, Thiersch. The boys had to fight doggedly and with their last ounce of strength during the last 200 meters before the finish in order to maintain their slight lead over the approaching Australians and Russians. Their famous trainer, Karl Adam, had a few anxious seconds. It was an extremely narrow but happy victory with such opponents.

Above: The rowers often went beyond the limits of their endurance in this thin air. Accompanying vehicles always hovered nearby with supplies of oxygen.

Below: The Russians gained their only rowing victory in the double sculls with Sass and Timoshinin. Holland won the silver, USA the bronze.

On the banks of Xochimilco, the Mexican spectators watched the canoe contests—for them
an unknown sport. It is a sport which is at home on the rivers of Europe and its top Olympic exponents
come from a broad base of thousands of nature-loving amateurs. The Hungarians were
predominant over the other nations in Mexico.

The weight lifters had an exclusive arena in the 'Teatro de los Insurgentes', a fully air-conditioned cinema, the gay mosaic façade of which will long be remembered by the many spectators from all over the world.

Above, from left to right:
Gold medal winner Baszanowski of Poland; in the center, the famous holder of the world record for the heavyweights, the Russian Zhabotinsky; and on the right, the winner of the gold medal in the Bantamweight, Nassiri of Iran.

Opposite page:
In this photo-study a Korean weight-lifter shows the drama and rigor which earn the weightlifters and their efforts enthusiastic applause again and again.

Right:
Honoring the victors in the Heavy-weight class. Gold for Zhabotinsky, Russia; silver for Reding, Belgium; and bronze for Joe Dube of the USA.

ALI GÜMÜŞ
"Tercuman," Istanbul

Wrestling's "Old Men" Sweep Mexico

Since 1896, the year in which the German Schumann was acclaimed as Olympic champion, wrestling, like no other sport, has been subject to changes. In St. Louis, 1904, there was not one champion, but seven, each representing a different weight class. Much has changed since then, from the dress to the mats to the weight of the wrestlers. Until the Olympics in Paris, 1924, the wrestlers fought until one had defeated the other. In Paris, the fight was limited to 30 minutes. Later on, these 30 minutes were reduced to 20 and, during the Olympics in London, to 12 and, after Tokyo, to nine minutes.

After the Olympic Games in Mexico, the number of weight classes was increased from eight to ten. The many changes in wrestling might constitute a danger for this sport and its future. Some effects are already evident. When the time was reduced to nine minutes, the bridge exercises lost importance. Wrestling became acrobatics. In Mexico City, the gold medals in wrestling went to those who had already been active in the sport for the last 12 to 15 years. The exercise methods and training required by the old wrestling system were much more severe and, in view of their techniques, the "old" wrestlers were superior to the younger ones. Greco-Roman champions like Kirov (Bulgaria), Varga (Hungary), Vesper (East Germany), Metz (East Germany), Radev (Bulgaria), and Free-Stylers like Nakata (Japan), Ueteka (Japan), Kaneko (Japan), Atalay (Turkey), Gurevitch (Russia) and Ayuk (Turkey) have been top wrestlers for 12 to 15 years. Among them, Mahmut Atalay can be considered as "grandfather," since he has been in the circle for the last 18 years.

Hristo Trakov (Bulgaria) who is considered the world's best Greco-Roman wrestler in the 57 kg (125 lbs.) class, was disqualified by the International Amateur Wrestling Federation Health Commission, which found ammonia in his wrestling suit during his match with David Hazewinkel (USA). In the middleweight (192 lbs.) group Lothar Metz of East Germany, who had been pursuing the gold medal since the Olympic Games in Rome, finally got it in Mexico, as did his countryman Rudolf Vesper in the welterweight group. Boyan Radev (Bulgaria), the "golden" man of the Olympics in Tokyo (1964), and who in 1967 during the world championship lost to the Russian Yakovenko and was beaten by the Hungarian Franc Kiss during the European Championship 1968, finally gained revenge by winning the gold medal in Mexico.

In freestyle wrestling, neither the Turks nor the Russians gained the desired or expected number of medals. In the three lighter weight classes, the Japanese proved their superiority. In the 70 kg (154 lbs.) class, the Persian Muvahed crowned his threefold world championship title with the Olympic medal thus proving once again that he is the best freestyle wrestler in the world.

Previous two pages:
Left page: The young West German, Rudolf Mang, has been weight-lifting since he was 13 years old and finds it great fun. Among the heavyweight élite in Mexico, he succeded in reaching 5th place.

Right page, above: A scene from the Greco-Roman contest between Schneider, East Germany, and Dutz, Belgium.

Center left: The flyweight wrestling contest between the Czech, Zeman, (bronze) and the West German, Lacour.

Center right: The lightweight wrestling contest between Horvat, Yugoslavia, (silver) and Rost, West Germany, (4th place).

Below: The tactic of biding one's time belongs to the wrestlers' repertoire. Here the Japanese, Hideo Fujimoto, (silver) awaits his chance against Hizur Alakoc, Turkey, who gained 5th place, in the featherweight contest.

Opposite page:
Above: Lothar Metz, East Germany, close to his victory over Nicolai Negut, Rumania, where he won the gold medal.

Below: The American Wayne Wells appears to have four legs in the free-style bantamweight wrestling contest. But two legs belong to the Japanese Iwao Horiuchi who was defeated by the American.

Gösta, Sture and Erik Pettersson from Sweden came to the Tokyo Games in 1964 accompanied by one "foreigner" called Hamrin, and received the bronze medal in the road team time trial. Three years later, at the world championships in Germany, the Petterssons were joined by their youngest brother, Tomas, who took Hamrin's place. The team of brotherhood succeeded in winning the title.

The following year, at the magnificent oval of Mexico City, the four brothers failed by 97 seconds to add gold to their family treasure. At the half way stage—51 kilometers of a total 102—the Swedes led by one second, but lacked punch towards the end and had to yield to the Dutch. They consoled themselves with silver, to which Gösta added another bronze medal in the individual road event, where young Tomas finished seventh.

Altogether quite satisfactory for this unique team whom nobody could blame for lacking... cohesion.

The Petterssons were not the only case in Mexico of brotherhood on wheels. The French had something similar to offer. To be precise, Pierre Trentin and Daniel Morelon are actually not tied by consanguinity, but ever since their childhood, when Daniel came to Paris as an apprentice mechanic, they have been close friends. They are the same age, belong to the same club, are managed by the same Louis Gérardin (a former world champion and now manager of the French national track team), live practically next door to each other in the same house at Créteil (Pierre's birthplace in the outskirts of Paris), and for some time Daniel worked at the little factory where Trentin and his father, himself once an excellent rider, manufacture handbags.

Fair Pierre and dark Daniel even share their sports laurels. As it happens, Trentin is generally more successful in even years, Morelon seems better in odd ones. They hold a number of world titles, but excel in the somewhat anachronistic tandem specialty, which they took up on a thirty-year-old model belonging to Gérardin.

In the meantime they have acquired a brand new one. On this new two-seater bike, the couple won the tandem event in Mexico City. Trentin brought home the individual time trial, with Denmark's Niels Fredborg as runner-up; Morelon took the scratch sprint, downing the Italian Giordani Turrini. This meant two gold medals each, but since Trentin had finished third in the sprint event, he was one bronze medal up on his mate.

This triumph proved a real paradox for, ever since the famous Parisian "Vel' d'Hiv'" was pulled down, France has been left without an indoor track. French riders have in fact very few training facilities and their cycling competition occurs exclusively on tracks abroad. Those who ought to know swear to it that track champions can only come out of these temples. But the two Frenchmen made it without any temple at all...

Under such circumstances it is even more amazing that France scored another track victory in Mexico. The hitherto unknown youngster, Daniel Rebillard, surprisingly won the individual pursuit. "I owe it to daddy," he claimed. Another family affair. "Dad," who had tried a professional career on the road—unsuccessfully—encouraged and coached the elder of his two boys... for road purposes, of course.

Only recently, young Daniel discovered the charms of the track, and showed so much pluck in the pursuit that Gérardin believed him good enough to go to Mexico. But only as a stand-in. As things went, teammate Darmet fell sick, and the beginner was "let loose"—with the unexpected result.

A harmless tap on the back, given by Kissner to his mate Henrichs, prevented West Germany from bringing home the team pursuit. The judges considered it as a "push," which is strictly prohibited, and the German team was disqualified, while Denmark received the gold medal.

When the road event started, Italy, as one of the leading countries in wheel riding, was without a victory. Pierfranco Vianelli put an end to that. He beat Leif Mortensen from Denmark by almost 90 seconds, with the elder Pettersson brother Gösta third. In this contest, just as taxing as a marathon, the winner showed the makings of a great champion. As a professional, though—for immediately after the Games, he decided to choose the money-making side.

LOUIS CLICTEUR
"Het Laatste Niews," Brussels

Brotherhood on Wheels

CIRO VERRATTI
Sportchief " Corriere della Sera,"
Milano

Fencing: An exquisitely Olympic Sport

Fencing is a sport which is congenial to the Olympics, a sport in which professionalism has not yet penetrated in an overwhelming manner as in other sports.

This is one of the reasons but not the only one for which fencing, even if it is an ancient sport, merits a place of honor in the modern Olympic Games. Especially considering that if once upon a time there were few nations that practised it, today the number of "fencing" nations has increased considerably. If today new classifications have been established in international fencing it is due to this fact too.

Now, as everyone knows, the strongest participants as a whole, are the Soviets, and in Mexico this was confirmed. However, we had the feeling that some crack was beginning to show itself in this perfect mechanism. It is not enough merely to count the win in a delicate sport like fencing, one should also look at the style of certain victories. To tell the truth, the Soviets in Mexico did not have the same authority, the same artistic and athletic superiority that they had demonstrated at the Olympic Games of Rome or at Tokyo and in the world championships which take place in the years when there are no Olympic Games.

This happened partly due to technical reasons and partly because of psychological motives. On the technical level the Soviets have let themselves be slightly influenced new and precarious theories, although they were once pure exponents of classical fencing. In other sports there is a steady technical evolution, above all in track and field, swimming and skiing. In fencing no evolution is possible since this sport, which is above all an art, reached its perfection long ago. "New" fencing is certainly not superior to classical fencing, just as modern painting is certainly not superior to ancient painting on an artistic level.

Then, on the psychological level there has virtually been a 'slaves revolt' as opponents are no longer awed by confrontation with a Soviet fencer. That one-time reverential fear is decreasing and the Russian fencers are no longer looked upon as men from Mars, but as common mortals.

Here it must be specified that the major opponents of the Soviets are no longer the Italians and the French. There was a time when Latin fencing ruled the world and the Italians especially were unrivalled. Then this supremacy mysteriously ended. France has since regained some gleam of its ancient glory, but Italy's decline inexplicably continues despite the efforts of the Italian Fencing Federation.

The major opponents of Russia in fencing are the Iron Curtain countries, in particular the Hungarians. The performance of the Hungarians, however, does not surprise us, in view of their glorious tradition. What does surprise us is the performance of the others, above all the Poles, who have suddenly appeared on the fencing scene. There is a fencer among them who has especially captivated the attraction and the general sympathy of everyone, and he is Jerzy Pawloski, a great sabreur, a magnificent opponent and a perfect gentleman— one of those who bring honor to fencing. He is 37 years old, but in fencing 37 years are not really so many. Men like Kovacs or Gerevich, two unforgettable Hungarians, continued to win in Olympic Games or in world championships at the ripe old age of forty-eight. Pawloski is a major in the army and his career has been rapid because he has been helped by his fencing victories. His fencing is lively and brilliant, like his intelligence, full of humanity, understanding and kindness.

The final match on the board in Mexico offered us an excellent, furious, unforgettable battle, full of uncertainties and emotions; but when it was over, we learned that Pawloski had won the Olympics. It was his first Olympic victory after three world championships, and there was a general explosion of enthusiasm in the great hall. Everybody wanted to run up to embrace him, even the ones who had been his opponents on the board. However, it was not easy to reach him because Pawloski was a captive of his companions who had caught hold of him and who were tossing him up into the air without ever getting tired of doing so. Jerzy was crying for the thrill of it and those tears of his remain our most vivid remembrance of the Olympic Games of fencing at Mexico City.

During the Olympic Games of 1960 in Rome, a young American student of theology named Gary Anderson stood behind the shooting line as a substitute. What he saw and heard he wrote down in his note book; he added sketches showing the positions of the competitors, took pictures of the favorites and the "also-rans", drew them into conversations and returned home to Nebraska with enough material to fill a textbook on the art of shooting.

From this moment on, he did not just study theology. As an elective during free hours, he added the subject of shooting. He re-evaluated the notes he took at Rome and thoroughly involved himself with psychology, anatomy and physiology. Because he did this with singular intensity, because he tested his theories again and again and searched for the best position to hold his rifle, because he analyzed his potential under various conditions and frequented all competitions of importance; in short because he—like nobody before him—recognized the fact that the two training components, theory and practice, are inseparable, the "student" advanced to become the best marksman in the world.

After a few semesters, Gary Anderson's name ranked at the top of the international elite: four world championships in Cairo (1962), the Olympic championship in Tokyo (1964), three more world championships in Wiesbaden (1966). And again, in Mexico City, he added another Olympic championship, again with a new world record count.

If today a chair were open at the centers of sports study in the USA, the USSR or anywhere else in the world to teach the sport of shooting, nobody could fill that chair better than Gary Anderson. In his notebooks and especially in his mind, all methods are listed which would enable mind, organs and muscles—in achieving technical perfection and precision—to shoot the smallest pattern possible.

So far, no marksman has succeeded in winning a gold medal in more than two Olympic Games. Anderson could become the first to achieve a hat trick. He has already begun work; thirty days after the final ceremonies in Mexico City, Gary and his young wife arrived in Munich, where the next Games will be held in 1972. First he took a course in German in order to enroll in a course in theology; but also in order to study—in his "elective" shooting course—other countries, their customs and specialties. His third try to capture a gold medal will profit from it in three years.

I asked Gary Anderson, "How can anybody shoot better than you?" He answered quickly, "By occupying himself even more with the subject, and by discovering methods which are successful even when nervousness or other factors disrupt the harmony between man and weapon." To achieve this unshakable unity between man and weapon is a task which Gary Anderson has been constantly working on since 1960 in Rome. He also has collected the best literature obtainable on shooting: his own notes from Rome, and the subsequent chapters written in Cairo, Tokyo, Wiesbaden and Mexico City.

The world record in his specialty—the 300 meters—has already been improved by Anderson by several rings. But those who know him are convinced he will drive the world record even closer to the absolute maximum. For Gary Anderson is not only the perfect student of marksmanship; he is also the perfect marksman.

KARL HEINZ LANZ
Editor "International Shooting Sport"

*Gary
Anderson –
the
Marksman-
Scholar*

*Gary Anderson, USA, during his series of
1,157 points in the free-rifle 300 m contest
with which he set a new world record,
a new Olympic record and won the gold
medal. He broke his own records and
repeated his gold medal from Tokyo 1964.*

The honoring of the victors in the free-rifle, three positions contest on the model shooting-range 'Oligone Olympico' in Mexico. Gold medal for Gary Anderson, USA, with 1,157 points, silver medal for Valantin Kornev, USSR, with 1,151 points and bronze medal for Kurt Müller, Switzerland, with 1,148 points.

John Writer, USA, (shown in center photo and on victory stand No. 2) during his practice for the small-bore rifle, three positions contest. He won the silver medal with 1,156 points following Bernd Klingner, West Germany, (gold medal with 1,157 points) and beating the Russian Parkhinovich (bronze medal with 1,154 points). The present world and Olympic record scored by Lones Wigger, USA, in his Olympic victory at Tokyo 1964, was not endangered.

*The greatest Olympic boxing matches took place in the famous old 'Arena Mexico'.
Baldwin, USA, fighting against the Cuban Garbey, who won the silver medal
for the Light-Middleweight. Baldwin and the German Günther Meier received the bronze
medals. (In Olympic boxing contests, both the defeated boxers in the semi-finals
receive a bronze medal as there are no fights for 3rd and 4th places.)*

*In the Lightweight contest Harris, USA, secured the gold medal in the fight against
Grudzien, Poland. Grudzien received silver in front of the Rumanian
Cutov and the Yugoslav Zvonimir.*

*In the Middleweight semi-final, Jones, USA, lost his opportunity in the fight against the
Englishman, Christopher Finnegan (gold). The Mexican spectators protested, but the judges
still backed Finnegan. Jones received the bronze medal together with the Mexican Zaragoza.*

Honoring the Lightweight victors. Harris, USA, gold, silver for Josef Grudzien, Poland, and bronze for Cutov, Rumania, and Zvonimir, Yugoslavia.
The young giant George Foreman, USA, 19 years old, hit his opponent, the Russian Iones Chepulis, so often and so accurately on the chin in the first round, that the referee stopped the fight in the second round. Gold for Foreman — he thanks the Mexican spectators for their applause with the sign of victory. His Russian opponent is marked by the heavy fight. Bambini of Italy and Rocha of Mexico received the bronze medals.

In the 'Salla de Armas', this splendid fencing hall in Mexico City (see the two previous pages), not only medals were contested in this most elegant sport, but also the high culture of the old fencing tradition represented by France and Italy found itself in opposition to the stormy and explosive fighting style of the Eastern nations and especially Russia. Hard pressed by Hungary, Poland and Rumania, Russia did not allow herself to be shaken from her predominant position. However, France and Italy also secured respect and recognition through their numerous medals. Nevertheless, the Russian fencing schools train a first-class reservoir of talents.

In the 4,000 meter team pursuit the Danish team Asmussen, Jansen, Lyngemark and Olsen
(above in red jerseys) won the gold medal through the disqualification of the four Germans, Hempel,
Link, Henrichs and Kissner (below).
The silver medal was not awarded to the Germans until November 27, 1968, in Lausanne
by the 'Federation Internationale de Cyclisme'.

*Above: Mexico plays Japan in the semi-final. The Japanese won 2—0 and thus
gained the bronze medal.
Left page: In the final between Bulgaria and Hungary the referee was
disappointing and allowed the game to degenerate into discreditable scenes. After he had sent
off three Bulgarians and then a Hungarian, the Mexican spectators finally lost their last
shred of patience and threw their cushions onto the field. The Hungarians eventually won 4—1.
Below: The honors of the soccer contest. The picture shows the victorious Hungarians
and the Japanese who had had a German coach. The Bulgarian team,
(silver medalists) are not in this picture.*

BRIAN GLANVILLE
The Sunday Times, London

Anyway, the Best Team Won...

For the purist, the logician, there are few less satisfactory tournaments than the Olympic soccer competition. The utter disparity between the kinds of teams entered by the various countries deprives it of any real significance.

This time, for example, Mexico, the hosts, fielded a side made up of young players with leading professional clubs—which led to a delightful exchange at the Press Conference following their defeat by France— the French fielded teams of genuine amateurs. Indeed, the last word was perhaps provided after the competition, when two of the gold-medal winning Hungarian team, Novak, the right-back and captain, and Lajos Szucs, the wing-half, were accorded the highest honor in the professional game—being chosen to play for the Rest-of-the-World against Brazil!

What one looks for in Olympic tournaments, then, is less significance than compensation, and there was some. If Szucs, by and large, was the outstanding player in the competition, his terrific shooting with either foot bringing him a hat trick of goals against Japan, the player most of us will remember is Japan's own centre-forward, Kamamoto.

One had heard of him—and his promise— beforehand, but one scarcely expected such a splendidly versatile and powerful performer. Indeed, had he played for one of the stronger Eastern European teams, he would have scored many more than the series of fine goals which he actually got. Tall, strongly built, very confident, an intelligent mover and passer, adept at controlling the ball with his chest, possessed of an excellent right foot, Kamamoto was the inspiration of a team which accomplished wonders.

I saw them beat the French with ease, drum

For the first time in 1968 the famous and magnificent Aztec Arena in Mexico City was the scene of an Olympic soccer contest in which modern soccer was predominant as the 'amateurs' had adopted the style of the professional teams.

a tattoo against the goalposts of a lucky Spanish eleven, lose to a Hungarian side just too powerful and experienced for them and finally—remarkably—thrash Mexico 2–0, to win the third place match; an achievement which provoked a vivid hail of cushions from the crowd. Nor can one easily forget the massed chant of "JA-pon! JA-pon!" (the *j* pronounced, after the Latin American fashion, as an *h*) when the Mexicans decided to change their allegiance to the visitors.

Needless to say, both goals were scored by Kamamoto, and the Mexican team really deserved to be three, rather than two, goals down at the interval. It was altogether a dreadful disappointment for the Mexicans, who were expected to benefit greatly from the advantage of playing 7,200 feet above sea level against teams unaccustomed to such remote heights.

This was the most intriguing aspect of the whole Olympic tournament; in effect, it served as a pilot for the 1970 World Cup. One had heard all sorts of alarming stories about the effect of altitude on sea level teams, and when one drove out to Puebla, which stands even higher than Mexico City, shortly before the Games began, one found no reassurance. The Czech Olympic team was playing the Mexican national eleven in the newly-opened Stadium, and in the last twenty minutes, their defenders were staggering about the penalty area like men in the last stages of exposure. Somehow, as the ball continually struck post or bar, they managed to hold out for a 1–1 draw, but the lesson seemed ominous.

In competition, however, most of the sea level teams adapted happily, as evidenced by the fact that three of them, the French, the Bulgarians—in the semi-final—and the Japanese managed to beat Mexico. Indeed, the only signs of exhaustion I saw in the colossal Aztec Stadium, where games in Mexico City were played, were shown by the Spaniards, whose team, after all, was playing another sea level one, Japan.

For all its inequalities and doubtful relevance, the tournament engendered mighty passions. During its course, no fewer than three Mexicans were stabbed to death for saying, correctly as it proved, they did not think Mexico would win the title. After the 4–1 victory by France over Mexico, M. André Grillon, the French team manager, said at the Press Conference that he was delighted his side had defeated a team of professionals. Instant uproar among the Mexican journalists. How did he know, they demanded, that these were professionals? M. Grillon, who once himself played right-back for France, cast a bland eye on them and replied that surely everybody knew. Would he, then, he was asked, officially protest? No, he replied, with equal blandness. After all, the French had been so kindly treated in Mexico.

There were one or two dire alarums in Guadalajara, notably in the match which pitted Israel against Ghana. Two Ghanaians were ordered off after a raging brawl. Each attacked the referee, each was subsequently given a long suspension. Yet curiously enough, the teams later ate pacifically, side by side, in the same restaurant. Such are the vagaries of violence.

As for the Final, what a farce that turned out to be; there is still dispute over whether Senor Diego De Leo, the Italo-Mexican referee, did the right thing in sending off Bulgarians in such abundance: three of them in the first half, to one Hungarian (the ludicrously unlucky Juhasz, embraced by a Bulgar as he left) in the second.

I remember coming away in the bus, after the game, and overhearing a protracted argument between a large, elderly American tourist who felt he hadn't had his money's worth (he hadn't!) and two embattled Danish journalists defending the referee. Morality—so ran the gist of their argument—must come before spectacle. In a phrase, the game's the thing.

I sympathized with both parties. It seemed to me that the foul which caused Bulgaria's Dimitrov to be sent off was not really worth expulsion; nor have subsequent arguments that the referee had cautioned him, held up some colored card for the world to see (according to the curious dispensations adopted by the tournament) and therefore had no choice, really convinced me.

In any event, the Bulgarians, as the saying goes, lost their cool; and the football match—as a football match—quickly ceased to exist. Still, the Hungarians were ahead by two goals to one at the time, and if the Final in no way measured up to the splendid one of 1964 in Tokyo, there is little doubt that it was won by the most talented team. A team which had two of its men chosen to represent the world. . .

Time after time, it was the same: silver, then bronze, then silver again and then bronze again. Despite their great abilities, the Yugoslav water poloists had never been able to climb on the highest pedestal, reserved for Olympic champions only. During the five Olympic Games since World War II, the gold medal in water polo had been won twice by Italy (1948 at London and 1960 at Rome) and three times by Hungary (1952 at Helsinki, 1956 at Melbourne and 1964 at Tokyo) and again and again the Yugoslavs had sworn: next time the gold medal will belong to us.

They finally did it in 1968. At the conclusion of the water polo events, gold medals were hung around the necks of the giants from the Adria. The Yugoslavs had finally reached the top.

And yet, the road to their greatest triumph had been very hazardous. When Italy defeated Yugoslavia, 6–5, in a game rocked by outbursts of bad tempers, the advance of the "Bahis" (so nicknamed because of their blue swim caps) to the semifinals seemed already blocked. Now, they had to win by a difference of 13 goals over Japan to achieve a goal average necessary to advance. The Nipponese, who had just begun to master the game of water polo, were beaten with two goals to spare, 17–2! Now, a glimmer of hope began to reappear; now, perhaps, even the Hungarians could be beaten.

This decisive semifinal game started with a Yugoslav goal in the very first minute, when Jankovics, the 22-year-old offensive star at Mexico, scored with a tremendous shot. From then on the Yugoslavs never gave up

GYÖRGY SZEPESI
Radio Budapest

The Yugoslavs Finally Did it

their advantage. Final score: Yugoslavia 8, Hungary 6.

The Yugoslavs met the Russians in the final game for the gold medal. It became the longest final in the Olympic history of water polo. At the end of regulation time the score was 11–11. During the two three-minute overtime periods, the Yugoslavs had steadier nerves; they scored twice more and finally took possession of their first gold medal in water polo.

And they deserved it too. Coach Szandic had waited ten long years for that moment and their goalkeeper Stipanics was so good that, with him in the nets, almost any team could have become Olympic champion.

Hungary was third and what a disappointment this caused among the ten million Hungarians. Their Olympic team had won ten gold, ten silver and 12 bronze medals over the years and yet the sports fanatics were extremely bitter about the failure of their water poloists to continue their supremacy in a sport which had almost become a Hungarian monopoly.

The bronze medal of Mexico was followed by long and heated discussions. For five months nobody could be found to become the new National coach and to steer the rocking ship away from the dangerous cliffs. Kálmán Markovits, who had played 150 times for Hungary himself, had been the Hungarian coach at Mexico City. He recognized the causes of his team's ineffectiveness. The Magyars had clung to the old-fashioned theory that a team which plays most beautifully and with the greatest technical skills will also play most successfully. However, at Mexico City, technique played a subordinate role to such qualities as physical fitness, speed and stamina.

Mexico also was the end of the penalty point system. Subsequently, F.I.N.A., on January 1, 1969, put into effect new rules, introducing the penalty minute as well as limiting the individual action to 45 seconds. These new rules open up totally new perspectives.

The popularity of water polo is on the rise all over the world. This was proven by the fact that never before were there as many countries to enter the qualifying rounds for the Olympic competition as in 1968. Another case in point were the water poloists of Australia. They had travelled to Mexico without the sanction of their Olympic Committee, paying their own fare. They were at Mexico City but could not participate because the International Olympic Committee did not want to embarrass the Australian officials any more. But this incident certainly proved how much the Australians love water polo.

Finally, the inevitable list of the All-World Water Polo team of the Olympic Games at Mexico City, a fantasy dear to the heart of every sports writer: Stipanics (Yugoslavia); Trumbics (Yugoslavia), Szivós (Hungary); Pizzo (Italy), Semjonow (USSR), Jankovics (Yugoslavia) and Sandics (Yugoslavia).

JAROSLAV BREZINA
"Stadion," Prague

A Successful Volleyball Encore

It was the day before the conclusion of the Olympic Games in Mexico. Practically the last medals were at stake, for only the Grand Prix des Nations of the equestrians was left on the final day. Mexican fans of this newest Olympic event—volleyball—filled the beautiful *gimnasio*, located next to the Olympic swimming pool, for the last time during the Olympic Games. The two final games were about to take place. Each of the two winners would collect a gold medal.

The first game had ended. The Japanese girls, the first Olympic volleyball champions in Tokyo (1964), could not cope with the offensively brilliant Russians and had been defeated by a score of 3–1. The first gold medal had already been awarded to the Soviet Union.

The red rectangle of the playing area was empty now. Soon the men of the USSR and Czechoslovakia were to meet in their game for first place and the gold medal. Excited debates filled the press box. We, the reporters from Czechoslovakia, were the center of attention and everybody wished us luck.

The Mexican fans too were on our side, ready to cheer the CSSR on to victory over the Russians. What had happened to this small Central European country in August left noticeable sympathies among the spectators.

To be quite honest, we ourselves were less optimistic this time than the day before, when we waited for the final in the women's gymnastic event. Vera Caslavska was our most reliable ace. Our volleyballers, unfortunately, raised more doubts than hopes. They had pulled out a few victories by the slimmest of margins and had even lost to Poland. Now, there remained only two alternatives for the World Champions: either a win and gold, or a defeat and bronze.

Sober evaluations made the Russians heavy favorites. But they had to play to beat us first and so we hoped... Otherwise we would not have missed an event which was topic number one in Mexico City at the moment: the wedding of Vera Caslavska, the Gymnast super star, to Josef Odlozil. We decided, reluctantly to be sure, to give preference to the youngest member in the family of Olympic sports, which had established itself so surprisingly fast.

It is indeed amusing to recall the events only 12 short years ago, when the International Olympic Committee met at Sofia in September of 1957. One point on the agenda of that particular Olympic Congress was to make volleyball an Olympic event. An excellent volleyball tournament, with teams from Bulgaria, Rumania, USSR and CSSR, had been arranged just for the delegates and officers of the Committee. The IOC members were to decide the fate of volleyball on Monday and they agreed to attend the tournament on Sunday.

Shortly after noon they appeared in their special loges, led by President Avery Brundage. A brilliant volleyball exhibition followed. Bulgaria and CSSR, the two opposing teams, did not really care about victory and defeat, they only wanted to demonstrate all the beauty and excitement volleyball has to offer. The crowd reacted promptly and became wildly enthusiastic about what they were shown. But the faces in the loges remained motionless and detached. After the first period the jury just got up and left. We

were crushed: this had to be the end of all our hopes.

When we went to the meeting on Monday to hear the verdict, we were shocked again: volleyball had unanimously been accepted as an Olympic event.

And now, after the great Olympic debut in Tokyo, the first encore had started in Mexico City. After a few exchanges, it became quite clear that the gold medal was out of reach for the World Champions. They could not find a formula to control the offensive moves of the Russians. All of their traditional fighting spirit, their combinations and technical tricks had been left behind in the dressing room. All hands in the arena, ready to applaud the successful play of the CSSR, remained silent.

It was all over in an hour and the cruel defeat by a score of 3–0 was justified. "How was this possible?" we were asked by our colleagues. What could we say? That we had expected it? That nothing else could have been expected after the relatively poor performances in the preceeding games? Perhaps, we had not solved the problem of rejuvenating our team. Perhaps, there had been mistakes in preparing the team. In any case, in this Olympic final, our team did not even come close to its potential ability. These problems will have to be solved by the World Champions themselves. More important and more encouraging was the fact that volleyball gained thousands of new fans, that countries which only recently became acquainted with the sport, like Peru, Korea, Mexico, etc., were able to field promising teams and that this interesting and exciting sport now has a secure place in the Olympic program!

Opposite:
Pakistan dominated the Olympic hockey tournament in Mexico. Surprisingly Australia managed to push itself into the traditional feud between India and Pakistan by taking second. India only succeeded in gaining the bronze to take home. In the picture is one of the outstanding Indian forwards. He embodies generations of Indian hockey art.

The waterpolo games in the 'Alberca Olimpica' were a pleasant diversion for the spectators after the dramatic swimming contests. After winning the silver medals in 1952, 1956 and 1960, Yugoslavia succeeded in being the Olympic victors for the first time in Mexico. It was a hard won gold medal against Russia (silver) and Hungary (bronze).

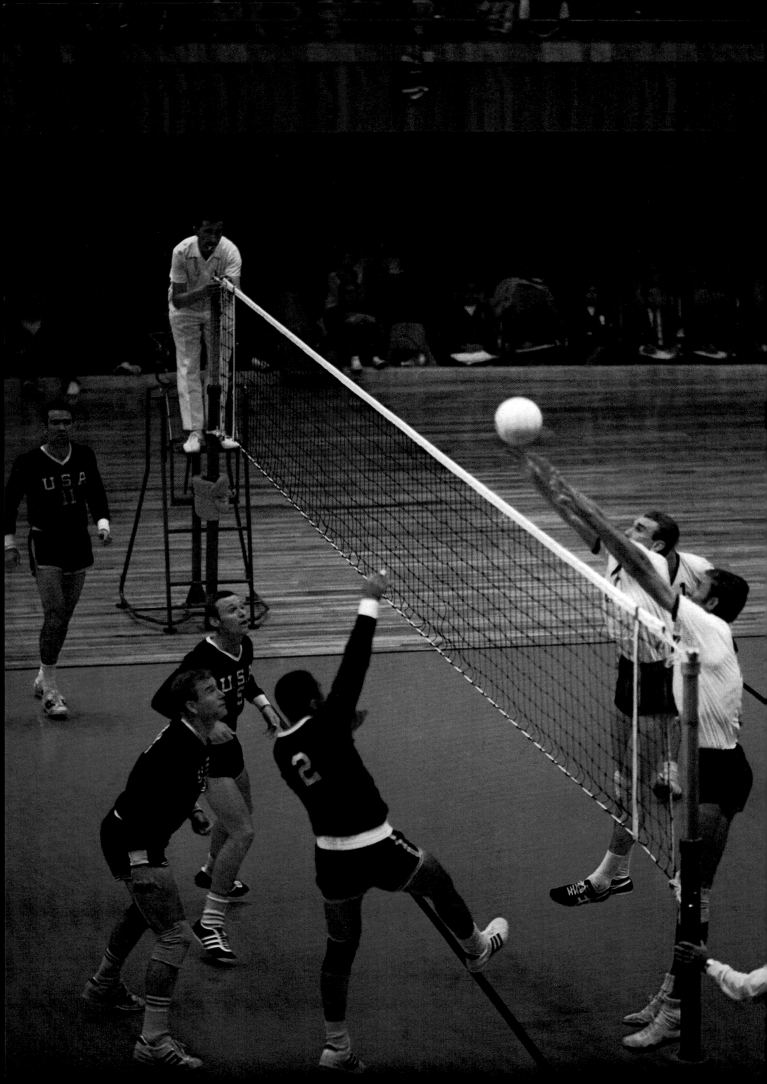

Volleyball was only included for the second time in the history of the Olympics, but one cannot imagine the Olympic Games without it anymore. The enthusiastic response of the spectators in Mexico made this contest an enormous success for the organizers. The volley-ball team from the USA may have been an outsider in this event, but it provided a great sensation by beating the Russians (gold) 3—1. The silver went to Japan, the bronze to Czecho-slovakia. In the picture above: the USA-team is defeated by the Czechs 3—1 in a dramatic game.

The USA basketball wizards were the Olympic champions for the seventh time in the tournament held in the "Palacio de los Deportes". Spencer Haywood and Joseph White simply overawed all their opponents. Their quiet coach, Henry Iba, never for a moment allowed any doubt to arise about the competence of his young USA-giants. But the European teams are catching up and hope to make Munich 1972 a European victory. (The following three pages) Henry Iba's boys smiled and played one of the nicest Olympic tournaments. The Yugoslavs gained the silver, the USSR the bronze medal.

MAURY WHITE
"Des Moines Register"

Hank's Kids Pull an Upset

Mexico City, Mexico — Although not as highly regarded as the Soviet Union and possibly Yugoslavia going into the Games of the XIX Olympiad, the United States won nine straight games to keep firm hold on a title it has claimed all seven times since basketball was added to the program in 1936.

Coached for the second straight Games by veteran mentor Hank Iba, but with an entirely different squad than in 1964, the USA defeated Yugoslavia, 65–50, in the title game to perpetuate its remarkable record of never having lost a game in Olympic competition. The championship contest was the second meeting of these two teams. The USA beat Yugoslavia earlier, 73–58, en route to a 7–0 record in Group A. Theoretically, that should have led towards a title meeting against the Soviet Union, which finished 7–0 in Group B.

But the enthusiastic crowds at the magnificent Sports Palace never saw this awaited match because Yugoslavia upset the Soviets in the semi-finals, 63–62, and the tall Soviets wound up third, after repeating a victory over Brazil. The two USA-Yugoslavia contests and the Yugoslavia-Soviet Union game were the highlights of the competition. Brazil's well-drilled team was too small and too old to keep up with the "Big Three."

Host Mexico, getting 19 points from Arturo Guerrero and 18 from Manuel Raga, warmed up a crowd of 22,000 on the final night by beating Poland, 75–65, for fifth place. It was Mexico's best finish since they won a bronze medal in 1936. Spain defeated Italy for seventh, Puerto Rico handled Bulgaria for ninth, Cuba nosed out Panama for eleventh, the Philippines defeated South Korea for thirteenth and Senegal took fifteenth from winless Morocco.

In the past the USA has always been favored for the Olympic basketball title. It wasn't this time because a number of college stars, particularly tall men, chose not to try out for the team, either because of grades or racial reasons or anxiety to start professional careers. Consequently, Iba had no player taller than 6-foot, 9-inch reserve Ken Spain and only one, forward James King, accustomed to his no-nonsense style of defense-oriented play. King played for Iba at Oklahoma State University.

On a summer trip to Europe, the USA won only one of three games each against both Yugoslavia and the Soviet Union. However, Iba did not accompany the squad then, nor did guard Joseph (JoJo) White nor forward Bill Hosket. The significance of these absences became apparent at the Olympics, where Iba's coaching genius and strong personality quickly molded a group of stars accustomed to different systems into a cohesive unit, led by White and center Spencer Haywood.

The 6–8 Haywood, a virtually unknown 19-year-old who was the youngest player ever to make the US squad, rebounded savagely and led the individual scoring with 145 points. White, a play-making senior from the University of Kansas, had 105.

The USA won seven games in Group A by an average spread of 28 points. The only close contest was a 61–56 victory over Puerto Rico, a game in which outside-shooters Mariano Ortiz and Adolf Porrata kept the USA worried.

In its first meeting with the USA when both were 4–0 in the eliminations, Yugoslavia led, 5–4, then lost the ball five straight times on errors, allowing White, Haywood and Calvin Fowler to build a lead that never vanished. White led the scoring with 24 points. Guard Ivo Daneu furnished 15 and the 6–9 Kresimir Cosic 14 for the losers. The quickness of the Americans, plus their patience in working for better shots, overcame a height deficiency.

Once the eliminations ended, the first team in each group met the second team in the opposite group for the semi-finals. The Soviet Union averaged 92 points in winning Group B and gave up an average 59. The USA averaged 85 and 57. These were the two best offenses and defenses in the field.

The most exciting game of title consequence was the semi-final meeting between Yugoslavia and the Soviet Union. Because of Vladimir Andreev and Sergei Kovalenko, both over 7 feet, the Soviets were powerful defensive rebounders. Yet, the Slavic giant-killers jumped into a 14–4 lead and never trailed in finishing the half leading 31–27.

205

Antoli Polivoda brought the Soviet Union's first lead at 34–33. The Soviets then opened a 40–35 margin, but soon ran into foul trouble.

Modest Paulauskas, a capable guard who led Soviet tournament scoring with 144 points, was whistled out and so was Andreev, a tall tower who had blocked seven shots. Yugoslavia also lost two players, but they were of lesser calibre. Polivoda's free throw brought the Soviet Union's last lead at 58–57 with 2:05 left. Cosic retrieved the advantage with a pair of free throws and Peter Skanski drove in for 2 of his 15 points, before Polivoda's goal cut the margin to one. Daneu intercepted a pass in the closing seconds and, as the Soviet Union pressed for the ball, substitute Vladimir Cvetovic was fouled. He calmly ensured victory with two free throws to make it 63–60. The Slavs then cleared the area to let Russia score a foul-free final goal.

Pandemonium broke out. Daneu was carried from the floor. Cosic sat on it and pounded with his fists. Other jubilant winners raced about, not caring that Brazil and US players were trying to take the court for warm-ups.

The second semi-final game was anti-climactic. The USA opened a 20–8 lead, went on to a 42–26 margin at halftime, and won, 75–63, despite Luis Menon's 24-point effort for the losers.

On the final night, Russia took the bronze with a 70–53 victory over Brazil, after jumping into a 25–14 lead against a zone defense. Carmo de Souza gave Ubiratan Maciel help under the boards in the second half and Brazil closed to 52–43. However, Polivoda (14 points) teamed with Paulauskas (17 points) in a Soviet hot spell that captured control with 6 minutes to go. Carlos Massoni led Brazil with 13.

In the gold medal game, Iba started the usual line-up of White (6–3) and Fowler (6–1) at the guards; Haywood (6–8) at center; Mike Silliman (6–6) and King (6–7) at the forwards. The USA game plan was to fastbreak as much as possible and hold Daneu, Dragutin Cernak und Radivoj Korack to a total of under 40 points.

Yugoslavia worked the boards hard for an 11–6 lead, but White's outside-shooting evened the game. The USA promptly started substituting freely and used all 12 players in the first half. The Slavs began using their two tall pivotmen, Trajko Rajkovic and Cosic, at the same time, but the USA led at halftime, 32–29. When the second half commenced, Iba's strategy of resting regulars in the high altitude paid off.

During a furious burst of near-perfect basketball, White and Haywood each scored 8 points as their team got 17 in a row to open a 49–29 lead. Yugoslavia had only five shots, and no rebounds, in this stretch. Not surprisingly, that splurge decided the game. The biggest lead was at 60–34. Haywood, who had been feared unable to play because of diarrhea, rebounded superbly (as did King) and scored 23 points. White had 14. Daneu led Yugoslavia with 13, and the three chosen "targets" totaled only 25.

Ranko Zeravica, the 36-year-old Yugoslav coach who was born one year after Iba started coaching, termed the USA defense the best he'd ever seen and praised the teamwork and tenacity of the winners. "The American team is playing every minute with five players," pointed out Zeravica. "All the other teams, including Yugoslavia, are playing with three players at a time. No other team had players such as Haywood and White."

Comparing the 1968 Olympic field to 1964, Iba thought ball handling had generally improved and more teams were using combination defenses, switching among man-for-man, zone and press.

The majority of the 16 teams had good big men and achieved acceptable play from the post position. The US guards and medium-sized forwards were all quick. This proved important in the victory.

Davis Peralta, a 5–7 guard from Panama, led tournament scoring by 19 points with 214. He was stopped only by the USA, when Fowler and Mike Barrett combined to hold him to six. The rest of the top 10 in scoring: Dong Pa Shin, Korea, 195; Mokhtar Sayad, Morocco, 186; Mieczyslaw Lopatka, Poland, 173; Pedro Rivas, Panama, 150; Manuel Raga and Arturo Guerrero, both Mexico, both 148; Spencer Haywood, United States, 147; Modest Paulauskas, Russia, 144; Wlamir Marques, Brazil, 142.

GYÖRGY SZEPESI

*Commentator of the
Hungarian Radio
and Television*

On the Top of the Eiffel Tower

Campo Militar, Mexico City. Lovely cacti, tiny brooks, nice walks; it could just as well be advertised for excursions. But the world's 48 best pentathletes–British, Hungarian, Australian, German, Soviet, Austrian, Swedish and French—do not find it delightful. For them it is a wild, grim ground, the scene of the first act of a modern sports drama, spread over five days. The event is riding; the course is 1,500 meters long, impeded by 23 jumps on a ground full of creeks. Much here depends on just how fortunate one's hand is as it reaches out for the ballot-box by the drawing of horses. Doctor Ferenc Török, for example, Tokyo's individual champion, is unlucky. He mounts his just-drawn tall horse, and cries desperately: "I feel like I'm on the top of the Eiffel tower." And all his efforts are in vain, the horse running frantically does not show him any mercy; the 1964 Olympic champion is destroying the fences, and his chances dwindle. Todt of West Germany, however, is still a greater enemy of Dame Fortune: his horse does not want to descend on the slipway for minutes; he does not get a single point... At the end of the first day, with all unknown names on the top, the laureate candidates are modestly hidden in the middle of the field.

The winner of the fencing event was decided by a Mexican peso coin. Even a marathon contest lasting 700 minutes did not decide the question in the *Minuca Magdalena* hall; the two Hungarians Török and Móna shared first place! Willie Gut, the first secretary, tosses up the coin, with an Indian figure on one side, and an eagle one the other. The winner is the eagle, the Mexican bird of Fortune, and this compensates Török for the riding: the eagle was his figure; he is the winner of the fencing event.

Björn Ferm of Sweden is remarkably quiet during this 12 hour fencing struggle. Between two exciting bouts, he produces a detective story from below his chair. His comment at the end of the fencing event is also true: "Modern pentathlon has five difficult obstacles and the final winner is the one who passes the last one as well..."

A delay of one hundredth of a second on the shooting stand—and all hopes vanish! After the strain produced by riding and fencing, excitement is crowned by shooting on the third day. The Swedes—Ferm, Jakobsson, Lilienwal—are worthy successors of their great predecessors, Dryssen, Thofelt and Hall. They are shooting sensationally, and though before the competition, experts forecast András Balczó of Hungary, winner of four world championships, as Olympic champion. It can be increasingly heard, that swimming and running may bring a breakthrough for Sweden's Ferm!

Swimming is usually a rest for the nerves but not in the pentathlon! Ferm, the surprise man, swam fantastically. Having heard his time, I reported: "Dear Hungarian listeners, Ferm can only be deprived of the Olympic pentathlon individual championship if Balczó runs a time 22 seconds better. This I hardly believe can be done."

The next day—*Campo Militar* again. Balczó has run with an all-out effort. This athlete is a tireless competitor of world class, but this time he can only be revived with the help of an oxygenflask. "Did Hungary win the team event?" he asks in an agonized voice. Hungarians surrounding him tell him—erupting, cheering—the answer: the team gold medal went to Hungary. But the individual! Ferm is still running; he started a minute later than Balczó, and if this one minute passes, and he is at least 22 seconds late, Balczó wins the individual event.

The hand hits 12, and now everyone starts counting aloud—seven, eight... nine, ten... Ferm is not in sight.—17, 18... The thin figure of the Swedish boy appears, sprinting half unconsciously but something drives him on...

19... 20 And Björn Ferm collapses home; but he is the individual Olympic gold medalist in the pentathlon. "What a sport," Balczó, the favorite, says later. "Unpredictable, that is why I like it. Ferm has more points, he is a brilliant competitor, I do not feel for a moment that I was unfortunate."

Says Sven Thofelt, Swedish President of the International Association of Modern Pentathlon, "Just before the race, I had a word with the new champion. I told him, 'Boy, this is the time to do something extraordinary.' And he was strong enough to take my advice. He won, and this is a splendid day for Sweden."

No one, today, wants to assume responsibility for the creation of the rules and competitions of the equestrian events during the 1968 Olympics. Why? Quite simply because it was a total failure. Actually, the results of the competition had a certain logic, for one's memory is of past equestrian competitions which were also messed up. First, the individual competition: it was an absurd compromise between the classical Cup competition and the abnormal formula of a power which is at once monstrous in its first place and pointless in its jump-offs. Thus, although America's William Steinkraus won the individual competition on his thoroughbred, Snowbound, he could not compete in the team competition because Snowbound was injured in the "B" section of the individual competition. In the same way, England's Marion Coakes, second in the *Campo Marte* with her Irish pony, Stroller, was eliminated in the Olympic Stadium.

In the team contests in the Stadium, during 90 rounds, not one rider went round clear (a staggering fact) and only three riders completed the course within the time limit: England's David Broome on Mister Softee, Italy's Raimondo d'Inzeo on Bellevue, and France's Marcel Rozier on Quo Vadis. On the other hand, Canada—which had no one in the first five in the individual competition—made the most of its team's consistency and won the team competition.

There were many names which will stand out in years to come, among them the European champion, Broome; West Germany's Alwin Schockemöhle, seventh in the *Campo Marte* and first in the Olympic Stadium; America's Kathy Kusner, first of the lady equestrians in Tokyo; and world champion Pierre Jonqueres d'Oriola of France, who once again failed to capture a gold medal. His team manager has written: *"For the second time, he is forced to realize that he has not the material (in his thoroughbred, Napier) which time would have allowed to mold to his hand. Without complete control, he is not the master, and that cannot be reconciled with his habits nor, above all, with his temperament. His thirst for possession is unquenchable; he is a great pilot, not a passenger."*

Certainly, within the framework of the Three-Day Event, the Olympic test of stamina is always a serious affair, a terrible testing of men and horses. But the endurance course at *Avandaro*, because of the great storm that took place there, must be the most terrible and also the most murderous of all time. Two horses drowned there, one of which was the Soviet mare, Barberina, who had just clocked one of the best times in the steeplechase. And it was only by a miracle that the Frenchman Sarrazin and his horse Joburg were able to finish the course and bring the French home to fourth place. An eye-witness of the course said: *"For an hour it was terrible: two horses and riders floundered, blinded... They fell, but hung on furiously, drawn by that line which became more and more imaginary, that of the finish... The water, which poured down from enormous clouds, flooded all the ground, and turned the stream into a tumultuous river, which swept along tree trunks in its powerful current."*

This extract from an official report puts the business into its proper perspective: *"The horses were in the impossible situation of having to recuperate during the second course and had to attack the cross country in conditions of fatigue, and with respiration difficulties. So the horses who had given their utmost in the steeplechase suffered in the cross country."*

The experts did not fail to remark that, with reference to the test of staying power between the dressage and the jumping, the difficulties had been increased with one particular aim—to give an advantage to those horses who were acclimatized, or by implication, to the horses of.... Mexico.

When everything is weighed, it was the British—and in particular their animals—who had the greatest successes in Mexico City's equestrian events. If one considers the first three placings in each of the six disciplines, awarding four, two and one points, respectively, the final standings would be as follows: Great Britain, nine points; West Germany, eight; the United States, seven; the USSR, six; Canada, four; and Australia and Switzerland, one apiece. Many of these teams used British stock, including the United States; in fact, France's Jean-Jacques Guyon won the Three-Day event on Pitou, which was a Norman crossbreed. Decidedly, English bloodstock is the best in the world.

FERNAND ALBARET
"L'Equipe"

Confusion
in
Mexico

The modern pentathlon was included in the modern Olympic Game in 1912 at the request of de Coubertin in order to make the Olympic movement more interesting and attractive for the military with running, shooting, fencing, swimming and riding. A number of soldiers still take part in this event, but in modern times the pentathlon has become a much admired special contest of especially good all-arounders.

Above: The Hungarian Mona during the pistol shooting. Together with his comrades, Balczo and F. Török, he won the prized team gold-medal for Hungary. Silver went to the USSR, bronze to France.

Fencing is an art that can be acquired for the modern pentathlon. Even pistol shooting at a range of 25 meters (78′11¹/₂″) and riding over a cross-country course can be brought up to a high standard with hard work and practice. But for swimming 300 meters (approx. 329 yards) and completing a 4000 meter cross-country run (approx. 4111 yards) a pentathlon athlete must be gifted.

Opposite: Like the modern pentathlon, the equestrian contests still retain much of the military tradition with dressage, cross-country trial and jumping. Not only officers, but also many gifted and enthusiastic civilians are to be found in these events both as competitors and champions. The cross-country trial is one of the most rigorous tests for horse and rider. Left in the picture: Thomas Brennan, Ireland, swims to the bank after being thrown from his horse 'March Hawk' at the water-ditch.

Below: In the individual placings, the French officer Guyon won the gold medal on his horse 'Pitou'. The Silver was gained by Allhusen, Gt. Britain, on 'Lochinvar' and bronze by Page, USA, on 'Foster'. The team championship was won by Great Britain with Allhusen, Meade and Jones ahead of the USA with Wofford, Page and Plumb. Australia gained the bronze medal with Cobcroft, Waine Roycroft and W. Roycroft.

Right:
For many years the two Italians, Raimondo and Piero D'Inzeo, have been counted among the big names in international jumping. Here is Piero on 'Fidux' in the individual jumping.

Left:
The Olympic stadium during the final team jumping.

Below:
Josef Neckermann, West Germany, gained the gold medal with the highest number of points in the team placings of the Dressage test. But in the individual placings the Russian Kizimov only allowed him to collect the silver medal.

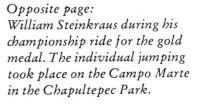

Opposite page:
William Steinkraus during his
championship ride for the gold
medal. The individual jumping
took place on the Campo Marte
in the Chapultepec Park.

In his capacity as president of the
'Federation Equestre International'
Prince Philip congratulates
William Steinkraus, USA, on
winning the gold medal in the
Jumping Test—Grand Prix,
individual placings.

The medal winners in the Jumping
Test—Grand Prix. Placings:
William Steinkraus, USA, gold,
on 'Snowbound', Marion Coakes,
Great Britain, silver, on 'Stroller',
and Broome, Great Britain,
bronze, on 'Mister Softee'.

Conversation between gold
medalists. William Steinkraus,
USA, and Josef Neckermann,
West Germany, during a friendly
chat at the side of the course.

Right: After the last medals had been won in the Grand Prix jumping contest, the Mexicans produced a 'Fiesta Olympica' in the Olympic stadium on the final evening of these wonderful games which left an unforgettable impression—especially on the foreign visitors. The Mexicans turned the Olympic Games into the biggest fiesta their country had ever had. Now they took leave of their guests. "Uno, dos, tres . . . Mexico, Mexico, Mexico"—ah! Munich 1972 shone forth as a distant promise from Europe!

Below:
The English girl, Marion Coakes, with her pony Stroller, was the darling of the knowledgeable spectators during the individual jumping on the Campo Marte. Fortune smiled and presented her with the silver medal.

Overleaf: As the Olympic Flame in the Olympic stadium expired, 10 naval cadets carried the Olympic flag out with measured tread surrounded by the silence of the hundred-thousand spectators.

DR. GERHARD SEEHASE

"Die Welt", Hamburg

The 1968 Olympic Games in Retrospect

"Munich 72" stood on the huge announcement board in the Olympic stadium. The Olympics are dead, long live the Olympics! Mexico buried her Olympic Games and celebrated the event as joyfully as a wedding. As the Olympic flame died down, after blazing over the stadium for fourteen days, jubilation and rejoicing filled the air. Where four years ago in Tokyo emotion reigned, here the theme of the closing ceremony was one of great joy, for the people in the stands showed their immediate and spontaneous reaction, which only needed a slight impulse to become the ceremony itself. The Mexicans had no need of a closing ceremony—they arranged it themselves.

Three times they sang the Mexican National Anthem, the last time as fervently as the first; they cheered every word which sounded like "Mexico" in the speech of President Avery Brundage; they twirled their yellow sombreros like a company of ballet dancers and finally they invaded the arena, a human carpet in perpetual motion, continually swirling and forming new patterns.

It was the Mexicans who were the big surprise. The bus driver who drove with one hand, collected the fares with the other and counted the bank notes with his third will always remain a phenomenon to the visitor from the United States or Europe. But myths do not die in the face of bare facts. Of course Mexican bus drivers do not really have three hands—but this is how it looks. Perhaps because the Mexican understands the economics of existence better than others, he has found a way to make one hand do the work of two. It seems as if this is the Mexican's secret of always finding time to be gay. The closing ceremony in the Olympic stadium proved it.

Many European and American visitors and press men could only smile helplessly under their sombreros at all the Mexican explosions around them. Some of them must surely have covered their heads protectively with their hands when fireworks were exploded directly above the spectators and burning missiles occasionally landed among the crowd.

This was *their* Olympic festival and they had a right to be proud of it, for in spite of all shortcomings and criticism, it was a success. Mexico played host to the world and everyone could be sure of hospitality as long as he did not expect a special elevator to lift him over all the ridiculous obstacles which certainly existed. For the Mexicans, anyway, this was a festival of joy beyond words. They made pilgrimages to the Olympic saints and shrines, they saw, they marvelled—and were always in the highest of spirits. The Mexicans and their town! Fortunately, when all is said and done, our own memories are more than just those of Olympia.

You climb a mountain of concrete. Your chest gets tight, breathing becomes heavy when you have finally reached the top. But you are rewarded for your effort with a fascinating view—the Estadio Azteka, the most beautiful football stadium in the world. From a dizzy height, the tiers cascade into a symmetrically laid out gorge, and below at last, the green quadrangle of lawn which absorbs the view as if looking through the other end of a telescope. Here is the true grandeur of the Mexican world, which even in its cool emptiness is an experience.

In the park of Chapultepec, some ten miles further north, you find the world in miniature, a colorful, warmhearted world—the Olympia of the children. They were invited from all over the world to take part in an open air painting competition.

The youngest was only seven years old, the oldest, 15. Thirty huge cardboard cubes about six feet tall could be daubed with paint. Each one of the young artists had one area of the four-sided cube to himself; nobody was allowed to help. Nothing was allowed to be sketched beforehand and as the enclosure was locked at night—the colors being waterproof—not even the anxious parents could *corriger la fortune*. "Our standards have to be just as strict as those of the adults in the Olympic stadium," said the attendant at the gates of this small world.

The Aztec stadium and the park of Chapultepec—these are contrasts that in Mexico belong together, and that is what makes it so fascinating. The hot sun which even at this time of year still blazes at noon, and the cool evenings. The cactus plantations and the Popocatepetl with its peak covered in perennial snow. The beautiful women and the strict customs. The martial appearance of the traffic policeman and the lenient hand behind his back, which—if asked nicely—even allows you to drive against the stream. In Mexico, opposites are united in the most curious way. He who wants to see Mexico as it really is has to look through a prism of a thousand different colors. The Olympic visitor who could not cope with the harmony of those contrasts was not the person to discover Mexico.

Contrasts? One has to fit in—in Mexico! In the capital, contrary to the provinces, traffic priorities do not exist. The experienced driver proceeds according to this principal: stop when a bus comes out from a side street; also stop when it's a taxi; otherwise the best man wins. Pedestrians who cannot jump stand no chance. Only children count; hardly a European town can boast of children's playgrounds as marvellously equipped as those of Mexico City. There is poverty—and there are wonderful social services for the poor. Mexico is baffling! In Mixhuca, a sports town near the Olympic stadium, are eighty football grounds available to the public, and lawns with no 'Keep off the grass' signs. Any street urchin can play here during the week.

Boxing is a merry art—if it weren't for the blows. In the boxing arena in Mexico City, it was the public who was the center of events. And they came full of the same happy expectations as a hungry man in a restaurant, dreaming of the steak he has ordered. Woe betide the waiter who serves the next table first! It was of course taken for granted that their boxers must win, even though the opponents looked the better men. The joy of victory began the moment their own man entered the ring. A disappointing defeat was always seen as a cruel injustice.

Still, the Mexicans were lucky enough to have a team to exult, as it contained a few genuine talents and was inspired by two Polish trainers. Gone to a great extent were their snarling posturings; they fought just as coolly and controlled as their opponents from the USA and Europe—and, of course, they enjoyed the support of their own public.

In this boxing arena the cheering was the most impressive aspect, even though it was often quite divorced from what went on in the ring. And so, the further away in the past the Games are, the more we are inclined to see a virtue even in unjust joy. "Mexico, Mexico, rah, rah, rah!"; that's how they coaxed their own man, Augustin Zaragoza, in a merciless fight against the Czech middleweight Jan Hejduk, even though Zaragoza could hardly stand on his feet in the last few minutes of the fight. "Zaragoza, winner on points." The hall went beserk with joy.

In this beautiful old sports palace designed for excellent viewing, from the very first day the seats were more in danger than the boxers. It was here that the Mexicans' wildest reactions were let loose. They came to witness two things: firstly, the Mexican victories, and secondly, plenty of fierce action. If both of these coincided, the acoustic pressure seemed to raise the roof.

The Mexicans' biggest disappointment happened in the Aztec Stadium. The Olympic soccer tournament was to be the ultimate crowning of their hopes—and they were bitterly disappointed several times. That the Mexican team didn't make it to the final they could still accept, but that they should lose to the Japanese in the match that decided the bronze medal was too much for the hot-blooded Mexican soccer fans to grasp.

For the first and only time during the whole games, Mexican competitors were really condemned by the Mexican crowd. Their disappointment was so great that the people in a matter of seconds transferred their support to the opposing side. But this only happened in the Aztec Stadium, where Mexico had met her Waterloo. The next day it was all forgotten.

Seen through Mexican eyes, the Olympics changed into a festival of national passions. Whenever they showed how they felt—and they were to show it often without understanding any of the finer points of the Games—their attitude was naive, fiery, sympathetic. Mexico for the Mexicans!

Day after day with bag and baggage, they queued in front of the gates of the Olympic village. Their idea of absolute bliss was to catch a glimpse of one of the Olympic gods, or even more, to obtain from one of them an autograph. Even the press came in for their share of adulation and were asked for autographs.

Even the traffic policemen queued outside the gates, their pea-whistles at the ready, a look of stern authority in their eyes. They continually whistled at cars which couldn't move anyway. They whistled aimlessly, like dogs bark. In the 'village' itself one didn't whistle, one photographed. Especially down by the swimming pool. For instance, the very attractive Luxembourg swimmer Arlette Wilnes, a wonderful girl with sweeping eyes. Who cared about gold medal chances? Here is a colorful world, a world without tradition, motley. It is a mistake to assume that among young people only the gold medal matters. Personal contacts naturally have their value as well.

Suddenly they were there, one of them perhaps five years old, the other, four. Both unbelievably dirty and yet unbelievably healthy. Mexican bambinos scrounging for pesos. Strangers are the best prey, and strangers we were. Avenue Juarey about six o'clock in the evening. We sit in the open and drink our beer *(Cerveza clara)*.

"Senor," says the five-year-old, and pushes a dirty piece of chocolate under my nose. We place our arm benevolently around the urchin's shoulders. The price of the chocolate rockets. One peso! We smile and say "Well, boy," pleased with their cleverness. The stranger's smile has registered: this one is friendly, this one is nice, this one is stupid. The escalation of Mexican logic makes the tot suddenly raise two dirty fingers. And miraculously the chocolate has become 100% more expensive in 9.9 seconds (new world record!): two pesos!

The big stranger from Germany searches in his purse, produces two pesos, receives the dirty chocolate and has confirmed with this exchange—as one can see in the eyes of the bambinos—the stupidity of the big mysterious stranger a hundred times over. And when they depart, they look from behind like fellows who have just broken the Bank of England.

In Mexico you have to look at least twice before you can grasp the simple truth.

Mexico celebrated the most colorful, gay and carefree Olympics of the last decades. The Mexicans could not understand why their visitors were constantly surprised at this world of contrasts. To themselves it seemed perfectly natural.

"Munich 72" was flashed onto the announcement board as the finale to these extremely colorful Olympic Games, and the Mexicans cheered even this huge illuminated message with enthusiasm. May the Germans stage a better festival if they can, but more cheerful it can hardly be.

DR. GERHARD SEEHASE

"Die Welt", Hamburg

Summing up

Mexico City—the Olympic Games at the dizzy height of 7,373 feet! This news made an impact on the sporting world and resulted in many dark predictions—but luckily, they were nearly all proved wrong. Death was not a competitor in Mexico as had been forecast. Not one single fatality occurred on the field of Olympic battle. What shook (and fascinated) the world was the performance explosion which neither coaches nor medical advisers had expected on such a scale.

For instance, the 29′2½″ long jump which Bob Beamon of the USA accomplished must be seen as an astounding leap into the year 2000. It is a conception both fascinating and horrifying, for here a standard has been achieved which must remain unsurpassed in the foreseeable future because it does not fit into any logical sequence. As this sensational distance was recorded on the Olympic scoreboard, we could all see how the spirit went out of the competition.

Up to now, athletic experts who saw in sport a well-ordered world of numbers and records—which were subject to a certain process of calculable continuity—had to despair of their own wisdom during these

Olympic Games. The presumption that our records would gradually approach absolute barriers collapsed in Mexico in a way that was almost painful. The biggest problem for international athletics in the near future will be how to live with these new records and how to overcome them.

The flood of new records in track and field, the centerpiece of the Olympic Games, swept away all the old conceptions. Fifteen world records were broken, two were equalled and in 25 out of the 36 events, the Olympic records were surpassed. The lion's share of the gold medals went to the USA. In general this may not have been surprising, but their tremendous lead over the other great power in world sport, the USSR, did cause surprise. The final tally makes it clear: 45 gold medals for the USA, 29 for the USSR.

After the Second World War, when the USSR sports machinery was set in motion, it was very well oiled and immediately produced astounding international results. The only annoying thing about it was that these successes were interpreted in Soviet terminology as "proof of the superiority of socialist culture." The Western nations had to take this as a challenge, although they were unable to give similar state support to their amateurs. This was bound to involve national prestige in the Olympic Games; in Mexico, however, the Soviet ideas of producing medal-winners to order were wrecked by the physiological and psychical conditions which the USA team in particular possessed.

But this was perhaps less of a sensation than the invasion of the African athletes into the élite group. It is true that some of these athletes found the same conditions in Mexico City as they have at home—mainly those from the high lands of Kenya and Ethiopia. Thus the appearance of the Africans in the arenas introduced new standards and raised problems which cannot be assessed at present. In Mexico City the old duel between East and West virtually came to an end. With an almost grotesque sense of assurance which was frequently void of any tactical sense, the colored athletes have invaded the domain dominated for decades by the Americans and Europeans. Take for instance the Kenyan, Kipchoge Keino, in the 1,500 meters. At 600 meters he already had a tremendous lead while the others were still jockeying for positions. Yet the experts with their traditional conceptions—that too much speed at the start would necessarily lead to an early collapse—were promptly proved wrong. Even the favorite from the USA, Jim Ryun, with his feared long final spurt, was unable to challenge him; Keino broke the tape with long easy strides, not taking any notice of the American behind him.

In Mexico the African competitors concentrated almost exclusively on track and field. But who can rule out the possibility that the whole of the Olympic landscape could change once they begin to feel at home in other Olympic fields like soccer football, boxing, cycling, gymnastics and swimming. Sport as a whole can only gain from the appearance of this new rival.

Mexico City has, all in all, set new standards One of them is the knowledge that Mexico, a country without rival in South American sport, has made a decisive stride into the future. When on the evening of October 26, 1968, the Olympic fire was extinguished, Mexico had stood the test which in itself can be of far-reaching importance for the development of its own sport.

It not only showed the admiring visitors from America and Europe magnificent sports facilities like the sports arena or swimming stadium, it also created a new overture of success which is directed as an invitation for the future—above all to the USA—for encouragement and support of their achievements through the sporting rivalry of further competitions. The Mexicans have earned the right to this rivalry through its Olympic Games—and the whole of Middle and South America will benefit from it too.

GRENOBLE

X OLYMPIC WINTER GAMES 1968

SERGE GROUSSARD

"L'Aurore," Paris

Pageant in the Snow

An air of wild excitement reigned in Grenoble, the capital of the French Alps, on that Tuesday 6th of February, 1968. The opening ceremony of the 10th Winter Olympics unfolded in the vast, horseshoe-shaped arena to the South of the valley encircled by the white ranges. But, with the dawn, what a pea-soup! Would the colossal event that 500 million television-viewers around the world would follow be shrouded in whitish shadows?

The manes of Hercules interceded. The wind purified the sky, and airy clouds traced pearl-grey ballets on the deep, fresh hue. Around the stadium, which looked in its powerful splendour like a magnificent casket, encrusted with diamonds, applauded the mountains, which the cold sun made resplendent. At 2 p.m., 70,000 people came together in the stands in furs and thick woollens. Five parachutists, whose billowing chutes were dyed in the colors of the Olympic rings, landed exactly in the centre of the area. The festival had begun.

Before the gateway of honor, Count Jean de Beaumont, President of the French Olympic Committee, received General de Gaulle. The Marseillaise was struck up. Then the trumpets from Aida brayed forth. These penetrating notes preceded the "Grand Triumphal March" by Jacques Bondon, a resolutely futuristic symphony which was going to punctuate the procession of the contingents with its brass, with its unexpected harmonies and with its choirs.

Quite properly, first came the standard with the blue and white horizontal stripes of Greece, where 2,744 years ago an analogous ceremony unfolded for the first time, full of purity and a lost harmony. One after the other, the cohorts of the competitors would appear and salute the official personalities with sloping flags, then line up facing them, on the vast, earthen arena.

A symbol of the divisions in the world today are the two German rivals who followed the Greeks. For them there was one flag, black, red, and gold, on which were painted five white rings. Western Germany was in deep blue, faced with light blue, beneath a peculiar, pointed bonnet. The East Germans had dressed their girls in bright red, while the hatted and gloved male champions were done up in maroon overcoats.

In the midst of the little Argentinian team stood out a powerful personage with a biblical beard. He was 57, and he was the doyen of the competitors: a tobogganist. He wore his pancho so proudly.

But the attention turned to the voluminous mass of Austrians, the girls in cute, white bonnets, the men in terrible, bottle-green frock coats. They were going to be Number One rival to their French hosts, who so much wanted to glean medals. The children of Vienna seemed to smile in advance, and refused to march in step.

"Olé! Olé" shouted the audience who warmed themselves up by stamping their feet in rhythm. It was Chile who had released those cries. They presented themselves like matadors—hats with interminable rims, capes of Aztec wool and loose sashes the color of fresh blood.

An electric current ran through the stands: disciplined, numerous, solemn, advanced the contingent from the USA! Mignonette anoraks with white band on the sleeves, night blue ski-pants, supple boots in creased sky-blue leather, they politely inclined their heads as they passed before General de Gaulle. The Chief of State replied with the same gesture of his long head with its pale crown and small white moustache.

225

And the technicolor film continue d... There were the Finns who had taken the snow as the background to their uniform, as they covered it with lavender-colored tracks. The British, a long serpent of garnet-colored velvet. The solitary Indian, who threw towards that august assembly a scarlet rose which the wind made dance on the ice...

The sparrows were bold enough to alight in the gangways sloping down between the tiers. The hostesses in costumes of ultramarine blue and cherry-colored stockings distributed blankets in the tribune of honor. The Empress of Iran, H. M. Farah Diba, was content with her jacket of wild mink, and welded her almond eye to the viewer of a camera. General de Gaulle, imposing and weighty in a dark gray overcoat, sat between Mme. de Gaulle and Mr. Avery Brundage, president of the International Olympic Committee.

Japanese sowers of chrysanthemums, Moroccans in white chechia and violet burnous, Poles waving in appreciated hommage little tricolor flags, and many others, went past at a lively pace.

After the powerful Soviet team, the French brought up the rear. They looked as if they were going hunting. On their heads the men wore a sort of stiff cap. Lower down, a Mao tunic of royal blue, a white, roll-necked pullover, a very tight, electric-blue pair of ski-pants, and a pair of shining, black boots.

The president of the organizing committee, M. Albert Michallon, descended to the podium, which consisted of a platform plated with aluminium and divided by vertical plates of glass. He asked Mr. Avery Brundage, who had followed him, to beg the president of the French Republic to open the 10th Olympic Games. Mr. Brundage began a short speech. He carries his 80 years lightly, this veteran decathlete who has never ceased to take care of his body, and there he stood, healthy and upright, his face round and smooth, his eyes sparkling behind his spectacles. At his invitation, up there in the first row of the official tribune, General de Gaulle rose up to his full height. He cried out in a powerful voice:

"Je proclame l'ouverture des 10e Jeux Olympiques d'hiver de Grenoble!"—"I proclaim the opening of the 10th Olympic Winter Games of Grenoble!"

He projected the name of Grenoble like a drum-roll.

The Olympic flag arrived! Eight soldiers from the 27th Alpine Brigade slowly bore it, stretched out between them, to the martial music of trumpets and saxophones. Along the curious mast of tapering aluminium the rings unfurled in their white background, with their symbolic colors: Europe blue, Africa black, America red, Asia yellow, Oceania green... And over there the white masts which overhung the short-lived and enormous arena, were in their turn adorned with the colors of all the nations which are recognized by the I.O.C. Below President de Gaulle, for so coincidence had it, stood out, shining, the fifty white stars and the red stripes of the USA. A deafening thundering: some huge "Frelon" helicopters were sowing a red rain of paper roses, more perfumed than real ones. In dozens of thousands, the bouquets of perfume flew towards the crowd, and towards the multi-colored swarming of the contingents, who covered the gravel area soaked by melting snow.

We had come to the moment in the ceremony which is the most simple, the most moving and the most true. The torch, lit with mirrors in the sun of Olympus, came into the stadium. It was borne by Alain Calmat, a silver medalist at figure skating in the previous Winter Games at Innsbruck. No choice could have been better than this doctor, a former student in hospitals in Paris, who knows exactly how to reconcile his studies and competition.

Fine featured and blue-eyed, with strong masculine legs like all skaters, celestial in his moulded, sea-blue and black outfit, he crossed the piste to a roar of applause. He ascended the platform of light blue planks, which rose gently up to the foot of the aluminium tower in 96 steps. The chestnut headed athlete climbed them at a smart pace, brandishing on high his torch, the yellow tongues of which were stirred up by the wind. Little by little, the whispy haze of mist half, obliterated him; he became unreal.

He seemed almost a mirage, who, moving

steadily, grew closer to the huge cupola turned up towards heaven on the summit of the black tower. He stood immobile on the highest step. He must have been a mountaineer not to feel vertigo. He turned towards the crowd, and presented his torch to them. His arm stretched out, he rested several moments thus, motionless as a statue. He turned round and, with a short movement caused a huge sheaf of flames to be born, gilded at their source, then a blinding red, then smoky, and at last yellow, becoming calm.

Afterwards there was the oath taken by that fine champion with his honest, bronzed face, the skier Léo Lacroix. But in that promise made in a distinct voice, there was this fragment of a phrase:
"... respectful of the rules..."
These rules, which before everything else, demand a sincere amateurism.
Gusts of wind bent the burning flame of the Olympic bowl towards the monumental wall of Vercors, with its steep slopes, full of heroic tales and its peaks trembling with snow. The rest no longer counted...

WOLF-DIETER ROESNER
"Internationale Sportkorrespondenz,"
West Germany

Biathlon Gold for an Unknown

Olympia can be a two faced lady: she can destroy favorites, but she can also raise unknowns to unexpected heights. Magnar Solberg was one of those unknowns during the Olympic Winter Games at Grenoble. The 31-year-old policeman from Trondheim was a total stranger, even to his fellow Norwegians, who are great fans of the biathlon. Although already advanced in years as an athlete, he had never participated in any important international competition, not to mention any Olympic Games.

His teammates, Ion Istad, world champion of 1966, as well as Ragnar Tveiten and Ola Waerhaug, ranked among the most experienced and successful biathlon specialists in the world. They were fast and strong on skies as well as accurate with their rifles. They justly deserved the confidence of their countrymen. But Magnar Solberg? Nobody knew why he was chosen as the fourth member of the Norwegian team. Solberg was terribly disappointing when he took part in a pre-Olympic competition in Switzerland and the Norwegians would have liked to have sent him back to Norway. And yet, the same Magnar Solberg won the biathlon gold medal at the Olympic Games. There were not too many spectators assembled that cold and wet morning of February 12th, when 60 competitors representing 14 nations started the 20 kilometer (about 12.4 miles) biathlon in one-minute intervals. The French did not particularily care for this event, which was added

to the Olympic program only eight years before at Squaw Valley. Many regarded it as a competition for soldiers, and anything military really is not compatible with the Olympic spirit.

This prejudice, however, is disclaimed by looking into the history of skiing. The oldest known picture of a skier, the rock painting of Roedoey, Norway, which was discovered in 1929 and dates back to 3000 B.C., shows a man on something which looks very much like today's skis' carrying a weapon in his hands. This ancient skier could be called the first biathlon athlete on record. All the other pictorial documents, especially the old Russian stone sketches, also show hunters on skis. In the books of Bishop Olaus Magnus of Uppsala, Sweden, dating back to 1539, numerous winter hunting scenes can be found. Interesting are the descriptive texts of these pictures. One of them reads: "Those are the Laplanders, who with opened and long woods tied to their feet roam swiftly at will over mountains and valleys to hunt..." It is a curious fact that the youngest Winter Olympic sport is actually older than all the others!

The modern biathlon competitor can therefore be compared to a hunter rather than to a soldier. Every 4.5 kilometers (4,923 yards) he has to fire five shots at a target 150 meters (492 feet) away. He has to shoot in a prone position at the first and third targets and standing up at the others. The target he has to hit is only 12.5 centimeters (five inches) or 35 centimeters (14 inches) in diameter.

Magnar Solberg hit the targets as if they were twice their size. With his third starting position, the unknown Norwegian began his lonely race behind the strong Russian Alexander Tokhonov and Poland's Stanislaw Szezepaniak. The course was wet and strenuous, but Solberg, six feet tall and weighing only 150 pounds, did not seem to notice it. He felt a strange driving force within him. With almost automatic motions, he unslung his rifle from his back and took aim with such a steady hand it was as if he had not been skiing at all. The Russian had skied a little faster, but did not shoot as well at the first two targets. This cost him two penalty minutes, which were added to his time of 1:12.40.4 hours. Solberg's time was 1:13.45.9 hours and he did not miss a single shot.

The first starters were already close to the finish line when the rain began to fall. The Olympic gods were against the reigning world champion, Victor Mamatov of Russia. His starting number was 58. The gods were also against the other favorites, Ion Istad and Ola Waerhaug. They all started in the last section and had no chance because of a progressively worsening course. Only the incredibly strong Russian Vladimir Goundartsev could manage to overcome those handicaps to win the bronze medal.

Gold fell upon a man, however, whom nobody had known before. Magnar Solberg experienced his greatest moment. Only after he had crossed the finish line did the strain become noticeable. There he had to admit to the photographers who wanted to take pictures of a happy champion: "I am very happy, but too tired to smile."

MARTIN MAIER
'Kurier,' Vienna

No Rooms for Cowards

"Why do you think more highly about the downhill race than any other alpine event?" I put this question to some of the most prominent skiers. I knew they did, but I was interested in finding out why. I asked the champion, Jean-Claude Killy. His answer: "Because the downhill tests character and courage."

Guy Perillat paused before giving his answer. Surrounded by new glory, the silver medalist wanted to find words worthy of him, words which would look good in print. Then he said: "Because the downhill does not leave room for a compromise. You're either in front or you perish—that's the law of the downhill race." Gerhard Nenning: "You have to take great risks and you've got to have heart." Karl Schranz: "The downhill demands everything a skier is able to give. No coward will ever win."

Over and over again the statement is repeated: no prize without courage. I continue my questioning: "Is there any danger in the downhill?" Everyone confirms this, but then quickly changes the subject. They do not want to talk about the danger.

French television showed a special one day after the event. In a close-up, Killy and Perillat were shown just after their victories were announced. They fell into each other's arms. One rested his head on the other's shoulder and there they stood, motionless, for a long time. Had they worn a uniform they would have looked exactly like two soldiers who had just survived a highly dangerous combat mission.

Next came the final jump over a wall before the last stretch in slow motion. Nenning's skis wobbled as if struck by a nervous disorder. A fall seemed inevitable, but in the air Nenning regained his balance—just like a cat landing on it's feet.

Each flight seemed to last an eternity, seemed to cover many hundreds of meters in slow motion. Perillat flew easiest; he flew like children dream about flying: simply to rise and to float in space. Killy's style was not as quiet; he seemed to continue his battle with the course in mid-air. Once he spread his arms as if to take a long voluptuous stretch. And most macabre were the faces. Crash helmet and goggles revealed only nose and mouth. The faces all looked alike, one after the other, mouths wide open as if screaming the battle cry of the downhill racer. Strange: talk about the downhill race always returns to the terminology of war . . . .

Accompanied by brilliant sunshine, the Xth Olympic Winter Games were opened on the afternoon of February 6, 1968, in Grenoble, surrounded by the famous Dauphine landscape. The rock faces of the Chartreuse, Vercora and Grandes Rousses with their snow-capped peaks set the winter scene for this technically perfect opening ceremony. For this, the snowless valley of Grenoble was thankful to the neighboring mountain giants. 'Sans peur et reproche' (without fear or reproach— that is the motto of the local inhabitants. In this spirit the organizers built this broad, open arena beside the other excellent sports facilities just for the opening ceremony. It cost many hundred-thousands of francs and is as big as the 'Place de la Concorde' in Paris.

The Olympic fire was lit in the arena by the French silver medal winner in figure skating, Dr. Alain Calmat. Léo Lacroix, silver medal winner in the downhill Alpine race in Innsbruck, 1964, gave the Olympic oath. During the shorter opening ceremonies for each of the competition facilities, the French also had colorful ideas for arousing an Olympic mood among the spectators as shown here on the big ski-jump at St. Nizier.

Right: During the 30 kilometer cross-country run on the 7th February in Autrans, the 27-year-old Italian post official, Franco Nones, caused a sensation. He was more than a match for all the Russian and Scandinavian cross-country élite and succeeded in obtaining the first gold medal of the games ahead of Martinsen, Norway, and the great Finnish cross-country skier, Maentyranta. Thus the Italian postman from the Dolomites was a good example for all the other outsiders, that they too had a chance of winning.

Below: Two unknown skiers who lay far behind the winners: Martin Ross (No. 19) Australia, and Tibor Holeczy (No. 23) Hungary.

In the Winter Olympic Games, the Nordic events with their cross-country runs and relay races in the midst of a peaceful winter landscape embody for many spectators the true characteristics of an Olympic contest.

Above: The ladies also take an active part in the Nordic events with 5 and 10 kilometer cross-country runs and a 3 x 5 kilometer relay. The 30-year-old physics teacher Toini Gustavsson of Sweden is shown here as she approached her victory during the 10 kilometer race in the woods surrounding Grenoble. She was also champion in the 5 kilometer cross-country run and gained silver with her two teammates in the relay.

Right above: The modern pentathlon in the Summer Games corresponds to the Biathlon contest in the Winter Games. The latter includes a 20 kilometer cross-country run and four types of target shooting. The Norwegian policeman, Magnar Solberg, was able to win the gold medal in the individual event ahead of the highly favored Russians because he did not chalk up one single miss in the shooting.

Right below: The Norwegian team is shown here during the relay changeover. They gained silver behind the Russians and were followed by Sweden with bronze.

The Alpine events in the Grenoble Winter Games, which took place on the slopes of the 7,400 feet high Croix de Chamrousse, proved to be a triumph for the Frenchman, Jean-Claude Killy. He won the downhill race, the giant slalom and the slalom. He fulfilled the greatest expectations of his country and became the darling of the French people. These two pages of pictures show Killy and others not only as skiers, but also as personalities.

The U.S.A. team lost the ice-hockey game against the Canadians 3—2. In 1960, the U.S.A. was the champion in this event at Squaw Valley, after they had won the silver medal four years previously in Cortina, 1956. However, in 1964 and 1968 other nations took over the leading rôle. But the U.S.A. fans of this fastest of all team games are hoping for a renaissance with a new generation of young players.

Above:

For years William Kidd has been one of the strongest and most durable USA skiers for the downhill race. After gaining respect among the European élite by winning the silver medal in Innsbruck, 1964, here in Grenoble he was to be found in the leading positions. Thus he even left skiers with world class, like the Austrians Karl Schranz and Gerhard Nenning, behind him.

In the Nordic combination, the Scandinavian supremacy of the last few decades has been broken by the two West Germans, Georg Thoma (in 1964) and Franz Keller (in 1968). Together with Alois Kaelin, Switzerland, who gained silver and Andreas Kunz, East Germany, with bronze, the Central Europeans were predominant in this event.

Franz Keller is shown here during his victorious cross-country run and jump.

The ice-hockey battles in the Grenoble ice-stadium were always savoured by the spectators. One can no longer image the Olympic Games without these rugged lightning attacks, man against man, and the cunning tactics which can change in a second. Above, the USA battles lone Czechoslovakia for the puck. Below, USA just misses tie-breaking goal against Sweden.

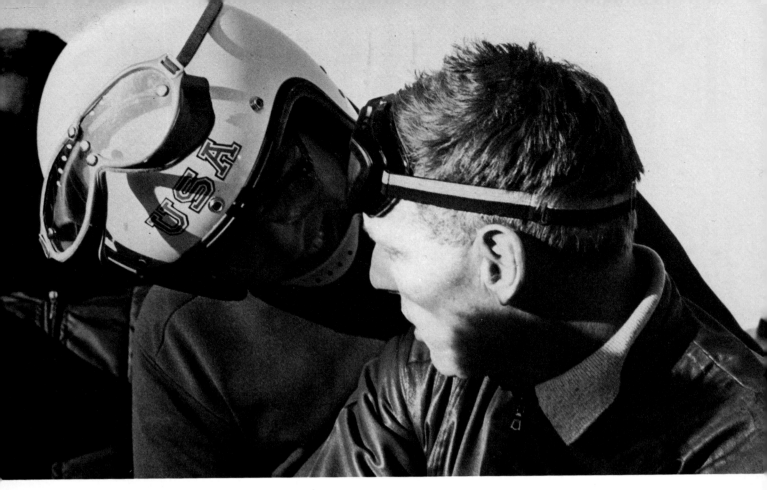

The Italian Eugenio Monti was the great champion of the bob-sled competitions. He gained the gold medal for Italy not only in the two-man-bob, but also in the four-man-bob.
Above: Monti having a friendly chat with the USA bob-driver, William Hickey.

KARL-HEINZ HUBA

"Sport Illustrierte," Munich

Eugenio Monti's Dream

It was 1964 at Innsbruck, Austria. The Olympic bobsled competition was held at the Heiligenwasserwiese on the foot of the Patscherkofel mountain. Eugenio Monti was anxiously awaiting the last run of his most dangerous rival in the two-man competition. Suddenly, there came a desperate cry for help over the loudspeaker system. A bolt supporting the runners had broken on the sled of Tony Nash from England, just as he was about to start his last run in an attempt to wrest the gold medal away from Monti.

The Italian did not hesitate very long. He went over to his bob, took out a bolt, the counterpart of the broken one, and hurried up the hill to the starting place. He himself repaired the sled of his rival: Tony Nash and his brakeman Nixon finally started—and became Olympic champions. It was Nash who later proposed Monti, when the International Sportswriters association met to award the first "Pierre de Coubertin Fair Play Trophy" of the UNESCO council for Education, Science and Culture. Thus, in May of 1965, Monti became the first recipient of this valuable trophy.

Eugenio Monti was born January 23, 1928, at Dobaccio near Bolzano, Italy. He developed into an outstanding Alpine skier and heir-apparent to the famous Zeno Colo. Before he got that far, however, severe injuries put a heavy damper on his ambitions. In 1952 at Sestriere, he took a bad spill and required an operation on his left knee. One year later, he fell again at Cervinia. This time, the same cartilage operation had to be performed on his other knee. This settled matters for Monti. In 1954, he won the Italian Collegiate championships once more in the long distance, the slalom and the Nordic combined, but the multi-talented athlete had discovered his interest in bobsledding at Cortina d'Ampezzo.

Monti began to typify more and more the new breed of bobsledders. He weighed just 145 pounds, was five-feet, nine-inches tall and a strong believer in physical fitness. Nobody could handle the Podar bob better than he. The world championships of the following years turned into "Monti Festivals." Nobody faced the dangerous challenge of the icy shoots at St. Moritz, Cortina or Garmisch as seriously as he. He left nothing to chance. He himself carried the runners of his bob to the races and meticulously supervised their proper treatment, which included continuous polishing with woolen cloths until seconds before the actual run. Monti turned the examination of a course into a sacred ceremony. He walked the course from start to finish and checked every small detail. Once he escaped disaster by jumping out of the course just in time when another bob came rumbling down in a high speed test run.

Monti, many times world champion, very much wanted to win his first Olympic championship at Innsbruck in 1964. However, he could not come to friendly terms with the course, just as he disliked the one at Alpe d'Huez four years later. He just did not care for courses solely planned by calculations on the drawing boards, where only the laws of mathematics and physics were applied. Monti was a driver by intuition. Nevertheless, he never lost his nerves during the races and he never took unnecessary risks. Most of his victories were won during the last run and he only broke course records when he had no other choice. Innsbruck was Monti's major disappointment. There was talk of the end of the "Era Monti" and he himself let it be known that he wanted to retire. However, Monti could keep his promise only one year. His brakeman Siorpaes had developed new ideas in the construction of the Podar bob. Monti added another world championship in the two-man bob in 1966. One year later, only poor conditions in *Alpe d'Huez* kept him from winning yet another one.

Monti had won nine world championships —but only two silver and two bronze medals in Olympic competition—when he came to Alpe d'Huez in 1968. Now 40 years old, Monti proved he had lost nothing of his fast reflexes and certainly nothing of his uncanny ability to be at his best when it really mattered: his victory in the two-man race could not have been any closer and his gold medal in the four-man bob was won by only nine-hundredths-of-a-second faster than the one of silver medalist Thaler of Austria.

Eugenio Monti's dream had finally come

245

true: he had won his tenth and 11th world championship and his first two gold medals. He promptly announced his retirement once more and this time there was no reason to suspect he would ever change his mind again.

F ear is the worst of evils in sports. Worse than the often quoted bad luck, worse even than a broken leg. An injury can stimulate. Fear paralyzes.

Such is the lesson that Czechoslovakia's ice hockey players learned from their unfortunate experience at the Grenoble Olympics, where they missed the unique chance of getting ahead of their rivals from the Soviet Union and, by that, putting a temporary end to the supremacy of the Russians, world champions since 1954.

When the last day of the ice hockey tournament dawned, things did not look too bright for the men around 27-year-old Soviet star Anatoli Firsov, from Moscow. Two days before, the Russians had been overwhelmed by Czechoslovakia in a fierce game, when the whirlwind-like rushing Czechs took a 3–1 lead in the first period, drew 1–1 in the second, and resisted heroically a brilliant Soviet rush in the third (1–2), thus scoring a final 5–4 victory which opened door to the gold medal for them.

It had been an extremely difficult job, as the computer revealed: the USSR totaled 31 shots at the goal against 26 of their opponents, and the final result was a lucky one, though quite in order.

At this stage, three teams were still possible champions: Czechoslovakia, defeated by Canada 2–3; the USSR, beaten by the Czechs; and Canada, surprisingly downed in the early stage of the competition by Finland, 2–5.

Alfred Hitchcock could not have staged it more dramatically. The final outcome depended on the two matches which concluded the Games. It was now or never for the three who had beaten each other. Czechoslovakia had to deal with Sweden. Then, last but not least, USSR and Canada were to close the session. Except for Sweden, who had nothing to lose, it was all or nothing for the three remaining. The Czechs, if they beat the Scandinavians,

were in any case ahead of the Soviets whom they had previously defeated. The Maple Leaf team, if victorious, held a final advantage on the Czechs who had succumbed to them earlier.

So it was obvious that the men from Bohemia, Moravia and Slovakia had the easiest part, and the odds were all the more in their favor, since they had the crowd on their side. Less so for political reasons, since the dramatic events in Eastern Europe took place several months later, but mainly because people like a change and the Soviets had been too long in command of ice hockey. Also, big Goliath is always less popular than little David.

Thus, all the Czechs had to do was to put away the Three Crown bearers from Scandinavia, who had not been brilliant throughout the event, except for one good game against the Soviet team.

He who does not seize his chance, does not deserve success. Paralyzed by the fear of losing, the Czechs started hesitatingly against Sweden. "Safety first" was their motto. Instead of pushing forward as they had done so well against the Russians, they sent out only two men against the Swedish defense, where number 7, 23-year-old Lennart Svedberg, one of the best full-backs of the whole tournament, withstood firmly.

The Czech tactics were madness and it is not sure there was method in it. Anyway, when Sweden took the lead towards the end of the second period, the match was practically over and done with. Tired as they grew after their gruelling match with the Russians, they had to be satisfied with a draw, after their most disappointing show since the tournament began. To put it crudely: they had lacked "guts" at the crucial moment.

The Czech setback meant freedom from fear for the Russians during the last match. They did not suffer from any inhibitions, ignored their apprehensions, and outclassed

EDGAR JOUBERT
Le Parisien libéré, Paris

Freedom from Fear

Canada in such a way that no doubt was ever permitted.

True, the North Europeans had been helpful: the Finns when they shocked Canada and the Swedes by holding the Czechs. But all these "ifs" and "buts" remained quite irrelevent. The Russians not only did not lose their nerves after their misfortune against the Czechs, but moreover played excellent hockey throughout the Grenoble fortnight. The very best team won. And that's what matters in the long run.

MARTIN MAIER
"Kurier," Vienna

A Cast in the Latest Style

There she was lying at the bottom of the hill with a small and pale face. Robin Morning of the USA women's Alpine skiing team, had broken her foot after a playful little swing down the course after the training had been completed. She had fallen and the first aid man had straightened out her scarf, pushing one edge behind her neck. I asked, "Can I be of help?" A silly question; what could a reporter do?

Robin could have angrily answered "No." Or she could have asked for a brandy, a piece of chocolate, perhaps, a hot tea or zwieback, just to take her mind of her misfortune. In the tales of amazon skiers and their heroics, Robin would have exclaimed "I will start anyway!" But not this Robin. As her face became even smaller and paler, I wanted to continue talking, as one talks to sick people or to little babies. Suddenly she asked "Do you think it will show?" She was afraid of a permanent scar or of her leg becoming shorter than the other.

This should not be dismissed by pointing out that girls just happen to be vain and that they would worry about the latest style in hospital gowns when their appendix is about to be removed. It rather points out a strong feminine virtue—not to lose poise while in distress.

I was not going to interview Robin Morning in her situation. After all, reporters are not hyenas. So I went back to press headquarters and got all my information there: Robin Morning, student at the University of Utah, 20, 5′1″, 105 pounds, born in Santa Monica, California. And, oh yes, her hobby: women's fashion.

She probably wore her cast in the latest style, in the newest Olympic look.

DENNIS L. BIRD
The Times, London

Artistry on Ice

The new *Stade de Glace* at Grenoble is one of the most beautiful ice rinks in the world. Built specially for the 1968 Winter Olympic Games, it lies like a great four-pointed star in the Mistral Park, near the center of the town. As you approach one of the entrances, at each corner of the building, the huge glass-and-wood-and-concrete structure soars above you like the bow of an ocean liner. Inside, there is not a single pillar to obstruct the view of 12,000 spectators; the massive, graceful curves of the roof are completely self-supporting.

Skating of equal beauty was to be seen in that splendid stadium during the two weeks of the Olympics. Most memorable of all was the performance of the Russians, Ludmila and Oleg Protopopov, in the pairs' event. Winners of the gold medal at the 1964 Winter Games in Innsbruck, the Leningrad couple were now aged 32 and 35—veterans indeed by skating standards. But they proved to be still in a class by themselves. Apart from two small technical errors, they presented a program that was immaculate, artistic, perfect almost beyond the bounds of belief. Most pairs begin with a lively introduction, fast and full of jumps and lifts. The Protopopov's began in magical quiet, to the cool beauty of Beethoven's "Moonlight" Sonata. Spirals . . . a parallel spin with the girl inverted . . . an overhead split-lift skated with dreamy grace . . . glides . . . another lift; and then a sudden change of mood as they did a difficult double-loop jump to the challenging, imperious opening bars of Beethoven's Fifth Symphony. The rest of their program was of similar quality —not technically as difficult as some, but far ahead of all the rest in artistry. Some of the loveliest movements were the simplest —for instance, the spirals where Ludmila glided away from her partner, and then returned as though drawn to him by a magnet, with the hint of a kiss. And their forward spiral together, the two united as one, and then the girl going forward alone as her partner stopped in supplication . . . it was sheer ballet on ice, and beautiful to behold.

Nothing else could compare, not even the runners-up from Moscow, Tatiana Zhuk and Alexander Gorelik, with the Protopopov's spectacular jumps and lifts. The USA pair champions, Seattle's Cynthia and Ronald Kauffman, had had hopes of the bronze medal. They started out in fine style, but Ronald slipped on their dramatic death-spiral, and some later errors put them down to seventh place in free-skating—just below the graceful Sandi Sue Sweitzer and her partner Roy Wagelein from Los Angeles. The Californians were one of the most pleasing pairs of the evening, but having done less well in the earlier compulsory exercises, they changed places with the Kauffmans in the final results. The third US pair Alicia (Jo-Jo) Starbuck and Kenneth Shelley, also from California, made a promising debut in international skating.

It was in the singles events that American skaters came into their own. Peggy Fleming, trained in Colorado Springs and world champion since 1966, built up a long lead of more than 77 points in the women's compulsory figures, those complex variants of the basic figure eight which President Charles de Gaulle had watched Peggy practise on the day the Games opened. In free skating Miss Fleming had no other competitor to fear; her only rival was herself. The strain of being favorite, with all its attendant publicity, told on her, and she was a little below her enchanting best. But no one else could compare with her artistic interpretation. She said afterwards that she free-skated "as in a dream." Her rapt concentration rendered her completely oblivious of her audience. For her, nothing existed but the ice and her music—Tschaikowsky, Verdi, Saint-Saëns, and Rossini. The onlooker felt almost like an interloper.

Gabriele Seyfert of East Germany, brimful of vitality, gave a powerful performance of great technical difficulty, and was unanimously placed second by the panel of nine judges. Albertina Noyes from Boston had a chance of the bronze medal, but some faulty jumps prevented her gaining it. It was the graceful Czech and European champion, Hana Maskova, who finished third, with a program full of high jumps cleanly landed. Fourteen-year-old Janet Lynn from Illinois finished ninth, and showed great promise. Her talent was amply confirmed less than a year later, when she succeeded Miss Fleming as US national champion.

The three US entrants in the men's event all took places in the top six against strong European and Canadian competition. It was a championship of surprises, with world champion Emmerich Danzer (Austria) finishing no higher than fourth, despite a brilliant display in free-skating; his compulsory figures had left him with a 32-point deficit which he could not make up. His compatriot, Wolfgang Schwarz, won only the first of the five compulsory figures and was second best in free skating, but his skating was consistent enough to enable him to beat his more erratic rivals for the gold medal. His program included many difficult jumps, among them a triple salchow, but his style was less polished than that of Timothy Wood (Detroit), the US champion. Wood had skated the best change-loop figure in the compulsories, and his smooth, stylish free program seemed to get progressively more difficult towards the end. Schwarz just gained a majority verdict over Wood, by five judges to four. Wood took the silver medal, and the other Americans Gary Visconti (Detroit) and John Misha Petkevich (Montana) were 5th and 6th, respectively.

The Russian Oleg Protopopov and his wife Ludmilla showed their mature ability once more in Grenoble and secured thereby the gold medal for Russia. But other Russian couples are also pushing themselves forward and hoping that they will be the champions of tomorrow.

248

USA's Peggy Fleming was the darling of the ice stadium in Grenoble as she floated over the glistening ice like a fairy, filling the spectators with pure delight. In contrast to the Olympic champions Sjoukje Dijkstra, Netherlands, and Regine Heitzer, Austria, who **performed** with great muscular strength, Peggy floated along like delicate thistledown. Her performance alone made the trip to Grenoble worthwhile.

Honoring the champions of the ladies' figure-skating. IOC-President Brundage performed this pleasurable task personally. Thus he honored Peggy Fleming's art which could not be bettered by the powerful Gabriele Seyffert, East Germany, who gained silver, or by Hanna Maskova, Czechoslovakia, who gained bronze. Opposite: Peggy during her Olympic performance.

The organizers compensated for the lack of snow in Grenoble by having some interesting ideas. At night the illumination of the streets and the snowy slopes of the nearby mountain giants helped to transform Grenoble into a dramatic Olympic city so that the grey of the day was forgotten.

Close on the heels of Schwarz, Austria, came 19-year-old Tim Wood, USA, with the silver medal for men's figure skating. In Sapporo, 1972, Tim will be 23 and if he sticks it out with the rigors of his training, he should then be at the height of his achievement.

Above:
World record holder Erhard Keller, West Germany, also gains the Olympic championship in the 500 meter speed skating.

Left:
Richard T. McDermott, U.S.A., speeds to silver medal triumph.

The speed skating in Grenoble was held on the 400 meter (approx. 411 yards)
long ice rink in the Paul Mistral Park. The French spectators were really impressed by the
swift gliding figures shooting round the oval course. In eight contests
from 500 meters (approx. 548 yards) to 10,000 meters (approx. 10,972 yards)
200 participants from 17 countries took part.

Above:
The medal winners in the 500 meter race: Left to right, McDermott, USA,
Keller, West Germany, and Thomassen, Norway.

Right:
In the ladies' 500 meter speed skating, the three merry USA girls, Jennifer Fish,
Diane Holum and Mary Meyers, all skated the same time behind the gold medalist
Ludmilla Titova, USSR. The jury could find no alternative but to award them each a silver
medal! When the three jolly girls stood together in second place,
Ludmilla found it just as amusing.

The Winter Olympic Games in Grenoble 1968 had a magnificent finale with the
ski-jumping contest on the large ski-jump at St. Nizier. The aura of a flying man always
clings to the ski-jumpers and it is this fascination that ensures the jumping
events a firm place in the Winter Olympic Games.

France viewed its Olympic Winter Games mainly through the Alpine ski races.
Therefore, for the French, the Winter Games really took place in Chamrousse where all the
ski races were held. The 7319 foot high Croix de Chamrousse, which lies 4875 feet
higher than Grenoble, was the scene of the greatest French success in Alpine
skiing that they had ever had. The finish for some of the men's and women's races
was on the slopes of the Seiglières in Casserouse.

Olympic flags with their five rings were also flying on all the bridges in Grenoble. For the many foreign visitors they were bridges of friendship and peace in a torn world.

CHAMROUSSE

Centre Olympique
Gare Routière

Centre de Presse

Sports de Glace

Accueil-Hébergement
...n·Bureau
...gszentrale

CHAMBÉRY
Centre Ville

Bd Gambetta

Numerous friendly hostesses in attractive red fur jackets and dark blue pants were everywhere, always ready to help. Within a few hours, the stranger was familiar with the streets of Grenoble through the perfect maps and information boards. This busy modern industrial town charmed the visitor into forgetting that the Winter Games did not really take place in Grenoble at all and that the snow could only be found miles away.

The organizers of the Winter Games built a beautifully modern ice-palace in the center
of Grenoble, where the ice-hockey tournament and figure skating contests took
place. After all the rigorous and exciting competitions were over, the final ceremony was held
here as well. Once more all the flags of the competing nations assembled and
already the flag from distant Nippon was hoisted beside the Tricolor as a first invitation
to the Olympic Winter Games in Sapporo, 1972.

SERGE GROUSSARD
"L'Aurore," Paris

Epilogue

On the evening of Sunday, the 18th of February, 1968, the capital of the French Alps was illuminated with a kaleidoscopic profusion of bright colors for the last hours of the Xth Winter Games. The ice stadium emerged from the shadows of the Mistral Park, dazzling and strange. With its two crossed and vaulted roofs, it reminded us irresistibly of some huge exotic butterfly settling on the grass, and its four façades with their projecting ridges glowed in the darkness like phosphorescent whalebone.

It was in this super-modern piece of architecture that the closing ceremony of the Xth Winter Olympic Games unfolded with extreme charm and elegance. First the pairs of ice dancers swirled across the ice, sometimes eddying and then flowing like an Alpine river after the snow has melted. In their wake came the figure-skaters, true Olympians, exhibiting their masterful control on the ice in a display to excite the imagination and envy of every beholder. The following procession of all the athletes moved by as a powerful and joyful exhibition of the brotherhood of man.

During the presentation of the medals to the victors of the contests on the last two days of the Games, the ice was covered with an enormous blue nylon carpet which was spread out by a clever mechanical contrivance. The three winners of the special slalom, which had been the topic of so much discussion on the previous evening, the cross-country skiers, the speed skaters, the jumpers—all passed by, one by one, to the podium for the impressive ceremonial of the hoisting of the flags.

Smiling, President Avery Brundage delivered the closing speech in French, inviting "the youth of all countries to assemble in four years at Sapporo, in Japan, to celebrate with us the XIth Winter Olympic Games." The sacred flame arrived and was extinguished, and then, with an air of melancholy, the strains of the "Song of Farewell" rose from the assembled throng. The Olympic spirit, united more than ever with the ideal forged by Pierre de Coubertin, left revitalised by the splendor, the performances and the crises of Grenoble.

These were our reflections as the crowd regretfully left the ice stadium. People dispersed into the cold crisp night under a sky riddled with stars. On the sidewalk, charming Japanese distributed tiny flags of white silk shining with the red sun of Oriental dawns. Some Japanese athletes also presented tiny artificial roses sheathed in perfumed lace. Then the sadness of seeing the great quadrennial festival finish vanished as one thought of the next meeting, over there, half a world away—a meeting in the beautiful islands of Japan with their historical associations and a modern and vital civilization whose origins are rooted way back in antiquity. Goodbye Grenoble 1968! Hello Sapporo 1972!

ALOYS BEHLER
"Die Welt," Hamburg

Three Ice Queens from USA

Happy occasions are rare for most of the participants in Olympic Games. Therefore, the events of February 9, 1968, deserve special mention. On this day, as eye–witnesses will readily confirm, even the Olympic gods were prompted to a discreet smile.

Among the 28 young ladies who competed in the skating rink of Parc Paul Mistral in the 500 meters, there were Mary, Dianne and Jenny from the United States. First it was Mary's turn. Her time was 46.3 seconds. Then came Dianne—and she also was clocked in 46.3 seconds. Finally, Jenny went on her way and when the electronic clock again stopped exactly at 46.3, it seemed like the punch line had been delivered to an already delightful story. This highly unusual development created waves of excitement around the ice oval. Mary, Dianne and Jenny giggled and squealed like youngsters who had just pulled off their biggest prank. They had hoped for one silver medal and now they had won three of them. The charming American three-stage rocket had blasted off with absolute perfection. Even the glitter of the gold medal, won in 46.1 seconds by the Russian girl Ludmila Titova, paled in comparison to the threefold silver lining of Mary's, Dianne's and Jenny's happiness. At this moment not one of three American girls would have cared to switch places with Ludmila.

Overwhelmed by their triple blessing, the three girls faced the inquisitive reporters and even the most hardboiled newsmen were infected by the high spirits of the trio. The first question put to them was about their ages. He was satisfied with Jenny's 18, he thought that Dianne (16) was too young, and to the delight of the group he expressed the thought that Mary (21) was too old. Little did he know that Mary had already made herself one year older than she really was. While Jenny stretched her long legs, while Dianne combed her shoulder length hair which seemed to be such a massive bulk that one wondered how all this could have been hidden under the tight skating cap, and while Mary looked around with undisguised pride, Ludmila sat next to them and enjoyed her triumph all by herself. It was impossible for her, who after all was the winner, to compete with these three cheerfully chirping American girls, whose amiable chatter filled the interviewing room. Laughing and chuckling, they replied to all answers, flirting with their newly-gained glory and capturing all newsmen with their charm. Now, only a few minutes after their Olympic efforts, they were not athletes any more, but simply daughters of Eve, enjoying the impact of their feminity.

They were unable to explain the coincidence which had lifted all three of them on the same pedestal of Olympic prominence. Perhaps spring, which had arrived on this very day, with temperatures way above the freezing point, may have given them wings. The ice had become dull, which may have favored the American skating style. With short, chopping strides the Americans had raced over the course, accelerated by strong arm movements and set afire by the "go go" chants of the American fans.

Later that night, Mary Meyers from St. Paul, Minnesota, Dianne Holm from Northbrook, Illinois, and Jennifer Fish from Strongsville, Ohio, were a happy crowd to the right of Ludmila Titova during the victory ceremonies. But they probably could not wait until this was over so that they could start dancing all through the night.

Are the Alpine girl skiers different from the other girls of today? To answer this question best, let me talk about one of those girl skiers, 24-year-old Nancy Greene of Canada. In 1967 she won the World Cup and in Grenoble, after placing second behind Marielle Goitschel in the slalom, she won the giant slalom.

Nancy who is a university assistant in Montreal, says "If I were not in love with snow and skiing, I would not be able to endure the hardships that go with today's races. To be precise: it does not strike me as a hardship, of course; how could I love it otherwise?"

Well, Nancy Greene has become a philosopher. Doesn't she have any other problems than skiing? She laughs: "You're misunderstanding me again." This "again" irritates me a little. Nancy continues: "Skiing is not a problem for me. If it were, it would become a burden. And if it were a burden, I wouldn't love it. And if I didn't love it, why would I do it?"

Her colleagues say she can entertain a party all by herself. One of them points her finger at her: "She talks as fast and persistent as an itinerant preacher." But she never has used any of the many excuses which are available to all skiers in great numbers, excuses like "my skis were too hard, too soft, too long, too short, too stiff, too temperamental" or "The snow was too deep, too slow, too powdery, too iced" or "Just as I started, the view became poor, the fog came, the sun blinded me ... etc."

Nancy Greene is full of wit. In Portillo she had hurt her shoulder during slalom training. She asked, puzzled: "Can anybody tell how I got blue marks from green bamboo posts?" (During training, bamboo posts were used). Nancy wears her freckles like jewelry. She has a stubby nose and likes to walk around in old, comfortable slacks. But when she enters a hotel lobby, every porter lifts his cap anyway. About a rival she said: "This is no lady. She cheated herself into her starting number." But as for Nancy, despite pants and an occasional curse, Nancy Greene is a lady.

MARTIN MAIER
"Kurier," Vienna

When Girl Skiers Become Philosophers

MARTIN MAIER

"Kurier," Vienna

Nobody is Helping Him

Honoré Bonnet, coach of France's Alpine team, told his skiers not to hang any victory photos from Portillo on the walls of the Olympic quarters-in Bachat-boulord. The athletes were not to be reminded of their earlier triumphs during the world championships. That could have made them too confident.

Bonnet had marched his team into the eye clinic for jet pilots of the French air force in Paris during the summer. There they were examined and the eyes of some of the skiers were corrected by contact lenses or by optical gymnastics. Bonnet refused to disclose the names of those wearing contact lenses.

I asked him which athletes would win. Bonnet answered "How can I help but favor all of my skiers? It should go without saying that I, as coach, have confidence in all my skiers." Then he continues: "I have no favorite. The individual is holy, untouchable, because the Alpine races are an individual sport like no other. The skier is all by himself during the race. Who can help him, if he is not helping himself?"

This sounded like he really wanted to say "Every coach is by himself. Who is helping me, if my team fails?" But his team helped him anyway: Killy, Perillat, Marielle Goitschel, Isabel Mir, Annie Famose ....

WALTER WEHRLE

Sportinformation Zürich

The Woes of the Tobogganers

The rare breed of tobogganers—they still have difficulties meeting the requirement of twelve participating nations to become an Olympic event—experienced many troubles and disappointments during their second Olympic competition. Their sleds, weighing approximately 40 pounds, suffered more than any other sport because of unfavorable weather influences. What had originally been forecast for the bobsled on the sun terrace of Alpe D'Huez, unfortunately, came true for the toboggan shoot located at Villard-de-Lans.

Almost daily the brave girls and boys had carried their sleds piggyback up to the starting point early in the morning, only to the told that the course never would have held up to the trial runs of 26 women and 57 men. The ice was approaching snow conditions and the sharp runners of the sleds zooming down at speeds close to 50 m. p. h. would surely have cut through to the concrete foundation of the shoot. Only four days before the end of the Games were the organizers able to hold three runs of the singles competition for men and women. Finally, on the very last day, the weather did cooperate and the course presented itself in perfect condition for the doubles. The second mishap had little to do with the sport itself; however, it had a direct influence upon the distribution of all three medals. There seemed to be no way to stop a sweep of East Germany in the girl's competition. After two runs, Ortrun Enderlein,

the undisputed queen of tobogganists, was leading. Her two teammates, Anna-Maria Müller and Angela Knösel, were in second and fourth positions. Suddenly, before the third and deciding run, one jury member discovered that the runners of the girls' sleds had been heated artificially. This had been strictly prohibited by a recent ruling. Other observers were summoned, and the jury had no choice; the East German trio was disqualified. This heavy blow was regrettably followed by an unpleasant war of words and accusations which damaged the prestige of tobogganning. In addition, it strained the friendly relations enjoyed by the participating nations. The scars will not disappear for many years to come.

This incident was even more unfortunate, since tobogganning was just beginning to gain widespread popularity. There was great admiration for the courageous athletes, especially for the girls, who looked more as though they belonged to a ballet troupe and appeared strangely out of place when they jumped fearlessly on their sleds in a running start to catapult themselves down the icy shoots. The most fragile looking doll of them all, Erika Lechner of Italy, turned in the fastest times and won the gold medal. World champion Thomas Köhler, East Germany, failed by a few hundredths of a second to overtake the Austrian Manfred Schmid, but he and his teammate Bohnsack did not miss their last chance and won the doubles competition.

How did it happen? A group of Norwegians, awaiting transportation in front of this quaint mountain community's town hall, were asked the question by a late arrival.

The cross-country enthusiasts, who were headed back for Grenoble, had just seen little Franco Nones, the 27-year-old Italian skier, streak to an unexpected triumph in the 30-kilometer event. They wondered how a European from the south could beat the Scandinavians at their own game.

"If it had been close," said the puzzled questioner in Norwegian, "maybe it would be easier to understand. But the Italian won as if he were racing alone. Where was Martinsen? Did he stop to rest?"

There was no doubt that Nones, a wiry athlete with amazing stamina, was in a class by himself. He won by a substantial 49.7 seconds over the hilly, 18.6-mile course and his victory margin was at least three city blocks.

Odd Martinsen, a 26-year-old forester, helped the Norwegians save some face by finishing second ahead of Eero Maentyranta, the 1964 Olympic double gold medal winner. Vladimir Voronkov of the Soviet Union was fourth.

It was fortunate from the standpoint of prestige that the Norwegians and Finns came home second and third. If Giulio de Florian, an Italian who placed fifth, had finished higher, the Scandinavians, as well as the highly rated Soviet skiers, really would have been embarrassed.

The day's major development was so unexpected that Fabio Conci, president of the Italian Ski Federation, wasn't on hand to see it. After all, Italy never had won a world championship cross-country event. Conci was at Chambrousse, more than 30 miles across the mountains to the east, watching the Alpine nonstop downhill, for which there were no medals.

The first-place and fifth-place finishes by the Italians proved again that determined training, backed by capable coaching, could produce progress in ski racing. The Italians have had Swedish coaches ever since 1952, when Sigvard Nordland was put in charge of the program.

Bengt-Herman Nilsson, another Swede, took over control in 1958. He was the recipient of almost as many slaps on the back as was Nones. Nilsson said at least part of today's success stemmed from training stints in Sweden.

"I've been taking the boys there every year," he said.

"We do our basic work in the mountains of northern Italy, but there's nothing like a Scandinavian country to give the men the right feel for the sport. I take them about 700 kilometers north of Stockholm."

It was generally agreed that wax had an important bearing on the outcome. When the skiers arose at dawn, the temperature was well below freezing. The Italians spread a green wax, made by a countryman, immediately under the boot portions of the skis. This type is suitable for cold snow. Then they applied the same manufacturers' "special" green wax, designed for very cold snow, over the skis' entire lengths.

The combination proved to be ideal. The morning remained cold, the temperatures climbing somewhat only after Nones had crossed the finish line.

In contrast, it was evident the favored Norwegians had guessed at the temperatures and as a result they waxed poorly. Norway was able to place only Martinsen, who had started 52nd, in the first 10. Gjermund Eggen, the winner of three world championship medals for Norway in 1966, was 34th. For the USA, the day was notable in that Mike Gallagher of Vermont and Mike Elliot of Colorado enabled America to reach a new high at the distance.

Gallagher placed 27th and Elliott 29th, Gallagher showed a 2½-minute improvement over his Federation International de Ski showing in 1966. "We are extremely happy," said Al Merrill of Lebanon, N.H., the Americans' head Nordic coach. "We are making progress. I'm convinced our more intensive training programs are paying off."

MICHAEL STRAUSS
The New York Times

Italian Nordic Skier Stuns Scandinavians on Opening Day

Reprinted with special permission of The New York Times

GAMES OF THE XIX OLYMPIAD

Mexico City

October 12–27, 1968

X OLYMPIC WINTER GAMES

Grenoble

February 6–18, 1968

V PAN-AMERICAN GAMES

Winnipeg

July 23 – August 6, 1967

A REVIEW OF

THE UNITED STATES TEAMS

and their participation and
performance in the great
international amateur sports festivals held
in Mexico City, Grenoble
and Winnipeg.

by

Arthur G. Lentz
Executive Director
United States Olympic Committee

The participants, the events and the fine achievements of our athletes in Mexico City, Grenoble and Winnipeg during the years of 1967 and 1968 are recorded in the following special section. The United States Olympic effort is a unique blend of the *individual* contributions of many. More than one thousand young American men and women who competed in the Games, as well as the hundreds of devoted administrators and staff personnel who so well served our Olympic and Pan-American Teams, are here gratefully acknowledged and saluted. Olympians, all!

Arthur G. Lentz

ARTHUR G. LENTZ
FOR
THE UNITED STATES OLYMPIC COMMITTEE

UNITED STATES OLYMPIC COMMITTEE ADMINISTRATION

President
Douglas F. Roby, Detroit, Mich.

1st Vice President
Franklin L. Orth, Washington, D.C.

2nd Vice President
Dr. Merritt H. Stiles, Spokane, Wash.

Secretary
Robert J. Kane, Ithaca, N.Y.

Treasurer
Julian K. Roosevelt, Oyster Bay, N.Y.

Presidents Emeriti
*Avery Brundage, Chicago, Ill.
*Kenneth L. Wilson, Wilmette, Ill.

Counselor
*Patrick H. Sullivan, New York, N.Y.

Associate Counselor and Chief of Mission
*Dr. Miguel A. de Capriles, New York, N.Y.

Executive Director
*Arthur G. Lentz, New York, N.Y.
+Everett D. Barnes, Hamilton, N.Y.

Assistant Treasurer
*William J. Bachert, Montclair, N.J.

* Non voting member
+ Served as acting director, June 1 – December 1, 1968

D. Roby

| F. Orth | M. Stiles | R. Kane | J. Roosevelt | A. Brundage | K. Wilson |

| P. Sullivan | M. de Capriles | A. Lentz | E. Barnes | W. Bachert | |

MEMBERS
U.S.O.C. BOARD OF DIRECTORS
(Serving as of October 1, 1968)

T. Alteneder	S. Barnes	L. Benton	E. Black	F. Brilando	R. Brown	C. Buck
Buckingham	H. Buse	A. Bushnell	A. Coward	J. de Capriles	R. Dixon	A. Duer	C. Fagan
L. Fisher	H. Friermood	J. Garland	H. Glassen	C. Gram	W. Greim	C. Hansen	A. Hart
J. Hawthorne	J. Hill	W. Hobson	D. Hull	J. Jack	G. Killian	P. Krumm	T. Lockhart
J. Mahoney	A. Martin	D. Matlin	J. McClelland	M. McLane	C. Neinas	W. Reed	C. Shenk
P. Smart	P. Sober	E. Steitz	B. Strean	J. Sulger	A. Wheltle	K. Wickham	G. Wilson

MEXICO 68

GAMES OF THE XIX OLYMPIAD · MEXICO CITY, MEXICO
OCTOBER 12 - 27, 1968

"GRANDIOSO," spelled out in four-inch high letters across the eight columns of a leading Mexico City newspaper on a Sunday morning following the opening ceremonies, could not have been a better choice as the single most descriptive word to herald the beginning of the Games of the XIX Olympiad. And, to the thousands who jam packed the many sports stadiums and the millions who viewed the course of events on their television sets, it was a word which most appropriately expressed their reaction to the continual flow of exciting and colorful happenings during the entire 16-day period in October of 1968.

Probably no staging of the world's greatest sports festival ever had greater impact than this triumphal setting in Mexico City. Despite all the frustrations of controversy raised by pseudo-application of political overtones and the carping criticism of self-appointed alarmists who saw only doom in the choice of high-altitude Mexico City as host, the Games of the XIX Olympiad not only began in magnificent style but ran their course with no let-down in high level presentation. The results were clear indication of a great achievement by the Organizing Committee and the thousands of individual workers needed to bring a highly-complex project into successful fruition.

For the United States of America, too, it was a grand and glorious venture. From the time its athletes paraded into *Estadio Olimpico,* dressed in the colorful and stylish apparel provided through generous contributions by American industry, to the final night of the basketball competition when the USA courtmen won the gold medal and kept intact a record of never having been beaten in this sport, there was more than enough proof of performance to keep this nation's Olympic and international prestige at the top.

Although it is difficult to properly compare team performances when standards, conditions and talent change so radically during the four-year period between Olympic Games, the 1968 USA delegation's overall success rates as the best in history. All told, the harvest of 45 gold medals, 28 silvers and 34 bronzes for a total of 107 awards is the greatest USA haul in the ultra-modern period of the Games which started in 1948. In addition, the winning of 26 fourth places, 16 fifths and 17 sixths is also a high level of production and indicates the depth of high grade talent.

Veteran and newcomer shared in top honors for the *Norte Americanos.* One must start with Al Oerter, discus thrower, who became the first athlete ever to win an athletic event four times in as many Games. And for the new-

comers, you begin with 16-year-old Debbie Meyer, who won three gold medals in her first Olympic swimming competition.

Successful title defenses by Wyomia Tyus in the women's 100 meter dash and by Gary Anderson in the free rifle shooting tests must be spotlighted as well as the 12 basketball players, grossly underestimated by national critics, who amazed everyone with their gold medal performance in their first Olympic experience. Linda Metheny, a 1964 Olympian, set new high standards for USA gymnasts by qualifying for the individual finals in balance beam, rating sixth, an unprecedented achievement for an American.

Veteran rider Bill Steinkraus' gold medal triumph in the equestrian jumping capped a five-time Olympic Games contention for such an honor, while Mrs. Janice-Lee Romary, competing in her sixth Olympic Games as a fencer, was accorded the honor of carrying the USA flag in the opening ceremonies, a "first" for the distaff side. Oerter, who carried the flag in the closing ceremonies, had been in contention with Mrs. Romary for the classic honor but graciously deferred.

There are, of course, many more who deserve mention, but they are accounted for in the reviews of each sport which follow on ensuing pages.

(continued on page 276)

UNITED STATES OF AMERICA MEDAL WINNERS AT MEXICO CITY 1968

GOLD MEDAL WINNERS

ATHLETICS Track & Field) — MEN (16)

ROBERT BEAMON, long jump; WILLIE DAVENPORT, 110 meter hurdles; LEE EVANS, 400 meters, 4 x 400 meter relay; RICHARD FOSBURY, high jump; *RONALD FREEMAN, 4 x 400 meter relay * CHARLES GREENE, 4 x 100 meter relay; JAMES HINES, 100 meters, 4 x 100 meter relay; *LAWRENCE JAMES, 4 x 400 meter relay; J. RANDEL MATSON, shot put; VINCENT MATHEWS, 4 x 400 meter relay; ALFRED A. OERTER, JR., discus; CAPT. MELVIN PENDER, USA, 4 x 100 meter relay; ROBERT SEAGREN, pole vault; RONALD RAY SMITH, 4 x 100 meter relay; TOMMIE SMITH, 200 meters; WILLIAM A. TOOMEY, decathlon.

ATHLETICS (Track & Field) — WOMEN (5)

MARGARET BAILES, 4 x 100 meter relay; *BARBARA FERRELL, 4 x 100 meter relay; MADELINE MANNING, 800 meters; MILDRETTE NETTER, 4 x 100 meter relay; WYOMIA TYUS, 100 meters, 4 x 100 meter relay.

* also won silver and/or bronze medals.

BASKETBALL — MEN (12)

MICHAEL BARRETT, USN; JOHN CLAWSON, USA; DONALD DEE; CALVIN FOWLER; SPENCER HAYWOOD; E. WILMER HOSKET; JAMES KING; GLYNN SAULTERS; CHARLES SCOTT; MICHAEL SILLIMAN, USA; KENNETH SPAIN; JOSEPH WHITE.

BOXING (2)

GEORGE FOREMAN, heavyweight; RONALD HARRIS, lightweight.

EQUESTRIAN (1)

WILLIAM C. STEINKRAUS, individual, Prix des Nations.

SHOOTING (1)

GARY L. ANDERSON, free rifle, 3-position.

SWIMMING & DIVING — MEN (12)

MICHAEL J. BURTON, 400 meter freestyle, 1500 meter freestyle; *CHARLES HICKCOX, 200 meter individual medley, 400 meter individual medley, 4 x 100 meter medley relay; DONALD MC KENZIE, 100 meter breaststroke, 4 x 100 meter medley relay; *JOHN NELSON, 4 x 200 meter freestyle relay; STEPHEN RERYCH, 4 x 100 meter freestyle relay, 4 x 200 meter freestyle relay; CARL ROBIE, 200 meter butterfly; DOUGLAS A. RUSSELL, 100 meter butterfly, 4 x 100 meter medley relay; *DONALD SCHOLLANDER, 4 x 200 meter freestyle relay; *MARK SPITZ, 4 x 100 meter freestyle relay, 4 x 200 meter freestyle relay; *KENNETH WALSH, 4 x 100 meter freestyle relay, 4 x 100 meter medley relay; BERNARD WRIGHTSON, springboard diving; ZACHARY ZORN, 4 x 100 meter freestyle relay.

SWIMMING & DIVING — WOMEN (12)

CATHARINE BALL, 4 x 100 meter medley relay; *JANE BARKMAN, 4 x 100 meter freestyle relay; *ELLIE DANIEL, 4 x 100 meter medley relay; *LINDA GUSTAVSON, 4 x 100 meter freestyle relay; SUE GOSSICK, springboard diving; *KAYE HALL, 100 meter backstroke, 4 x 100 meter medley relay; *JAN MARGO HENNE, 100 meter freestyle, 4 x 100 meter freestyle relay; CLAUDIA KOLB, 200 meter individual medley, 400 meter individual medley; DEBORAH MEYER, 200 meter freestyle, 400 meter freestyle, 800 meter freestyle; *SUSAN PEDERSEN, 4 x 100 meter freestyle relay, 4 x 100 meter medley relay; LILLIAN DEBRA WATSON, 200 meter backstroke; *SHARON WICHMAN, 200 meter breaststroke.

* also won silver and/or bronze medals.

YACHTING (5)

PETER BARRETT, Star class — crew; GEORGE S. FRIEDRICHS, Dragon class — helmsman; BARTON W. B. JAHNCKE, Dragon class — crew; LOWELL O. NORTH, Star class, helmsman; GERALD C. SCHRECK, Dragon class — crew.

SILVER MEDALS

ATHLETICS (Track & Field) — MEN (5)

EDWARD CARUTHERS, high jump; ERVIN HALL, 110 meter hurdles; **LAWRENCE JAMES, 400 meters; JAMES RYUN, 1500 meters; GEORGE WOODS, shot put.

ATHLETICS (Track & Field) — WOMEN (1)

**BARBARA FERRELL, 100 meters.

** also won gold medal.

BOXING (1)

ALBERT ROBINSON, featherweight.

EQUESTRIAN (3)

° MICHAEL O. PAGE, team 3-day event; JOHN M. PLUMB, team 3-day event; JAMES C. WOFFORD, team 3-day event.

° also won bronze medal.

ROWING (2)

LAWRENCE A. HOUGH, USN, pairs without coxswain; ANTHONY P. JOHNSON, pairs without coxswain.

SHOOTING (2)

THOMAS I. GARRIGUS, trapshooting; JOHN H. WRITER, USA, small bore rifle, 3-position.

SWIMMING & DIVING — MEN (8)

GREGORY BUCKINGHAM, 200 meter individual medley; GARY HALL, 400 meter individual medley; **CHARLES HICKCOX, 100 meter backstroke; MITCHELL IVEY, 200 meter backstroke; JOHN KINSELLA, 1500 meter freestyle; **DONALD A. SCHOLLANDER, 200 meter freestyle; **MARK SPITZ, 100 meter butterfly; **KENNETH WALSH, 100 meter freestyle.

SWIMMING & DIVING — WOMEN (6)

**ELLIE DANIEL, 100 meter butterfly; **LINDA GUSTAVSON, 400 meter freestyle; **JAN MARGO HENNE, 200 meter freestyle; PAM KRUSE, 800 meter freestyle; **SUSAN PEDERSEN, 100 meter freestyle, 200 meter individual medley; LYNN VIDALI, 400 meter individual medley.

** also won gold medal.

WRESTLING (freestyle) (2)

DONALD BEHM, bantamweight; RICHARD SANDERS, flyweight.

BRONZE MEDALS

ATHLETICS (Track & Field) — MEN (7)

RALPH H. BOSTON, long jump; JOHN CARLOS, 200 meters; THOMAS FARRELL, 800 meters; **RONALD FREEMAN, 400 meters; **CHARLES GREENE, 100 meters; GEORGE YOUNG, 3000 meter steeplechase; LAWRENCE YOUNG, 50,000 meter walk.

** also won gold medal.

BOXING (4)

JOHN BALDWIN, light middleweight; ALFRED JONES, middleweight; HARLAN MARBLEY, light flyweight; JAMES WALLINGTON, light welterweight.

EQUESTRIAN (1)

***MICHAEL O. PAGE, individual 3-day event.

*** also won silver medal.

ROWING (2)

WILLIAM P. MAHER, double sculls; JOHN H. NUNN, double sculls.

SWIMMING & DIVING — MEN (9)

JOHN FERRIS, 200 meter butterfly, 200 meter individual medley; JAMES HENRY, springboard diving; JOHN HORSLEY, 200 meter backstroke; BRIAN JOB, 200 meter breaststroke; RONALD MILLS, 100 meter backstroke; ***JOHN NELSON, 200 meter freestyle; ***MARK SPITZ, 100 meter freestyle; ROSS WALES, 100 meter butterfly; EDWIN YOUNG, platform diving.

*** also won gold and/or silver medals.

SWIMMING & DIVING — WOMEN (10)

***JANE BARKMAN, 100 meter freestyle; ****ELLIE DANIEL, 200 meter butterfly; ****LINDA GUSTAVSON, 100 meter freestyle; ***KAYE HALL, 200 meter individual medley; KEALA O'SULLIVAN, springboard diving; ANN PETERSON, platform diving; SUSAN SHIELDS, 100 meter butterfly; JANE SWAGGERTY, 100 meter backstroke; ***SHARON WICHMAN, 100 meter breaststroke.

*** also won gold medal.
**** also won gold and silver medals.

WEIGHTLIFTING (1)

JOSEPH D. DUBE, heavyweight.

275

(continued from page 274)

An analysis of medal achievement shows that of 294 male participants, a total of 86 athletes won 59 golds, 23 silvers and 24 bronzes (in some cases an individual won more than one medal in his classification). The USA girls, numbering 23 out of a total entry of 95, hauled in 17 golds, seven silvers and ten bronzes (with several winning more than one in any classification). Thus a total of 109 athletes out of a total delegation of 389 (actually 387 since two modern pentathlon competitors also qualified for the men's fencing team) can be credited with 149 medals overall.

Considerable improvement was seen in the sports of men's and women's athletics (track and field), boxing, cycling, equestrian (men and women), women's gymnastics, men's and women's swimming and diving, men's volleyball, water polo and wrestling. In some cases it was not medal success but higher placings that indicated the improvement.

Basketball, of course, could not rise any higher than the top rung it has occupied since the sport was first contested in 1936, while yachting — winner of two silvers and three bronzes in the five 1964 contesting classes — went up to two golds this time, but was not able to get any other placings.

Off in various degrees from 1964 performances were the teams in men's and women's canoeing and kayaking, men's and women's fencing, men's gymnastics, modern pentathlon, rowing, shooting, women's volleyball and weightlifting.

Consider now the performances in the various competitions, only two of which did not see a United States entry. These were soccer football (the USA was eliminated in zone preliminaries in 1967) and field hockey (in not winning the 1967 Pan-American Games title, the US was eliminated from the Olympic tests by international federation rule).

DISTRIBUTION OF MEDALS AT GAMES OF XIX OLYMPIAD – MEXICO CITY – 1968

ALL COMPETITIVE MEDAL PLACINGS (Official listings)				Nation	ACTUAL MEDALS DISTRIBUTED (See explanation below)			
(G) 1st	(S) 2nd	(B) 3rd	Total Places		(G) 1st	(S) 2nd	(B) 3rd	Total Medals
45	28	34	107	UNITED STATES	83	31	35	149
29	32	30	91	Soviet Union	64	60	60	184
10	10	12	32	Hungary	33	19	28	80
11	7	7	25	Japan	16	29	25	70
9	9	7	25	East Germany	13	19	19	51
5	10	10	25	West Germany	16	11	18	45
5	2	11	18	Poland	5	2	28	35
5	7	5	17	Australia	5	38	10	53
3	4	9	16	Italy	5	7	19	31
7	3	5	15	France	11	5	10	26
4	6	5	15	Rumania	5	9	8	22
7	2	4	13	Czechoslovakia	7	7	15	29
5	5	3	13	Great Britain	8	5	5	18
3	4	2	9	Kenya	3	7	2	12
3	3	3	9	Mexico	3	3	3	9
2	4	3	9	Bulgaria	2	22	3	27
3	3	2	8	Yugoslavia	13	14	2	29
1	4	3	8	Denmark	4	6	6	16
3	3	1	7	Netherlands	6	7	1	14
2	1	2	5	Iran	2	1	2	5
1	3	1	5	Canada	3	3	4	10
0	1	4	5	Switzerland	0	3	10	13
2	1	1	4	Sweden	4	4	1	9
1	2	1	4	Finland	1	2	1	4
0	4	0	4	Cuba	0	10	0	10
0	2	2	4	Austria	0	2	3	5
0	1	3	4	Mongolia	0	1	3	4
1	0	2	3	New Zealand	5	0	2	7
0	1	2	3	Brazil	0	1	3	4
2	0	0	2	Turkey	2	0	0	2
1	1	0	2	Ethiopia	1	1	0	2
1	1	0	2	Norway	4	2	0	6
1	0	1	2	Tunisia	1	0	1	2
0	1	1	2	Belgium	0	1	2	3
0	1	1	2	South Korea	0	1	1	2
0	0	2	2	Argentina	0	0	2	2
0	1	1	2	Uganda	0	1	1	2
1	0	0	1	Pakistan	18	0	0	18
1	0	0	1	Venezuela	1	0	0	1
0	1	0	1	Cameroon	0	1	0	1
0	0	1	1	Greece	0	0	1	1
0	0	1	1	India	0	0	18	18
0	1	0	1	Jamaica	0	1	0	1
0	0	1	1	Taiwan	0	0	1	1
174	169	183	526	Totals	344	336	353	1033

EXPLANATION — In the official competitive placings (see left column above), only one medal is credited to a nation for each team sport classification championship. For example, the United States, in winning the basketball crown, was credited with only one medal placing although, in fact, all of its 12 players actually received a gold. Similarly were treated the team sports of soccer football, volleyball, water polo, and field hockey as well as relay teams in swimming and in track and field. Crews in yachting, rowing, and canoeing also counted only one competitive medal placing as did any team classifications in equestrian, cycling, fencing, gymnastics, and modern pentathlon.

However, in an attempt to determine the actual number of medals received by nations, a second table has been used, based on the following numerical values:

Only one medal is credited for a first, second, or third place in an individual event. However, multiple credits are awarded in this manner:

ATHLETICS — four each in all relay events, for men and women. BASKETBALL — 12 each. CANOEING — two in the tandems and four in four-man events. CYCLING — two for the tandem events. MODERN PENTATHLON — three each in the team event. FIELD HOCKEY — 18 players team categories. FENCING — four each in the team events. GYMNASTICS — six each in the team events. MODERN PENTATHLON — three each in the team event. FIELD HOCKEY — 18 players credited. ROWING — two each in the pairs and double sculls, three in the pairs with coxswain, four for the four-oars, five for the fours with coxswain, nine for the eights with coxswain. SOCCER FOOTBALL — 19 players credited. VOLLEYBALL — 12 players each for men's and women's teams. WATER POLO — 11 players credited. SWIMMING — four each in all relay events for men and women. YACHTING — three each in the 5.5 meter and Dragon events, two each in the Star and Flying Dutchman classes.

In explanation of the apparent discrepancy in the total number of medals awarded, duplicate gold medals were awarded in the men's gymnastics horizontal bar competition and in the women's gymnastics free exercise finals. No silver medals were awarded in those events. In boxing, the two losers in semi-final bouts each were awarded a bronze medal.

At the close of competition in Mexico City, the award of the silver medal in the cycling team pursuit race was held up pending investigation of alleged infraction of the rules by the second-place winning unit.

Consequently there are five more gold medal placings awarded than silvers and 11 more bronzes than the third-place totals indicate.

DISTRIBUTION OF UNITED STATES MEDALS WON IN GAMES OF XIX OLYMPIAD – MEXICO CITY – 1968

ALL COMPETITIVE MEDAL PLACINGS (Official listings)								ACTUAL MEDALS DISTRIBUTED (see explanation below)			
(G) 1st	(S) 2nd	(B) 3rd	Diplomas 4th	5th	6th	Total Medals	Sport category	(G) 1st	(S) 2nd	(B) 3rd	Total Medals
12	5	7	4	4	5	24	Athletics – men	18	5	7	30
3	1	0	2	2	4	4	Athletics – women	6	1	0	7
1	0	0	0	0	0	1	Basketball	12	0	0	12
2	1	4	0	0	0	7	Boxing	2	1	4	7
0	0	0	1	0	0	0	Canoeing M/W	0	0	0	0
0	0	0	0	0	0	0	Cycling	0	0	0	0
1	1	1	2	0	1	3	Equestrian M/W	1	3	1	5
0	0	0	0	0	0	0	Fencing M/W	0	0	0	0
Did not compete			–	–	–	–	Field Hockey	–	–	–	–
0	0	0	0	0	0	0	Gymnastics – men	0	0	0	0
0	0	0	0	0	1	0	Gymnastics – women	0	0	0	0
0	0	0	0	0	0	0	Modern Pentathlon	0	0	0	0
0	1	1	1	3	1	2	Rowing	0	2	2	4
1	2	0	2	0	3	3	Shooting	1	2	0	3
11	8	10	4	0	2	29	Swimming – men	20	8	10	38
12	7	10	5	4	1	29	Swimming – women	18	7	10	35
0	0	0	0	0	0	0	Volleyball – men	0	0	0	0
0	0	0	0	0	0	0	Volleyball – women	0	0	0	0
Did not compete			–	–	–	–	Soccer Football	–	–	–	–
0	0	0	0	1	0	0	Water Polo	0	0	0	0
0	0	1	1	0	0	1	Weightlifting	0	0	1	1
0	2	0	2	1	1	2	Wrestling (F.S.)	0	2	0	2
0	0	0	0	1	1	0	Wrestling (G.R.)	0	0	0	0
2	0	0	0	0	0	2	Yachting	5	0	0	5
45	28	34	26	16	17	107	Totals	83	31	35	149

EXPLANATION — In the official competitive listings (see left column above) only one medal is credited to a nation, regardless of whether or not more than one individual was involved in its winning. For instance, the USA won the basketball gold medal, receiving credit for only one award but actually all 12 players did receive the honor. The USA relay teams in track and field and in swimming for both men and women each had four competitors receiving medals, as did the USA Three-Day equestrian team of three riders. The rowing crews in double sculls and pairs each numbered two in personnel while, in yachting, the Star class (two in crew) and in the Dragon class (three in crew) were won by the USA.

PERSONNEL OF UNITED STATES DELEGATION AT GAMES OF THE XIX OLYMPIAD – MEXICO CITY – 1968

Sport Classification	Athletes M	W	T	Managers M	W	T	Coaches M	W	T	**Technical M	W	T	Overall M	W	T
Athletics (Track-field)	67	26	93	5	1	6	7	–	7	–	–	–	79	27	106
Basketball	12	0	12	2	0	2	2	0	2	–	–	–	16	0	16
Boxing	11	0	11	1	0	1	2	0	2	–	–	–	14	0	14
Canoeing & Kayaking	12	4	16	1	0	1	0	1	1	1	0	1	14	5	19
Cycling	18	0	18	1	0	1	2	0	2	2	0	2	23	0	23
*Equestrian	6	6	12	1	0	1	2	0	2	2	0	2	11	6	17
Fencing	15	5	20	2	0	2	2	0	2	1	0	1	20	5	25
Gymnastics	7	7	14	2	0	2	1	1	2	0	1	1	10	9	19
Modern Pentathlon	4	0	4	1	0	1	1	0	1	–	–	–	6	0	6
Rowing	32	0	32	2	0	2	2	0	2	1	0	1	37	0	37
Shooting	12	0	12	2	0	2	–	–	–	1	0	1	15	0	15
Swimming & Driving	38	35	73	3	1	4	7	0	7	–	–	–	48	36	84
Volleyball	12	12	24	1	1	2	3	0	3	–	–	–	16	13	29
Water Polo	11	0	11	1	0	1	1	0	1	–	–	–	13	0	13
Weightlifting	7	0	7	1	0	1	1	0	1	–	–	–	9	0	9
Wrestling	16	0	16	2	0	2	2	0	2	–	–	–	20	0	20
Yachting	14	0	14	2	0	2	–	–	–	–	–	–	16	0	16
Medical staff													4	2	6
Training staff													9	1	10
USOC Administration staff													34	7	41
Olympian advisory staff													5	1	6
OVERALL TOTALS	294	95	389	30	3	33	35	2	37	9	1	8	419	112	531
International officials													33	2	35
													452	114	566

* Does not include grooms.
** Includes armorers for shooting and fencing, riggers for boats, pianist for gymnastics, mechanic for cycling, veterinarian for equestrian.

ALL-TIME MEDAL PLACINGS – GAMES OF THE OLYMPIADS – 1896 THRU 1968 – INCLUSIVE

Rank	Nation	(1st) Gold	(2nd) Silver	(3rd) Bronze	Total
1	UNITED STATES OF AMERICA	550	382	343	1275
2	Great Britain	139	189	148	476
3	Soviet Union	161	155	148	464
4	*Germany	108	150	135	393
5	Sweden	119	118	150	387
6	France	119	120	122	361
7	Italy	111	95	88	294
8	Hungary	96	77	89	262
9	Finland	80	69	93	242
10	Australia	55	45	59	159
11	Japan	52	52	43	147
12	Switzerland	37	50	48	135
13	Netherlands	38	43	46	127
14	Denmark	27	48	48	123
15	Canada	23	37	46	106
16	Czechoslovakia	36	37	30	103
17	Poland	23	28	51	102
18	Norway	37	28	29	94
19	Greece	21	38	33	92
20	Belgium	20	35	30	85
21	Austria	15	22	28	65
22	Rumania	15	16	25	56
23	South Africa	16	15	22	53
24	Argentina	13	18	13	44
25	Turkey	23	11	7	41
26	Bulgaria	7	15	10	32
27	Yugoslavia	10	14	7	31
28	*East Germany	9	9	7	25
	*West Germany	5	10	10	25
30	Iran	4	8	12	24
	Mexico	6	8	10	24
32	Estonia	6	6	9	21
33	New Zealand	11	1	9	20
34	Cuba	6	10	3	19
35	Egypt	6	4	5	15
36	Brazil	3	2	9	14
37	India	7	3	2	12
38	Ireland	4	2	4	10
	Kenya	3	4	3	10
40	Jamaica	3	6	0	9
	Uruguay	2	1	6	9
	Korea	0	4	5	9
43	Spain	1	4	2	7
	Chile	0	5	2	7
45	Trinidad-Tobago	0	2	4	6
	Portugal	0	2	4	6
	Philippines	0	1	5	6
48	Pakistan	2	1	2	5
49	Ethiopia	3	1	0	4
	Tunisia	1	1	2	4
	Mongolia	0	1	3	4
52	Venezuela	1	0	2	3
	Latvia	0	2	1	3
54	Luxembourg	1	1	0	2
	United Arab Republic	0	1	1	2
	Ghana	0	1	1	2
	Lebanon	0	1	1	2
	South Korea	0	1	1	2
	Panama	0	0	2	2
	Uganda	0	1	1	2
	Taiwan	0	1	1	2
	West Indies Federation	0	0	2	2
63	Peru	1	0	0	1
	Bahamas	1	0	0	1
	Ceylon	0	1	0	1
	Haiti	0	1	0	1
	Cameroon	0	1	0	1
	Iceland	0	1	0	1
	Singapore	0	1	0	1
	Iraq	0	0	1	1
	Puerto Rico	0	0	1	1
	Nigeria	0	0	1	1
	Totals	2037	2018	2024	6079

* Germany credited with only one national entry thru 1964; East and West Germany competed separately starting with 1968.

ATHLETICS (Track & Field)
MEN

In comparison with its 1964 performance at Tokyo, the United States men's track and field team did very well indeed in Mexico City. Not only did the team equal the 1964 output of 12 golds and five silvers, but it garnered seven bronzes, a gain of four medals in all, while participating strongly in the competitions which saw Olympic records tumble in 17 of the 24 events. Only in the long distance running and walking events, and in the gruelling decathlon test, did the Olympic record book escape revision. It was the greatest assault on standards the Games have experienced.

The USA repeated in nine title defenses against the world's best and regained three more crowns, albeit relinquishing superiority in three other classifications. The sprints, 100, 200 and 400 meters, along with both relays, again were won in smashing style. Success continued in the pole vault, discus throw, shot put, and the 110 meter hurdles ... a pretty good exchange for unsuccessful title defenses in the 400 meter hurdles, 5000 and 10,000 meter runs.

All USA winners were outstanding in probably the best entry fields ever drawn to the Games, with Al Oerter's fourth straight Olympic gold medal triumph in the discus throw and young Bob Beamon's astounding long jump performance providing the most extraordinary moments.

The USA men's track and field team more than met the challenge of the world.

Now for a brief review of USA showings in the respective events:

100 meters – James Hines realized his life-long ambition to be an Olympic champion with a last-second surge at the tape, besting Lennox Miller of Jamaica and USA teammate Charlie Greene with a Games and world mark of 9.9 seconds. Both Miller and Greene equalled the Olympic mark of 10.0 set in 1964 by the incomparable Bob Hayes. How tremendously fast was this final field is indicated by the USA's Mel Pender, who finished sixth with a time of 10.1 seconds!

200 meters – Tommie Smith surmounted a leg injury sustained in the semi-finals to win the furlong race in world and Olympic record time of

J. Bacheler   R. Beamon   C. Bell   B. Gittins   C. Greene   A. Hall

R. Boston   R. Brown   E. Burke   E. Hall   R. Haluza   J. Hines

J. Carlos   G. Carlsen   C. Carrigan   G. James   G. Klopfer   Kutschinski

E. Caruthers   L. Coleman   H. Connolly   R. Laird   T. Laris   M. Liquori

F. Covelli   W. Davenport   R. Daws   D. Maggard   J. Matson   V. Matthews

R. Day   T. Dooley   L. Evans   C. Mays   K. Moore   M. Murro

T. Farrell   R. Fosbury   R. Freeman   V. Nelson   Nightingale   A. Oerter

278

19.8 seconds. Expert attention by US Olympic medicos and his own burning desire to prove his claim as world's best at the distance brought Smith home a winner. Peter Norman of Australia caught the USA's John Carlos at the tape for second place, although both runners were credited with Olympic record-breaking times of 20.0 seconds each. Larry Questad, the third USA runner, was sixth in 20.6 seconds.

400 meters – The only sweep of the men's competition was credited to the United States in this event, with Lee Evans, Larry James, and Ronald Freeman finishing in that order. Evans ran a great race and his world and Olympic mark of 43.8 seconds is ample proof. Just the same, he needed an all-out performance since James was clocked in 43.9 and Freeman in 44.4.

4 x 100 meter relay – The USA quartet of Charles Greene, Mel Pender, Ronnie Ray Smith, and James Hines won this in the fantastic time of 38.2, nipping Cuba by one-tenth of a second. Hines pulled out all the stops in the anchor leg to beat off Cuba's challenge. It was the closest relay race in the history of the Games for, in fact, West Germany's sixth place time of 38.7 bested the old Olympic mark of 39.0 flat set in 1964 by the US.

4 x 400 meter relay – An even more fantastic time was set by the USA in winning this race. Vince Mathews, Ronald Freeman, Larry James, and Lee Evans formed the gold medal combination that won in the world and Olympic record time of 2:56.1, fully three seconds faster than second place Kenya. The USA clocking meant an average of 44.02 seconds per runner and it is conceivable that Evans ran close to 43 flat in the anchor effort.

800 meters – Tommy Farrell, who placed sixth at Tokyo, ran a heady race in the finals but could not quite cope with Australia's Ralph Doubell, who won in the Olympic record-breaking and world record-equalling time of 1:44.3. Tom finished behind Doubell and second place W. Kiprugut of Kenya with a time of 1:45.4, just three-tenths off the existing Olympic mark set in 1964 by New Zealand's stellar Peter Snell. Ronald Kutschinski, USA runner, was eliminated in the semi-finals while Wade Bell, the third American entry and a pre-Games favorite to win, was eliminated in the first preliminary heats. Bell had been sick for two days and even before the race began, he fell ill on the track, yet he courageously tried to run. It was to no avail.

1500 meters – Jim Ryun's bid to bring the US its first gold medal in this event since 1908 was turned down by Kenya's Kipchoge Keino, a runner
(continued)

M. Pender   J. Pennel   L. Questad

W. Reilly   D. Romansky   J. Ryun

L. Scott   R. Seagren   L. Silvester

R. Sloan   D. Smith   R. Smith

T. Smith   Tr. Smith   G. Stenlund

N. Tate   W. Toomey   Vanderstock

T. von Ruden   T. Waddell   A. Walker

A weary Bill Toomey begins the 1500 meters, final event of the grueling decathlon.

279

R. Whitney G. Woods G. Young

L. Young B. Durbin T. Haydon

P. Jordan B. Lewis H. Lodge

J. Oelkers M. Portanova F. Potts

C. Roesch S. Wright

whom Jim had bested at lower altitudes several times and whom he had beaten with a "kicking" sprint in the semi-finals two days before. Keino, who had competed in the 10,000 and 5000 meter events, seized the lead in the second lap while Ryun was settling down in the pack, conserving energy for the last-lap surge. When the third lap opened, it was evident that the race was getting away from Ryun, for Keino gradually built up a 40-meter margin. At the bell lap, Ryun moved up to fifth place and in the backstretch he made his bid, but Keino had too much of an advantage, hitting the tape ahead of the American by at least

20 meters. Jim's silver medal performance was timed in 3:37.8, remarkable for the altitude and a time which would have beaten Snell in 1964. As it was, Keino broke Herb Elliott's Olympic mark by seven-tenths of a second. The two other Americans in the finals, Tom Von Ruden and young Martin Liquori, finished in ninth and 12th places respectively. Von Ruden's time was 3:49.2 and Liquori's 4:18.2.

5000 meters – Jack Bacheler, lone USA qualifier for the finals, was hospitalized and could not compete, while Louis Scott and Bob Day, other American entrants, were eliminated in the preliminary heats.

10,000 meters – Tracy Smith was the leader for the USA in this race, placing 11th with 30:14.6. Tom Laris was 16th in 30:26.2 and Van Nelson, Pan-American champion, was 28th in 31:40.2.

110 meter hurdles – Willie Davenport, who in 1964 was eliminated in the semi-finals, reached his pinnacle with a magnificent win in this event, thus continuing unbroken US domination since 1932. Willie cleared the barriers in Olympic record time of 13.3, edging out teammate Ervin Hall by one-tenth. Leon Coleman, third USA entrant, was fourth in 13.6.

400 meter hurdles – For the first time since 1932, no USA hurdler won this event, yet America can have some consolation in having trained the young man who smashed world and Olympic records with an electrifying time of 48.1 seconds. The winner was Boston College-trained David Hemery of Great Britain. In a final which saw the fifth place hurdler equal 1964's winning time, the best the USA could do was a fourth place by Geoff Vanderstock (49.6) and a sixth place by Ron Whitney (51.2). Boyd Gittins, another USA entry, was injured in training and had to be withdrawn from the preliminaries.

3000 meter steeplechase – George Young's courageous bid for victory in this demanding race was forestalled by Kenyans, Amos Biwott and B. Kogo. After a stretch duel George finished third in the respectable time of 8:51.8, just eight-tenths behind the winner. Two other Americans were eliminated in the preliminary heats, Bill Reilly rating fifth in the third heat and Conrad Nightingale sixth in the first heat.

Marathon run – Kenneth Moore, who led the pack at 10 kilometers, was the best American in this race, finishing

14th with a time of 2:29:49.4. George Young, who had competed in the steeplechase, was 16th with 2:31:15.0, while Ron Daws, third USA entry, was 22nd with 2:33:53.0.

20,000 meter walk – Rudy Haluza made a great effort to win a medal in this event but could only finish fourth in the time of 1:35:00, slightly more than a minute behind the Russian winner. Two other USA entrants, Tom Dooley and Ron Laird, were 17th with 1:40:08.0 and 25th with 1:44:38.0 respectively.

50,000 meter walk – The United States gained a medal in the Olympic walking events for the first time in history when Larry Young finished third. Larry's time was 4:31:55.4. The USA's Goetz Klopfer was 10th in 4:39:13.8 and David Romansky, USA, was 26th in 5:38:03.4. The medal performance and relative high rankings in both walking events indicate that the US has improved greatly in this sport.

High jump – The unusual "backward" high jumping style of the USA's Dick Fosbury brought back the gold medal in this event and the "Fosbury flop" created a sensation in *Estadio Olimpico*. Before he launched himself at the crossbar, Fosbury would rock back and forth for seconds, apparently until he was positive that he would clear the height. Then be would lunge toward the standards, turn his back in mid-air and literally "flop" over the bar. Thousands in the stadium actually rocked with him and figuratively "flopped" over the bar with him. At any rate, Fosbury won at the Olympic record height of 7'4¼" with teammate Ed Caruthers second at 7'3⅝". The USA's Reynaldo Brown placed fifth at 7'0¼."

Pole vault – Bob Seagren had all the nerve of a second-story worker and a crack poker player in his successful bid for the pole vault championship. It was like filling an "inside straight" when Bob, after passing at such heights as 17'2¾" and 17'6¾", finally cleared 17'8½" to win the gold on the matter of fewer misses. West Germany's G. Schiprowski also cleared that height but down along the line during the seven hours of competition, he had one more missed attempt than Bob.

Hard luck man of the Games was the USA's John Pennel, who finally finished in fifth place with a leap of

17′6³/₄″. Twice he was thwarted from a successful leap when the stadium band blared out with a fanfare just as he was in the middle of his effort. The USA's other pole vaulter, young Casey Carrigan, a 17-year-old prep star who had a career best of 17 feet, failed to make the qualifying height in the previous day's preliminaries.

Long jump – It was almost unbelievable... that leap of 29′2¹/₂″ by the USA's Bob Beamon in the long jump finals. On his first try, just before a rainstorm, Bob ran down the runway, soared into the air, and – for a breathless instant – it seemed he'd never come down. But he did and it was an incredible world and Olympic mark; Bob had jumped almost two feet farther than anyone had ever done before. When the realization of his tremendous feat dawned on him, Bob's astonishment, then glee, and finally his profound humility, portrayed a range of Olympian emotion that brought home to every viewer – whether at the *Estadio* or at the TV set – the magnitude of glory that accompanies an Olympic Games triumph by an individual. Ralph Boston, wonderful competitor that he is, earned his third Olympic medal, a bronze, at 26′9¹/₄″, also bettering the Olympic mark. The third USA entrant, Charles Mays, who had qualified for the final, fouled on all three of his attempts.

Triple jump – Even if you surpass American, Olympic, and even world records, it does not always follow that you win. Such was the misfortune of the USA's Art Walker, who placed fourth in the triple jump with 56′2″.

A Russian won it at 57′0³/₄″ and notably the first five finishers bettered the existing world mark. Even the 1964 winner, Jozef Schmidt of Poland, broke the Olympic mark but placed only seventh. For the USA, Norman Tate and David Smith failed to gain the finals, missing out in the preliminary qualifying trials.

Discus throw – Olympic history had a new indelible line on the pages when the USA's Al Oerter, almost counted out because of his sporadic seasonal performance, summoned his old skill and strength to hurl the discus to a new Olympic record of 212′6¹/₂″. That meant a fourth straight gold medal in the event, an unprecedented performance for any Olympian. A fifth straight at Munich in 1972? Could be, for Al Oerter is just the kind of a fellow who can do it. His triumph at Mexico City was easily the most popular in the USA camp.

Jay Silvester, the USA's leader in the trials and a claimant for a world record, was off form and had to settle for fifth place with 202′7³/₄″ and the USA's Gary Carlsen clinched sixth with a toss of 195′1″.

Shot put – As expected, the big Texan, Randy Matson, won the shot put and while he did not approach his world mark of 71-feet plus, he did hit an Olympic high of 67′4³/₄″. Second place went to teammate George Woods on 66′0¹/₄″ and Dave Maggard picked up fifth place on 63′9″.

Javelin throw – Mike Murro was United States' best in this event, placing ninth on a toss of 262′8³/₄″. Gary Stenlund and Frank Covelli, other

US entrants, did not qualify for the finals. The three winners in this test easily exceeded the existing Olympic mark which had stood since 1956.

Hammer throw – The veteran trio of hammer tossers – Hal Connolly, Al Hall, and Ed Burke – failed to get any honors because a trio of Hungarians and two Russians rang up marks well out of range of the Americans. Connolly, who had won the gold in 1956, did not get in the finals, fouling out on the technicality of not entering the ring properly, while Hall never approached his form and missed qualifying. Burke placed 12th on a heave of 215′7¹/₂″.

Decathlon – The durable, extremely talented, and dedicated Bill Toomey brought back the decathlon title to the USA after a hiatus of two Olympiads. While he did not approach his world best, Bill tallied 8193 points to beat off the challenge of West Germany's H. Walde by 82 points. In the grueling two-day competition, Bill ran a 45.6-second 400 meters and long jumped 25′9³/₄″ to build up a lead, but it took the final event to decide things. All Toomey needed was to finish ahead of Walde and the other West German, K. Bendlin, who were in the last flight with him. In a driving rainstorm, Toomey – who has run the 1500 in 4:30 – deliberately set a slow pace at the outset and won in 4:57.1.

Toomey's 8193 total set an Olympic mark under the new scoring system begun in 1964. Two other Americans ranked high; Tom Waddell was sixth with 7720 points and Rick Sloan was seventh with 7692.

America's Charlie Greene wins a preliminary heat of the 100 meter dash. In the final, Greene finished third behind Jim Hines of the US and American-trained Lennox Miller of Jamaica.

TEAM PERSONNEL

ATHLETICS (Track & Field) — MEN

Jack Bacheler, Gainesville, Fla. (5000 meters)
Robert Beamon, Jamaica, N.Y., (long jump)
Wade Bell, Eugene, Oregon (800 meters)
Ralph H. Boston, Nashville, Tenn. (long jump)
Edward A. Burke, Newport Beach, Calif.
   (hammer throw)
Reynoldo Brown, Compton, Calif. (high jump)
John Carlos, San Jose, Calif. (200 meters)
Gary Carlsen, Los Angeles, Calif.
   (discus throw)
Casey Carrigan, Orting, Wash. (pole vault)
Edward J. Caruthers, Santa Ana, Calif.
   (high jump)
Leon Coleman, Boston, Mass. (100 meter
   hurdles)
Harold Connolly, Culver City, Calif.
   (hammer throw)
Frank Covelli, Long Beach, Calif.
   (javelin throw)
Willie Davenport, Warren, Ohio
   (110 meter hurdles)
Ronald H. Daws, Minneapolis, Minn.
   (marathon run)
Robert Day, Los Angeles, Calif. (5000 meters)
Thomas Dooley, Daly City, Calif.
   (20 km. walk)
Lee Edward Evans, San Jose, Calif.
   (400 meters & 4x400 meter relay)
Thomas Farrell, Forest Hills, N. Y.
   (800 meters)
Richard Fosbury, Medford, Oregon
   (high jump)
Ronald Freeman, Elizabeth, N. J.
   (400 meters & 4x400 meter relay)
Boyd Gittins, Bellevue, Wash.
   (400 meter hurdles)
Charles Edward Greene, Seattle, Wash.
   (100 meters & 4x100 meter relay)
Albert Hall, Charlton, Mass.
   (hammer throw)
Ervin Hall, Philadelphia, Pa.
   (100 meter hurdles)

Rudy Haluza, Riverside, Calif. (20 km. walk)
James Hines, Oakland, Calif.
   (100 meters & 4x100 meter relay)
Larry James, White Plains, N.Y.
   (400 meters & 4x400 meter relay)
Goetz Klopfer, Baton Rouge, La.
   (50 km. walk)
Ronald Kutschinski, Grand Rapids, Mich.
   (800 meters)
Ronald Laird, Pomona, Calif. (20 km. walk)
Thomas Laris, Walnut Creek, Calif.
   (10,000 meters)
Martin Liquori, Cedar Grove, N. J.
   (1500 meters)
David Maggard, Mountain View, Calif.
   (shot put)
J. Randel Matson, Pampa, Texas (shot put)
Vincent Matthews, Queens Village, N. Y.
   (4x400 meter relay)
Charles Mays, Jersey City, N. J. (long jump)
Kenneth Moore, Eugene, Oregon
   (marathon run)
Mark Murro, Newark, N. J. (javelin throw)
Van Arthur Nelson, Minneapolis, Minn.
   (10,000 meters)
Conrad Nightingale, Halstead, Kansas
   (3000 meter steeplechase)
Alfred Oerter, Jr., West Islip, N. Y.
   (discus throw)
Capt. Melvin Pender, USA
   (100 meters & 4x100 meter relay)
John Pennel, Enrico, Calif. (pole vault)
Larry Questad, Los Angeles, Calif.
   (200 meters)
William Reilly, Oceanport, N. J.
   (3000 meter steeplechase)
David Romansky, Pennsville, N. J.
   (50 km. walk)
James Ryun, Wichita, Kansas (1500 meters)
Louis Scott, Detroit, Michigan (500 meters)
Robert Seagren, Los Angeles, Calif.
   (pole vault)
L. Jay Silvester, Smithfield, Utah
   (discus throw)
Richard Don Sloan, Anaheim, Calif.
   (decathlon)

David Smith, Los Angeles, Calif. (triple jump)
Ronnie Ray Smith, Los Angeles, Calif.
   (4x100 meter relay)
Thomas Smith, Lemoore, Calif. (200 meters)
Tracy Smith, Arcadia, Calif. (10,000 meters)
Gary Stenlund, Athens, Ohio (javelin throw)
Norman Tate, East Orange, N. J.
   (triple jump)
William Toomey, Laguna Beach, Calif.
   (decathlon)
Geoff Vanderstock, Los Angeles, Calif.
   (100 meter hurdles)
Thomas Von Ruden, San Pedro, Calif.
   (1500 meters)
Dr. Thomas Waddell, Washington, D. C.
   (decathlon)
Arthur Walker, Los Angeles, Calif.
   (triple jump)
Ronald Whitney, Boulder, Colo.
   (400 meter hurdles)
George Woods, Los Angeles, Calif.
   (shot put)
George Young, Casa Grande, Ariz.
   (marathon run & 3000 meter steeplechase)
Larry Young, San Pedro, Calif. (50 km. walk)

Staff Personnel

G. Payton Jordan, Los Altos, Calif.
   (Head Coach)
Michael A. Portanova, Tarzana, Calif.
   (Head Manager)
Brice B. Durbin, Topeka, Kansas
   (Asst. Manager)
Ben G. Lewis, Washington, D. C.
   (Asst. Manager)
Hilmer Lodge, Pala, Calif. (Asst. Manager)
Carl J. Roesch, Buffalo, N. Y. (Asst. Manager)
Edward M. Haydon, Chicago, Ill.
   (Asst. Coach)
John Oelkers, New Orleans, La.
   (Asst. Coach)
Frank C. Potts, Boulder, Colo. (Asst. Coach)
Stanley V. Wright, Houston, Texas
   (Asst. Coach)

Anchoring the United States record-breaking 4 x 100 meter relay team was Jim Hines, who also won a gold medal in the 100 meters.

ATHLETICS (Track & Field)
WOMEN

Like the men's team, the USA women's track and field contingent improved on its showing of 1964, although in total medal-placings, the count was the same... four. At Mexico City, however, the haul was three golds and one silver, while in point-placings (fourth, fifth, and sixth) the girls pulled in eight as compared to a solitary fourth place in 1964. Competition was tough, Olympic records falling in nine events.

Wyomia Tyus led the team with two gold medal triumphs. Not only did she repeat as 100 meter champion but she anchored the USA 4 x 100 meter relay team to an Olympic and world record victory. In addition, Madeline Manning broke up the European monopoly in the 800 meters, speeding to a decisive win in world record-equalling time.

100 meters – Wyomia Tyus never faltered in her bid to repeat gold medal success in this event and in the finals, she nipped teammate Barbara Ferrell in the surge to the tape. Wyomia was clocked in world and Olympic record time of 11 seconds, while Barbara was second in 11.1, a time shared by the third and fourth place finishers. In fifth place was the USA's Margaret Bailes, timed in 11.3 seconds.

200 meters – The USA trio of Tyus, Ferrell, and Bailes easily gained the finals, but in the stretch run for the title showdown, none seemed able to pick up a final burst of speed. As a result, Miss Ferrell finished fourth in 22.9, while Miss Tyus (23.0) and Miss Bailes (23.1) were sixth and seventh respectively.

4 x 100 meter relay – The first five teams placing in the finals of the relay all bettered existing Olympic and world marks but the US combination of Barbara Ferrell, Margaret Bailes, Mildrette Netter, and Wyomia Tyus won by a convincing margin. Its time was 42.8, with Cuba ranking next at 43.3.

400 meters – Jarvis Scott, lone USA entry to place in the 400 meters, was sixth in a time of 52.7 seconds, the two other USA entries, Lois Drinkwater, and Esther Stroy, were eliminated in the semi-finals.

800 meters – Madeline Manning's excellent pacing and impressive finishing sprint brought the USA into the winner's circle for the first time ever

in this event. Madeline broke the Olympic record and equalled the world mark with her time of 2:00.9. USA teammate Doris Brown was fifth with 2:03.9, while Frances Kraker, third USA entry, was eliminated in the first round trials.

80 meter hurdles – Pat Van Wolvelaere of the USA equalled the Olympic record of 10.5 in the 80 meter hurdle finals but it gained only fourth place for her as two Australians and a Taiwan girl had better times. Mamie Rallins and Judy Dyer of the US reached the semi-finals but were then eliminated.

High jump – None of the USA entrants were able to qualify for the competition proper and hence were eliminated. They were Eleanor Montgomery, who had placed eighth in 1964, Estelle Baskerville and Sharon Callahan.

Long jump – A leap of more than 21 feet was needed just to get into the final six rankings and the USA's Martha Watson and veteran Willye White just couldn't make it. Miss Watson placed 10th with 20'4" and Willye, who first competed in the 1956 Games and placed second, was 11th at Mexico City on 19'11½".

Shot put – The lone USA entry, Maren Seidler, was 11th in this event dominated by East Germans, who shattered world and Olympic marks every time they entered the ring. Miss Seidler's best toss was 48'9".

Discus throw – The USA discus throwers were Mrs. Olga Fikotova Connolly (winner in 1956) and Carol Moseke. Mrs. Connolly's toss of 173'9" was good for sixth place, but Miss Moseke rated only 14th with 158'4½".

Javelin throw – The best the United States entries could do in this event was ninth place, Barbara Friedrich gaining that position on a toss of 175'10". RaNae Bair was 11th with 174'4".

Pentathlon – A sixth place by Pat Winslow was the USA's best in this two-day test of skill and endurance for women. Pat scored 4877 points but this was 221 below the winning mark. The other US entry, Cathy Hamblin, tallied 4330 points for 24th place.

TEAM PERSONNEL

ATHLETICS (Track & Field) — WOMEN

Mrs. Margaret Johnson Bailes, Portland, Oregon (100 & 200 meters, 4x100 meter relay)

ATHLETICS – WOMEN

M. Bailes   R. Bair   E. Baskerville

D. Brown   S. Callahan   O. Connolly

I. Davis   L. Drinkwater   J. Dyer

B. Ferrell   B. Friedrich   C. Hamblin

F. Kraker   M. Manning   Montgomery

C. Moseke   M. Netter   M. Rallins

J. Scott   M. Seidler   E. Stroy

283

ATHLETICS – WOMEN

W. Tyus

V. Wolvelaere

M. Watson

W. White

P. Winslow

M. West

C. Ford

S. Ferenczy

BASKETBALL

M. Barrett

J. Clawson

D. Dee

C. Fowler

S. Haywood

W. Hosket

J. King

G. Saulters

C. Scott

M. Silliman

K. Spain

J. White

RaNae Jean Bair, San Diego, Calif.
(javelin throw)
Estelle Baskerville, Columbus, Ohio
(high jump)
Mrs. Doris Brown, Seattle, Wash. (800 meters)
Sharon Callahan, Whittier, Calif. (high jump)
Mrs. Olga Fikotova Connolly, Culver City,
Calif. (discus throw)
Iris Davis, Pompano Beach, Calif.
(4x100 meter relay)
Lois Anne Drinkwater, Phoenix, Arizona
(400 meters)
Julia May Dyer, Chicago, Ill. (80 meter
hurdles)
Barbara Ferrell, Los Angeles, Calif.
(100 & 200 meters, 4x100 meter relay)
Barbara Ann Friedrich, Spring Lake Heights,
N. J. (javelin throw)
Cathy Hamblin, Albuquerque, N. M.
(pentathlon)
Francie Kraker, Ann Arbor, Mich.
(800 meters)
Madeline Manning, Cleveland, Ohio
(800 meters)
Eleanor Inez Montgomery, Cleveland, Ohio
(high jump)
Carol Moseke, Cedar Rapids, Nebr.
(discus throw)
Mildrette Netter, Rosedale, Miss.
(4x100 meter relay)
Mamie Rallins, Chicago, Ill. (80-meter
hurdles)
Jarvis Scott, Los Angeles, Calif. (400 meters)
Maren Seidler, Plainfield, N. J. (shot put)
Esther Stroy, Washington, D. C. (400 meters)
Wyomia Tyus, Griffin, Georgia (100 & 200
meters, 4x100 meter relay)
Patty Jean Van Wolvelaere, Renton, Wash.
(80 meter hurdles)
Martha Rae Watson, Long Beach, Calif.
(long jump)
Willye B. White, Chicago, Ill. (long jump
& 4x100 meter relay)
Pat Winslow, San Mateo, Calif. (pentathlon)

Staff Personnel
Miss Maralyn West, Cleveland, Ohio
(Manager)
Conrad A. Ford, New York, N. Y. (Coach)
Sandor Ferenczy, Cleveland, Ohio (Coach)

BASKETBALL

Sweet are the fruits of victory, and when it is accomplished against the world's best and amid dolorous predictions of possible failure, it is doubly sweet. Entering the 1968 tests with many "experts" downgrading them as a collection of players not quite up to usual standards, the USA basketball team confounded its critics by winning the gold medal for the seventh straight Olympiad, and achieved the triumph in a manner which should be underlined as "truly great."

Despite the decision of several highly-ranked players to pass up the chance to play in the Games, and disappointing showings in international play during a European tour in early spring, the USA won all nine of its games and kept intact an unbeaten record since the sport first came on the Olympic program. And all this was

in the face of the strongest opposition ever assembled at the Games.

As in Tokyo in 1964, this was a "team" victory, resulting not from overpowering brilliance by a collection of individual stars, but from dedication by a solid, single-purpose unit that followed a carefully conceived and well-prepared-for plan to its ultimate goal. The 12 players on the squad placed "team play" above all other considerations and their ready response to the coaching of Hank Iba, who also charted the Tokyo triumph, made it possible to reach the top. It was a winning combination.

Previously unheralded and certainly underrated Spencer Haywood, a 19-year-old native of Detroit who had played his first year with Trinidad (Colorado) Junior College, was the hub around which Iba and his assistant, Henry Vaughn (also at Tokyo), fashioned a smoothly operating team. The youngest player ever selected to play for the US in Olympic competition, Haywood, 6–8 in height and weighing 225 pounds, provided the team with more than enough "firepower," rebounding strength, and all-around ability. With him were Captain Mike Silliman and Jim King up front and backcourt men, JoJo White and Cal Fowler; Mike Barrett, John Clawson, Don Dee, Bill Hosket, Glynn Saulters, Charles Scott, and Kenneth Spain provided unfailing support.

This was a well-conditioned team, again a tribute to the determination of the players and the constant adherence to training plans. It first was evident near the close of the altitude training period at Alamosa, Colo., and more apparent in the games played with national professional teams, where victories were scored over Denver and New York clubs, against one loss to Cincinnati.

At Mexico City, the United States was placed in Group A and in successive games defeated Spain, 81–46, Senegal, 93–36, and the Philippines, 96–75. Next came Yugoslavia, co-favored with Russia to win the gold medal. The US was well-prepared for this first showdown and after a fairly close first half, built up a substantial lead in the closing period to finally emerge a 73–58 winner. Following that win, the USA moved on to victories over Panama, 95–60, and Italy, 100–61, then closed out the preliminary group play by edging Puerto Rico, 61–56, in a ragged tilt. Yugoslavia finished second in the group standings and moved with the USA into the straight elimination finals against Russia and Brazil, who emerged the leaders in Group B.

In the championship playoffs, the US downed Brazil, 75–63, while Yugoslavia upset Russia, 63–62. That put the USA and Yugoslavia into the championship game, this time with the Yanks favored.

The first half of the title game was a tensely-played contest, but after trailing most of the time, the USA went ahead, 32–29, at halftime, Glynn Saulters scoring a field goal just four seconds before the horn sounded. When play resumed, the issue was decided almost immediately, as the USA, paced by Haywood and White, exploded for

17 straight points and coasted to a 65–50 decision. The 25,000 spectators who jam-packed the arena were left stunned.

TEAM PERSONNEL

BASKETBALL

Michael Barrett, USN, Norfolk, Va.
Cpl. John Clawson, USA, Naperville, Ill.
Donald Dee, Dodge City, Kansas
Calvin Fowler, Akron, Ohio
Spencer Haywood, Detroit, Mich.
Wilmer Hosket, Columbus, Ohio
James King, Akron, Ohio
Glynn Saulters, Lisbon, La.
Charles Scott, New York, N. Y.
Capt. Michael Silliman, USA, Louisville, Ky.
Kenneth Spain, Houston, Texas
Joseph White, St. Louis, Mo.

Staff Personnel

Henry Iba, Stillwater, Okla. (Coach)
Ben Carnevale, New York, N. Y. (Manager)
G. Russel Lyons, Boulder, Colo.
 (Asst. Manager)
Henry Vaughn, Akron, Ohio (Asst. Coach)

UNITED STATES BASKETBALL TEAM

Name	G	Mins.	Pts.	FGA	FGM	FTA	FTM	PF
Haywood	9	252	145	89	64	38	17	15
White	9	222	105	98	46	16	13	16
Silliman	9	230	81	78	35	12	11	18
Scott	9	211	72	49	25	32	22	20
Hosket	8	125	69	49	31	16	7	23 (1)
Fowler	9	187	58	44	26	10	6	24
Barrett	9	164	56	56	26	8	4	17 (1)
Saulters	8	69	42	30	16	10	10	9
Spain	8	77	35	17	15	14	5	11
Dee	7	75	33	33	13	12	7	13 (1)
Clawson	8	70	29	25	13	4	3	9
King	8	118	14	10	5	6	4	20 (1)
USA Totals	9	1800	739	578	315	178	109	195 (4)
Opponents	9	1800	485	513	190	168	105	240 (11)

Field Goal Percentages: USA 54.5; Opponents 37.
Foul Goal Percentages: USA 61.2; Opponents 62.5
Points Per Game: USA 82.1; Opponents 53.9.
NOTE: G — Games; Mins. — Minutes Played; Pts. — Total Points Scored; FGA — Field Goal Attempts; FGM — Field Goals Made; FTA — Free Throw Attempts; FTM — Free Throws Made; PF — Personal Fouls. (Figures in parentheses alongside personal fouls indicates disqualifications on five fouls.)

Final Standings — Basketball

1. UNITED STATES
2. Yugoslavia
3. Soviet Union
4. Brazil
5. Mexico
6. Poland
7. Spain
8. Italy
9. Puerto Rico
10. Bulgaria
11. Cuba
12. Panama
13. Philippines
14. Korea
15. Senegal
16. Morocco

BOXING

The best medal haul for US boxers since 1952 was evidence that the 1968 team was a finely conditioned and well-handled group. Two golds were annexed with one silver and four bronzes out of 11 weight classes. The sportsmanship showed by USA entrants was excellent and heavyweight George Foreman capped it all with his

conduct while accepting the gold medal. Spectators and TV-viewers alike saw this young man bow graciously to the judges in accepted international style, hold an American flag in his hand, and then sing out clearly the words to his national anthem.

The United States performances:
Light Flyweight – Harlan Marbley lost in the semi-finals to the eventual

BASKETBALL

B. Carnevale

H. Iba

G. Lyons

H. Vaughn

BOXING

J. Baldwin

G. Foreman

S. Goss

R. Harris

A. Jones

H. Marbley

A. Muniz

A. Redden

A. Robinson

D. Vasquez

J Wallington

P. Duffy

R. Gault

R. Rogers

285

CANOEING

P. Beacham   T. Cooper   L. Cutler

W. Gates   J. Glair   E. Heincke

M. Hickox   W. Jewell   M. Larson

J. Pickett   A. Weigand   P. Weigand

F. Fox   V. Moore   Rademaker

M. Smoke   L. Abbott   G. Grigoleit

G. Miller

titlist, Francisco Rodriguez of Venezuela, by decision.

Flyweight – David Vasquez was eliminated in the second round matches by L. Rwabogo of Uganda by decision. The latter won a bronze medal.

Bantamweight – Samuel Goss was eliminated in the first round matches, losing the decision to N. Giju of Rumania.

Featherweight – Albert Robinson lost to Antonio Roldan of Mexico through disqualification in the championship bout when the referee charged him with butting, although films later put question to the decision. Although rules prohibit the award of a silver medal in such an infraction, the jury did give Robinson the trophy but did not change the ruling on alleged butting.

Lightweight – Ronald Harris won the gold medal by decision over Jozef Grudzien of Poland after outpointing C. Cutov of Rumania in the semi-finals.

Light Welterweight – James Wallington lost by decision to Enrique Regueiferos of Cuba in the semi-finals. The latter won the silver medal.

Welterweight – In the quarter-final matches, Armando Muniz was decisioned by M. Guilloti of Argentina.

Light Middleweight – John Baldwin was eliminated in the semi-finals by Cuba's Ricardo Garbey, who went on to earn the silver medal.

Middleweight – Alfred Jones lost by decision to the eventual champion, Christopher Finnegan of Great Britain, when they met in the semi-finals.

Light Heavyweight – Arthur Redden was eliminated in the first round by G. Stankov of Bulgaria.

Heavyweight – George Foreman won the championship by TKOing I. Chepulis of Russia in the second round of the title bout. George advanced to the finals also via the TKO route over G. Bambini of Italy.

Since the defeated semi-finalists in each weight division did not meet in a special match to determine third place, each was awarded a bronze medal. In this ruling, Marbley, Wallington, Baldwin, and Jones won bronzes for the USA.

TEAM PERSONNEL

BOXING

John Baldwin, Detroit, Mich. (light middleweight)
Sam Goss, Trenton, N. J. (bantamweight)
George Foreman, Pleasanton, Calif. (heavyweight)
Ronnie Harris, Canton, Ohio (lightweight)
Alfred Jones, Detroit, Mich. (middleweight)
Harlan Marbley, Washington, D. C. (light flyweight)
Armando Muniz, Artesia, Calif. (welterweight)
Arthur Redden, USMC, Wilmington, Dela. (light heavyweight)
Albert Robinson, USN, Phoenix, Ariz. (featherweight)
David Vasquez, New York, N. Y. (flyweight)
James Wallington, Jr. USA, Fayetteville, N. C. (light welterweight)

Staff Personnel

Robert Gault, Washington, D. C. (Coach)
Francis Pat Duffy, Yeadon, Pa (Manager)
Sgt. Raymond Rogers, USMC, Camp LeJeune, N. C. (Asst. Coach)

CANOEING AND KAYAKING (MEN AND WOMEN)

Medals eluded the United States men and women canoeists although Mrs. Marcia Jones Smoke, a bronze medalist in 1964, did come close by placing fourth in the women's kayak singles. The men's best showing was in the Canadian singles where Andreas Weigand finished eighth.

United States performances were:

Kayak singles (men) – John Glair was eliminated in the semi-finals.

Kayak tandem (men) – Paul Beacham and Peter Weigand were eliminated in the repechages.

Kayak fours (men) – The quartet of Lester Cutler, Ernst Heincke, Mervil Larson, and John Pickett was eliminated in the repechages.

Canadian singles (men) – Andreas Weigand finished eighth in the finals.

Canadian tandem (men) – William Gates and Malcolm Hickox reached the semi-finals but were eliminated.

Kayak singles (women) – Mrs. Marcia Jones Smoke placed fourth.

Kayak tandem (women) – Mrs. Marcia Jones Smoke and Mrs. Sperry Jones Rademaker placed seventh in the finals.

TEAM PERSONNEL

CANOEING & KAYAKING — Men's Team

Maj. Paul Beacham, USA, Columbus, Ga. (K)
Toby Cooper, Long Beach, Calif. (C)
Lester Cutler, Costa Mesa, Calif. (K)
William J. Gates, Dedham, Mass. (C)
John Glair, Traverse City, Mich. (C)
Ernest Heincke, Cos Cob, Conn. (K)
Malcolm Hickox, Port Credit, Ontario (C)
William H. Jewell, Newport Beach, Calif. (K)
Mervil C. Larson, Carpinteria, Calif. (K)
John R. Pickett, Dallas, Pa. (K)
Andreas Weigand, Arlington, Va. (C)
Peter M. Weigand, Newport Beach, Calif. (K)

Women's Team

Miss Francine Fox, Washington, D. C. (K)
Mrs. Sperry Jones Rademaker, Windemere, Fla. (K)
Mrs. Marcia Jones Smoke, Buchanan, Mich. (K)
Miss Virginia M. Moore, Honolulu, Hawaii (K)

Staff Personnel
Gert Grigoleit, Sacramento, Calif.
(Manager & Coach)
Miss Lee Abott, Oneonta, N. Y.
(Asst. Women's Coach)
A. Gordon Miller, Brooklyn, N. Y. (Boatman)

CYCLING

Although United States cyclists did not win medals or high rating, the caliber of their performances revealed improvement over 1964 showings. Best for the USA were Jackie Simes and Tim Mountford, both veteran riders. Simes was 12th in the final rankings for competitors in the 1000 meter individual time trial and also reached

and James Van Boven placed 20th with a time of 2:24:13.50.

TEAM PERSONNEL

CYCLING

John C. Allis, San Pedro, Calif. (road race)
David Brink, Berkeley, Calif. (4000 m. individual pursuit)
Dan Butler, Davis, Calif. (road race)
David Chauner, Rosemont, Pa. (4000 m. individual pursuit)
Harry W. Cutting, Riverside, Calif. (4000 m. team pursuit)
Jack Disney, Monrovia, Calif. (tandem sprint)
John Howard, Springfield, Mo. (road race)
Wayne LeBombard, Milwaukee, Wis. (4000 m. team pursuit)
Steven Maaranen, Lomita, Calif. (4000 m. team pursuit)

D. Chauner   H. Cutting   J. Disney

J. Howard   LeBombard   S. Maarenen

O. Martin   T. Mountford   R. Parsons

Typical of the Mexicans' ingenuity was this sculpture of a cyclist, built to stand just outside the main entrance to the velodrome, site of the cycling competition.

the quarter-finals with Mountford before being eliminated.

The USA performances:

1000 meter individual time trial – Jackie Simes placed 12th.

1000 meter scratch sprint – Jackie Simes and Tim Mountford were eliminated in final repechages of quarter-finals.

Tandem – Jack Disney and Charles Pranke were eliminated in the repechages.

4000 meter individual pursuit – David Brink placed 18th in final rankings.

4000 meter team pursuit – The team of David Chauner, Harry Cutting, Steven Maaranen and John Vande Velde did not qualify for the quarter-finals, their time of 4:32.87 being the 16th best.

196 kilometer individual road race – John Howard placed 44th with time of 4:52:45.8 while Dan Butler and David Chauner also competed, no places taken.

100 kilometer team time trial – The United States combination of Jack Howard, Oliver Martin, John Allis

Pfc. Oliver Martin, USA, New York, N. Y. (road race)
Tim H. Mountford, Sherman Oaks, Calif. (1000 meter sprint)
Robert Parsons, LaCanada, Calif. (road race)
Michael Miles Pickens, San Diego, Calif. (road race)
Charles William Pranke, Santa Monica, Calif. (tandem sprint)
Jackie Simes III., USA, Closter, N. J. (1000 meter sprint)
John C. VandeVelde, Glen Ellyn, Ill. (4000-m. team pursuit)
James W. Van Boven, Hillsborough, Calif. (road race)
Walt Wessberg, Granada Hills, Calif. (road race)

Staff Personnel
Alfred J. Toefield, New York, N. Y. (Manager)
Robert Hansing, Los Angeles, Calif. (Coach)
Robert Tetzlaff, Los Gatos, Calif. (Coach)
Jerry L. Rimoldi, San Diego, Calif. (Mechanic)
Peter Senia, Brooklyn, N. Y. (Mechanic)

M. Pickens   C. Pranke   J. Simes

J. Van Boven   VandeVelde   W. Wessberg

A. Toefield   R. Hansing   R. Tetzlaff

J. Allis   D. Brink   D. Butler

J. Rimoldi   P. Senia

EQUESTRIAN

K. Freeman

M. Page

J. Plumb

J. Wofford

F. Chapot

M. Chapot

C. Hoffman

K. Kusner

Steinkraus

K. Downton

E. Master

D. Plumb

W. Stone

de Nemethy

J. Lynch

J. O'Dea

J. Denny

EQUESTRIAN

Although the coveted gold medal in the Grand Prix des Nations team jumping – for which they were one of the highly-regarded favorites – escaped their efforts, the USA equestrian team did gain three medals in other events and also rated two fourth-place honors. Biggest achievement and a highly popular one was the winning of the gold in the individual jumping by veteran Olympian William Steinkraus. It was the first gold medal for Bill, who was competing in his fifth straight Olympic Games, and the first such individual award ever won by an American rider.

A silver medal was picked up by the United States three-day event team and a bronze in the individual phase of that competition also found its way into the USA collection.

United States performances:

Individual dressage – Mrs. Kyra Downton (on Kadett) placed 21st, Miss Edith Master (on Helios) was 23rd, and Mrs. Donnan Sharp Plumb (on Attache) was 24th.

Team dressage – United States team of above riders placed eighth.

Three-Day event (individual) – Michael O. Page (on Foster) was third with 52.31 penalty points. James C. Wofford (on Kilkenny) was sixth with 74.06 and Michael Plumb was 14th with 119.50.

Three-Day event (team) – United States team of Wofford, Plumb and Page, was second on 245.87 penalty points.

Grand Prix jumping (individual) – William Steinkraus won the coveted gold medal on Snowbound, turning in a perfect score in the morning round and being charged with only one penalty of four points in the afternoon. Frank Chapot, riding San Lucas, missed out on the bronze medal when a check of riding time found him only seconds slower than the British rider with whom he was deadlocked in penalty points. Miss Kathryn Kusner, other US entry, riding Untouchable, placed 21st.

Grand Prix jumping (team) – The trio of Mrs. Mary Chapot, Miss Kusner and Frank Chapot ran into trouble at the start and the accumulated total of 117.50 penalty points put the US down to fourth place.

TEAM PERSONNEL

EQUESTRIAN (MEN & WOMEN)
Three-Day Event Team
Kevin Freeman, Portland, Oregon
Michael Owen Page, Briarcliff, N. Y.
John Michael Plumb, Bedminster, N. J.
James C. Wofford, Milford, Kansas

Jumping Team
Frank Chapot, Wallpack, N. J.
Mrs. Mary Mairs Chapot, Wallpack, N. J.
Carol Hoffman, North Branch, N. J.
Kathy Kusner, Monkton, Md.
William Steinkraus, Noroton, Conn.

Dressage Team
Mrs. Kyra G. Downton, Atherton, Calif.
Miss Edith Master, New York, N. Y.
Mrs. Donnan Sharp Plumb, Bedminster, N. J.

Staff Personnel
Whitney Stone, New York, N. Y. (Manager)
Bertalan deNemethy, Gladstone, N. J. (Jumping Coach)
Major John Lynch, Gladstone, N. J. (Three-Day Event Coach)
Dr. Joseph O'Dea, Genasco, N. Y. (Veterinarian)
Jacques Denny, Unionville, Pa. (Veterinarian)

FENCING (MEN AND WOMEN)

United States fencers, largely veterans of Olympic competition, found medals well out of their grasp. Best showing was a sixth place rating in the team sabre.

United States performances:

Individual foil (men) – Larry Anastasi, Jeffrey Checkes, and Herbert Cohen all were eliminated in the second round pool competition.

Individual epee (men) – Stephen Netburn lost out in the final round of 16 fencers on direct elimination while David Micahnik and Paul Pesthy were eliminated in the second round pools.

Individual sabre (men) – Alfonso Morales gained the direct elimination quarter finals but lost out to the eventual fourth place winner, V. Nazlimov of Russia. Anthony (Jack) Keane and Alex Orban were eliminated in second round pools.

Individual foil (women) – Mrs. Janice Lee Romary and Harriet King advanced to the second round pools but were then eliminated. Veronica Smith lost out in the first round pools.

Team foil (men) – The USA team of Albert Axelrod, Herbert Cohen, Uriah Jones and Larry Anastasi lost to Great Britain, 9–7, and later with Jeffrey Checkes replacing Jones, the team lost to Russia, 12–4. That eliminated the team in the first round pool.

Team epee (men) – Paul Pesthy, Stephen Netburn, David Micahnik and Lt. Daniel Cantillon formed the team which lost to Italy, 10–6, and with Robert Beck replacing Cantillon, also lost to Russia, 10–5, in the first round pool, thus being eliminated.

Team sabre (men) – The US quartet of Alex Orban, Anthony Keane, Thomas Balla, and Robert Blum defeated Argentina, 11–5, to gain the direct elimination bracket but lost to Italy, 8–6, Alfonso Morales replacing Blum in the lineup. In the repechage, Orban, Blum, Morales and Keane combined to defeat West Germany, 9–7, but in the classification match to determine 5th and 6th places, the same combination lost to Poland, 9–5.

Team foil (women) – The team formed by Harriet King, Janice Lee Romary, Maxine Mitchell and Sally Pechinsky lost in the first round pool to Hungary, 13–3, and then was eliminated by Italy, 10–6. Veronica Smith replaced Mrs. Romary in the second match.

TEAM PERSONNEL

FENCING
Men's Team
Lawrence J. Anastasi, Swarthmore, Pa. (foil)
Albert Axelrod, Scarsdale, N. Y. (foil)
J. Thomas Balla, Philadelphia, Pa. (sabre)
*Dr. Robert L. Beck, San Antonio, Texas (epee)
Robert M. Blum, New York, N. Y. (sabre)
Lt. Daniel J. Cantillon, USA, Ft. Sam Houston, Texas (epee)
Jeffrey Alan Checkes, Brooklyn, N. Y. (foil)
Herbert Cohen, Ney York, N. Y. (foil)
Uriah Jones, Killingworth, Conn. (foil)
Anthony Jack Keane, East Brunswick, N. J. (sabre)
David M. Micahnik, Philadelphia, Pa. (epee)
Alfonso H. Morales, Santa Monica, Calif. (sabre)
Stephen S. Netburn, New York, N. Y. (epee)
Alex Orban, Bronx, N. Y. (sabre)
*Paul K. Pesthy, San Antonio, Texas (epee)

* also on modern pentathlon team

Women's Team
Miss Harriet King, Jackson Heights, N. Y. (foil)
Mrs. Maxine Mitchell, Los Angeles, Calif. (foil)
Sally Pechinsky, West Peabody, Mass. (foil)
Mrs. Janice Lee Romary, Woodland Hills, Calif. (foil)
Miss Veronica Smith, Washington, D. C. (foil)

Staff Personnel
Norman Lewis, Kew Gardens, N. Y. (Team Captain)
William Latzko, West New York, N. J. (Team Manager)
Michel Alaux, New York, N. Y. (Coach)
Csaba Elthes, New York (Coach)
Daniel R. Dechaine, Jr., Los Angeles, Calif. (Technician)

GYMNASTICS — MEN

The United States male gymnasts maintained their international rating by placing seventh in the team all-around standings, equalling what they did at Tokyo four years back. However, the best individual showing was David Thor's 24th place on 110.60 points. None of the US gymnasts qualified for the individual championships in free exercise, long horse, rings, side horse, parallel bars, and horizontal bars

FENCING

L. Anastasi

A. Axelrod

J. Balla

W. Latzko

M. Alaux

C. Elthes

R. Beck

R. Blum

D. Cantillon

D. Dechaine

J. Checkes

H. Cohen

U. Jones

GYMNASTICS – MEN

J. Allen

S. Cohen

Freudenstein

A. Keane

H. King

D. Micahnik

S. Hug

R. Loyd

Roethlisberger

M. Mitchell

A. Morales

S. Netburn

D. Thor

J. Beckner

W. Meade

A. Orban

S. Pechinsky

P. Pesthy

GYMNASTICS – WOMEN

D. Bolin

W. Cluff

K. Gleason

J. Romary

V. Smith

N. Lewis

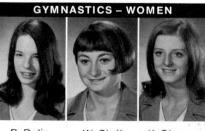
L. Metheny

C. Mulvihill

C. Rigby

GYMNASTICS – WOMEN

J. Tanac   V. Edwards   M. Grossfeld

P. Melcher

which were a test between Japanese and Russian entries.

Fred Roethlisberger placed 34th with 109.70 points, Steve Hug was 36th on 109.60; Steven Cohen was 46th with 108.75; Sid Freudenstein was 57th with 108.00 and Kanati Allen was 80th with 105.45.

The USA team total was 548.90 as compared with Japan's winning total of 575.90.

TEAM PERSONNEL

GYMNASTICS — MEN

Kanati Allen, Los Angeles, Calif.
Stephen Cohen, Philadelphia, Pa.
Sidney Freudenstein, Oakland, Calif.
Stephen Hug, Northridge, Calif.
Richard Loyd, Winnsboro, La.
Frederick Roethlisberger, Menomonee Falls, Wis.
David Thor, Reseda, Calif.

Staff Personnel

William T. Meade, Carbondale, Ill. (Manager)
Jack Beckner, Studio City, Calif. (Coach)

GYMNASTICS — WOMEN

Satisfactory improvement in both team and individual standings can be credited to the USA women's gymnastics team. It rose from ninth place at Tokyo in 1964 to sixth place at Mexico City, scoring 369.75 points to the winning Russian team's 382.85. Even more gratifying were the individual ratings, none of the team placing lower than 39th. In 1964, only two Yankees had places as good as 34th and 36th.

But the best showing was by Linda Metheny who gained the finals of the individual championships in balance beam. She scored 19.225 points to tie East Germany's K. Janz for fourth place. It was the first time since 1932

that any US gymnast had even qualified for the individual championship, much less ranked so high.

In the individual all-around tests, young Cathy Rigby led the way with 16th place on 74.95. Linda Metheny was 28th with 74.00, Joyce Tanac was 30th with 73.65, Kathy Gleason was 31st with 73.60, Colleen Mulvihill was 34th with 73.05 and Wendy Cluff was 39th with 71.80.

TEAM PERSONNEL

GYMNASTICS — WOMEN

Wendy Cluff, Torrance, Calif.
Kathy Gleason, Buffalo, N. Y.
Linda Metheny, Tuscola, Ill.
Colleen Mulvihill, Champaign, Ill.
Cathy Rigby, Los Alamitos, Calif.
Joyce Tanac, Seattle, Wash.

Staff Personnel

Vannie Edwards, Shreveport, La. (Manager)
Mrs. Muriel Grossfeld, New Haven, Conn. (Coach)
Miss Patricia Melcher, New Haven, Conn. (Pianist)

MODERN PENTHALON

R. Beck   M. Lough   J. Moore

P. Pesthy   P. Hains   H. Johnston

MODERN PENTATHLON

The United States, usually a contender for team honors in this sport (it won the silver medal at Tokyo), could do no better than fourth place this time, scoring 13,280 points to the winning total of 14,325 by Hungary. In individual rankings, James Moore placed 11th, Robert Beck, 23rd, and Maurice Lough, 30th.

TEAM PERSONNEL

MODERN PENTATHLON

*Dr. Robert Beck, San Antonio, Texas
Capt. Maurice Thomas Lough, USA, San Antonio, Texas

Major James W. Moore, USA, San Antonio, Texas
*Paul K. Pesthy, San Antonio, Texas

* also on fencing team

Staff Personnel

Maj. Gen. Peter C. Hains, III, USA-ret., Gibson Island, Md. (Manager)
Howard L. Johnston, San Antonio, Texas (Coach)

ROWING

For the first time in history, the United States failed to win at least one gold medal in this sport. A silver in the pair oars without coxswain and a bronze in the double sculls was the best the oarsmen could do at Mexico City, a disappointing showing at best.

Here are the American performances:

Single sculls – John Von Blom placed fourth with a time of 8:00.51, two places higher than Don Spero accomplished in 1964.

Double sculls – In a close race, the combination of John H. Nunn and William P. Maher placed third behind Russia and the Netherlands. Their time was 6:54.21, about one length behind the winners. (The USA was second in 1964.)

Pair oars without coxswain – Until East Germany closed the gap and surged to a deck-length win within the last 50 meters, the US pair of Lawrence Hough and Anthony Johnson appeared to have the gold medal. However, East German's thrust won by a few feet in the time of 7:26.56 to USA's 7:26.71.

Pair oars with coxswain – The shell rowed by William Hobbs and Richard Edmunds and coxed by Stewart MacDonald, placed fifth and never was in contention.

Four oars without coxswain – The United States crew of Peter Raymond, Raymond Wright, Charles Hamblin and Lawrence Terry placed fifth in this final, being timed in 6:47.70 as compared to East Germany's winning 6:39.18.

Four oars with coxswain – Still another fifth place was taken by the USA crew of Luther Jones, William Purdy, Anthony Martin, Gardner Cadwalader and coxswain John Hartigan. Its time was 6:51.41. New Zealand won in 6:45.62. Only consolation was that the USA beat Russia by two lengths.

Eight oars with coxswain – Harvard University's crew, which had rated pre-Games speculation as a possible medalist, never did get into contention and finished sixth and last. Its only time for some glory came in a fine finish during the repechages to gain a berth in the finals. The crew was composed of Stephan Brooks, Curtis Canning, Andrew Larkin, Scott Steketee, Franklin Hobbs, Jacques Fiechter, Cleve Livingston, David Higgins and coxswain Paul Hoffman. Its time was 6:14.34, some two lengths behind the winning West Germany combination.

TEAM PERSONNEL

ROWING

Stephen H. Brooks, Weston, Mass.
(stroke, 8-oar)
Gardner Cadwalader, Ambler, Pa.
(No. 3, 4 w/c)
Curtis Ray Canning, Salt Lake City, Utah
(No. 7, 8-oar)
Richard R. Edmunds, Springville, N. Y.
(bow, 2 w/c)
Arthur T. Evans, III, Cincinnati, Ohio
(stroke, 8-oar)
Jacques Fiechter, Plymouth Meeting, Pa.
(No. 3, 8-oar)
Douglas I. Foy, Mountain Lakes, N. J.
(spare)
Charles B. Hamblin, Chaumont, N. Y.
(No. 2, 4-oar)
Mark Harrington, Simsbury, Conn. (spare coxswain)
John D. Hartigan, Philadelphia, Pa.
(cox, 4 w/c)
David D. Higgins, Worcester, Mass.
(bow, 8-oar)
Franklin W. Hobbs, Concord, Mass.
(No. 4, 8-oar)
William Hobbs, Concord, Mass.
(Stroke, 2 w/c)
Paul Hoffman, St. Thomas, Virgin Islands
(cox, 8-oar)
Lawrence A. Hough, Arlington, Va.
(stroke, 2-oar)
Anthony P. Johnson, Arlington, Va.
(bow, 2-oar)
Luther Jones, Blackfoot, Idaho (stroke 4 w/c)
Andrew Larkin, Kensington, Conn.
(No. 6, 8-oar)
J. Cleve Livingston, Carmichael, Calif.
(No. 2, 8-oar)
Michael Livingston, Carmichael, Calif. (spare)
Stewart MacDonald, Belmont, Mass.
(cox, 2 w/c)
Thomas D. McKibbon, Laguna Niguel, Calif.
(spare)
William Patrick Maher, Detroit, Mich.
(bow, doubles)
Anthony E. Martin, III, Philadelphia, Pa.
(No. 2, 4 w/c)
John H. Nunn, Cincinnati, Ohio (stroke, doubles)
Edward Porter, Bath, Maine (spare)
William K. Purdy, Hindsdale, Ill. (bow, 4 w/c)
Peter Harlow Raymond, Princeton, N. J.
(stroke, 4-oar)
Scott N. Steketee, Toledo, Ohio
(No.5, 8-oar)
Lawrence Terry, Jr., Harvard, Mass.
(bow, 4-oar)

ROWING

S. Brooks   Cadwalader   C. Canning

C. Livingston M. Livingston S. MacDonald

R. Edmunds   A. Evans   J. Fiechter

W. Maher   A. Martin   T. McKibbon

D. Foy   C. Hamlin   M. Harrington

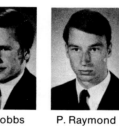  

J. Nunn   E. Porter   W. Purdy

J. Hartigan   D. Higgins   F. Hobbs

P. Raymond   S. Steketee   L. Terry

W. Hobbs   P. Hoffman   L. Hough

J. Von Blom   R. Wright   C. Findlay

A. Johnson   L. Jones   A. Larkin

J. Gardiner   H. Parker   J. Frailey

John Von Blom, Alamitos, Calif. (singles)
Raymond G. Wright, Seattle, Wash.
(No. 3, 4-oar)

Staff Personnel

Conn Findlay, Belmont, Calif. (Manager)
James A. Gardner, Midway, Wash.
(Asst. Mgr.)
Harry Parker, Cambridge, Mass. (Asst. Coach)
Jack Frailey, Boston, Mass. (Asst. Coach)
Campbell Galt, Cambridge, Mass. (Boatman)

C. Galt

MEXICO 68

SHOOTING

The United States harvest of medals in shooting was a meager one at Mexico City compared to Tokyo's total of seven, and it is hard to explain the dropoff since the team was a veteran one. Team officials and shooters alike were at a loss to determine the reason, for training preparations and discipline were at the same high level as before. However, the fact that Olympic and/or world marks were equalled or broken in all but one event may be the best explanation.

The lone gold medal was won by Gary L. Anderson, winner at Tokyo,

SHOOTING

G. Anderson   J. Foster   T. Garrigus

D. Hamilton   E. Herring   W. McMillan

J. McNally   R. Rodale   L. Stafford

A. Vitarbo   L. Wigger   J. Writer

H. Reeves   E. Crossmann   F. Green

and in repeating, a new world record holder in the free rifle with a score of 1157. A silver was taken by Sgt. Thomas Garrigus, USAF, with 196 hits on 200 targets and likewise by Lt. John Writer with a score of 1156 in the small bore rifle, three position tests.

United States performances:

Free rifle, 3 position – Gary Anderson was first with a world record total of 1157 while Major John Foster, US Army, tied for sixth on 1140.

Small bore rifle, prone position – Gary Anderson was eighth with 595 and Major Lones Wigger, a silver medalist in 1964, was down the line with 592.

Small bore rifle, 3 position – Lt. John Writer was second with 1156, losing to West Germany's Bernd Klinger by just one point. Fourth place went to Major John Foster with 1153.

Free pistol – Staff sergeant Arnold Vitarbo, USAF, tied H. Vollmar of East Germany for third place with a tally of 559 but lost out on number of bullseyes. ADRM 1/C Donald Hamilton, USN, placed 16th with 549.

Rapid fire pistol – Lt. Col. William McMillan, USMC, gold medalist in 1960, ranked only 17th with 584 and S/Sgt. James McNally, US Army, was 25th with 580.

Trapshooting – Sgt. Thomas Garrigus, USAF, was second with 196 × 200, two behind Great Britain's John Braithwaite, who equalled world and Olympic marks. E-4 Larry Stafford, US Army, was 26th with 189 × 200.

Skeet shooting – Staff sergeant Earl Herring, USAF, placed 16th with a score of 190 and Robert Rodale was 19th with 189.

TEAM PERSONNEL

SHOOTING

Gary L. Anderson, Axtell, Nebr. (rifle)
Major John Robert Foster, USA, Columbus, Ga. (rifle)
Sgt. Thomas Irvin Garrigus, USAF, Hillsboro, Oregon (clay pigeon)
PO 1C Donald Leslie Hamilton, USN, Brookline, Mass. (pistol)
SM SGT. Earl Francis Herring, USAF, San Antonio, Texas (skeet)
Major William Willard McMillan, USMC, Carlsbad, Calif. (pistol)
S/Sgt. James Henderson McNally, USA, Columbus, Ga. (pistol)
S/Sgt. Albert David Rodale, Allentown, Pa. (skeet)
Sp4 Larry Ray Stafford, USA, Thornton, Colo. (clay pigeon)
S/Sgt. Arnold Vitarbo, USAF, Edison, N. J. (pistol)

Major Lones W. Wigger, Jr., USA, Carter, Mont. (rifle)
Lt. John Henry Writer, USA, LaGrange, Ill. (rifle)

Staff Personnel

Harry Reeves, Andrews, N. C. (Team Captain)
Col. Edward B. Crossman, USA-ret., Arlington, Va. (Team Adjutant)
Capt. Franklin C. Green, USAF, San Antonio, Texas (Armorer)

SWIMMING AND DIVING MEN

The wholesale record-busting at the US Nationals and at the US Olympic Trials made it clear to everyone that the United States swimming and diving teams for men and for women had to be a dead cinch to take most of the honors at the Games. Except for a bit of shuffling among individual titles, everything came out just the way it was expected.

Rated to win 22 or 23 gold medals, the United States did just that. The men accounted for 11, the girls for 12 and, all told, the *Norte Americanos* won a total of 58 medals out of a possible 89 (the relays cutting down the total opportunities by 10).

For the men, the pacesetters were Charles Hickcox, John Nelson, Michael Burton, Don Schollander, Mark Spitz and Kenneth Walsh. Hickcox won three golds and a silver; Spitz won two golds one silver and one bronze, Walsh won two golds and one silver, Burton won two golds, and the "elder statesman" Schollander, winner of four golds in 1964, had a gold and a silver to his credit.

The men scored a 1–2–3 sweep in two events and scored at least one medal in every one of the 17 events on the program.

United States performances:

100 meter freestyle – Kenneth Walsh was second to Australia's Mike Wenden, who equalled the world mark of 52.2 seconds. Walsh was timed in 52.8. Mark Spitz was third in 53.0 and Zachary Zorn was eighth in 53.9.

200 meter freestyle – Don Schollander made a gallant try to get the gold in this event, losing only when Australia's Wenden set a new Olympic mark of 1:55.2. Don placed second in 1:55.8. John Nelson was third in 1:58.1 while Stephen Rerych, who had qualified for the finals, was forced to withdraw because of illness.

400 meter freestyle – Michael Burton showed his world class by winning this final in Olympic record time of 4:09.0. John Nelson was sixth in 4:17.2 and Brent Berk was eighth in 4:26.0.

1500 meter freestyle – Burton further clinched his claim to distance honors with an Olympic record time of 16:38.9 to win with ease the swimming "mile," a performance astounding because of the altitude. John Kinsella was a surprising and highly-pleased second with 16:57.3 and John Nelson was eighth with 18:05.1.

100 meter breaststroke – Don McKenzie surprised everyone with his convincing win in this event usually monopolized by Europeans. He set a new Olympic mark of 1:07.7 in besting two Russians. David Perkowski and Kenneth Merten were eliminated in the semi-finals.

200 meter breaststroke – In this race, won by Mexico's 17-year old Felipe Munoz, Brian Job did the USA credit by placing third in 2:29.9. Phillip Long was seventh in 2:33.6, while Kenneth Merten was eliminated in the preliminary heats.

100 meter backstroke – Charles Hickcox made a desperate try to win four gold medals when he swam in this final, but Roland Matthes of East Germany – who also won the 200 meter event – set a new Olympic record of 58.7. Charlie could do only 1:00.2 for second place. Ronald Mills was third in 1:00.5 and Larry Barbiere was fourth in 1:01.1.

200 meter backstroke – Like Hickcox, the USA's Mitchell Ivey had to contend with Matthes and another Olympic record performance, so he placed second in 2:10.6 while Jack Horsley with 2:10.9 and Gary Hall with 2:12.6 were third and fourth, respectively.

100 meter butterfly – Doug Russell equalled the Olympic mark of 55.9 in leading the USA sweep, with Mark Spitz second in 56.4 and Ross Wales third in 57.2.

200 meter butterfly – Carl Robie won this in the fine time of 2:08.7 with John Ferris third in 2:09.3. The other USA entry, Spitz, was eighth.

200 meter individual medley – The incomparable Charles Hickcox picked up the first of his three golds by winning his specialty in Olympic record time of 2:12.0. This led to a sweep with Greg Buckingham second in 2:13.0 and John Ferris third in 2:13.3.

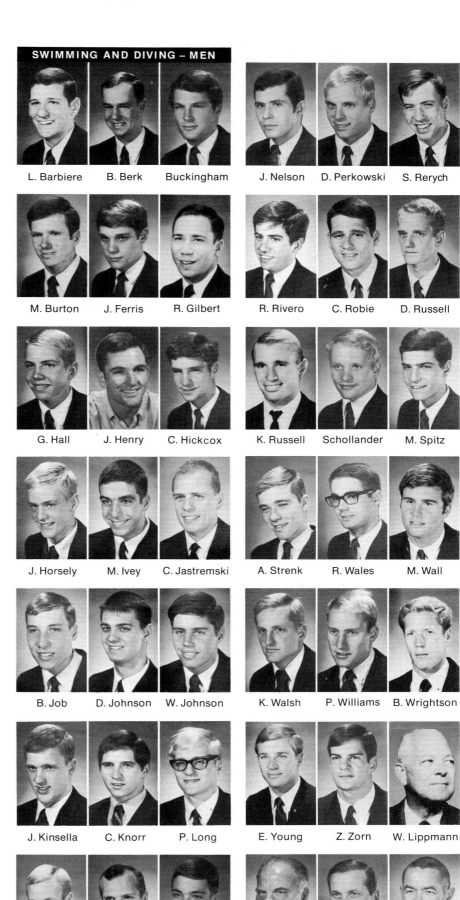

SWIMMING AND DIVING – MEN

L. Barbiere   B. Berk   Buckingham   J. Nelson   D. Perkowski   S. Rerych

M. Burton   J. Ferris   R. Gilbert   R. Rivero   C. Robie   D. Russell

G. Hall   J. Henry   C. Hickcox   K. Russell   Schollander   M. Spitz

J. Horsely   M. Ivey   C. Jastremski   A. Strenk   R. Wales   M. Wall

B. Job   D. Johnson   W. Johnson   K. Walsh   P. Williams   B. Wrightson

J. Kinsella   C. Knorr   P. Long   E. Young   Z. Zorn   W. Lippmann

D. McKenzie   K. Merten   R. Mills   E. Olson   G. Haines   D. Gambril

293

SWIMMING AND DIVING – MEN

D. Smith   R. O'Brien

SWIMMING AND DIVING – WOMEN

S. Atwood   T. Auda   C. Ball

J. Barkman   K. Brecht   L. Bush

P. Caretto   C. Corcione   E. Daniel

D. Giebel   S. Gossick   L. Gustavson

K. Hall   J. Henne   T. Hewitt

C. Jamison   S. Jones   M. King

400 meter individual medley – Hickcox had to beat off the challenge of a teammate, Gary Hall, to win this in 4:48.4. Hall was second in 4:48.7 and Greg Buckingham fourth in 4:51.4.

4 x 100 meter freestyle relay – The US set a new world mark of 3:31.7 in winning this relay. The winning quartet was comprised of Zach Zorn, Steve Rerych, Mark Spitz, and Ken Walsh.

4 x 200 meter freestyle relay – Don Schollander's great anchor performance brought the USA home a winner over Australia's challenging team and the time was good, 7:52.3.

4 x 100 medley relay – A new world record was set in the US medley relay triumph. The time was 3:54.9 for the four swimmers, Charles Hickcox, Don McKenzie, Doug Russell and Ken Walsh.

Springboard diving – Bernard Wrightson, exhibiting great form, amassed 170.15 points to score a decisive win in this event. James Henry was third with 158.09 and Keith Russell sixth with 151.75.

Platform diving – The best USA effort here was a third place showing by Edwin Young on 153.93 points, only .11 less than the winning Italian, Klaus Dibiasi. Keith Russell was fourth with 152.34 and Richard Gilbert was 17th.

TEAM PERSONNEL
SWIMMING & DIVING — MEN

Brent T. Berk, Honolulu, Hawaii
(200 & 400 freestyle)
Larry Barbiere, Medford Lake, N. J.
(100 backstroke)
Mike Burton, Carmichael, Calif.
(400 & 1500 freestyle)
Greg Buckingham, Atherton, Calif.
(200 & 400 indv. medley)
John Ferris, Sacramento, Calif.
(200 butterfly, 200 indv. medley)
Rick Gilbert, Ft. Worth, Texas
(platform diving)
Gary Hall, Garden Grove, Calif.
(200 backstroke, 400 indv. medley)
James Henry, Dallas, Texas
(springboard diving)
Charles Hickcox, Phoenix, Ariz.
(100 backstroke, 200 & 400 indv. medley)
Jack Horsley, Seattle, Wash. (200 backstroke)
Mitchell Ivey, Santa Clara, Calif.
(200 backstroke)
Lt. Chester A. Jastremski, USA, Toledo, Ohio
(relays)
Brian Job, Cortland, Ohio (200 breaststroke)
David Johnson, Wilmington, Del. (relays)
William Johnson, Los Angeles, Calif. (relays)
John Kinsella, Oak Brook, Ill. (1500 freestyle)
Charles Knorr, Columbus, Ohio (alternate-diving)
Philip Long, Wayne, Pa. (200 breaststroke)
Donald W. McKenzie, Woodland Hills, Calif.
(100 breaststroke, 4x100 medley relay)
Ken Merten, Pacoima, Calif.
(100 & 200 breaststroke)

Ronald P. Mills, Ft. Worth, Texas
(100 backstroke)
John M. Nelson, Pompano Beach, Fla.
(200, 400 & 1500 freestyle)
David Perkowski, Westfield, N. J.
(100 breaststroke)
Stephen K. Rerych, Paterson, N. J.
(200 freestyle, 4x100 and 4x200 freestyle relays)
Raymond E. Rivero, Santa Clara, Calif.
(relay)
Carl Robie, Drexel Hill, Pa. (200 butterfly)
Douglas A. Russell, Midland, Texas
(100 butterfly)
Keith Russell, Mesa, Ariz. (springboard & platform diving)
Donald Schollander, Jacksonville, Fla.
(200 freestyle, 4x200 freestyle relay)
Mark Spitz, Santa Clara, Calif. (100 & 200 butterfly, 100 freestyle, relays)
Andrew Strenk, Los Angeles, Calif. (relays)
Ross Wales, Youngstown, Ohio
(100 butterfly)
Michael A. Wall, Los Gatos, Calif. (relays)
Kenneth M. Walsh, Ponte Vedra, Fla.
(100 freestyle, 4x100 freestyle relay)
Peter Williams, Pittsburgh, Pa. (relays)
Bernard Wrightson, Phoenix, Ariz.
(springboard diving)
Edwin Young, Phoenix, Ariz. (platform diving)
Zachary Zorn, Buena Park, Calif.
(100 freestyle, 4x100 freestyle relay)

Staff Personnel

William A. Lippman, Jr., Los Angeles, Calif.
(Manager)
Edwin Olaf Olson, San Francisco, Calif.
(Asst. Mgr.)
George F. Haines, Santa Clara, Calif. (Coach)
Donald I. Gambril, Huntington Harbour, Calif.
(Asst. Coach)
Dick A. Smith, Phoenix, Ariz. (Diving Coach)
Ronald O'Brien, Columbus, Ohio
(Asst. Diving Coach & Asst. Mgr.)

SWIMMING AND DIVING WOMEN

At least nine of the women's team can be classed as multiple medalists. Jan Margo Henne and Susan Pedersen each won four, while Ellie Daniel, Linda Gustavson, Kaye Hall, and Debbie Meyer won three each. Debbie, however, had the best collection, three golds in as many tries in freestyle races. Jane Barkman, Claudia Kolb and Sharon Wichman each won two. Interestingly, the Misses Henne, Daniel and Gustavson each included gold, silver, and bronze medals in their collections.

The USA girls won 11 of the 14 swimming final races, and added another first in springboard diving, besides engineering three 1 – 2 – 3 sweeps.

United States performances:

100 meter freestyle – Jan Margo Henne led a US sweep in this, winning in the time of 1:00.0, with Sue Pedersen second in 1:00.3 and Linda Gustavson third in 1:00.3.

200 meter freestyle – Deborah Meyer started on her triple crown by setting an Olympic record of 2:10.5 in this final. It was another USA sweep, with Miss Henne second in 2:11.0 and Jane Barkman third in 2:11.2.

400 meter freestyle – Miss Meyer continued her Olympic record-breaking by taking this one in 4:31.8 with Linda Gustavson second in 4:35.5. Pam Kruse almost made it a sweep but finished fourth in 4:37.2.

800 meter freestyle – Debbie completed the hat trick with another Olympic record, this being clocked in 9:24.0. Pam Kruse was second in 9:35.7 and Patty Caretto was fifth in 9:51.3.

100 meter breaststroke – Sharon Wichman was the USA's best in this, finishing third in 1:16.1, the race being won in Olympic record time by Yugoslavia's Djurdjica Bjedov (1:15.8). Catharine Ball was sixth in 1:16.7, while Susan Jones was eliminated in the semi-finals.

200 meter breaststroke – Sharon Wichman surprised the Europeans by winning this toughie in 2:44.4. Catherine Jamison was fifth in 2:48.4 while Catie Ball was forced to withdraw from the finals because of illness. She later left the team and returned home upon advice of team physicians.

100 meter backstroke – A world mark was set at 1:06.2 when Kaye Hall took the championship, beating out the challenge of favored Elaine Tanner of Canada. Jane Swaggerty was third in 1:08.1 and Kendis Moore fourth in 1:08.3.

200 meter backstroke – Lillian (Pokey) Watson was the winner here in Olympic record time of 2:24.8 and again the Canadian, Elaine Tanner, was the challenger. Kaye Hall picked up the bronze medal with 2:28.9, while Susan Atwood failed to qualify for the finals.

100 meter butterfly – In a very close race, Lynn McClements of Australia edged the USA's Ellie Daniel for the gold medal. Her time was 1:05.5 while Ellie was timed in 1:05.8. Susan Shields was third in 1:06.2 and Toni Hewitt was seventh in 1:07.5.

200 meter butterfly – Ada Kok of the Netherlands, an odds-on favorite, proved her claim in this event, winning in Olympic-record time of 2:24.7, just nipping East Germany's H. Lindner by one-tenth of a second. Ellie Daniel was third in 2:25.9, Toni Hewitt was fourth in 2:26.2 and Diane Giebel sixth in 2:31.7.

200 meter individual medley – Claudia Kolb led a USA sweep in winning her specialty, setting an Olympic record of 2:24.7. Sue Pedersen was second with 2:28.8 and Jan Henne was third in 2:31.4.

400 meter individual medley – Miss Kolb added another gold to her collection by taking this one in 5:08.5, well ahead of second-place Lynn Vidali, who was timed in 5:22.2. Sue Pedersen was fourth in 5:25.7.

4 x 100 meter freestyle relay – The USA quartet of Jane Barkman, Linda Gustavson, Sue Pedersen and Jan Henne won this handily and set an Olympic mark of 4:02.5.

4 x 100 meter medley relay – Another decisive win and another Olympic record performance was turned in by the United States. The team of Kaye Hall, Catharine Ball, Ellie Daniel and Sue Pedersen set the new mark at 4:28.3.

Springboard diving – Sue Gossick, who was fourth in 1964, was excellent in the execution of her dives and her total of 150.77 points easily took the title. Young Keala O'Sullivan's steady performance earned her the third place slot on 145.23 points. Lt. Micki King, USAF, was leading until final two dives, then injured herself on the board, losing points on that dive and getting a low rating on her final attempt. However, her 137.38 points gave her fourth place.

Platform diving – Ann Peterson was the only Yankee to get in the medal picture here, scoring 101.11 points, some eight behind the winning Czechoslovakian, Milena Duchkova. Lesley Bush, 1964 champion, had a very poor first dive and was never in contention, finishing 19th in a field of 24 divers. Mrs. Barbara Talmage, the USA's third entrant, placed 10th with 87.29.

SWIMMING AND DIVING – WOMEN

V. King   C. Kolb   P. Kruse   K. Thomas   L. Vidali   L. Watson

D. Meyer   K. Moore   K. O'Sullivan   E. Wetzel   S. Wichman   K. Treadway

S. Pederson   A. Peterson   S. Pitt   O. Mucha   S. Chavoor   F. Elm

S. Shields   J. Swaggerty   B. Talmage   H. Billingsley   mexico 68

TEAM PERSONNEL

SWIMMING & DIVING — WOMEN

Terry Auda, Indianapolis, Ind. (relays)
Susie Atwood, Long Beach, Calif.
   (200 backstroke)
Catharine Ball, Jacksonville, Fla.
   (100 & 200 breaststroke, 4x100 medley relay)
Jane Barkman, Wayne, Pa. (200 freestyle,
   4x100 freestyle relay)
Kimla M. Brecht, Whittier, Calif. (relays)
Lesley Bush, Princeton, N.J.
   (platform diving)
Patty Caretto, Whittier, Calif. (800 freestyle)
Cathy Marie Corcione, Long Branch, N.J.
   (relays)
Ellie Daniel, Elkins Park, Pa.
   (100 & 200 freestyle, 4x100 medley
   relay)
Diane Giebel, Cherry Hill, N.J.
   (200 butterfly)
Sue Gossick, Tarzana, Calif.
   (springboard diving)
Linda Lee Gustavson, Santa Cruz, Calif.
   (100 & 400 freestyle)
Kaye Hall, Tacoma, Wsh.
   (100 & 200 backstroke, 4x100 medley
   relay)
Jan Margo Henne, Oakland, Calif.
   (200 indv. medley, 100 & 200 freestyle)
Toni Hewitt, Newport Beach, Calif.
   (100 & 200 butterfly)
Catherine Jamison, Portland, Oregon
   (200 breaststroke)
Susan Jean Jones, Palo Alto, Calif.
   (100 breaststroke)
Lt. Micki King, USAF, Pontiac, Mich.
   (springboard diving)
Victoria King, Sacramento, Calif. (relays)
Claudia Kolb, Santa Clara, Calif.
   (200 & 400 indv. medley)
Pam Kruse, Pompano Beach, Calif.
   (400 & 800 freestyle)
Debbie Meyer, Sacramento, Calif.
   (200, 400, & 800 freestyle)
Kendis Moore, Phoenix, Ariz.
   (100 backstroke)
Keala O'Sullivan, Kailua, Hawaii
   (springboard diving)
Sue Jane Pedersen, Sacramento, Calif.
   (200 & 400 indv. medleys, 100 freestyle,
   also 2 relays)
Ann Peterson, Bellevue, Wash.
   (platform diving)
Sue Pitt, Highland Park, N.J. (relays)
Susan Shields, Louisville, Ky. (100 butterfly)
Jane Swaggerty, Stockton, Calif.
   (100 & 200 backstroke)
Barbara Talmage, Walnut Creek, Calif.
   (platform diving)
Kathleen Thomas, Arlington, Va. (relays)
Lynn Vidali, San Francisco, Calif.
   (400 indv. medley)
Lillian Debra Watson, Santa Clara, Calif.
   (200 backstroke)
Eadie Wetzel, Wilmette, Ill. (relays)
Sharon Wichman, Ft. Wayne, Ind.
   (100 & 200 breaststroke)

Staff Personnel

Kenneth W. Treadway, Bartlesville, Okla.
   (Manager)
Mrs. Olive Mucha, Portland, Oregon
   (Asst. Manager)
Sherman Chavoor, Carmichael, Calif. (Coach)
Frank Elm, East Brunswick, N.J.
   (Asst. Coach)
Hobert Billingsley, Bloomington, Ind.
   (Diving Coach)

VOLLEYBALL — MEN

The United States, though improved from 1964, met stern opposition to its medal hopes and got only seventh place on four wins against five defeats. However, one of the wins was a cherished upset of the eventual champion, Russia, the only blot on the Soviet record. The USA downed the Russians three games to two, also scored wins over Belgium (3–0), Brazil (3–0) and Mexico (3–1). Losses were to Japan (0–3), Czechoslovakia (1–3), East Germany (0–3), Poland (0–3), and Bulgaria (2–3).

FINAL STANDINGS — Men's VOLLEYBALL

	Matches Won	Lost	Points
1. Soviet Union	8	1	17
2. Japan	7	2	16
3. Czechoslovakia	7	2	16
4. East Germany	6	3	15
5. Poland	6	3	15
6. Bulgaria	4	5	13
7. UNITED STATES	4	5	13
8. Belgium	2	7	11
9. Brazil	1	8	10
10. Mexico	0	9	9

TEAM PERSONNEL

VOLLEYBALL — MEN

John K. Alstrom, Beverly Hills, Calif.
David M. Bright, Malibu, Calif.
Winthrop Davenport, Jr., Santa Monica,
   Calif.
Horace Smith Duke, Irving, Texas
Thomas A. Haine, Honolulu, Hawaii
John T. Henn, San Diego, Calif.
Robert Stanley May, Jr., West Los Angeles,
   Calif.
Daniel E. Patterson, Los Angeles, Calif.
Larry D. Rundle, Santa Monica, Calif.
Jon C. Stanley, USAF, Laie, Hawaii
Rudy Suwara, El Segundo, Calif.
Pedro Velasco, Honolulu, Hawaii

Staff Personnel

John C. Lowell, Laie, Hawaii (Manager)
James E. Coleman, Downers Grove, Ill.
   (Coach)

VOLLEYBALL — WOMEN

The USA women's volleyball team, hopeful of a good showing and possible improvement over the fifth-place finish at Tokyo, ran into stiffer competition than expected. The result — seven straight match defeats and last place in an eight-team field. The girls simply could not cope with the strong

VOLLEYBALL - MEN

J. Alstrom

D. Bright

W. Davenport

H. Duke

T. Haine

J. Henn

R. May

D. Patterson

L. Rundle

J. Stanley

R. Suwara

P. Velasco

J. Lowell

J. Coleman

VOLLEYBALL - WOMEN

P. Bright

K. Heck

F. Hopeau

N. Norgensen

L. Lewis

M. McFadden

VOLLEYBALL – WOMEN

M. McReavy   N. Owen   B. Perry

M. Perry   S. Peterson   J. Ward

M. Liba   H. Cohen   G. Chambliss

opposition, losing 3–1 decisions to Russia, Peru, Korea, and Czechoslovakia and 3–0 decisions to Japan, Poland, and Mexico.

FINAL STANDINGS — Women's VOLLEYBALL

	Matches		
	Won	Lost	Points
1. Soviet Union	7	0	14
2. Japan	6	1	13
3. Poland	5	2	12
4. Peru	3	4	10
5. Korea	3	4	10
6. Czechoslovakia	3	4	10
7. Mexico	1	6	8
8. UNITED STATES	0	7	7

TEAM PERSONNEL

VOLLEYBALL — WOMEN

Mrs. Patti Bright, Malibu, Calif.
Ann Heck, Balbas, Island, Calif.
Fanny R. Hopeau, Honolulu, Hawaii
Ninja Jorgensen, Los Angeles, Calif.
Laurie Lewis, Los Angeles, Calif.
Micki McFadden, Honolulu, Hawaii
Marilyn McReavy, Big Lake, Texas
Nancy Owen, Rolling Hills Estate, Calif.
Barbara B. Perry, Long Beach, Calif.
Mary Perry, Van Nuys, Calif.
Sharon Peterson, Honolulu, Hawaii
Jane Ward, Huntington Beach, Calif.

Staff Personnel

Dr. Marie Liba, Madison, Wis. (Manager)
Harlan Cohen, Los Angeles, Calif. (Coach)
Gene Chambliss, Dallas, Texas (Asst. Coach)

WATER POLO

The US Pan-American championship water polo team provided eight of the 11 players on the Olympic aggregation which competed at Mexico City. The experience of international play was noticeable and the USA finished fifth in the final standings, an improvement of four notches over 1964. Qualified observers claimed the competition was the fiercest of any in history, with Yugoslavia winning the title in an overtime 13–11 defeat of Russia.

In the preliminary pool round, the Yankees defeated Brazil, 10–5, Spain, 10–7, and West Germany, 7–5, while losing to Russia, 8–3, and Hungary, 5–1. A 6–6 tie was played with Cuba. This record left the USA in third place in its group, not enough to get into the straight elimination semi-finals. However, it did qualify for the semi-finals of classification competition for fifth through eight places. The US downed the Netherlands first, 6–5, then whipped East Germany (8–2 victors over Cuba) to take fifth place, 6–4.

All told, the USA chalked up five victories, two losses, and one draw while compiling 49 goals to its opponent's 43. Bruce Bradley led the scoring with 18 goals, Gary Scheerer and Barry Weizenberg each had eight, Russell Webb six, Stan Cole three, and David Ashleigh, John Parker and Dean Willeford each had two.

TEAM PERSONNEL

WATER POLO

David Michael Ashleigh, Modesto, Calif.
Steven William Barnett, Campbell, Calif.

FINAL STANDINGS — WATER POLO

1. Yugoslavia
2. Soviet Union
3. Hungary
4. Italy
5. UNITED STATES
6. East Germany
7. Netherlands
8. Cuba
9. Spain
10. West Germany
11. Mexico
12. Japan
13. Brazil
14. Greece
15. United Arab Republic

Myron Bruce Bradley, Long Beach, Calif.
Stanley Clark Cole, Whittier, Calif.
Ronald E. Crawford, Torrance, Calif.
John Michael Parker, Los Altos, Calif.
Gary Peter Sheerer, Los Angeles, Calif.
Anton Ludwig Van Dorp, USAF, Camarillo, Calif.
Russell Irving Webb, USN, Los Angeles, Calif.
Charles Barry Weitzenberg, Los Altos, Calif.
Leslie Dean Willeford, Huntington Beach, Calif.

Staff Personnel

K. Monfore Nitzkowski, Huntington Beach, Calif. (Manager)
Arthur F. Lambert, Los Altos, Calif. (Coach)

WATER POLO

D. Ashleigh   S. Barnett   M. Bradley

S. Cole   R. Crawford   J. Parker

G. Sheerer   A. Van Dorp   R. Webb

Weitzenberg   D. Willeford   K. Nitzkowski

A. Lambert

WEIGHTLIFTING

Bartholomew   J. Dube   P. Grippaldi

R. Knipp   F. Lowe   G. Pickett

J. Puleo   G. Otott   J. Terpak

WEIGHTLIFTING

A bronze medal in the heavyweight division was the lone bright spot for the US weightlifters. It marked the second straight Olympic Games in which a gold medal eluded the *Norte Americanos*, who had once been a power in the sport. The lone medal was taken by Joseph Dube.

United States performances:

Bantamweight – No USA entry.

Featherweight – No USA entry.

Lightweight – No USA entry.

Middleweight – Russell Knipp was fourth with 962.5 pounds; Frederick Lowe was eighth with 946.0 pounds.

Light heavyweight – Joseph Puleo failed to make a legal press and was disqualified.

Middle heavyweight – Philip Grippaldi was seventh with 1050.5 pounds and Robert Bartholomew was ninth with 1006.5 pounds.

Heavyweight – Joseph Dube won third with a lift of 1221 pounds. Ernest Pickett was disqualified for failure to make a legal press.

TEAM PERSONNEL
WEIGHTLIFTING

Robert Bartholomew, Catasqua, Pa.
(middle heavyweight)
Joseph D. Dube, Doctor's Inlet, Fla.
(heavyweight)

Philip Grippaldi, Belleville, N.J.
(middle heavyweight)
Russell Knipp, Chicago, Ill. (middleweight)
Fredrick H. Lowe, Lambertville, Mich.
(middleweight)
George Ernst Pickett, Randallstown, Md.
(heavyweight)
Joseph R. Puleo, Detroit, Mich.
(light heavyweight)

Staff Personnel
Major George E. Otott, USMC, Quantico,
Va. (Manager)
John B. Terpak, York, Pa. (Coach)

WRESTLING

Freestyle

Freestyle wrestlers for the United States improved on 1964's record by taking two silvers, as well as two fourth places, one fifth and one sixth out of eight divisions. Richard Sanders, flyweight, and Donald Behm, bantamweight, were the silver medalists. It was one of the best US showings ever.

United States performances:

Flyweight – Richard Sanders placed second to champion Shigeo Nakata of Japan, who defeated him in the final round-robin title showdown. Sanders also defeated S. Sukhbaatar of Mongolia. In reaching the final round, Sanders scored four victories, all by falls.

Bantamweight – Although he reached the final round robin, Donald Behm could not rate higher than second since his decision over Russian A. Aliev cost him one penalty point. Earlier, Behm had worked his way through the sixth round with four wins (one by fall) and a draw.

Featherweight – Bobby Douglas, captain of the team, was injured in his first round match with S. Abassy of Iran, which he lost by decision, and was forced to withdraw from further competition.

Lightweight – Wayne Wells took fourth place, although he was eliminated in the sixth round when decisioned by Bulgaria's V. Enio, the eventual silver medalist. Up to that time, Wells had won three decisions, won another match by pin, and had one draw.

Welterweight – Steve Combs reached the fourth round before being eliminated by D. Robin of France, eventual silver medalist. Before that, Combs had scored two decisions and had one loss by decision.

Middleweight – Thomas Peckham placed fourth in this class, losing to silver medalist M. Jigjid of Mongolia in the final round. Prior to this, he

WRESTLING

D. Behm   S. Combs   B. Douglas

L. Kristoff   J. Lewis   T. Peckham

R. Sanders   T. Wells   M. Gorriaran

T. Evans   Baughman   Hazewinkel

J. Hazewinkel   W. Holzer   L. Lyden

R. Roop   H. Schenk   R. Tamble

D. Torio   H. Wittenberg

had scored two draws, won one match by decision and two more by pins.

Light heavyweight – Jesse Lewis rated sixth in this competition being eliminated in the fourth round on decision to S. Moustafov of Bulgaria. Until that time, Jesse had scored two decision victories and one draw.

Heavyweight – Larry Kristoff finished in fifth place, being eliminated in the fourth round on a pin by Russia's Aleksandr Medved, the eventual champion. Earlier he had scored two wins by decision and one more by disqualification of his opponent.

Greco-Roman

A fifth and a sixth place was the best showing for United States wrestlers in the Greco-Roman division. United States performances were:

Flyweight – Richard Tamble was eliminated in the second round, losing a match decision for the second time.

Bantamweight – David Hazewinkel reached the fourth round before being eliminated when he lost a decision to E. Ibrahim of Afghanistan. Prior to that he had won one match by pin, won another through disqualification of his opponent, and lost one by decision.

Featherweight – James Hazewinkel also reached the fourth round before being eliminated on a decision loss to D. Gualintchev of Bulgaria. Up to that time, he had scored one win by fall, another by decision, and had gained a referee's decision in a third match.

Lightweight – Werner Holzer tied with Russia's G. Sapunov for sixth place, although he was eventually eliminated in the fifth round by losing a decision to K. Rost of West Germany. In earlier matches, he scored one victory by a pin and one by decision. He also lost a match by a fall.

Welterweight – Larry Lyden lost two straight decisions and was eliminated in the second round.

Middleweight – Captain Wayne Baughman, who did not place in 1964 at Tokyo, captured fifth place this time. However, he was pinned by silver medalist V. Olenik of Russia in the fifth round, thus being eliminated. Prior to this, he had scored two wins by fall, won another by decision, after losing by decision in his initial match.

Light heavyweight – Henk Schenk was disqualified in his first round match and drew in his second, thus being eliminated.

Heavyweight – Robert Roop was eliminated in the third round. He was

pinned by A. Roshin, Soviet Union, in 2:48. Previously he had won his first match by fall, then lost via the same route in the second round.

TEAM PERSONNEL

WRESTLING — FREESTYLE

Donald Behm, Lansing, Mich. (bantamweight)
Steven Combs, Deerfield, Ill. (welterweight)
Bobby Douglas, Bridgeport, Ohio (featherweight)
Larry Kristoff, Carbondale, Ill. (heavyweight)
Jess Lewis, Aumsville, Oregon (light heavyweight)
Thomas Peckham, Ames, Iowa (middleweight)
Richard Sanders, Portland, Oregon (flyweight)
Turner Wells, Houston, Texas (lightweight)
Staff Personnel
Manuel Gorriaran, Providence, R. I. (Manager)
Thomas Evans, Norman, Okla. (Coach)

WRESTLING — GRECO-ROMAN

Wayne Baughman, USAF, Colorado Springs, Colo. (middleweight)
David Hazewinkel, USA, Coon Rapids, Minn. (bantamweight)
James Hazewinkel, USA, Coon Rapids, Minn. (featherweight)
Werner Holzer, Des Plaines, Ill. (lightweight)
Larry Lyden, Hopkins, Minn. (welterweight)
Robert Roop, Carbondale, Ill. (heavyweight)
Henk Schenk, USA, Bend, Ore. (light heavyweight)
Richard Tamble, Alamosa, Colo. (flyweight)

Staff Personnel
Dominick Torio, Toledo, Ohio (Manager)
Henry Wittenberg, Bronx, N.Y. (Coach)

Middleweight Wayne Baughman of the USA gains a decision over Mexico's A Alvarez in the second round of Greco-Roman competition.

YACHTING

Although their total medal haul was only two as compared to 1964's five, this time the medals were all gold for the United States yachtsmen. Championships were scored in the Dragon and Star Classes. At Tokyo, the US won two seconds and three thirds.

T. Allen   P. Barrett   S. Colgate

F. Cox   R. Doyle   G. Friedrichs

B. Jahncke   D. James   R. James

J. Marshall   L. North   G. Schreck

C. Van Duyne   S. Walker   P. Smart

C. Kober

United States performances:

5.5 Meter class – The US entry, skippered by Gardner Cox and crewed by Dr. Stuart Walker and Stephen Colgate, finished eighth in the final standings with 74.7 points, as compared to Sweden's winning total of just eight points. Sweden won five series of the race. A fourth place was the best single race showing by the US boat.

Dragon class – The United States, by scoring four firsts and two seconds for a total of six points, easily outclassed this field. George Friedrichs was the helmsman while Barton Jahncke and Gerald Schreck were the crew.

Flying Dutchman class – The United States placed 10th in this division, tallying 97.4 points with a third place its best single race showing. Robert James, Jr. was the helmsman with David James as crew.

Star class – Lowell North skippered the US entry to victory in this class and had as crew member, Peter Barrett, who had won a silver medal in the 1964 Finn class at Tokyo. North had been a bronze medalist in the Dragon class in 1964. The champions won three races, had one second and two thirds for an aggregate of 14.4 points, winning handily.

Finn class – Carl Van Duyne, who had won the silver medal at the 1967 Pan-American Games, was way down the list with 117.7 points, placing 13th. His best race was a third-place finish.

TEAM PERSONNEL

YACHTING

Thomas Allen, Buffalo, N.Y. (alternate)
Peter Jones Barret, Newport Beach, Calif. (Star, crew)
Stephen Colgate, New York, N.Y. (5.5 meter, crew)
F. Gardner Cox, Villanova, Pa. (5.5 meter, skipper)
Robert Edward Doyle, Salem, Mass. (alternate)
George Shelby Friedrichs, Jr., New Orleans, La. (Dragon, skipper)
Barton W. B. Jahncke, Metairie, La. (Dragon, crew)
David N. James, Mobjack, Va. (Flying Dutchman, crew)
Robert L. James, Jr., Bena, Va. (Flying Dutchman, skipper)
John K. Marshall, Stamford, Conn. (alternate)
Lowell North, San Diege, Calif. (Star, skipper)
Gerald Click Schreck, Matairie, La. (Dragon, crew)
Carl I. Van Duyne, Short Hills, N.J. (Finn)
Dr. Stuart Hodge Walker, Annapolis, Md. (5.5 meter, crew)

Staff Personnel
Paul H. Smart, Darien, Conn. (Manager)
Charles McC. Kober, Long Beach, Calif. (Asst. Manager)

Mexico provided excellent facilities for the yachting competition, held in Acapulco.

X OLYMPIC WINTER GAMES · GRENOBLE, FRANCE
FEBRUARY 6 - 18, 1968

If United States efforts for medals at the X Olympic Winter Games held in Grenoble, France, brought only meager returns in comparison to other nations, the triumphs nonetheless were significant ones. Basically, the entries in all the sports events performed well and their respective placings, in the main, bore out the predictions by Olympic experts who had viewed USA prospects in advance of the competitions.

The one gold medal counted upon... the one emblematic of the world's best in the ladies singles figure skating... was won in breathtaking style by the USA's lovely champion, Miss Peggy Fleming. Four silvers were taken in the speed skating events and one in the men's figure skating singles, while a bronze was added in the women's speed skating tests. The overall total of seven medals was one better than in the 1964 Games, but the caliber of USA triumphs was much higher. At Innsbruck in 1964, the USA won a single gold medal, one silver, and four bronzes for a total of six.

Miss Fleming's victory in figure skating was a dazzling one and capped four years of training for the petite brunette who had set the Olympic title as her goal right after she had placed sixth at Innsbruck in 1964. Not only did she build up a commanding lead in the compulsory phases of the tests, but in the freestyle finale, her performance was so splendid that the judges unanimously awarded her the near-perfect score of 5.9 points out of a possible 6.0 figure, a feat never before achieved in Olympic competition.

Tim Wood added a silver medal in the men's singles of the figure skating, pushing the champion Wolfgang Schwarz of Austria to the limit before losing by the narrow margin of 1904.1 to 1891.6.

While Peggy Fleming's expected triumph provided the first cheering

note for the United States, the heart-stopping thrill for USA followers was the veteran Terry McDermott's winning of the silver medal in the men's 500 meter speed skating final. An

unheralded entry in 1964, Terry had won the lone USA gold medal and had set the Olympic record in his 500 meter race at Innsbruck. Four years older and handicapped by lack of continued

One of the biggest stories of the Winter Games was the three-way tie for second place in the women's 500 meter speed skating competition by a trio of young American girls: Jennifer Fish, Dianne Holum and Mary Myers.

training during the interim between Games, Terry's flaming competitive spirit drove him to the runnerup honors and, except for a fleeting fraction of a second, might have had him in the winner's circle.

Three particular young ladies also thrilled the spectators and brought acclaim to the United States. Products of an intensive US Olympic Committee development program, the trio wrote their names indelibly in the Olympic annals. Misses Mary Meyers, Jennifer Fish and Dianne Holum all were timed in 46.3 seconds as each competed in their respective 500 meter sprints and each received a silver medal. Only once before had there been a triple tie for second place in a speed skating event – two USA men and a Norwegian gaining that distinction in 1948 – but never before had three from the same nation accomplished that feat! Miss Holum also won a bronze medal by finishing third in the 1000 meter race.

To the total of seven medals, the United States entries picked up one fourth place, five fifth places and four sixth places to attain an unofficial fourth place ranking among the competing nations, one step higher than in 1964.

Admittedly, the Olympic Games are recognized as athletic competitions among individuals rather than among nations, and no type of national scoring, except for medal placings, is sponsored officially. However, in order to truly assess the overall strength of the competing nations, comparisons must be made and then evaluated on a common denominator basis.

Just as an experiment, and not presented as an official recognition, a comparison of performances was made first in 1964 and then in 1968 to determine the leading nations within each of the respective sports. Points were awarded to each nation depending

UNITED STATES GOLD MEDAL WINNER

Peggy Fleming (Figure Skating)

UNITED STATES SILVER MEDAL WINNERS

Jennifer Fish (Speed Skating)
Dianne Holum (Speed Skating)
Mary Meyers (Speed Skating)
R. Terence McDermott (Speed Skating)

UNITED STATES BRONZE MEDAL WINNER

Dianne Holum (Speed Skating)

DISTRIBUTION OF MEDALS AT X OLYMPIC WINTER GAMES – GRENOBLE, FRANCE – 1968

ALL COMPETITIVE MEDAL PLACINGS (Official listings)				Nations Competing	ACTUAL MEDALS DISTRIBUTED (See explanation below)			
1st (G)	2nd (S)	3rd (B)	Total		1st (G)	2nd (S)	3rd (B)	Total
6	6	2	14	Norway	11	9	2	22
5	5	3	13	Soviet Union	26	6	5	37
3	4	4	11	Austria	3	8	4	15
4	3	2	9	France	4	3	2	9
3	3	3	9	Holland (Netherlands)	3	3	3	9
3	2	3	8	Sweden	3	7	6	16
2	2	3	7	West Germany	2	3	5	10
1	5	1	7	UNITED STATES	1	5	1	7
0	2	4	6	Switzerland	0	2	7	9
1	2	2	5	Finland	1	2	5	8
1	2	2	5	East Germany	2	2	2	6
4	0	0	4	Italy	8	0	0	8
1	2	1	4	Czechoslovakia	1	19	1	21
1	1	1	3	Canada	1	1	18	20
0	0	1	1	Rumania	0	0	2	2
35	*39	32	106	Totals	66	70	63	199

* Includes ties for second place; duplicate silver medals were awarded, with a resulting decrease in bronze medals.

Did not win medals — Argentina, Australia, Bulgaria, Chile, Denmark, Great Britain, Greece, Hungary, Iceland, India, Iran, Japan, Korea, Lichtenstein, Liberia, Morocco, Monaco, New Zealand, Poland, Spain, Turkey, Yugoslavia.

RANKINGS BY INDIVIDUAL SPORT

BIATHLON — Ski and Shooting

Rank	Nation	Events	Pts.	Int'l Pts.
1	Soviet Union	2	17	7
2	Norway	2	12	5
3	Poland	2	6	4
4	Finland	2	4	2½
5	Sweden	2	4	2½
6	East Germany	2	1	1

BOBSLED

Rank	Nation	Events	Pts.	Int'l Pts.
1	Italy	2	15	7
2	Austria	2	8	5
3	Rumania	2	7	3½
3	West Germany	2	7	3½
5	Switzerland	2	4	2
6	Great Britain	2	2	1
7	UNITED STATES	2	1	0

FIGURE SKATING

Rank	Nation	Events	Pts.	Int'l Pts.
1	UNITED STATES	3	19	7
2	Soviet Union	3	14	5
3	Austria	3	12	4
4	East Germany	3	8	3
5	Czechoslovakia	3	4	1
5	France	3	4	1
5	West Germany	3	4	1
8	Hungary	3	1	0

ICE HOCKEY

Rank	Nation	Events	Pts.	Int'l Pts.
1	Soviet Union	1	7	7
2	Czechoslovakia	1	5	5
3	Canada	1	4	4
4	Sweden	1	3	3
5	Finland	1	2	2
6	UNITED STATES	1	1	1
7	West Germany	1	0	0
8	East Germany	1	0	0

LUGE

Rank	Nation	Events	Pts.	Int'l Pts.
1	East Germany	3	18	7
2	West Germany	3	17	5
3	Austria	3	14	4
4	Poland	3	9	3
5	Italy	3	7	2
6	Czechoslovakia	3	1	1

ALPINE SKIING

Rank	Nation	Events	Pts.	Int'l Pts.
1	France	6	58	7
2	Austria	6	35	5
3	Switzerland	6	16	4
4	Canada	6	12	3
5	UNITED STATES	6	4	1½
5	Great Britain	6	4	1½
7	Italy	6	1	0
7	Poland	6	1	0
7	West Germany	6	1	0

NORDIC SKIING

Rank	Nation	Events	Pts.	Int'l Pts.
1	Norway	10	54	7
2	Sweden	10	40	5
3	Soviet Union	10	34	4
4	Finland	10	17	3
5	Czechoslovakia	10	15	2
6	Italy	10	12	1
7	Finland	10	11	0
7	Switzerland	10	11	0
9	Austria	10	10	0
10	East Germany	10	8	0
11	West Germany	10	7	0
12	Poland	10	3	—

SPEED SKATING

Rank	Nation	Events	Pts.	Int'l Pts.
1	Netherlands	8	53½	7
2	Norway	8	37	5
3	UNITED STATES	8	21½	4
4	Soviet Union	8	20	3
5	Finland	8	19½	2
6	Sweden	8	16½	1
7	West Germany	8	7	0

on the final placement of their individual entries; then the nations were ranked according to the best totals. The top rankings in each of the sports then were graded for international points and a final overall tabulation resulted.

Points were awarded to the first six place winners in each event on a 7-5-4-3-2-1 basis. After each sport category had been ranked, international points also on a 7-5-4-3-2-1 basis were awarded to the top six ranking nations in each sport division. A chart appears on

accompanying pages and illustrates this interesting evaluation.

Surprisingly enough, Norway – which won the most medals at Grenoble – ranked only third in overall performance, the Soviet Union and Austria outranking the Norwegians. The Soviet Union was the top-ranking nation in the sports of biathlon and ice hockey, placed second in figure skating, third in Nordic skiing and fourth in speed skating for a total of 26 international points. Austria's runnerup spot was earned on second rankings in alpine skiing and bobsledding, a tie for second in luge and a third in figure skating. The Norwegians scored second place rankings in biathlon and speed skating while taking first in the Nordic skiing. They did not place in other sports.

The United States' fourth place total of 13½ points was earned by a tie for fifth place in Alpine skiing, a first in figure skating, a sixth in ice hockey and a third in speed skating.

Scanning the all-time medal placings, one finds the United States still in second place to Norway, but the continuing upsurge of the Soviet Union has put that nation in third place, just one medal away. A tally of the all-time medal placings for the Olympic Winter Games is on an accompanying page.

Complete summaries of the various competitions are carried in the regular Olympic Winter Games section of this book. However, a brief review of what United States athletes did follows.

COMPARISONS BY SPORTS INDICATE SOVIET UNION LEADS AUSTRIA, NORWAY AND USA IN Xth GAMES

Note: The following performance comparison system rates the nations two ways: (1) Rates each nation within each of the eight sports, (2) Credits each nation with "international points" in the overall standings. Both ratings are on a 7-5-4-3-2-1- point score.

All rankings within a single sport, therefore, are decided on the basis of number of points earned for the first six placewinners, either individual, pairs, doubles, four-man or team — without regard to number of events.

The figures in parentheses indicate the number of "sport top rankings" within a sport in the overall compilation among nations, and the events in which a nation was top ranked within an individual sport.

Final Rank	Competing Nation	ALS Pts.	BIA Pts.	BOB Pts.	FSK Pts.	IHO Pts.	LUGE Pts.	NOS Pts.	SSK Pts.	Total
1	Soviet Union (2)	—	7	—	5	7	—	4	3	26
2	Austria	5	—	5	4	—	4	—	—	18
3	Norway (1)	—	5	—	—	—	—	7	5	17
4	UNITED STATES (1)	1½	—	—	7	1	—	—	4	13½
5	Sweden	—	2½	—	—	3	—	5	1	11½
6	East Germany (1)	—	1	—	3	—	7	—	—	11
7	Italy (1)	—	—	7	—	—	2	1	—	10
8	Finland	—	2½	—	—	2	—	3	2	9½
8	West Germany	—	—	3½	1	—	5	—	—	9½
10	Czechoslovakia	—	—	—	1	5	1	2	—	9
11	France (1)	7	—	—	1	—	—	—	—	8
12	Canada	3	—	—	—	4	—	—	—	7
12	Netherlands (1)	—	—	—	—	—	—	—	7	7
12	Poland	—	4	—	—	—	3	—	—	7
15	Switzerland	4	—	2	—	—	—	—	—	6
16	Rumania	—	—	3½	—	—	—	—	—	3½
17	Great Britain	1½	—	1	—	—	—	—	—	2½

Legend: ALS — Alpine Skiing; BIA — Biathlon; BOB — Bobsled; FSK — Figure Skating; IHO — Ice Hockey; LUGE — Luge (toboggan); NOS — Nordic Skiing; SSK — Speed Skating.

DISTRIBUTION OF UNITED STATES MEDALS WON AT X OLYMPIC WINTER GAMES IN 1968

(G) 1st	(S) 2nd	(B) 3rd	4th	5th	6th	Medal Totals Only	Sport Classification	(G) 1st	(S) 2nd	(B) 3rd	Total
0	0	0	0	0	0	0	Biathlon	0	0	0	0
0	0	0	0	0	1	0	Bobsled	0	0	0	0
1	1	0	1	1	2	2	Figure Skating	1	1	0	2
0	0	0	0	0	1	0	Ice Hockey	0	0	0	0
0	0	0	0	0	0	0	Luge	0	0	0	0
0	0	0	0	2	0	0	Ski-Alpine	0	0	0	0
0	0	0	0	0	0	0	Ski-Nordic	0	0	0	0
0	4	1	0	2	0	5	Speed Skating	0	4	1	5
1	5	1	1	5	4	7	Totals	1	5	1	7

Medals and Event Placings — Diplomas (4th 5th 6th)

PERSONNEL OF UNITED STATES DELEGATION AT X OLYMPIC WINTER GAMES – 1968

Sport classification	Athletes M	W	T	Managers M	W	T	Coaches M	W	T	Overall M	W	T
Biathlon	6	0	6	1	0	1	2	0	2	9	0	9
Bobsled	14	0	14	1	0	1	1	0	1	16	0	16
Figure Skating	6	6	12	2	0	2	0	0	0	8	6	14
Ice Hockey	18	0	18	2	0	2	1	0	1	21	0	21
Luge	8	3	11	2	0	2	2	0	2	12	3	15
Ski-Alpine	7	8	15	2	0	2	2	0	2	11	8	19
Ski-Nordic (X-Country)	10	0	10	1	0	1	3	0	3			
Ski-Nordic (Jumping)	6	0	6	—	—	—	—	—	—			
Ski-Nordic (Combined)	4	0	4	—	—	—	—	—	—	24	0	24
Speed Skating	12	6	18	1	0	1	1	0	1	14	6	20
Medical services										9	1	10
Administration										22	3	25
Totals	*91	23	114	12	0	12	12	0	12	146	27	173

* Actual total — one athlete competed in two sports: Nordic Skiing (cross country) and Biathlon.

ALL-TIME MEDAL PLACINGS – OLYMPIC WINTER GAMES – 1924–1968 INCLUSIVE					
Rank	Nation	(1st) Gold	(2nd) Silver	(3rd) Bronze	Total
1	Norway	44	43	36	123
2	UNITED STATES	24	32	20	76
3	Soviet Union	28	23	24	75
4	Austria	19	27	23	69
5	Finland	21	26	19	66
6	Sweden	21	20	21	62
7	*Germany	14	11	10	35
8	Switzerland	10	11	12	33
9	France	12	8	9	29
10	Canada	10	5	13	28
11	Italy	7	3	5	15
12	Holland (Netherlands)	4	5	4	13
13	Great Britain	3	2	6	11
14	Czechoslovakia	1	4	3	8
15	*West Germany	2	2	3	7
16	Hungary (tied with)	0	1	4	5
	*East Germany	1	2	2	5
18	Belgium	1	1	2	4
19	Poland	0	1	2	3
20	Japan tied with	0	1	0	1
	North Korea and	0	1	0	1
	Rumania	0	0	1	1

*Credited through 1964 as single unit

303

BIATHLON

W. Bowerman   J. Chaffee   Ehrensbeck

W. Spencer   R. Wakely   E. Williams

C. Parker   C. Burns   S. Johanson

BOBSLED

H. Clifton   R. Crowley   D. Dunn

P. Duprey   J. Hickey   W. Hickey

R. Huscher   P. Lamey   M. Luce

B. Said   P. Savage   G. Sheffield

BIATHLON

(SKIING AND SHOOTING)

In spite of experience and a well-organized training effort in this difficult sport which combines cross country skiing and rifle shooting, the United States entries were not able to equal or better their performances of 1960 and 1964. Capt. William Spencer, US Army, slipped from 30th to 37th place this time, while a newcomer to the team, Cpl. Ralph Wakely, also of the Army, scored a 27th place to pace the USA team. The other two finishers were 45th and 49th. In the relay event, staged for the first time, the USA finished eighth among 13 nations.

Biggest problem for the US entries seemed to be a dropoff in rifle shooting accuracy. Each contestant is timed in covering a distance of approximately 12 miles cross country, but is charged with an extra minute for each miss of a target along the way.

United States placings:

Individual biathlon – Cpl. Ralph Wakely, USA, 27th, 1:27:32.9 (5 minutes penalty time); Capt. William Spencer, USA, 37th, 1:30:17.7 (10 minutes penalty time); Edward G. Williams, 45th, 1:32:24.5 (9 minutes penalty time); Pfc. Jonathan Chaffee, USA, 49th, 1:34:21.1 (11 minutes penalty time).

4 x 10,000 meter relay – The United States team of Wakely, Williams, Spencer and Cpl. John R. Ehrensbeck, USA, placed 8th with an overall time of 2:28:35.5 (incurring 9 penalty tours for missed targets).

TEAM PERSONNEL

BIATHLON

Lt. William Jay Bowerman, USA, Eugene, Oregon
Pfc. Jonathan K. Chaffee, USA, Lyme, N.H.
*Cpl. John Robert Ehrensbeck, USA, Utica, N.Y.
Capt. William A. Spencer, USA, Fort Richardson, Alaska
Cpl. Ralph C. Wakely, USA, Murray, Utah
Edward G. Williams, Rosendale, N.Y.

Staff Personnel

Maj. Cleo C. Parker, Jr., USA, Fort Richardson, Alaska (Manager)
M/Sgt. Clyde Burns, USA, Fort Richardson, Alaska (Rifle coach)
Sven Johanson, Fort Richardson, Alaska (Ski Coach)

*Also on nordic ski team

BOBSLED

H. Siler   C. Timm   P. Martin

J. Lamy

BOBSLED

With a host of newcomers relatively inexperienced in international competition, the United States bobsled entries recorded performances which were the least creditable of any showing in the Games by a USA entry. Best showing was a sixth place in the two-man event and tenth in the four-man event.

United States placings:

Two-man sleds – 6th, United States No. 1 team of Paul Lamey and Robert Huscher, 4:46.03 for the four runs; 11th, United States No. 2 team of Howard Clifton and Michael Luce, 4:49.31.

Four-man sleds – 10th, United States No. 2 team of Boris Said, Dr. David Dunn, Robert Crowley, Philip Duprey, 2:19.56 for the two runs; 15th, United States team of William Hickey, Howard Clifton, Michael Luce, and Paul Savage, 2:20.37.

TEAM PERSONNEL
BOBSLED

Howard Clifton, Elnora, N.Y.
Robert Crowley, Saranac Lake, N.Y.
Dr. David K. Dunn, Elm Grove, Wis.
Philip M. Duprey, Raybrook, N.Y.
A/1C J. James Hickey, USAF, Plattsburgh, N.Y.
William D. Hickey, Keeseville, N.Y.
Adr/2 Robert W. Huscher, USN, Valley Stream, N.Y.
Lt. Paul E. Lamey, USN, Manchester, N.H.
Michael L. Luce, Keene Valley, N.Y.
Boris Said, Jr., Fair Haven, Vt.
Paul D. Savage, Ausable Forks, N.Y.
A/1C Gary J. Sheffield, USAF, Lake Placid, N.Y.
A/1C Howard B. Siler, USAF, Newport News, Va.
A/1C Charles E. Timm, USAF, Neenah, Wiss.

Staff Personnel
Patrick H. Martin, Massena, N.Y. (Manager)
James E. Lamy, Saranac Lake, N.Y. (Coach)

FIGURE SKATING
(MEN AND WOMEN)

United States figure skaters returned to their usual top ranking in the sport with Peggy Fleming and Tim Wood leading the way. La Belle Peggy, world champion and heavy favorite in the ladies' singles, was simply magnificent, not only building up a commanding lead in the compulsories, but clearly dominating the field in the freestyle as probably no other champion ever has.

Tim Wood, after ranking a close second in the compulsories, had a chance to pick up enough points in the freestyle to possibly win the gold in the men's singles. But his third place finish in these rankings dropped him to the runner-up spot in the overall competition.

Albertina Noyes, like Peggy Fleming a holdover from 1964, improved greatly on her Innsbruck debut to place fourth in the ladies' singles. Two other 1964 Olympians, Cynthia and Ron Kauffman, had two bad falls and could place only sixth in the pairs.

United States placings:

Ladies' singles – Peggy Fleming, 1st, 1970.5 points; Albertina Noyes, 4th, 1797.3; Janet Lynn, 9th, 1698.7.

Men singles – Tim Wood, 2nd, 1891.1 points; Gary Visconti, 5th, 1810.2; John Petkevich, 6th, 1806.2.

Pairs – Cynthia and Ron Kauffman, 6th, 297.0 points; Sandi Sue Sweitzer and Roy Wagelein, 7th, 294.5; Alicia Starbuck and Kenneth Shelley, 13th, 276.0.

TEAM PERSONNEL

FIGURE SKATING (MEN & WOMEN)

Peggy Gale Fleming, Colorado Springs, Colo. (singles)
Cynthia Kauffman, Seattle, Wash. (pairs-A)
Ronald Kauffman, Seattle, Wash. (pairs-A)
Janet Lynn, Rockford, Ill. (singles)
Albertina Noyes, Arlington, Mass. (singles)
John Petkevich, Great Falls, Mont. (singles)
Kenneth Shelley, Downey, Calif. (pairs-C)
Alicia Starbuck, Downey, Calif. (pairs-C)
Sandi Sue Sweitzer, Burbank, Calif. (pairs-B)
Gary Visconti, Detroit, Mich. (singles)
Roy Wagelein, Los Angeles, Calif. (pairs-B)
Timothy Lyle Wood, Bloomfield Hills, Mich. (singles).

Staff Personnel

John R. Shoemaker, San Francisco, Calif. (Manager)
Carl W. Gram, New York, N.Y. (Assistant Manager)

IOC president Avery Brundage awards the figure skating gold medal to Peggy Fleming.

K. Shelley   A. Starbuck   S. Sweitzer

FIGURE SKATING (MEN AND WOMEN)

P. Fleming   C. Kauffman   R. Kauffman

G. Visconti   R. Wagelein   T. Wood

J. Lynn   A. Noyes   J. Petkevich

J. Shoemaker   C. Gram

H. Brooks   J. Cunniff   J. Dale

C. Falkman   R. Gaudreau   P. Hurley

T. Hurley   L. Lilyholm   J. Logue

J. Morrison   L. Nanne   R. Paradise

L. Pleau   B. Riutta   D. Ross

P. Rupp   L. Stordahl   D. Volmar

Williamson   D. Neiderkorn   D. Clark

ICE HOCKEY

The United States missed a fifth-place rating in the final Class A ice hockey standings when it was held to a 1–1 tie by Finland in the final game of the championship division round robin. Never ranked as a title threat in pre-Games speculation, the USA sextet won two games, lost four and tied one.

Although a nucleus of the athletes trained together in the Minneapolis-St. Paul area, Coach Murray Williamson had a difficult task in moulding a winning team from a relatively inexperienced squad. Lack of international competitive experience was also apparent and the handicaps were simply too much to overcome.

The first match pitted the United States against Czechoslovakia, eventual silver medalist, and after a 1–1 deadlock in the first period, the Czechs scored twice in each of the remaining periods to win, 5–2. Eventual fourth-place winner Sweden was the next foe and in a rough game, the Americans were beaten, 4–3. The first period was scoreless, and both teams traded goals twice before the Swedes broke loose for a 4–2 lead in the second period.

The going got worse in the third match since the incomparable Soviet Union team was the foe. The Russians took advantage of a weakened USA lineup when either one or two players sat in the penalty box to roll up a 6–0 advantage in the first period. Russia outscored the USA, 4–2, in the next period but the last period went without a tally for either side, when Pat Rupp took over as USA goalie. The one bright spot for the Americans came when defenseman Don Ross scored, the first goal tallied against the Soviet Union in the tournament.

Traditional foe Canada squeaked out a 3–2 win over the USA by scoring two last period goals. The USA had led, 2–1, in the first period on goals by Larry Pleau and Bruce Riutta.

Then things brightened. A win over West Germany by an 8–1 score was followed by a 4–2 conquest of East Germany. With a chance to place fifth, the USA played Finland but a 1–1 deadlock achieved in the first period held up to the end. For all games, goalie Pat Rupp had 184 saves to lead his team in that department. Pleau scored two goals and four assists to lead the team in points.

TEAM PERSONNEL

ICE HOCKEY

Herbert Paul Brooks, St. Paul, Minn.
John Paul Cunniff, Boston, Mass.
John Byron Dale, St. Paul, Minn.
Craig Falkman, Golden Valley, Minn.
Robert R. Gaudreau, Providence, R.I.
Paul M. Hurley, St. Paul, Minn.
Thomas F. Hurley, Bloomington, Minn.
Leonard P. Lilyholm, St. Paul, Minn.
James B. Logue, North Andover, Mass.
John L. Morrison, Minneapolis, Minn.
Louis V. Nanne, Minneapolis, Minn.
Robert H. Paradise, St. Paul, Minn.
Pfc. Lawrence W. Pleau, USA,
  Ft. Campbell, Ky.
Bruce Riutta, Houghton, Mich.
Donald F. Ross, St. Paul, Minn.
Patrick L. Rupp, Minneapolis, Minn.
Larry D. Stordahl, Edina, Minn.
Douglas S. Volmar, Minneapolis, Minn.

Staff Personnel

Murray R. Williamson, Minneapolis, Minn.
  (Coach and Manager)
Donald L. Neiderkorn, South St. Paul, Minn.
  (Assistant)
Donald M. Clark, Cumberland, Wis.
  (Asst. Manager)

LUGE (MEN AND WOMEN)

Prospects for high ranking in the sport of luge never were bright for the USA. First of all, there were no Olympic-type facilities in the States and the squad could not get in much training at a Canadian base before departing on a tour of Europe to gain much-needed experience. Not much help was gained on the tour because of lack of training time, and even in Grenoble, unseasonably warm weather often prevented use of the Olympic run for pre-competition testing. The weather conditions also caused many postponements of the official competition. Disputes over alleged infractions of the rules also helped spoil what could have been a spectacular round.

The ladies representing the USA had less than two years of any kind of luging experience, placing 14th, 16th, and 17th in a small field of 21 entries for the singles. Against the vastly-experienced European entries, the USA cause was a doomed one.

At one time, the men's two-seater races were cancelled and the USA sleds were packed up and shipped home. The races were suddenly rescheduled at the last moment, and one USA pair got to the starting line but could not qualify during the practice runs. In men singles, the highest ranking for the USA was 26th.

United States placings:
Men's singles (four-run total) Kim Layton, 26th, 2:58.64; Jim Murray, 28th, 3:00.00; Michael Hessel, 30th,

3:00.62; Robin Partch, 46the, 3:29.67.

Men's pairs – United States entries did not qualify.

Ladies singles (four-run total) – Kathleen Roberts, 14th, 2:33.60; Ellen Williams, 16th, 2:35.15; Sheila Johansen, 17th, 2:35.47.

TEAM PERSONNEL
LUGE (MEN & WOMEN)

J. Michael Hessel, Eugene, Ore.
Lt. Lewis J. Janousek, USAF, Dallas, Texas
Sheila M. Johansen, Billings, Mont.
A/1C Kim Alfred Layton, USAF, Tahoe City, Calif.
James E. Moriarty, St. Paul, Minn.
James D. Murray, Avon, Mont.
A/1C Terrance E. O'Brien, USAF, South Portland, Maine
Robin T. Partch, St. Cloud, Minn.
A/2C Robert B. Pettit, USAF, Spokane, Wash.
Kathleen A. Roberts, Miles City, Mont.
Ellen Williams, Old Tappan, N.J.

Staff Personnel
David G. Rivenes, Miles City, Mont. (Manager)
Sgt. Maj. Volley Cole, USA, Portland, Oregon (Team Advisor)
Capt. Bruce Medley, USAF, Billings, Mont. (Coach)
Francis Feltman, Sun Valley, Idaho (Asst. Coach)

SKIING — ALPINE (MEN AND WOMEN)

Best performances in the men's alpine competitions are credited to Vladimir "Spider" Sabich, Jim Heuga, Billy Kidd and Rick Chaffee. Sabich placed fifth in the slalom with Heuga seventh and Chaffee ninth. Kidd did not finish his heat in the slalom and was disqualified. However he led the USA in the giant slalom with a fifth place finish.

Men's downhill – Billy Kidd, 18th, 2:03.40; Dennis McCoy, 21st, 2:04.82.

Men's slalom – Vladimir Sabich, 5th, 1:40.49; Jimmy Heuga, 7th, 1:40.91; Frederick Chaffee, 9th, 1:41.19. Note – Billy Kidd fell and did not finish.

Men's giant slalom – Billy Kidd, 5th, 3:32.37; Jimmy Heuga, 10th, 3:33.89; Vladimir Sabich, 14th, 3:36.15; Frederick Chaffee, 15th, 3:36.19.

Hopes for success in the women's events were thwarted by (1) a severe leg injury to Robin Morning before the competition; (2) injuries in practice which slowed down the development of Wendy Allen; and (3) a dislocated shoulder suffered by Karen Budge on her way to the starting line in the downhill, an unfortunate freak accident. Nonetheless the highest finishes for USA girls were a 12th in the giant slalom for Judy Nagel, a last minute addition to the team, and a 17th in

the downhill by Christina "Kiki" Cutter, also a late entry.

Biggest misfortune was sustained in the slalom. At the end of the first run, the USA had all four girls in the first seven positions. Then a review of films taken of the competition disqualified all but Miss Nagel for having missed one or more gates. Miss Nagel, shaken by the setback to her teammates and under the ensuing pressure of having the best time of all qualifiers for the second run, missed an early gate in the final and also was disqualified.

Women's downhill – Kiki Cutter, 17th, 1:44.94; Sandra Shellworth, 21st, 1:46.53; Suzanne Chaffee, 28th, 1:48.50.

LUGE (MEN AND WOMEN)

 J. Hessel
 L. Janousek
S. Johansen

 K. Layton
 J. Moriarty
 J. Murray

 T. O'Brien
 R. Partch
 R. Pettit

 K. Roberts
 E. Williams
 D. Rivenes

 V. Cole
 B. Medley
 F. Feltman

SKIING-ALPINE (MEN AND WOMEN)

W. Allen
J. Barrows
K. Budge

F. Chaffee
 S. Chaffee
 C. Cutter

 J. Elliott
 R. Fortna
J. Heuga

 W. Kidd
 D. McCoy
 R. Morning

 J. Nagel
 V. Sabich
S. Shellworth

 R. Beattie
 J. Barrier
G. Eaton

 C. Ferries

307

L. Damon

Ehrensbeck

M. Elliott

W. Hampton

C. Merrill

A. Tokle

M. Gallagher

E. Gillette

R. Gray

J. Caldwell

C. Kellogg

G. Krog

J. Lufkin

C. Matis

W. Bakke

J. Balfanz

J. Martin

D. Norby

J. Rand

A. Watt

J. Bower

M. Devecka

J. Miller

J. Speck

T. Upham

Note – Karen Budge was injured before starting and did not compete.

Women's slalom – Kiki Cutter, Rosie Fortna and Wendy Allen disqualified on first run; Judy Nagel disqualified on second run; all for missing gates.

Women's giant slalom – Judy Nagel, 12th, 1:57.39; Suzanne Chaffee, 17th, 1:58.38; Kiki Cutter, 21st, 1:59.52; Wendy Allen, 22nd, 2:00.03.

Only once before, in 1956, were USA girls blanked in medal quests. However, for the men, the only medals ever won were in 1964 when Billy Kidd and Jimmy Heuga won silver and bronze medals respectively in the slalom. That same year, Jean Saubert won a silver in the women's giant slalom and a bronze in the slalom.

TEAM PERSONNEL
SKIING-ALPINE (MEN & WOMEN)

Wendy Allen, San Pedro, Calif.
James Barrows, Steamboat Springs, Colo.
Karen Budge, Jackson, Wyo.
Frederick Chaffee, Rutland, Vt.
Suzanne Chaffee, Rutland, Vt.
Christina Cutter, Bend, Ore.
Jere Elliot, Steamboat, Springs, Colo.
Rosie Fortna, Warren, Vt.
James Heuga, Squaw Valley, Calif.
William Kidd, Stowe, Vt.
Dennis McCoy, Bishop, Calif.
*Robin Morning, Santa Monica, Calif.
Judy Ann Nagel, Enumclaw, Wash.
Vladimir Sabich, Kyburz, Calif.
Sandra Shellworth, Boise, Idaho

Staff Personnel

Robert Beattie, Boulder, Colo.
　(Coach and Team Leader)
James Barrier, Yakima, Wash. (Manager)
Pfc. Gordon Eaton, USA, Littleton, N.H.
　(Men's Coach)
Charles Ferries, Boulder, Colo.
　(Women's Coach)
*Injured prior to competition and entry withdrawn

SKIING — NORDIC

In all but the jumping events, Nordic ski representatives from the United States improved on 1964 showings, though the results were still far away from high rankings. The best US performance in the men's 15,000 meter cross country race was 34th place, four steps higher than four years ago. In the 30,000 meter run, the US ranking rose three places to 27th and in the 50,000 meter test, the ranking was 22nd as compared to 28th in 1964. The 4 x 10,000 meter relay team also improved one step, ranking 12th. But 33rd and 34th places in the 70 and 90 meter special jumping events, respectively, fell far below the performance of four years ago.

In the Nordic combined test (cross country and jumping), the USA's best was 13th place, two rungs higher than 1964's showing. No entries were placed in the women's cross country events.

United States placings:

15,000 meter cross country – Michael Gallagher, 34th, 52:02.4; Michael Elliott, 41st, 52:40.8; Robert Gray, 48th, 53:24.8; Lawrence Damon, 55th, 55:07.2.

30,000 meter cross country – Gallagher, 27th, 1:41.58.2.; Elliott, 29th, 1:42.22.6; Charles Kellogg, 51st, 1:50.03.7; Jon Lufkin, 55th, 1:51:21.2.

50,000 meter cross country – Gallagher, 22nd, 2:36:26.1; Elliott, 30th, 2:40:38.5; Damon, 32nd, 2:41:25.2; Kellogg, 36th, 2:44:00.4.

4 x 10,000 meter cross country relay – The United States team of Gallagher, Elliott, Gray and John Bower finished 12th in 2:21:30.4.

Nordic Combined (15,000 meter cross country and 70 meter jumping) – John Bower, 13th, 411.16 points; Georg Krog, 22nd, 383.76; James Miller, 26th, 378.38; Thomas Upham, 39th, 325.17.

70 meter special jumping – John Balfanz, 33rd, 189.7 points; William Bakke, 40th, 180.8; Jay Rand, 42nd, 178.4. No other placings.

90 meter special jumping – Bakke, 34th, 175.5 points; Rand, 35th, 174.7; Balfanz, 42nd, 169.8; Jay Martin, 43rd, 163.8.

TEAM PERSONNEL
SKIING-NORDIC
Cross Country

Lawrence Damon, Burlington, Vt.
*Cpl. John Robert Ehrensbeck, USA, Utica, N.Y.
2/Lt. Michael Elliott, USA, Durango, Colo.
Michael Gallagher, Killington, Vt.

SPEED SKATING (MEN AND WOMEN)

The men and women speed skaters earned the most medals for the USA, five in all, and performed very well even in those events where medals escaped their efforts. This reflected well on the Olympic development program and the intensive training afforded by the splendid facilities at West Allis, Wisconsin, site of the only Olympic-style artificially refrigerated track in the US.

No medal winner earned an accolade more than Terry McDermott, the USA's defending champion in the men's 500 meters. It is doubtful if a title holder ever had to give it a bolder try. The weather conditions were against Terry. He was skating last in a field of 14 pairs with the sun high overhead and beaming down on the track, turning the ice into a spongy mush.

It was apparent that Terry was going to make a truly great attempt, even against bad ice conditions and four years of relative inactivity. When he took his place at the start, determination bulged his jaw and one could sense this was an all-out attempt. He tossed away his skating cap, dug in, and then flashed down the starting straightaway. His time was 10.1 seconds for the first 100 meters, an indication that this could be a winning race if the pace was maintained.

The luck of the draw had placed him on the inside track at the start, requiring him to cross over and skate the final 250 meters on the outside – a tricky maneuver which can cost valuable fractions of seconds in time. But

Dianne Holum won a silver medal in 500 meter speed skating and a bronze in the 1000.

no obstacle or challenge was too much for the "old man" of the team on this St. Valentine's Day morning. With his wife and mother in the stands cheering him on, he rounded the far turn after the crossover, then headed down the final straightaway, fighting time and fatigue. Finally in the last 40 meters, he faded ever so slightly but just enough to keep him from the gold medal. His time of 40.5 seconds was just two-tenths of a second from the eventual champion, Erhard Keller of West Germany.

After the race, one member of the press said to him, "Terry, it was a gutsy race." Terry's reply was typical: "That's the way I skate." Gold medalist Keller paid McDermott a great tribute in a post-race interview. "What Terry did today was sheer guts," said the young dental student. "If he had started in the earlier heats while the ice was still good, I'd have lost. It's as simple as that."

Opening day of the speed skating competitions found the US 500 meters sprinters magnificent in the women's division. Mary Meyers, a junior at the University of Minnesota and the 1967 world champion, was off with the second pair and immediately placed her name at the top of the scoreboard with a splendid 46.3 clocking. Seven pairs later, Ludmila Titova, 21-year old all-events champion from the

Soviet Union, sped around the oval to take over first place with a 46.1-second clocking. This eventually proved good enough for the gold medal, but the USA still challenged strongly.

In the very next heat, 16-year-old Dianne Holum, a Northbrook, Ill. high school student, tucked her long flowing brown locks under her skating cap and burst into an all-out effort. She fell just short, but her time of 46.3 put her into a second place tie with teammate Mary Meyers.

There was no more excitement until the final pair, when the Soviet star, Irina Egorova, raced the USA's Jennifer Fish, an 18-year-old Baldwin-Wallace college freshman. The crowd roared with approval when Miss Fish turned in a flashy 46.3 clocking to effect a triple USA deadlock for silver medal honors, the first time in history that three skaters from one nation had achieved that feat.

Two days later, Miss Holum provided the US with a bronze medal by finishing third in the women's 1000 meters, beaten only by Holland's Carolina Geijssen and the Soviet Union's Titova.

The men showed slight improvement, with the top entry in the 1500 meters finishing 19th as compared to 25th four years ago. In the 10,000 meters, the US scored 21st and 25th as compared to 30th at Innsbruck.

SPEED SKATING (MEN AND WOMEN)

J. Ashworth   N. Blatchford   R. Capan

D. Carroll   W. Cox   T. Dorgan

J. Fish   T. Gray   D. Holum

W. Lanigan   LeBombard   T. McDermott

M. Meyers   Omelenchuk   M. Passarella

E. Rudolph   J. Wurster   R. Wurster

G. Howie   K. Henry

United States placings:

Ladies 500 meters – Mary Meyers, Jennifer Fish and Dianne Holum all tied for 2nd, each with a time of 46.3 seconds.

Ladies 1000 meters – Dianne Holum, 3rd, 1:33.4; Jeanne Ashworth, 7th, 1:34.7; Jennifer Fish, 23rd, 1:38.4.

Ladies 1500 meters – Dianne Holum, 13th, 2:28.5; Jeanne Ashworth, 16th, 2:30.3; Mrs. Jeanne Omelenchuk, 25th, 2:35.5.

Ladies 3000 meters – Jeanne Ashworth, 10th, 5:14.0; Mrs. Jeanne Omelenchuk, 11th, 5:14.9; Toy Dorgan, 14th, 5:17.6.

Men's 500 meters – Terry McDermott, 2nd, (tied with Magne Thomassen, Norway), 40.5; Neil Blatchford and John Wurster, 5th, (tied with Arne Herjuanet, Norway) 40.7; Thomas Gray, 21st, 41.6.

Men's 1500 meters – Richard Wurster, 19th, 2:08.4; Wayne LeLombard, 23rd, 2:11.2; William Lanigan, 24th, 2:11.7; Roger Capan, 34th, 2:13.6.

Men's 5000 meters – Lanigan, 24th, 7:57.7; William Cox, 25th, 7:58.1; LeBombard, 28th, 8:03.8.

Men's 10,000 meters – Lanigan, 21st, 16:50.1; Cox, 25th, 17:08.2.

TEAM PERSONNEL
SPEED SKATING (MEN & WOMEN)

Jeanne Ashworth, Wilmington, N.Y.
Neil Blatchford, Northbrook, Ill.
Roger Capan, Champaign, Ill.
Daniel J. Carroll, St. Louis, Mo.
William Cox, St. Paul, Minn.
Toy Joan Dorgan, Springfield, Ill.
Jennifer Fish, Strongsville, Ohio
A/1C Thomas J. Gray, USAF, Milwaukee, Wis.
Dianne Holum, Northbrook, Ill.
William Lanigan, Bronx, N.Y.
Wayne LeBombard, West Allis, Wis.
Terry McDermott, Birmingham, Mich.
Mary Margaret Meyers, St. Paul, Minn.
Mrs. Jeanne Omelenchuk, Warren, Mich.
Michael Passarella, Chicago, Ill.
Edward Rudolph, Northbrook, Ill.
John Wurster, Ballston Spa, N.Y.
Richard Wurster, Ballston Spa, N.Y.

Staff Personnel

Gordon E. Howie, Oconomowoc, Wis. (Manager)
Kenneth C. Henry, Lake Bluff, Ill. (Coach)

V PAN-AMERICAN GAMES · WINNIPEG, CANADA
JULY 23 - AUGUST 6, 1967

It was the very last gold medal to be awarded and, added to the staggering total amassed in a sweeping harvest by United States athletes at the Vth Pan-American Games, it might well have been dismissed as merely another statistic in the final accounting . . . except for one thing!

It was emblematic of a championship never before achieved in Pan-American competition, a triumph long overdue and, to the followers of USA athletic fortunes, the most satisfying of scores of brilliant performances by the 429 men and women who represented this nation in the fifth staging of the Western Hemisphere sports extravaganza.

When the United States defeated Cuba in a playoff series to win the baseball crown for the first time, it not only provided a storybook finish for the record but, without question, was the highlight of the exciting and well-conducted international sports carnival held in Winnipeg, Canada, July 23 through August 6, 1967.

All told, the United States captured 120 gold medals, 63 silvers, and 42 bronzes, easily dominating the Games which included competition in 22 different sports and five more exclusively for women. To some observers, this seemed to be an embarrassment of riches, yet the competition was the fiercest in Pan-American Games history. The USA entered its best available talent in all phases of the program and while its strength overcame the challenges of 27 other nations, the tests were rigid, attesting to the upward surge of abilities in those countries.

The United States was the only nation to enter a full complement of athletes, and only one of the 332 men listed, pole vaulter Paul Wilson, missed competition, illness preventing his participation. As expected the USA dominated the sports of athletics (track and field), swimming and diving, fencing, gymnastics, judo, rowing, shooting, weightlifting, wrestling, and yachting, while also triumphing in such team sports as baseball, men's basketball, men's and women's volleyball and water polo. Only in the sport of soccer football were USA efforts unrewarded by a medal.

The total of 225 medals does not constitute a record, however, since the USA tallied 245 in the 1959 Games at Chicago. Just the same, the total for 1967 is just as impressive. Both in 1959 and in 1967, the USA tallied 120 gold medals, but in 1959 nations were permitted to enter three athletes in each of the track and field and each of the swimming and diving events, instead of the present limit of two each.

In the 1955 Games at Mexico City, the USA gleaned 182 medals, including 87 golds, and in 1963 at Sao Paulo, Brazil, the total was 193, including 109 first place awards. Only in 1951 when the Games were inaugurated in Buenos Aires, Argentina, did the USA total fail to lead the way. Argentina amassed 153 medals while the USA, with a comparatively token entry of only 126 athletes, was second with 97, including 46 golds.

The Vth Pan-American Games got away impressively on Sunday, July 23, despite a heavy rainstorm. More than 22,000 persons jammed the main stadium to capacity to witness the opening ceremonies and to cheer Prince Philip, representing Queen Elizabeth, as he stood bareheaded throughout the downpour to greet the nations as they paraded on to the field.

The 28 nations participating marched through the rain in parade finery and just when the Canadian delegation appeared, last in line because it was the host, the sun broke out and provided a shining finish to the rituals. The United States, dressed in colorful attire, was led by Don Schollander, four gold medal winner swimmer in the 1964 Olympic Games at Tokyo, as flag bearer.

Two weeks later, August 6, a near capacity crowd again thronged the main stadium to witness the final sports event, the Grand Prix des Nations equestrian jumping competitions, and then join in the closing ceremonies. In contrast to the opening day weather, the sun shone brilliantly throughout the day. Carrying the USA flag in the final assembly of athletes was Ralph Boston, Pan-American and former Olympic long jump champion.

Trials to select the USA athletes were held in Minneapolis, Minnesota, imme-diately prior to the Games. Finals were staged in 12 sports and squads chosen earlier in the other sports joined together for training prior to departure for Winnipeg.

America's Randy Matson, who is the world recordholder in the shot put, easily won the competition at Winnipeg with a Pan-Am record toss of 65-1, which was more than a foot better than the silver medalist's best.

Before the Games opened, the Pan-American Sports Organization (PASO) held its formal meetings and selected Cali, Colombia, as the site for the VIth Pan-American Games. Cali, a city of 800,000 located about 3000 feet above sea level, will hold the Games in late July or early August of 1971.

In the voting for the site selection, Cali narrowly edged out Champ, Missouri, an industrial community adjacent to St. Louis, which had sought the honor.

A review of accomplishments in each sport follows:

DISTRIBUTION OF UNITED STATES MEDALS WON AT FIFTH PAN-AMERICAN GAMES IN 1967

(1) G	(2) S	(3) B	(4)	(5)	(6)	Medal Totals Only	Classification	(1) G	(2) S	(3) B	Total
22	13	4	3	0	0	39	*Athletics-Men	28	13	4	45
8	5	2	2	1	1	15	*Athletics-Women	8	5	2	15
1	0	0	0	0	0	1	Baseball	18	0	0	18
1	0	0	0	0	0	1	Basketball-Men	12	0	0	12
0	1	0	0	0	0	1	Basketball-Women	0	12	0	12
3	0	4	0	0	0	7	Boxing	3	0	4	7
0	1	3	2	0	0	4	Cycling	0	1	6	7
3	2	1	2	2	0	6	Equestrian M&W	6	7	1	14
4	4	1	2	0	1	9	Fencing M&W	13	7	1	21
0	0	1	0	0	0	1	Field Hockey (Men)	0	0	16	16
6	4	6	1	1	2	16	Gymnastics-Men	10	4	6	20
5	5	4	5	5	3	14	Gymnastics-Women	9	5	4	18
2	2	2	0	0	0	6	Judo	2	2	2	6
6	1	0	0	0	0	7	Rowing	25	1	0	26
11	3	2	1	0	0	16	Shooting M&W	28	3	2	33
0	0	0	0	0	1	0	Soccer Football	0	0	0	0
14	9	6	0	0	1	29	Swimming-Diving (M)	23	9	6	38
14	9	4	2	0	0	27	Swimming-Diving (W)	20	9	4	33
2	2	2	1	0	0	6	Tennis M&W	4	2	2	8
1	0	0	0	0	0	1	Volleyball-Men	12	0	0	12
1	0	0	0	0	0	1	Volleyball-Women	12	0	0	12
1	0	0	0	0	0	1	Water Polo	10	0	0	10
5	0	0	0	0	0	5	Weightlifting	5	0	0	5
8	0	0	0	0	0	8	Wrestling	8	0	0	8
2	2	0	0	0	0	4	Yachting M&W	5	3	0	8
120	63	42	21	9	9	225	Totals	261	83	60	404

PERSONNEL OF UNITED STATES DELEGATION AT FIFTH PAN-AMERICAN GAMES 1967

Sport classification	Athletes M	W	T	Managers M	W	T	Coaches M	W	T	*Technical M	W	T	Overall M	W	T
Athletics (Track & Field)	46	22	68	3	1	4	6	0	6	0	0	0	55	23	78
Baseball	18	0	18	1	0	1	2	0	2	0	0	0	21	0	21
Basketball	12	12	24	1	1	2	3	1	4	0	0	0	16	14	30
Boxing	10	0	10	1	0	1	2	0	2	0	0	0	13	0	13
+Canoeing	9	5	14	1	0	1	1	0	1	0	0	0	11	5	16
Cycling	16	0	16	1	0	1	2	0	2	1	0	1	20	0	20
Equestrian	6	5	11	1	0	1	2	0	2	1	0	1	10	5	15
Fencing	12	4	16	2	0	2	2	0	2	1	0	1	17	4	21
Field Hockey	16	0	16	2	0	2	0	0	0	0	0	0	18	0	18
Gymnastics	6	7	13	2	0	2	1	1	2	0	1	0	9	9	18
Judo	6	0	6	1	0	1	1	0	1	0	0	0	8	0	8
Rowing	32	0	32	2	0	2	2	0	2	1	0	1	37	0	37
Shooting	23	1	24	2	0	2	0	0	0	3	0	3	28	1	29
Soccer Football	18	0	18	1	0	1	1	0	1	0	0	0	20	0	20
Swimming & Diving	25	26	51	3	2	5	6	0	6	0	0	0	34	28	62
Tennis	3	3	6	1	0	1	0	0	0	0	0	0	4	3	7
Volleyball	12	12	24	1	1	2	2	0	2	0	0	0	15	13	28
Water Polo	10	0	10	1	0	1	2	0	2	0	0	0	13	0	13
Weightlifting	7	0	7	1	0	1	1	0	1	0	0	0	9	0	9
Wrestling	8	0	8	1	0	1	1	0	1	0	0	0	10	0	10
Yachting	7	1	8	1	0	1	0	0	0	1	0	1	9	1	10
Medical Services													3	2	5
Trainers													8	2	10
Student managers													32	0	32
USOC Administration & Staff													32	4	36
Overall totals	302	98	400	38	5	43	37	2	39	8	1	9	452	114	566

* includes armorers for shooting and fencing, riggers for boats, pianist for gymnastics, mechanic for cycling, veterinarian for equestrian.

+ sport of canoeing was held as Olympic demonstration event and no official medals were awarded.

Note: A total of 15 grooms including stable manager (13 men, 2 women) were with equestrian team but not accredited as official members of the USA delegation.

UNITED STATES MEDALISTS IN 1967 PAN-AMERICAN GAMES GOLD MEDAL WINNERS

(*) Retained 1963 Pan-American Games Championship

ATHLETICS (Track & Field) — MEN (25)

WADE BELL, 800 meters; *RALPH BOSTON, long jump; JERRY BRIGHT, 4 x 100 relay; JOHN CARLOS, 200 meters; GARY CARLSEN, discus; ED CARUTHERS, high jump; RON COPELAND; 4 x 100 relay; FRANK COVELLI, javelin; CHARLES CRAIG, triple jump; LEE EVANS, 400 meters and 4 x 400 relay; THOMAS GAGE, hammer throw; RON LAIRD, 20,000 meter walk; J. RANDEL MATSON, shot put; VINCENT MATHEWS, 4 x 400 relay; EARL MC CULLOUCH, 110 meter hurdles and 4 x 100 relay; CHRIS MC CUBBINS, 3000 meter steeplechase; VAN NELSON, 5000 & 10,000 meters; BOB SEAGREN, pole vault; ELBERT STINSON, 4 x 400 relay; EMMETT TAYLOR, 4 x 400 relay; WILLIAM A. TOOMEY, decathlon; WILLIE TURNER, 4 x 100 relay; THOMAS VON RUDEN, 1500 meters; RON WHITNEY, 400 meter hurdles, and LARRY YOUNG, 50,000 meter walk.

ATHLETICS (Track & Field) — WOMEN (8)

BARBARA FERRELL, 100 meters; BARBARA ANN FRIEDRICH, javelin; MADELINE MANNING, 800 meters; *ELEANOR MONTGOMERY, high jump; CAROL JEAN MOSEKE, discus; MRS. CHERRIE SHERRARD, 80 meter hurdles; WYOMIA TYUS, 200 meters, and MRS. BILLIE PAT WINSLOW, pentathlon.

BASEBALL (18)

RAYMOND BLOSSE, P.; DANIEL CARLSON, C.; JOHN CURTIS, P.; LT. BARRY DeBOLT, USA, P.; DENNIS LAMB, 3B; GEORGE GREER, OF; JACK KRAUS, OF; MICHAEL LISETSKI, 2B; MARK MARQUESS, 1B; TIMOTHY PLODINEC, P.; JOSEPH SADELFELD, P.; LT. KENNETH SMITH, SS; STEVEN SOGGE, C & 3B; JAMES SPENCER, OF; PAUL SPLITTORFF, P.; KENNETH SZOTKIEWICZ, SS; TAYLOR TOOMEY, P.; WILLIAM A. WRIGHT III, C.

BASKETBALL — MEN (12)

RAY CAREY, DAREL CARRIER, JOHN CLAWSON, USA, LLOYD DOVE, CALVIN FOWLER, Captain; HENRY LOGAN, KENDALL RHINE, LT. MICHAEL SILLIMAN, USA, STEVE SULLIVAN, WESTLEY UNSELD, JOSEPH H. (Jo Jo) WHITE, and JAMES WILLIAMS.

BOXING (3)

SGT. ARTHUR REDDEN, USMC, light heavyweight; JAMES WALLINGTON, USA, light welterweight; FOREST WARD, heavyweight.

EQUESTRIAN (6)

Individual

MRS. KYRA DOWNTON, dressage; J. MICHAEL PLUMB, Three-Day Event.

Team

ERNEST R. ECKHARDT, MICHAEL O. PAGE, J. MICHAEL PLUMB, JAMES C. WOFFORD, Three-Day Event.

FENCING (13)

Individual

ANTHONY KEANE, Sabre.

Team

HARRIET KING, MAXINE MITCHELL, JANICE-LEE ROMARY, VERONICA SMITH, Women's Foil. FRANK ANGER, PAUL PESTHY, RALPH SPINELLA, CARL BORACK, Men's Epee. THOMAS BALLA, WALTER FARBER, ANTHONY KEANE, CSABA GALL, Men's Sabre.

GYMNASTICS — MEN (8)

Team

FRED ROETHLISBERGER, MARK COHN, DAVID THOR, RICHARD LOYD, ARNO LASCARI.

Individual

FRED ROETHLISBERGER — All-Around; Horizontal Bar; Parallel Bars (tie); RICHARD LOYD — Parallel Bars (tie); MARK COHN — Pommel Horse (Side Horse).

Army Sgt. First Class Edward Teague was on America's gold medalist rapid fire pistol shot team at the Pan-American Games.

GYMNASTICS — WOMEN (6)

Team

MARIE WALTHER, JOYCE TANAC, DEBORAH BAILEY, DONNA SCHAENZER, LINDA METHENY.

Individual

LINDA METHENY — All-Around; Floor Exercises; Side Horse Vault; Balance Beam.

ROWING (25)

Eights — IAN GARDINER, stroke; CURTIS CANNING, no. 7; ANDREW LARKIN, no. 6; SCOTT STEKETEE, no. 5; FRANKLIN HOBBS, no. 4; JACQUES FIECHTER, no. 3; CLEVE LIVINGSTON, no. 2; DAVID HIGGINS, bow, and PAUL HOFFMAN, coxswain.
Fours with Coxswain — HUGH FOLEY, bow; CLEM KOPF, no. 2; JOSEPH HENWOOD, no. 3; WILLIAM STOWE, stroke, and ROBERT ZIMONYI, coxswain.
Fours without Coxswain — SEAN SHEA, bow; LAWRENCE GLUCKMAN, no. 2; Lt. ROBERT BRAYTON, USAF, no. 3; Ens. LEE DEMAREST, USN, stroke.
Pairs with Coxswain — GARDINER CADWALADER, PERRY MEEK, and JAMES FUHRMAN, coxswain.
Pairs without Coxswain — ANTHONY JOHNSON and Ens. LAWRENCE HOUGH, USN.
Double Sculls — JAMES DIETZ and JAMES STORM.

JUDO (2)

ALLEN JAMES COAGE, heavyweight; HAYWARD NISHIOKA, middleweight.

SHOOTING (28)

Individual

Free Pistol — Staff Sgt. HERSHEL ANDERSON, USA.
Center Fire Pistol — FRANCIS HIGGINSON, USMC.
Skeet — LT. ALLEN W. MORRISON, USMC.
Small Bore Rifle — LT. MARGARET L. THOMPSON, USA.

Team

Free Pistol — S/Sgt. HERSHEL ANDERSON, USA; Major FRANKLIN GREEN, USAF; S/Sgt. ARNOLD VITARBO, USA; M/Sgt. WILLIAM BLANKENSHIP, USA.
Small Bore Rifle — Capt. BRUCE MEREDITH, USA; GARY ANDERSON; Capt. RHODY NORNBERG, USAF; DAVID ROSS III.
Rapid Fire Pistol — Major WILLIAM McMILLAN, USMC; SFC EDWIN TEAGUE, USA; M/Sgt. WILLIAM BLANKENSHIP, USA; SFC AUBREY SMITH, USA.
Small Bore Rifle (Three Positions) — GARY ANDERSON, Lt. MARGARET THOMPSON, USA; Capt. BRUCE MEREDITH, USA; JOHN WRITER.
Center Fire Pistol — M/Sgt. WILLIAM BLANKENSHIP, USA; FRANCIS HIGGINSON, USMC; ADR 1 DONALD HAMILTON, USN; BONNIE HARMON.
Skeet — ROBERT RODALE, ROBERT SCHUEHLE, AOCS ALLEN BUNTROCK, USN; Lt. ALLEN MORRISON, USMC.
(continued)

DISTRIBUTION OF MEDALS AT FIFTH PAN-AMERICAN GAMES WINNIPEG, CANADA – 1967

ALL COMPETITIVE MEDAL PLACINGS * (Official listings)				Nation	ACTUAL MEDALS DISTRIBUTED * (See explanation below)			
1st	2nd	3rd	Total		1st	2nd	3rd	Total
120	63	42	225	UNITED STATES	262	83	60	405
12	37	43	92	Canada	12	84	76	172
8	14	26	48	Cuba	11	51	67	129
5	14	23	42	Mexico	22	33	52	107
9	14	11	34	Argentina	34	23	20	77
11	10	5	26	Brazil	27	36	10	73
2	2	3	7	Trinidad-Tobago	2	17	20	39
0	1	3	4	Panama	0	1	25	26
1	1	3	5	Puerto Rico	1	1	23	25
0	1	2	3	Bermuda	0	18	2	20
1	4	5	10	Venezuela	1	7	11	19
1	2	5	8	Colombia	1	2	11	14
0	2	1	3	Peru	0	13	1	14
1	1	3	5	Chile	3	1	6	10
0	0	3	3	Jamaica	0	0	9	9
0	1	4	5	Uruguay	0	1	7	8
0	1	2	3	Ecuador	0	2	4	6
0	1	0	1	Barbados	0	1	0	1
0	0	1	1	Guyana	0	0	1	1
0	0	1	1	Netherland-Antilles	0	0	1	1
171	169	185	525	**TOTALS	376	374	406	1156

Did not win medals – Guatemala, British Honduras, Paraguay, El Salvador, Virgin Islands.

* NOTE – In official medal placings, only one medal is credited to a nation winning a sport where team classification exists. For example, the United States won the gold medal in basketball; however, there were 12 players on the team, each of whom received a gold medal. Similarly, all medalists in team sports such as water polo (10), volleyball (12), baseball (18), field hockey (16), and soccer (18), were awarded. While the numbers varied with the sport, relay teams in swimming and athletics (track and field), crews in rowing and yachting, and teams in cycling, equestrian, fencing, gymnastics, shooting, tennis, also were recognized. As a result, the figures to the right of the above column indicate the ACTUAL number of medals distributed.
** Apparent discrepancy in these totals results from the fact that, in some championship finals, duplicate awards were made for first place, thus eliminating silver medals. This accounts for the apparent discrepancy in the totals. Also, in boxing and in judo, both the third and fourth place winners received bronze medals.

ALL TIME MEDAL PLACINGS – PAN-AMERICAN GAMES – 1951–1967 INCLUSIVE

Rank	Nation	(1st) Gold	(2nd) Silver	(3rd) Bronze	Total	Rank	Nation	(1st) Gold	(2nd) Silver	(3rd) Bronze	Total
1	UNITED STATES	482	274	186	942	17	Guatemala	1	2	5	8
2	Argentina	118	135	96	349	18	Ecuador	0	2	3	5
3	Canada	33	91	96	220	19	**British-Guiana	1	0	3	4
4	Mexico	35	53	111	199		Barbados	0	1	3	4
5	Brazil	40	58	52	150	21	Haiti	0	1	1	2
6	Cuba	24	41	53	118		Bahamas	2	0	0	2
7	Chile	22	31	41	94	23	Dominican Republic	1	0	0	1
8	Venezuela	6	23	28	57	24	Costa Rica	0	1	0	1
9	Uruguay	6	12	18	36	25	**Guyana	0	0	1	1
10	Peru	2	9	14	25						
11	Panama	2	7	11	20		Have not won medals				
12	Columbia	4	5	6	15		Paraguay	0	0	0	0
	*Jamaica	0	4	11	15		Virgin Islands	0	0	0	0
14	*West Indies Federation	2	4	8	14		British Honduras	0	0	0	0
15	*Trinidad-Tobago	3	5	5	13		El Salvador	0	0	0	0
16	Netherland-Antilles	0	5	7	12						

* Competed as federation of Jamaica, Trinidad, Tobago, and Barbados in Games of 1959.
** Competed as British Guiana until 1967.

313

SWIMMING — MEN (13)

MICHAEL BURTON, 1500 meter freestyle; GREGORY CHARLTON, 400 meter freestyle and 4 x 200 freestyle relay; F. MICHAEL FITZMAURICE, 4 x 100 freestyle relay; DON HAVENS, 100 meter freestyle; CHARLES HICKCOX, 100 meter backstroke and 4 x 100 medley relay; DOUGLAS RUSSELL, 200 meter individual medley and 4 x 100 medley relay; DONALD SCHOLLANDER, 200 meter freestyle and 4 x 100 and 4 x 200 freestyle relay; MARK SPITZ, 100 & 200 meter butterfly and 4 x 100 and 4 x 200 freestyle relay and 4 x 100 medley relay; WILLIAM UTLEY, 400 meter individual medley; KENNETH WALSH, 4 x 100 freestyle relay and 4 x 100 medley relay; RUSSELL WEBB, 4 x 100 medley relay.
BERNICE WRIGHTSON, Springboard; WIN YOUNG, Platform.

SWIMMING — WOMEN (12)

CATHARINE BALL, 100 & 200 meter breaststroke and 4 x 100 medley relay; ERIKA BRICKER, 100 meter freestyle; LESLEY BUSH, platform diving; PAM CARPINELLI, 4 x 100 freestyle relay; ELEANOR DANIEL, 100 meter butterfly and 4 x 100 medley relay; WENDY FORDYCE, 4 x 100 freestyle relay and 4 x 100 medley relay; SUE GOSSICK, springboard diving; LINDA GUSTAVSON, 4 x 100 freestyle relay; CLAUDIA KOLB, 200 & 400 meter individual medley and 200 meter butterfly; PAMELA KRUSE, 200 meter freestyle, 4 x 100 freestyle relay; DEBORAH MEYER, 400 & 800 meter freestyle; KENDIS MOORE, 4 x 100 medley relay.

TENNIS (3)

JANE ALBERT, women doubles and mixed doubles, captain; PATSY RIPPY, women doubles; Lt. ARTHUR ASHE, USA, mixed doubles.

VOLLEYBALL — MEN (12)

JOHN ALSTROM, ROBERT CLEM, WINTHROP DAVENPORT, H. SMITTY DUKE, captain; THOMAS A. HAINE, JOHN HENN, DANIEL PATTERSON, LARRY RUNDLE, ALLEN SCATES, JON STANLEY, RUDY SUWARA, PEDRO VELASCO.

VOLLEYBALL — WOMEN (11)

ANN HECK, NINJA JORGENSEN, LAURIE ANN LEWIS, MARILYN MC REAVY, LINDA MURPHY, NANCY OWEN, MARY JO PEPLER, BARBARA PERRY, MARY MARGARET PERRY, SHARON PETERSON, JANE WARD, captain.

WATER POLO (10)

DAVID ASHLEIGH, STEVEN BARNETT, WILLIAM BIRCH, STANLEY COLE, GREGORY HIND, GARY SHEERER, JONATHAN SHORES, ANTON L. VAN DORP, CHARLES WEITZENBERG, DEAN WILLEFORD.

WEIGHTLIFTING (5)

JOSEPH DUBE, heavyweight; PHILIP GRIPPALDI, middle heavyweight; WALTER IMAHARA, featherweight; RUSSELL KNIPP, middleweight; JOSEPH PULEO, captain, light heavyweight.

WRESTLING (8)

Lt. R. WAYNE BAUGHMAN, USAF, middleweight; GERALD R. BELL, lightweight; HARRY HOUSKA, light heavyweight; PATRICK J. KELLY, welterweight; LARRY D. KRISTOFF, heavyweight; RICHARD SANDERS, bantamweight; RICHARD SOFMAN, flyweight; MIKE YOUNG, featherweight.

YACHTING (5)

Flying Dutchman — HARRY C. MELGES, JR., helmsman, and WILLIAM R. BENTSEN, crew.
Lightning — BRUCE GOLDSMITH, helmsman and Mrs. GOLDSMITH and HUGO CAREY LONG, crew.

SILVER MEDALS

ATHLETICS (Track & Field) — MEN (13)

RICHARD BABKA, discus; SAMUEL BAIR 1500 meters; ROBERT BEAMON, long jump; JERRY BRIGHT, 200 meters; OTIS BURRELL, high jump; WILLIE DAVENPORT, 110 meter hurdles; VINCENT MATTHEWS, 400 meters; CONRAD NIGHT-INGALE, 3000 meter steeplechase; RUSSELL ROGRES, 400 meter hurdles; LOUIS SCOTT, 5000 meters; GARY STENLUND, javelin; NEIL STEINHAUER, shot put; WILLIE TURNER, 100 meters.

ATHLETICS (Track & Field) — WOMEN (5)

RANAE BAIR, javelin; Mrs. DORIS BROWN, 800 meters; BARBARA FERRELL, 200 meters; LYNN GRAHAM, shot put; MAMIE RALLINS, 80-meter hurdles.

BASKETBALL — WOMEN (12)

Mrs. CAROLE ASPEDON, captain; CATHERINE BENEDETTO, MYRNA JEAN DEBERRY, MARY LOIS FINLEY, BETTY GAULE, LOLA HAM, ANN MATLOCK, CAROLYN MILLER, ANNETTE RUTT, BARBARA SIPES, MAURIECE SMITH and DIXIE WOODALL.

CYCLING (1)

1000 meters Time Trial — JACK SIMES III.

EQUESTRIAN (7)

Team

Dressage — Mrs. KYRA G. DOWNTON, Mrs. DONNAN SHARP PLUMB, Mrs. DIANE FERMIN-DIDOT.
The Nation's Cup — FRANK D. CHAPOT, Mrs. CHAPOT, KATHRYN H. KUSNER, WILLIAM C. STEINKRAUS.

FENCING (7)

Individual

HARRIET KING, women foils; ALBERT AXELROD, men foils; FRANK D. ANGER, men epee.

Team

Men Foils — ALBERT AXELROD, JEFFREY CHECKES, EDWIN RICHARDS, ROBERT RUSSELL.

GYMNASTICS — MEN (4)

Pommel Horse (Side Horse) — RICHARD LOYD.
Floor Exercises — RICHARD LOYD.
Still Rings — FRED ROETHLISBERGER and MARK COHN.

GYMNASTICS — WOMEN (5)

All-Around — JOYCE TANAC; **Floor Exercises** — JOYCE TANAC; **Side Horse Vault** — DONNA SCHAENZER; **Balance Beam** — DEBORAH BAILEY; **Uneven Parallel Bars** — LINDA METHENY.

JUDO (2)

TOSHIYUKI SEINO, light middleweight; JAMES WESTBROOK, open.

ROWING (1)

Singles Sculls — JOHN NUNN.

SHOOTING (3)

Small Bore Rifle — Capt. RHODY NORNBERG, USAF; **Center Fire Pistol** — M/Sgt. WILLIAM BLANKENSHIP, USA; **Skeet** — ROBERT SCHUEHLE.

SWIMMING — MEN (9)

FRED HAYWOOD, 100 meter backstroke; CHARLES HICKCOX, 200 meter backstroke; ROBERT MOMSEN, 200 meter breaststroke; KEITH RUSSELL, springboard diving; WILLIAM UTLEY, 200 meter individual medley; ROSS WALES, 100 meter butterfly; KENNETH WEBB, 400 meter individual medley; RUSSELL WEBB, 100 meter breaststroke; ZACHARY ZORN, 100 meter freestyle.

SWIMMING — WOMEN (7)

LEE DAVIS, 200 meter butterfly; KAYE HALL, 100 meter backstroke; Lt. MICKI KING, USAF, springboard diving; CLAUDIA KOLB, 200 meter breaststroke; PAMELA KRUSE, 400 meter freestyle; KENDIS MOORE, 200 meter backstroke; SUSAN PEDERSEN, 800 meter freestyle and 200 and 400 meter individual medley.

TENNIS (2)

Pfc. HERBERT FITZGIBBON, USA, men singles; PATSY RIPPY, women singles.

YACHTING (3)

CARL VAN DUYNE, finn; ALAN LEVINSON, helmsman and HARRY LEVINSON, crew, snipe.

BRONZE MEDALS

ATHLETICS (Track & Field) — MEN (4)

GEORGE FRENN, hammer; GOETZ KLOPFER, 50,000 meter walk; TOM LARIS, 10,000 meters; DAVID THORESON, decathlon.

ATHLETICS (Track & Field) — WOMEN (2)

FRANZETTA PARHAM, high jump; WILLYE B. WHITE, long jump.

CYCLING (6)

TIM MOUNTFORD, 10 mile road race; CARL LEUSENKAMP, 2 lap sprint.
4000 Meters Team Pursuit — MICHAEL CONE, HARRY CUTTING, WESLEY CHOWEN, WILLIAM KUND.

EQUESTRIAN (1)

MICHAEL O. PAGE, three-day event.

FENCING (1)

PAUL PESTHY, men epee.

FIELD HOCKEY (16)

E. NEWBOLD BLACK IV, DUDLEY CONNORS, RICHARD GAINER, KULBIR ISSAR, JOCELYN KALIGIS, MICHAEL LICHTENFELD, THOMAS LINGENFELTER, VANCE LUDEKE, FRANCISCO NOODT, JUERGEN RICHARDS, ROBERT RUSSELL THOMPSON, FRANZ VAN DER LEE, CHRISTOPHER WATERS, HERMANN WAETGE, LEE YODER, HANS ZUCKER.

GYMNASTICS — MEN (6)

All-Around — MARK COHN; **Horizontal Bar** — DAVID THOR; **Parallel Bars** — ARNO LASCARI; **Pommel Horse (Side Horse)** — DAVID THOR; **Floor Exercises** — DAVID THOR; **Long Horse Vault** — FRED ROETHLISBERGER.

GYMNASTICS — WOMEN (4)

All-Around — MARIE WALTHER; **Floor Exercises** — DONNA SCHAENZER; **Side Horse Vault** — MARIE WALTHER; **Uneven Parallel Bars** — KATHY GLEASON.

JUDO (2)

LARRY FUKUHARA, lightweight; WILLIAM PAUL, light heavyweight.

SHOOTING (2)

Rapid Fire Pistol — Sgt./FC EDWIN TEAGUE, USA; **Small Bore Rifle (Three Positions)** — GARY ANDERSON.

SWIMMING — MEN (4)

MICHAEL BURTON, 400 meter freestyle and 200 meter butterfly; CHARLES GOETTSCHE, 200 meter backstroke; KENNETH MERTEN, 100 and 200 meter breaststroke; ANDREW STRENK, 1500 meter freestyle.

SWIMMING — WOMEN (4)

CATHY FERGUSON, 200 meter backstroke; CYNTHIA GOYETTE, 100 meter breaststroke; ANN PETERSON, platform diving; POKEY WATSON, 100 meter freestyle.

TENNIS (2)

Lt. ARTHUR ASHE, USA, men singles; JANE ALBERT, women singles.

ATHLETICS (TRACK & FIELD) MEN

Undoubtedly the best men's track and field team to compete for Pan-American honors almost succeeded in its quest for a complete monopoly of gold medals. Only in two of the 24 championship events did other than a USA athlete mount the victory stand. Oddly these were the shortest and longest races, the 100 meters and the marathon run.

The domination also was expressed in the winning of medals (gold, silver, or bronze) in 23 events, placing first and second in 12 events, and garnering the maximum of two medals in 16 of the 24 championship tests.

Adding 13 silvers and four bronzes to the gold medals won, USA athletes took a total of 39 medals out of a possible 46, the two relay events offering only one medal opportunity each.

Ralph Boston, long jumper, and a newcomer in the distance runs, Van Nelson, shared the individual honors. Boston was the only defending champion to repeat, setting a new Pan-American record. Nelson was the only athlete to win two gold medals, racing to triumph in both the 5000 and 10,000 meter runs in record breaking style.

As a matter of fact, Pan-American records were broken in nine track events and in six field events, with one record being established in the 50,000 meter walk as the event was held for the first time. All record performances were registered by USA athletes and virtually all were comparable to Olympic standards.

Some of the USA triumphs were close to world record performances as witness John Carlos' time of 20.5 seconds in the 200 meters, Lee Evans winning the 400 meters in 44.9, Earl McCullouch edging out Willie Davenport with a 13.4 clocking in the 110 meter hurdles, Boston's leap of 27'2½" in the long jump, Ed Caruthers scaling 7'2¼" in the high jump, and the USA relay victories netting times of 39.0 and 3:02.0 in the 4×100 and 4×400 meter events respectively.

Wade Bell's defeat of Canada's Bill Crothers in the 800 meters supplied an extra thrill for the spectators while Henry Jerome delighted his Canadian cohorts by nipping the US's Willie Turner in the 100 meters, each being timed in a record equalling 10.2, although an aiding wind did cause disallowance of a record share.

TEAM PERSONNEL

ATHLETICS (Track & Field) — MEN

Richard (Rink) Babka, Manhattan Beach, Calif. (discus throw)
Samuel Bair, Scottdale, Pa. (1500 meters)
Robert Beamon, Jamaica, N.Y. (long jump)
C. Wade Bell, Ogden, Utah (800 meters)
Ralph Boston, Nashville, Tenn. (long jump)
Charles A. (Jerry) Bright, Oakland, Calif. (100 & 200 meters, 400 meter relay)
Otis Burrell, Los Angeles, Calif. (high jump)
John Carlos, New York, N.Y. (200 meters)
Gary Carlsen, Rock Island, Ill. (discus throw)
Ed Caruthers, Santa Ana, Calif. (high jump)
Ron Copeland, Los Angeles, Calif. (400 meter relay)
Frank Covelli, Long Beach, Calif. (javelin throw)
Charles Craig, Fresno, Calif. (triple jump)
Willie Davenport, Warren, Ohio (110 meter hurdles & 400 meter relay)
Ron Daws, Minneapolis, Minn. (marathon run)
Thomas Dooley, Daly City, Calif. (20 km. walk)
Lee Evans, San Jose, Calif. (400 meters & 1600 meter relay)
George Frenn, Royal Oak, Mich. (hammer throw)
Thomas Gage, Billings, Mont. (hammer throw)
Darrell Horn, Berkeley, Calif. (triple jump)
Goetz Klopfer, Baton Rouge, La. (50 km. walk)
Ron Laird, Pomona, Calif. (20 km. walk)
Tom Laris, Walnut Creek, Calif. (10,000 meters)
Vincent Mathews, Queens Village, N.Y. (400 meters and 400 & 1600 meter relays)
J. Randel Matson, Pampa, Texas (shot put)
Chris McCubbins, Enid, Okla. (3000 meter steeplechase)
Earl McCullouch, Long Beach, Calif. (110 meter hurdles & 400 meter relay)
James McDonagh, Bronx, N.Y. (marathon run)
Van Nelson, Minneapolis, Minn. (5000 & 10,000 meters)
Conrad Nightingale, Burrton, Kan. (3000 meter steeplechase)
Russell Rogers, Newark, N.J. (400 meter hurdles)
Robert Rovere, Knoxville, Tenn. (400 meter relay)
Louis Scott, Detroit, Mich. (5000 meters)
Robert Seagren, Los Angeles, Calif. (pole vault)
Neil Steinhauer, Eugene, Oregon (shot put)
Gary Stenlund, Athens, Ohio (javelin throw)
Elbert Stinson, Texarkana, Texas (1600 meter relay)
Emmett Taylor, Akron, Ohio (1600 meter relay)
David Thoreson, Santa Barbara, Calif. (decathlon)
William A. Toomey, Laguna Beach, Calif. (decathlon)
Willie Turner, Yakima, Wash. (100 meters & 400 meter relay)
Jere Van Dyk, Vancouver, Wash. (800 meters)
Thomas Von Ruden, Los Angeles, Calif. (1500 meters)
Ron Whitney, Boulder, Colo. (400 meter hurdles and 1600 meter relay)
* Paul Wilson, Downey, Calif. (pole vault)
Larry Young, San Pedro, Calif. (50 km. walk)
* Injured, did not compete

Staff Personnel

Aldo Scandurra, Pt. Washington, N.Y. (Manager)
Richard R. Abbot, Macomb, Ill. (Asst. Mgr.)
Gaston F. Lewis, Wilberforce, Ohio (Asst. Mgr.)

ATHLETICS – MEN

PHOTOGRAPH NOT AVAILABLE

R. Babka   S. Bair   R. Beamon

C. Bell   R. Boston   C. Bright

O. Burrell   J. Carlos   G. Carlsen

E. Caruthers   R. Copeland   F. Covelli

C. Craig   W. Davenport   R. Daws

T. Dooley   L. Evans   G. Frenn

T. Gage   D. Horn   G. Klopfer

315

R. Laird   T. Laris   V. Mathews

T. Von Ruden   R. Whitney   P. Wilson

PHOTO-GRAPH NOT AVAILABLE

J. Matson   C. McCubbins   E. McCulloch

L. Young   A. Scandurra   R. Abbot

J. McDonagh   V. Nelson   Nightingale

G. Lewis   Warmerdam   C. Cooper

R. Rogers   R. Rovere   L. Scott

A. Francis   S. Wright

R. Seagren   N. Steinhauer   G. Stenlund

C.A. (Dutch) Warmerdam, Fresno, Calif. (Coach)
Carl Cooper, Tucson, Ariz. (Asst. Coach)
Alex Francis, Ft. Hays, Kan. (Asst. Coach)
Stanley V. Wright, Houston, Texas (Asst. Coach)

E. Stinson   E. Taylor   D. Thoreson

W. Toomey   W. Turner   J. Van Dyk

OFFICIAL SUMMARIES
ATHLETICS (Track & Field) — MEN

* New Pan-American Games Record

100 Meters — 1. Henry Jerome, Canada 10.2; WILLIE TURNER, USA 10.2; 3. Hermes Ramirez-Cajigal, Cuba 10.3; 4. JERRY BRIGHT, USA 10.4; 5. Michael Fray, Jamaica 10.4; 6. Ivan Moreno, Chile 10.5; 7. Ronald Monseque, Trinidad/Tobago. Pablo McNeil, Jamaica, did not start.

200 Meters — 1. JOHN CARLOS, USA 20.5*; 2. JERRY BRIGHT, USA 20.9; 3. Pablo Montes Casanova, Cuba 21.0; 4. Pedro Antonio Grajales, Colombia 21.3; 5. Michael Fray, Jamaica 21.4; 6. Bernard Nottage, Bahamas 21.9; 7. Henry Jerome, Canada 31.1. Don Domansky, Canada, did not start.

400 Meters — 1. LEE EVANS, USA 44.9*; 2. VINCENT MATTHEWS, USA 45.1; 3. Don Domansky, Canada 45.8; 4. Juan Franceschi, Puerto Rico 46.3; 5. Ross McKenzie, Canada 46.7; 6. Pablo Montes Casanova, Cuba 46.8; 7. Pedro Antonio Grajales, Colombia 47.0; 8. Clifton Forbes, Jamaica 47.1.

800 Meters — 1. WADE BELL, USA 1:49.2; 2. Bill Crothers, Canada 1:49.9; 3. Brian Mac-

Laren, Canada 1:50.3; 4. JERE VAN DYK, USA 1:50.3; 5. Alexander McDonald, Jamaica 1:52.3; 6. Neville Myton, Jamaica 1:52.5; 7. Lennox Yearwood, Trinidad/Tobago 1:52.8; 8. Roberto Silva Martinez 1:53.4.

1500 Meters — 1. TOM VON RUDEN, USA 3:43.4; 2. SAM BAIR, USA 3:44.1; 3. David Bailey, Canada 3:44.9; Jose Socorro Neri Valenzuela, Mexico 3:45.7; 5. Byron Dyce, Jamaica 3:46.6; 6. Raymond Haswell, Canada 3:46.7; 7. Jorge Grosser, Chile 3:48.0; 8. Ricardo Palomares Miranda, Mexico 3:48.4.

5000 Meters — 1. VAN NELSON, USA 13:47.4*; 2. LOUIS SCOTT, USA 13:54.0; 3. Juan Maximo Martinez, Mexico 13:54.0; 4. Robert Finlay, Canada 14:15.2; 5. Osvaldo Roberto Suarez, Argentina 14:19.4; 6. Valentin Robles Romero, Mexico 14:20.2.

10,000 Meters — 1. VAN NELSON, USA 29:17.4*; 2. David Ellis, Canada 29:18.4; 3. TOM LARIS, USA 29:21.6; 4. Juan Maximo Martinez, Mexico 29:27.2; 5. Victor Manuel Mora, Colombia 30:57.8; 6. Ron Wallingford, Canada 31:03.4.

Marathon — 1. Andrew Boychuk, Canada 2 hr. 23 min. 2.4 secs.; 2. Augustin Calle Osorio, Colombia 2 hr. 25:50.2; 3. Alfredo Penaloza Carmona, Mexico 2 hr. 27:48.2; 4. Felix Carmona Romero, Mexico 2 hr. 29:10.8; 5. JAMES McDONAGH, USA 2 hr. 29:24.6; 6. Victoriano Lopez Coco, Guatemala 2 hr. 41:34.2. Note: RON DAWS, USA, dropped out.

20,000 Meter Race Walk — 1. RONALD LAIRD, USA 1 hr. 33 min. 5.2 sec.; 2. Jose Pedraza Zuniga, Mexico 1 hr. 34:50.6; 3. Felix Capella, Canada 1 hr. 35:44.6; 4. THOMAS DOOLEY, USA 1 hr. 36:49.8; 5. Yvon Grouix, Canada 1 hr. 39:18.0; 6. Calzado Carbonella, Cuba 1 hr. 45:08.8.

50,000 Meter Race Walk — 1. LARRY YOUNG, USA 4 hr. 26 min. 20.8 sec.; 2. Felix Capella, Canada 4 hr. 35:59.6; 3. GOETZ KLOPFER, USA 4 hr. 37:59.2; 4. Karl-Heinz Merschenz, Canada 4 hr. 54:11.4; 6. Pablo Colin Martinez, Mexico 5 hr. 15:06.4. Only finishers.

110 Meter High Hurdles — 1. EARL McCULLOUCH, USA 13.4*; 2. WILLIE DAVENPORT, USA 13.5; 3. Juan Morales Echevarria, Cuba 14.3; 4. Richard Harvey, Jamaica 14.5; 5. Hernando Arrechea Serrano, Colombia 14.7; 6. Brian Donnelly, Canada 14.8.

400 Meter Intermediate Hurdles — 1. RON WHITNEY, USA 50.7; 2. RUSS ROGERS, USA 51.3; 3. Robert McLaren, Canada 51.4; 4. Miguel Olivera Alvarez, Cuba 51.7; 5. Juan Carlos Dyrzka, Argentina 52.0; 6. Santiago Gordon, Chile 52.8.

3000 Meter Steeplechase — 1. CHRIS McCUBBINS, USA 8:38.2*; 2. CONRAD NIGHTINGALE, USA 8:51.2; 3. Domingo Amaizon, Argentina 8:55.0; 4. Hector Villanuva Osario, Mexico 9:00.6; 5. Flavio Buendia Jiminez, Mexico; 9:09.6; 6. Albertino Etchechury, Uruguay 9:13.0.

4 x 100 Meter Relay — 1. UNITED STATES (EARL McCULLOUCH, JERRY BRIGHT, RON COPELAND, WILLIE TURNER) 39.0*; 2. Cuba 39.2; 3. Colombia 39.9; 4. Trinidad/Tobago 40.1; 5. Jamaica 40.2; 6. Puerto Rico 40.7; 7. Canada 40.7; 8. Peru 41.0.

4 x 400 Meter Relay — 1. UNITED STATES (ELBERT STINSON, EMMETT TAYLOR, VINCENT MATTHEWS, LEE EVANS) 3:02.0*; 2. Canada 3:04.8; 3. Jamaica 3:05.9; 4. Peru 3:09.9; 5. Colombia 3:10.4; 6. Trinidad/Tobago 3:10.8; 7. Mexico 3.11:5. No eighth place.

FIELD EVENTS

Pole Vault — 1. BOB SEAGREN, USA 16-1* (4.90 m); 2. Robert Raftis, Canada 15-7 (4.75 m); 3. Robert Yard, Canada 14-7¼ (4.45 m); 4. Jan Bernardo Barney, Argentina

14-7¼ (4.45 m); 5. Arturo Esquerra Castaneda, Mexico 14-1¼ (4.30 m); 6. Cesar Leon Quintero Urrutia, Colombia 13-7½ (4.15 m). Note: PAUL WILSON, USA, scratched because of injury.

High Jump — 1. ED CARUTHERS, USA 7-2¼* (2.19 m); 2. OTIS BURRELL, USA 7-1 (2.16 m); 3. Roberto Abugattas Aboind, Peru 6-8½ (2.05 m); 4. Wilf Wedman, Canada 6-6½ (2.00 m); 5. Teodoro Palacios Flores, Guatemala 6-6½ (2.00 m); 6. Roberto Guido Pozzi, Argentina 6-6½ (2.00 m).

Long Jump — 1. RALPH H. BOSTON, USA 27-2½* (8.29 m); 2. ROBERT BEAMON, USA 26-6 (8.07 m); 3. Wesley Clayton, Jamaica 25-5½ (7.66 m); 4. Jose Hernandez Estrada, Cuba 24-7¼ (7.50 m); 5. Samuel Cruz, Puerto Rico 24-3¾ (7.41 m); 6. Michel Charland, Canada 24-2¼ (7.37 m).

Triple Jump — 1. CHARLES CRAIG, USA 54-3¼ (16.54 m); 2. Nelson Prudencio, Brazil 54-0 (16.45 m); 3. Jose Estrada Hernandez, Cuba 52-4 (15.95 m); 4. DARRELL HORN, USA 52-0 (15.85 m); 5. Jorge Toro, Puerto Rico 50-9½ (15.48 m); 6. William Greenough, Canada 50-7½ (15.43 m).

Shot Put — 1. J. RANDEL MATSON, USA 65-1* (19.83 m); 2. NEIL STEINHAUER, USA 63-9¾ (19.45 m); 3. David Steen, Canada 60-8¾ (18.51 m); 4. George Puce, Canada 60-7¾ (18.48 m); 5. Jose Carlos Jacques, Brazil 53-4 (16.25 m); 6. Mario Norberto Peretti, Argentina 51-3½ (15.63 m).

Discus — 1. GARY CARLSEN, USA 188-8 (57.50 m); 2. RINK BABKA, USA 186-8 (56.88 m); 3. George Puce, Canada 184-8 (56.20 m); 4. Barbaro Canizares Poey 169-11 (51.80 m); 5. Javier Moreno Escalona, Cuba 167-9 (51.14 m); 6. Jose Carlos Jacques, Brazil 161-3 (49.16 m).

Javelin — 1. FRANK COVELLI, USA 243-8 (74.28 m); 2. GARY STENLUND, USA 242-8 (73.96 m); 3. Justo Pastor Perello Girart, Cuba 236-1 (71.96 m); 4. Jorge Pena, Chile 228-7 (69.68 m); 5. Edmundo Medina, Mexico 227-10 (69.44 m); 6. William Heikkla, Canada 219-5 (66.88 m).

Hammer — 1. TOM GAGE, USA 214-4* (65.32 m); 2. Enrique Samuello Ricardo, Cuba 212-2 (64.66 m); 3. GEORGE FRENN, USA

Chris McCubbins and Conrad Nightingale finished one-two in the 3000 meter steeplechase.

210-3 (64.08 m); 4. Jose Alberto Vallejo, Argentina 197-11 (60.32 m); 5. Roberto Chapchap, Brazil 182-6 (55.62 m); 6. Michael Cairns, Canada 181-1 (55.18 m).

Decathlon — 1. WILLIAM A. TOOMEY, USA 8044 points* (100-10.8 853 pts.; L.J. 24-10¾ 939; Shot Put 43-8 685; H.J. 6-3½ 788; 400-47.3 933; 110 Hurdles 15.1 837; Discus 131-10 689 Pole Vault 13-5½ 832; Javelin 221-10 852; 1500 4:23.3 636). 2. Hector Thomas, Venezuela 7312; 3. DAVID THORESON, USA 7295; 4. Dave Dorman, Canada 7024; 5. Steve Spencer, Canada 6796. Note: Only finishers.

ATHLETICS (TRACK & FIELD) WOMEN

The comeback of Olympic champion Wyomia Tyus in winning the 200 meters, Eleanor Montgomery's successful defense of high jump laurels, the emergence of young Barbara Ferrell as the best in the 100 meters, and talented Mrs. Pat Winslow's triumph in the pentathlon shared the USA spotlight in the women's track and field competition. In eight of the 11 events, the USA ranked first, was responsible for five of the six new Games records and also equalled one mark. Overall, the girls added five silvers and two bronzes for a total of 15 medals.

Madeline Manning and Doris Brown staged a stirring duel for honors in the 800 meters, the former winning in a last surge in the home stretch. The first five finishers broke the existing Games record. Miss Tyus was timed at 23.7 seconds in winning the 200 meters, bettering the existing record but it was ruled that an aiding wind was beyond the allowable limit.

Canada's Nancy McCredie successfully defended her shot put title when she beat out the USA's Lynn Graham with her final throw, but relinquished her discus crown to USA's Carol Moseke when her entry was withdrawn from that event. Willye White, a USA team member starting with the 1956 Olympic Games, gave her best long jump record ever but could get only third place.

The 4 x 100 meter relay record held by the USA was broken by a full second when Cuba's speedy quartet won the event, as the USA and Mexican units were disqualified for passing the baton outside of the zone.

TEAM PERSONNEL

ATHLETICS (Track & Field) — WOMEN

RaNae Jean Bair, San Diego, Calif. (javelin throw)
Mrs. Doris Elaine Brown, Seattle, Wash. (800 meters)

 R. Bair    D. Brown   J. Burnett

 D. Debusk   B. Ferrell    B. Friedrich

 L. Graham    J. Johnson    R. Kletchka

 J. MacFarlane    M. Manning    Montgomery

 C. Moseke    F. Parham    M. Rallins

 M. Seidler    C. Sherrard    W. Tyus

v. Wolvelaere   M. Watson   W. White

317

ATHLETICS – WOMEN

B. Winslow   M. Sexton   J. Bibbs

H. Brown

Jane Elizabeth Burnett, Chevy Chase, Md.
(200 meters & 400 meter relay)
Mrs. Devon Dee Debusk, Costa Mesa, Calif.
(400 meter relay)
Barbara Ann Ferrell, Los Angeles, Calif. (100
& 200 meters, 400 meter relay)
Barbara Ann Friedrich, Spring Lake Heights,
N.J. (javelin throw)
Lynn Graham, Pasadena, Calif. (shot put)
Janet Johnson, Seattle, Wash. (pentathlon)
Ranee Kletchka, Lincoln, Nebr. (discus throw)
Janet Macfarlane, Gridley, Calif. (100 meters
& 400 meter relay)
Madeline Manning, Cleveland, Ohio
(800 meters)
Eleanor Montgomery, Cleveland, Ohio (high
jump)
Carol Jean Moseke, Cedar Rapids, Nebr.
(shot put)
Franzetta Parham, Isleton, Calif. (high jump)
Mamie Rallins, Chicago, Ill. (80 meter hurdles
& 400 meter relay)
Maren Seidler, Berkeley Heights, N.J.
(shot put)
Mrs. Cherrie Sherrard, Oakland, Calif.
(80 meter hurdles)
Wyomia Tyus, Griffin, Ga. (200 meters &
400 meter relay)
Pat Van Wolvelaere, Renton, Wash.
(400 meter relay)
Martha Watson, Long Beach, Calif. (long
jump)
Willye White, Chicago, Ill. (long jump &
400 meter relay)
Mrs. Billee Pat Winslow, San Mateo, Calif.
(pentathlon)

Staff personnel

Dr. Maria Sexton, Wooster, Ohio (Manager)
James Bibbs, Ecorse, Mich. (Coach)
Dr. Harmon Brown, San Francisco, Calif.
(Asst. Coach)

OFFICIAL SUMMARIES

ATHLETICS (Track & Field) — WOMEN

* New Pan-American Games Record
** Ties Pan-American Games Record

100 Meters — 1. BARBARA FERRELL, USA
11.5**; 2. Miguelina Cobian, Cuba 11.6; 3.
Irene Piotrowski, Canada 11.7; 4. Cristina
Hechevarria, Cuba 11.9; 5. Vilma Charlton,
Jamaica 11.9; 6. JANET MACFARLANE, USA
11.9; 7. Thora Best, Trinidad/Tobago 12.1; 8.
Emma Giron Olivares, Mexico 12.3.

200 Meters — 1. WYOMIA TYUS, USA 23.7;
2. BARBARA FERRELL, USA 23.8; 3. Miguelina
Cobian, Cuba 23.8; 4. Irene Piotrowski,
Canada 23.9; 5. Vilma Charlton, Jamaica 24.0;
6. Una Morris, Jamaica 24.0; 7. Violeta Quezada
Diaz, Cuba 24.4; 8. J. Maddin, Canada
24.8.
800 Meters — 1. MADELINE MANNING, USA
2:02.3*; 2. DORIS BROWN, USA 2:02.9; 3.
Abigail Hoffman, Canada 2:04.6; 4. Roberta
Pico, Canada 2:07.5; 5. Irenice Maria Rodrigues,
Brazil 2:08.5; 6. Alicia Beatriz Enriguez,
Argentina 2:15.1; 7. Aurelia Penton
Conde, Cuba 2:15.4; 8. Lucia Balderas Quiroz,
Mexico 2:20.7.
80 Meter Hurdles — 1. CHERRIE SHERRARD,
USA 10.8*; 2. MAMIE RALLINS, USA
10.8; 3. Thora Best, Trinidad/Tobago 10.9; 4.
Carlotta Ulloa, Chile 11.1; 5. Aura Vidal Barreto,
Venezuela 11.5; 6. Cristina Hechevarria,
Cuba 11.5; 7. Norma Enriqueta Basilio, Mexico
11.8; 8. Jenifer Meldrum, Canada 12.1.
4 x 100 Meter Relay — 1. Cuba 44.6*; 2.
Canada 45.5; 3. Jamaica 47.1. Note: United
States and Mexico disqualified for passing
baton out of zone.
High Jump — 1. ELEANOR MONTGOMERY,
USA 5-10* (1.78 m); 2. Susan Nigh, Canada
5-7³/₄ (1.72 m); 3. FRANZETTA PARHAM, USA
5-6¹/₂ (1.69 m); 4. Maria Da Cypriano, Brazil
5-5¹/₄ (1.66 m); 5. Aida Dos Santos, Brazil 5-1
(1.55 m); 6. Audrey Reid, Jamaica 5-1 (1.55 m).
Long Jump — 1. Irene Martinez Tartabull,
Cuba 20-9* (6.33 m); 2. Aura Vidal Barreto,
Venezuela 20-4¹/₄ (6.20 m); 3. WILLYE B.
WHITE, USA 20-3 (6.17 m); 4. MARTHA WATSON,
USA 20-1¹/₂ (6.14 m); 5. Joan Hendry,
Canada 20-³/₄ (6.12 m); 6. Marcia Garbey Montell,
Cuba 19-7³/₄ (5.99 m).
Shot Put — 1. Nancy McCredie, Canada
49-9³/₄ (15.18 m); 2. LYNN GRAHAM, USA
48-9³/₄ (14.88 m); 3. Maureen Dowds, Canada
47-1 (14.35 m); 4. MAREN SEIDLER, USA
46-3¹/₂ (14.11 m); 5. Hilda Ramirez Serrano,
Cuba 46-2¹/₄ (14.07 m); 6. Rosa Molina, Chile
44-10³/₄ (13.68 m).
Discus — 1. CAROL MOSEKE, USA 161-7
(49.24 m); 2. Carol Martin, Canada 157-4
(47.94 m); 3. Caridad Aquero Acosta, Cuba
153-2 (46.68 m); 4. Marlene Kurt, Canada
150-7 (45.90 m); 5. RANEE KLETCHKA, USA
150-2 (45.78 m); 6. Hilda Ramirez Serrano,
Cuba 146-5 (44.62 m).
Javelin — 1. BARABARA FRIEDRICH, USA
174-9* (53.26 m); 2. RANAE BAIR, USA 169-5
(51.64 m); 3. Jane Dahlgren, Canada 149-2
(45.46 m); 4. Blanca Umana Andrade, Colombia
144-7 (44.06 m); 5. Maria Moreno Dieguez,
Cuba 141-3 (43.46 m); 6. Beryl Rodrigues,
Canada 130-9 (39.84 m).
Pentathlon — 1. PAT DANIELS WINSLOW,
USA 4860* [80 m hurdles — 11.6; Shot Put —
43-10 (13.36 m); High Jump — 5-4¹/₂ (1.64 m);
Long Jump — 19-2¹/₄ (5.85 m); 220 m — 24.0];
2. Jenifer Wingerson Meldrum, Canada 4724;
3. Aida Dos Santos, Brazil 4531; 4. Aura Vidal
Barreto, Venezuela 4385; 5. Lesley Shonk,
Canada 4329; 6. JANET JOHNSON, USA 4241.

BASEBALL

George Greer, until he strode to the
plate in the last of the ninth inning of
the final playoff baseball game, had
never played on a championship team.
But with one stroke of his bat, the
University of Connecticut athlete
corrected that injustice and wrote a
Horatio Alger finish to the most

BASEBALL

R. Blosse   D. Carlson   J. Curtis

B. Debolt   G. Greer   J. Kraus

D. Lamb   M. Lisetski   M. Marquess

T. Plodinec   J. Sadelfield   K. Smith

S. Sogge   J. Spencer   P. Splittorff

Szotkiewicz   T. Toomey   W. Wright

M. Karow   L. Timm   V. Yelkin

suspense-packed competition of the Games. With one out, the bases jammed and the score tied at 1–1, George slashed the first pitch by Cuban ace hurler Manual Alarcon into right field, scoring Ray Blosse with the winning run that culminated in the USA's initial baseball championship.

The title finish had all the earmarks of a dime-novel setting. In the regular double round-robin schedule, the USA twice lost to Cuba but finished second to the Castro nine in the standings. The rules then provided that the two top teams meet in a special three game playoff to decide the gold medal. The USA nine won the first playoff game, 8–3, dropped the second, 7–5, but made the grade in the third and deciding tilt.

The moment of truth came after a rain squall almost washed out the game late on the final Saturday night of competition. Blosse had yielded only four Cuban singles and a run for nine innings, his opponent allowing only one USA hit, a single by Steve Sogge.

The rainstorm broke just as the USA came to bat in the ninth and, for a time, it seemed that all efforts to complete the game were for naught. If the game could not continue, it would have to be replayed on Sunday,

60 miles away from Winnipeg since the stadium was reserved for the closing ceremonies.

But the fates were to nod favorably on the USA. As play was resumed after the lengthy interval, Cuban hurler Alarcon momentarily lost control and issued a base on balls to his rival, Blosse, a cardinal sin for any pitcher. First baseman Mark Marquess followed with a sacrifice bunt, advancing Blosse to second, left fielder Jack Kraus drew a walk, and second baseman Mike Lisetski singled to load the sacks. That left it up to Greer, who responded magnificently.

Once the joyful demonstration by the winners diminished to a controllable elation, Coach Marty Karow pushed Greer out to accept the gold medal on behalf of the team. The USA had not elected a team captain but who could have denied Greer's right to represent his mates?

The title triumph marked the most intense preparation the USA had ever undertaken to win the championship of a sport which originated in this country. The squad assembled late in June at Minneapolis and trained rigorously until the departure for Winnipeg. The 18-man squad was composed of 16 college undergraduates and two US Army officers. They were serious in

their intent and no group deserved a gold medal more than this one.

Cuba opened its title defense in the regular schedule by nipping the USA, 4–3, then winning their second round encounter, 9–2. The USA twice defeated Mexico, Puerto Rico, and Canada for a final record of 6 wins, 2 defeats, one game behind Cuba's 7–1 record (Canada's only win was at the Cubans' expense).

Sogge led the USA hitters with a fine .386 batting average, Greer posting second with .355. As a team, the United States hit at a .276 clip.

TEAM PERSONNEL

BASEBALL

Raymond Blosse, Marlow Heights, Md.
Daniel Carlson, Des Plaines, Ill.
John D. Curtis II, Smithtown, N.Y.
Lt. Barry Debolt, USA, Lawton, Okla.
George E. Greer, Chatham, Mass.
Jack W. Kraus, San Antonio, Texas.
Dennis L. Lamb, Chandler, Ariz.
Michael Lisetski, Northampton, Pa.
Mark E. Marquess, Stockton, Calif.
Timothy Plodinec, Aliquippa, Pa.
Joseph R. Sadelfield, Cincinnati, Ohio
Lt. Kenneth W. Smith, USA, Richfield, Minn.
Steven G. Sogge, Gardena, Calif.
James H. Spencer, Richland, Wash.
Paul W. Splittorff, Jr. Arlington Heights, Ill.
Kenneth Szotkiewicz, Wilmington, Del.
T. James Toomey, Laguna Beach, Calif.
William A. Wright III, Hermitage, Tenn.

Staff personnel

Martin G. Karow, Columbus, Ohio (Coach)
LeRoy C. (Cap) Timm, Ames, Iowa (Asst. Coach)
Virgil V. Yelkin, Omaha, Nebr. (Manager & Asst. Coach)

BASKETBALL — MEN

Led by the stellar Westley Unseld, whose all-around play was outstanding, the USA men's basketball team won the team title handily. Unseld not only scored 104 points but grabbed the most rebounds, and his accurate passes to teammates earning him the nickname of "Unselfish". Other standouts were Jo Jo White, Cal Fowler, Darel Carrier and Lt. Michael Silliman. White led all scorers with 125 points while Carrier was second with 108.

Playing in Group A for the preliminary portion of the schedule, the United States swept by Colombia, Peru, Panama and Puerto Rico in that order, winning by margins of from 28 to 88 points. Meanwhile Mexico led the qualifiers from Group B with successive wins over Argentina, Cuba, Brazil, and Canada. Three teams

(continued)

OFFICIAL SUMMARIES
BASEBALL

Final Standings		Regular W	L	Playoff W	L	Overall W	L
1	*UNITED STATES	6	2	2	1	8	3
2	Cuba	7	1	1	2	8	3
3	Puerto Rico	4	4	–	–	4	4
4	Mexico	2	6	–	–	2	6
5	Canada	1	7	–	–	1	7

* defeated Cuba in playoffs (first two teams in regular round robin standings qualified).

Scores of Games

Cuba 4, United States 3
Mexico 3, Canada 1

United States 4, Mexico 1
Cuba 3, Puerto Rico 0

United States 8, Puerto Rico 3
Mexico 3, Canada 1

Cuba 6, Canada 4
Puerto Rico 4, Mexico 3

United States 14, Canada 10
Cuba 4, Mexico 1

Cuba 9, United States 1
Mexico 7, Canada 3

United States 6, Mexico 3
Cuba 6, Puerto Rico 5

United States 7, Puerto Rico 3
Mexico 7, Canada 3

Canada 10, Cuba 9
Puerto Rico 7, Mexico 6

United States 14, Canada 2
Cuba 6, Mexico 5

Title Playoff Games

United States 8, Cuba 3
Cuba 7, United States 5
United States 2, Cuba 1

BASKETBALL – MEN

R. Carey D. Carrier J. Clawson

L. Dove C. Fowler H. Logan

K. Rhine M. Silliman S. Sullivan

W. Unseld J. White J. Williams

C. Bloedorn H. Fischer J. Kundla

qualified for the final round from each of the two groups.

In the final round robin, the USA whipped Cuba, repeated triumphs over Puerto Rico and Panama, then downed Argentina and Mexico – the latter team coached by former USA Olympian Les Lane – for the sweep of five games and the title. Mexico lost to the USA by 19 points, the closest challenge for the champions.

TEAM PERSONNEL

BASKETBALL — MEN

Ray Carey, Midland, Texas
Darel Carrier, Bartlesville, Okla.
Cpl. John Clawson, USA, Naperville, Ill.

Lloyd Dove, Brooklyn, N.Y.
Calvin Fowler, Akron, Ohio
Henry Logan, Asheville, N.C.
Kendall Rhine, Dupo, Ill.
Lt. Michael Silliman, USA, Louisville, Ky.
Steve Sullivan, East Orange, N.J.
Westley Unseld, Louisville, Ky.
Joseph H. White, St. Louis, Mo.
James Williams, Norristown, Pa.

Staff personnel

Harold Fischer, San Francisco, Calif. (Coach)
John Kundla, Minneapolis, Minn. (Asst. Coach)
Charles E. Bloedorn, Akron, Ohio (Manager)

BASKETBALL — WOMEN

The USA women cagers were unsuccessful in their bid for a repetition of 1963 honors, losing twice to Brazil, the ultimate champion (who had bowed in the title game four years before). However, the United States twice defeated Canada, Mexico, and Cuba to wind up in second place.

The final two victories, over Canada (by one point) and Cuba (by seven), were realized when Lois Finley came off the bench to spark winning rallies.

Scorers were led by Barbara Ann Sipes (108) and Carole Aspedon (92).

TEAM PERSONNEL

BASKETBALL — WOMEN

Mrs. Carole Phillips Aspedon, Hamburg, Iowa
Catherine Benedetto, Olympia, Wash.
Myrna Jean DeBerry, DeWitt, Ark.
Mary Lois Finley, Claude, Texas
Betty Gaule, Clearfield, Iowa
Lola Faye Ham, LaVerne, Okla.
Judith A. Matlock, Pryor, Okla.
Carolyn J. Miller, Palestine, Texas
Annette Kay Rutt, Sterling, Ill.
Barbara Ann Sipes, Kansas City, Mo.
Mauriece Smith, Overland Park, Kan.
Dixie Delores Woodall, Kansas City, Mo.

OFFICIAL SUMMARIES

BASKETBALL — MEN

Final Standings		Group Play W	Group Play L	Title Round W	Title Round L	Overall Total W	Overall Total L
1	UNITED STATES	4	0	5	0	9	0
2	Mexico	4	0	4	1	8	1
3	Panama	2	2	2	3	4	5
4	Cuba	2	2	2	3	4	5
5	Puerto Rico	3	1	1	4	4	5
6	Argentina	2	2	1	4	3	6
7	*Brazil	2	2	2	0	4	2
8	*Peru	1	3	1	1	2	4
9	*Canada	0	4	0	2	0	6
10	**Colombia	0	4	—	—	0	4

* competed in Centennial ranking playoffs for teams not qualifying for championship round.
** did not compete in lower ranking playoff games.

Scores in Group A Preliminary

United States 131, Colombia 43
Puerto Rico 81, Panama 66

United States 93, Peru 37
Panama 99, Colombia 54

United States 122, Panama 73
Puerto Rico 57, Peru 54

Puerto Rico 61, Colombia 49
Panama 84, Peru 77

United States 80, Puerto Rico 52
Peru 82, Colombia 48

Scores in Group B Preliminary

Mexico 71, Argentina 64
Cuba 77, Canada 66

Mexico 71, Cuba 66
Brazil 70, Argentina 62

Mexico 66, Brazil 65
Argentina 71, Canada 69

Argentina 65, Cuba 64
Brazil 102, Canada 89

Cuba 64, Brazil 49
Mexico 80, Canada 76

Scores in Championship Round

United States 91, Cuba 71
Mexico 58, Puerto Rico 50
Argentina 75, Panama 65

United States 89, Puerto Rico 53
Mexico 64, Argentina 56
Panama 80, Cuba 75

United States 90, Panama 44
Mexico 60, Cuba 51
Panama 77, Puerto Rico 71

United States 106, Argentina 55
Mexico 81, Panama 73
Cuba 66, Puerto Rico 61

United States 93, Mexico 74
Cuba 73, Argentina 71
Panama 84, Peru 77

BASKETBALL – WOMEN

C. Aspedon C. Benedetto M. DeBerry

M. Finley B. Gaule L. Ham

J. Matlock C. Miller A. Rutt

B. Sipes M. Smith D. Woodall

A. Cox O. Ruble M. Downing

Staff personnel

Alberta Lee Cox, Raytown, Mo. (Coach)
Olan G. Ruble, Mt. Pleasant, Iowa (Asst. Coach)
Margaret R. Downing, Magnolia, Ark. (Manager)

BOXING

United States boxers scored a placing in seven of the 10 weight divisions, winning three golds and four bronzes. Emerging champions were 18-year old heavyweight Forest Ward; James Wallington, a classy light welterweight; and Art Redden, light heavyweight. Bronzes were awarded to Harlan Marbley, flyweight; Albert Robinson, feather-

OFFICIAL SUMMARIES

BASKETBALL — WOMEN

Final Standings		First Round W	First Round L	Second Round W	Second Round L	Overall Total W	Overall Total L
1	Brazil	4	0	4	0	8	0
2	UNITED STATES	3	1	3	1	6	2
3	*Canada	1	3	2	2	3	5
4	Mexico	2	2	1	3	3	5
5	Cuba	0	4	0	4	0	8

Scores First Round Games

Brazil 60, United States 42
Canada 70, Cuba 48

Brazil 69, Canada 55
United States 48, Mexico 44

Brazil 85, Cuba 50
Mexico 62, Canada 56

United States 59, Canada 46
Mexico 67, Cuba 52

Brazil 61, Mexico 46
United States 62, Cuba 48

Scores Second Round Games

Brazil 59, United States 54
Canada 78, Cuba 47

Brazil 78, Canada 61
United States 52, Mexico 42

Brazil 74, Cuba 51
Canada 51, Mexico 43

United States 43, Canada 42
Mexico 49, Cuba 39

Brazil 61, Mexico 58
United States 51, Cuba 44

weight; Ronald Harris, lightweight; and Jesse Valdez, welterweight.

The USA's Ward knocked out his Cuban opponent in the first round of the heavyweight title bout, after having eliminated his foe from Argentina in the second round of his opening match.

Cuba also won three gold medals but added three silvers and one bronze to command team honors. Argentina won two golds and four silvers.

TEAM PERSONNEL

BOXING

Robert Lee Green (bantamweight), Washington, D.C.
Ronald W. Harris, Canton, Ohio (lightweight)
Leonard Hutchins, Detroit, Mich. (middleweight)
SP5 Harlan Marbley, USA, Washington, D.C. (flyweight)
Sgt. Arthur Redden, USMC, Wilmington, Del. (light heavyweight)
AN Albert Robinson, USN, Phoenix, Arix. (featherweight)
Cpl. Richard Royal, USMC, New York, N.Y. (welterweight)
Jesse Valdez, Houston, Texas (light middleweight)
SP4 James Wallington, USA, Philadelphia, Pa. (light welterweight)
Forest Ward, Brooklyn, N.Y. (heavyweight)

Staff personnel

Lt.Col. Ralph F. Mendenhall, USA, Washington, D.C. (Manager)
Dr. Victor J. DiFilippo, Upper Montclair, N.J. (Coach)
Sgt. Kenneth Miura, USA, Honolulu, Hawaii (Asst. Coach)

United States light welterweight James Wallington celebrates his gold medal victory.

OFFICIAL SUMMARIES

BOXING

Both defeated semi-finalists received bronze medals.

Flyweight: Final — Francisco Rodriguez, Venezuela decisioned Ricardo Delgado Nogales, Mexico. Semi-Finals — Rodriguez decisioned HARLAN MARBLEY, USA; Nogales decisioned Walter Henry, Canada. Quarter-Finals — Rodriguez won over Luis Cese, Cuba on disqualification; Henry decisioned Jaime Cabera, Ecuador; MARBLEY decisioned Servilio De Oliveira, Brazil. First-Round — MARBLEY won by TKO over Roberto Maynard, Panama, in second; De Oliveira decisioned Pedro Antonio Bendek, Colombia; Cese decisioned Cornell Hall, Jamaica.

(continued)

BOXING

R. Green   R. Harris   L. Hutchins

H. Marbley   A. Redden   A. Robinson

R. Royal   J. Valdez   J. Wallington

F. Ward   Mendenhall   V. DiFilippo

K. Miura

Bantamweight: Final — Juvencio Martinez Gonzalez, Mexico decisioned Fermin Espinosa Reyes, Cuba. Semi-Finals — Gonzalez decisioned Armando Mendosa, Venezuela; Reyes decisioned Guillermo Velasquez, Chile. Quarter-Finals — Gonzalez decisioned Domingo Casco, Argentina; Reyes won by "walk over" over Esteban De Jesus Rivera, Puerto Rico; Mendosa won by disqualification over Kenneth Campbell, Puerto Rico; Velasquez decisioned Frank Scott, Canada. First Round — Rivera won by disqualification over Marcial Gutieviez Yanguez, Panama; Reyes decisioned ROBERT GREEN, USA.

Featherweight: Final — Miguel Garcia, Argentina decisioned Eduardo Lugo, Cuba. Semi-Finals — Garcia decisioned Freytes Caban Ortiz, Puerto Rico; Lugo decisioned ALBERT ROBINSON, USA. Quarter-Finals — Garcia decisioned Alfredo Rojas, Chile; Lugo decisioned Marco Antonio Morgan, Panama; Ortiz decisioned Wayne Boyce, Canada; RO-

BINSON decisioned Jose Bernal Silva, Mexico. First Round — Lugo decisioned Errol West, Jamaica; Morgan won by TKO, over Hernan Torres Prens, Colombia.

Lightweight: Final — Enrico Blanco, Cuba decisioned Luis Minami, Peru. Semi-Finals — Blanco decisioned RONALD HARRIS, USA; Minami won by disqualification over Juan Rivero, Uruguay. Quarter-Finals — Blanco won by TKO over Gerald Ratte, Canada; Minami decisioned Luis Gonzalez, Chile; HARRIS decisioned Antonio Duran Aguirre, Mexico; Rivero decisioned Linden Topey, Jamaica. First Round — Minami decisioned Victor Marquez, Venezuela; Rivera won by TKO over Jovina Rodrigues De Oliveira, Brazil; Gonzalez won by disqualification over Carlos Alberto Curia, Argentina.

Light Welterweight: Final — JAMES WALLINGTON, USA won by TKO over Hugo Oscar Sclarandi, Argentina. Semi-Finals — WALLINGTON won by TKO over Alfredo Morales Cornejo, Mexico; Sclarandi decisioned Guillermo Salcedo, Venezuela. Quarter-Finals — WALLINGTON decisioned Dick Findlay, Canada; Sclarandi decisioned Reinaldo Ortiz, Puerto Rico; Morales Cornejo decisioned Gustavo Villalobos, Peru; Salcedo decisioned Luis Reyes, Uruguay; First-Round — WALLINGTON decisioned Felix Betancourt, Cuba; Morales Cornejo decisioned Bernardo Olea, Chile; Findlay decisioned Kenneth Nelson, Jamaica.

Welterweight: Final — Andres Modina Casanola, Cuba decisioned Omar Guilloti, Argentina. Semi-Finals — Modina Casanola won by TKO over Alfonso Ramirez, Mexico; Guilloti decisioned JESSE VALDEZ, USA. Quarter-Finals — Modina Casanola decisioned Fred Fuller, Canada; Guilloti won by TKO over David Dakers, British Honduras; VALDEZ decisioned Walter Gossi, Uruguay; Ramirez won by "walk over" over Roberto Camargo, Brazil. First Round — Modina Casanola won by TKO over Linfer Contreras Paternas, Colombia; Fuller decisioned Ulises Duran, Chile; Camargo won by TKO over Seymour Wright, Jamaica; Ramirez decisioned Juan Perez Milero, Puerto Rico.

Light Middleweight: Final — Rolando Garbey, Cuba won by TKO over Victor Emilio Gallindez, Argentina. Semi-Finals — Garbey decisioned Augustin Zaragosa Revna, Mexico; Gallindez decisioned Donato Paduano, Canada. Quarter-Finals — Garbey won by TKO over Juan Evangelista Cordoba Galan, Colombia; Paduano decisioned RICHARD ROYAL, USA; Zaragosa decisioned Miguel De Oliveira, Brazil.

Middleweight: Final — Jorge Victor Ahumada, Argentina won by TKO over Carlos Fabre, Brazil. Semi-Finals — Ahumada winner by retirement over Joaquin Delis Aguero, Cuba; Fabre decisioned Carlos Franco, Uruguay. Quarter-Finals — Franco won by TKO over LEONARD HUTCHINS, USA.

Light Heavyweight: Final — ARTHUR REDDEN, USA decisioned Juan Jose Torres, Argentina. Semi-Finals — REDDEN decisioned Manuel Castanon Rodrigues, Mexico; Torres decisioned Marijan Kolar, Canada. Quarter-Finals — REDDEN decisioned Jose Gajardo, Chile; Torres decisioned Jose Del Carmen Rondon, Venezuela; Castanon Rodrigues won by TKO over Angel Hernandez Borroto, Cuba.

Heavyweight: Final — FOREST WARD, USA won by TKO over Jose Luis Cabrera Tartabul, Cuba. Semi-Final — WARD won by TKO over Ricardo Aguad.

CANOEING — MEN & WOMEN

Although not on the program of championship events, the sport of canoeing and kayak-racing offered interesting competition as an Olympic Development project for United States, Mexican, and Canadian contestants. The two-day regatta held on the Winnipeg Floodway, although not carrying Pan-American Games medal significance, was closely contested and bore out the intention of the organizers, that of providing international testing of Olympic talent potential.

Mrs. Marcia Jones Smoke, who won a bronze medal in the Tokyo Olympic Games, led the USA women's contingent by winning the 500 meter kayak singles final, doubling with her sister, Mrs. Perry Jones Rademaker, to place first in the 500 meter kayak tandem, and then teaming up again with her sister and two others, Francine Fox and Pat Petraitis, to win the 500 meter kayak fours. Miss Fox was a silver medalist at Tokyo in the tandem.

United States kayakers won four of the seven men's events. Kenneth Wilson, who first represented the USA in the sport when he competed at Melbourne's Olympic Games in 1956, won the 10,000 meter singles and placed second in each of the 500 and 1000 meter solo races. John Van Dyke and Paul Beacham placed first in both the 1000 and 10,000 meter tandem events while Billy Ray Bragg and Robert Haris teamed to win the 500 meter tandem.

In the four Canadian style races, John Glair, an Army private, was the only USA paddler to win a first place, taking the 10,000 meter singles. He also placed second in the 1000 meter singles.

TEAM PERSONNEL

CANOEING — MEN & WOMEN
(Olympic Development Team)

Pfc. Michael Ray Ansley, USA, St. Charles, Ill.
(C-2 1000 & 10,000 meters)
Pfc. Steven Roy Ansley, USA, St. Charles Ill.
(C-2 1000 & 10,000 meters)
Paul Beacham, Columbus, Ga. (K-2 1000 & 10,000 meters)
Billy Ray Bragg, Los Angeles, Calif.
(K-2 500 meters, K-4 1000 meters)
Francine Anne Fox, Washington, D.C.
(K-4 500 meters)
John Glair, Battle Creek, Mich.
(C-1 1000 meters)
Robert Haris, Radnor, Pa. (K-2 500 meters, K-4 1000 meters)
Virginia Moore, Honolulu, Hawaii
(K-4 500 meters)

CANOEING

M. Ansley S. Ansley P. Beachem

B. Bragg F. Fox J. Glair

R. Haris V. Moore F. Petraitis

J. Pickett S. Rademaker M. Smoke

J. van Dyke K. Wilson W. Smoke

G. Grigoleit

Frances Pat Petraitis, Ann Arbor, Mich.
(K-4 500 meters)
John R. Pickett, Dallas, Pa. (K-1 10,000 meters,
K-4 1000 meters)
Mrs. Sperry Jones Rademaker, Windermere,
Fla. (K-2 500 meters, K-4 500 meters)
Mrs. Marcia Jones Smoke, Niles, Mich.
(K-1 500 meters, K-2 500 meters)
John L. Van Dyke, Falls Church, Va. (K-2 1000
& 10,000 meters, K-4 1000 meters)

Kenneth Wilson, Bronx, N.Y. (K-1 500 &
1000 meters)

Staff Personnel

William Smoke, Niles, Mich. (Manager)
Gert Grigoleit, Sacramento, Calif. (Coach)

CYCLING

The best US showing in five Pan-American Games can be credited to the United States cyclists. Carl Leusenkamp rode well to place third in the two-lap sprint race. The 4000 meter pursuit team of Wes Chowen, Mike Cone, Harry Cutting, and Bill Kund picked up a bronze medal in their specialty, as did Tim Mountford in the 10-mile scratch road race. Best showing medal-wise was Jack Simes' second place in the 1000 meter time trial finals.

Other standout performances were turned in by David Brink, placing fourth in the 4000 meter individual pursuit and by Michael Pickens, who enjoyed similar success in the 110 mile individual road race.

TEAM PERSONNEL

CYCLING

David L. Brink, Berkeley, Calif. (400 meter
indv. pursuit)
Daniel Butler, Davis, Calif. (road race)
David M. Chauner, Rosemont, Pa. (4000 meter
indv. pursuit)
Wesley John Chowen, Los Angeles, Calif.
(4000 meter team pursuit)
Michael Cone, Palo Alto, Calif. (4000 meter
team pursuit)
Harry W. Cutting III, Riverside, Calif.
(4000 meter team pursuit)
Preston Handy, New York, N.Y. (1000 meter
time trial)
William Kund, Glendale, Calif. (4000 meter
team pursuit)
Carl Leusenkamp, Silver Spring, Md.
(1000 meter sprint)
Tim Mountford, Sherman Oaks, Calif.
(1000 meter time trial)
David Mulkey, Sunnyvale, Calif. (road race)
Robert Parsons, Berkeley, Calif. (road race)
Michael Pickens, San Diego, Calif. (road race)
Jack Simes III, Closter, N.J. (1000 meter time
trial)
Sam Zeitlin, Brooklyn, N.Y. (1000 meter sprint)
Nicholas Zeller, Portland, Ore. (road race)

Staff Personnel

Alfred J. Toefield, Floral Park, N.Y. (Manager)
Robert Paul Tetzlaff, Campbell, Calif. (Coach)
Augustus Husse, Columbus, Ohio (Asst. Coach)
Peter Senia, Sr., Brooklyn, N.Y. (Mechanic)

OFFICIAL SUMMARIES

CYCLING

Two-Lap Sprints — 1. Roger Gibbon, Trinidad/Tobago; 2. Oscar Garcia, Argentina; 3. CARL LEUSENKAMP, USA; 4. Daniel Larreal, Venezuela.
1000 Meter Time Trial — 1. Roger Gibbon, Trinidad/Tobago 1:09.33; 2. JACK SIMES III,

CYCLING

D. Brink R. Butler D. Chauner

W. Chowen M. Cone H. Cutting

P. Handy W. Kund Leusenkamp

T. Mountford D. Mulkey R. Parsons

M. Pickens J. Simes S. Zeitlin

PHOTOGRAPH NOT AVAILABLE

N. Zeller A. Toefield R. Tetzlaff

A. Husse P. Senia

323

In Pan-American competition, a South American tries to overtake an American cyclist.

USA 1:09.94; 3. Carlos Alberto Vazquez, Argentina 1:12.03; 4. Jocelyn Lovell, Canada 1:12.81; 5. Luis Carlos Saldarriaga, Colombia 1:13.69; 6. Jose Mercado, Mexico 1:13.71.

4000 Meter Individual Pursuit Final — 1. Martin Rodriguez, Colombia 4:58.31; 2. Juan Merlos, Argentina 5:11.56; 3. Radames Trevino, Mexico 5:06.03; 4. DAVID BRINK, USA 5:09.35.

4000 Meter Team Pursuit Final — 1. Argentina (Juan Merlos, Carlos Alvarez, Ismael Moran, Vincente Chancay) 4:44,58; 2. Mexico 4:45.44; 3. USA (WES CHOWEN, MIKE CONE, HARRY CUTTING, WILLIAM KUND) 4:47.24; Colombia 4:51.17.

10 Mile Scratch Race — 1. Carlos Alvarez, Argentina 23:11.4; 2. Vincente Chancay, Argentina; 3. TIM MOUNTFORD, USA.

100 Kilometer Team Time Trial — 1. Argentina (Delmo Delmastro, Carlos Alvarez, Luis Bautista Breppe, Juan Cavallieri) 2 hrs. 20 min. 49 sec.; 2. Mexico 2 hr. 22:17; 3. Colombia 2 hr. 25:46; 4. Uruguay 2 hr. 27:36; 5. Chile 2 hr. 27:56; 6. Canada 2 hr. 30:17; 7. USA 2 hr. 30:21.

110 Mile Road Race — 1. Marcel Roy, Canada 5 hrs. 3 min. 5 sec.; 2. Vincente Chancay, Argentina; 3. Heriberto Diaz, Mexico; 4. MICHAEL PICKENS, USA; 11. DAVID MULKEY, USA. Note: There were 41 starters and final placings were taken for the first eleven.

EQUESTRIAN MEN & WOMEN

Strong showings in all three classifications of competition enabled the United States riders to emerge with overall honors. J. Michael Plumb won the gold medal and Michael Page the bronze in the three-day individual tests, both joining James Wofford and Ernest Eckhardt to take first place in the team category. Mrs. Kyra Downton captured the individual medal in the dressage and, with teammates Mrs. Fermin-Didot and Mrs. Donnan Sharp Plumb, took second place in the team event.

The jumping competition on the closing day of the Games was great although the United States, favored to win, was upset in both the team and individual phases. The veteran team of Mrs. Mary Mairs Chapot, Frank Chapot, Kathryn Kusner, and Olympian William Steinkraus were nosed out by a fine quartet of Brazilians.

In the individual testing, Canada's James Day took the gold medal, defeating Nelson Pessoa Filho of Brazil on a time basis when both scored eight penalty points in a special jump-off. Kathryn Kusner tied with three others for third place but was eliminated in the special jump-off when Captain Mendivil Yucupicio of Mexico turned in a perfect tour of the course.

TEAM PERSONNEL
EQUESTRIAN — MEN & WOMEN

Frank D. Chapot, Wallpack, N.J. (jumping)
Mrs. Mary Mairs Chapot, Wallpack, N.J. (jumping)
Mrs. Kyra G. Downton, Atherton, Calif. (dressage)

Ernest R. Eckhardt, Purcellville, Va. (3-Day)
Mrs. Diane Fermin-Didot, Paris, France (dressage)
Kathryn H. Kusner, Monkton, Md. (jumping)
Michael O. Page, Briarcliff Manor, N.Y. (3-Day)
J. Michael Plumb, Bedminster, N.J. (3-Day)
Mrs. Donnan Sharp Plumb, Bedminster, N.J. (dressage)
William C. Steinkraus, Noroton, Conn. (jumping)
James C. Wofford, Somerville, N.J. (3-Day)

Staff Personnel

Whitney Stone, New York, N.Y. (Manager)
Bertalan de Nemethy, Gladstone, N.J. (Jumping Coach)
Stephen Von Visy, Peapack, N.J. (3-Day Coach)
Dr. James O'Dea, Avon, N.Y. (Veterinarian)

OFFICIAL SUMMARIES
EQUESTRIAN
PRIX DES NATIONS — (Nation's Cup)
(Name of horse in parentheses)

Individual Final Standings — 1. James Day (Canadian Club), Canada; 2. Nelson Pessoa Filho (Gran Geste), Brazil; 3. Capt. Manuel Mendivil Yucupicio (Veracruz), Mexico. The first two finished with zero penalty points in regular competition. In the jump-off both riders had eight penalty points, Day declared the winner on the basis of time. In the jump-off for third place, Captain Mendivil received zero penalty points while Antonio Eduardo Simoes (Samusai), Brazil had four penalty points and MISS KATHRYN KUSNER (Untouchable), USA and Jose Roberto Fernandez (Canral), Brazil had 16 penalty points.

Team Final Standings — 1. Brazil (Col. Reynoldo Pedro Ferreira, Jose Roberto Fernandez, Antonio Eduardo Simoes, Nelson Pessoa Filho); 2. USA (MRS. MARY MAIRS CHAPOT; FRANK CHAPOT; MISS KATHRYN KUSNER; WILLIAM STEINKRAUS); 3. Canada.

Three-Day Event — Individual

1. J. MICHAEL PLUMB, USA (Plain Sailing) plus 82.40; 2. Norman Elder, Canada (Ranee Doe) plus 49.80; 3. MICHAEL PAGE, USA (Foster) plus 31.65; 4. JAMES WOFFORD, USA (Kilkenny) minus 60.40; 5. ERNEST ECKHARDT, USA (The Stranger) minus 68.0; 6. Robin Hahn, Canada (Warden) minus 84.35.

Three-Day Event — Team

1. USA (PLUMB, PAGE, WOFFORD, ECKHARDT). No silver or bronze since other countries eliminated.

Mrs. Mary Chapot was a silver medalist on the US Prix des Nations team at Winnipeg.

EQUESTRIAN (MEN AND WOMEN)

F. Chapot

M. Chapot

K. Downton

E. Eckhardt

PHOTO-
GRAPH
NOT
AVAILABLE
Fermin-Didot

K. Kusner

M. Page

J. Plumb

D. Plumb

Steinkraus

J. Wofford

W. Stone

B. deVemethy

S. Von Visy

J. O'Dea

Dressage — Individual

1. MRS. KYRA DOWNTON, USA (Kadett) 1,352 points; 2. Capt. Patricio Escudero, Chile (Prete) 1,309; 3. Majoor Guillermo Squella, Chile (Copihue) 1,279.5 4. MRS, DIANE FERMIN-DIDOT, USA (Auverne) 669; 5. Inez Fischer-Credio, Canada (D'Eaubonne) 653; 6. Capt. Mario Diaz, Chile (Madrigal) 651. Note: First three riders competed in ride-off for first three placings.

Dressage — Team

1. Chile (Major Squella, Capt. Diaz, Capt. Escudero) 2,158 points; 2. USA (MRS. DOWNTON, MRS. FERMIN-DIDOT, MRS. DONNAN SHARP PLUMB) 1,929 points; 3. Canada (Miss Christilot Hanson, Miss Inez Fischer-Credio, Mrs. Jean MacKenzie) 1,699 points.

FENCING — MEN & WOMEN

United States fencers, with many experienced Olympic performers in the lineup, grabbed most of the medal honors in the individual competition. Winner of two golds was Anthony Keane, who took the individual sabre test for men and joined Walter Farber, Thomas Balla, and Csaba Gall for a first place in the team sabre.

Other golds were won by the men's epee team of Frank Anger, Paul Pesthy, Ralph Spinella, and Carl Borack and by the women's foil team comprised of Harriet King, Janice Romary, and Maxine Mitchell. Miss King also placed second in the women's individual foil, bowing only to the skilled Pilar Roldan of Mexico.

Anger and Pesthy were second and third respectively in the individual epee, Albert Axelrod and Robert Russell placed second and fourth respectively in the individual foil. The latter two, with Edwin Richards and Jeffrey Checkes, were second in the team foil division. Farber placed fourth in the individual sabre.

TEAM PERSONNEL

FENCING — MEN & WOMEN

Frank David Anger, Cambridge, Mass. (epee)
Albert Axelrod, Scarsdale, N.Y. (foil)
Thomas Balla, Philadelphia, Pa. (sabre)
Carl Borack, Beverly Hills, Calif. (epee)
Jeffrey Checkes, Brooklyn, N.Y. (foil)
Walter V. Farber, New York, N.Y. (sabre)
Csaba Gall, New York, N.Y. (sabre)
Anthony Keane, East Brunswick, N.J. (sabre)
Harriet King, San Francisco, Calif. (foil)
Maxine Mitchell, Los Angeles, Calif. (foil)
Paul K. Pesthy, San Antonio, Texas (epee)
Edwin Alan Richards, Boston, Mass. (foil)
Janice-Lee Romary, Woodland Hills, Calif. (foil)
Robert Russell, New York, N.Y. (foil)
Veronica Smith, Washington, D.C. (foil)
Ralph Spinella, Waterbury, Conn. (epee)

Staff Personnel

Delmar Calvert, Los Angeles, Calif. (Coach)
Csaba Elthes, New York, N.Y. (Coach)
Stanley S. Sieja, Princeton, N.J. (Manager)
Edmond F. Zeisig, Milwaukee, Wis. (Team Captain)
Dan DeChaine, Los Angeles, Calif. (Armorer)

OFFICIAL SUMMARIES

FENCING

Individual Epee

1. Arthur Telles, Brazil; 2. FRANK ANGER, USA; 3. PAUL PESTHY, USA. Other finalists: Peter Dakonyi, Canada; Felix Almada, Mexico; and Fernando Taboada, Argentina.

(continued)

FENCING (MEN AND WOMEN)

F. Anger

A. Axelrod

T. Balla

C. Borack

J. Checkes

W. Farber

C. Gall

A. Keane

H. King

M. Mitchell

P. Pesthy

E. Richards

J. Romary

R. Russell

V. Smith

R. Spinella

D. Calvert

C. Elthes

S. Sieja

E. Zeisig

D. DeChaine

325

FIELD HOCKEY

 E. Black

 D. Connors

 R. Gainer

 J. Schroeter

 B. Thompson

 Van Der Lee

 K. Issar

 J. Kaligis

 M. Lichtenfeld

 H. Waetge

 C. Waters

 D. Yoder

 Lingenfelter

 W. Luedeke

 F. Noodt

 H. Zucker

J. Greer

v. Walleghem

OFFICIAL SUMMARIES

FIELD HOCKEY

Final Rank	Nation	Regular Schedule			Title Series			Overall Total		
		W	L	T	W	L	T	W	L	T
1	Argentina	5	0	2	2	0	0	7	0	2
2	Trinidad-Tobago	4	2	1	1	1	0	5	3	1
3	UNITED STATES	4	3	0	1	1	0	5	4	0
4	Canada	5	0	2	0	2	0	5	2	2
5	Jamaica	1	1	5	–	–	–	1	1	5
6	Mexico	2	4	1	–	–	–	2	4	1
7	Bermuda	0	5	2	–	–	–	0	5	2
8	Netherlands-Antilles	0	6	1	–	–	–	0	6	1

Scores of Regular Scheduled Matches

Argentina 5, United States 0
Canada 2, Trinidad-Tobago 0
Jamaica 0, Mexico 0 (tie)
Bermuda 1, Netherlands-Antilles 1 (tie)

Argentina 1, Canada 1 (tie)
United States 2, Mexico 1
Jamaica 0, Bermuda 0 (tie)
Trinidad-Tobago 1, Netherlands-Antilles 0

Argentina 5, Mexico 0
United States 3, Netherlands-Antilles 0
Trinidad-Tobago 4, Bermuda 0
Canada 1, Jamaica 1 (tie)

Argentina 2, Trinidad-Tobago 0
Canada 3, United States 1
Jamaica 3, Netherlands-Antilles 0
Mexico 3, Bermuda 0

Argentina 0, Jamaica 0 (tie)
Trinidad-Tobago 3, United States 0
Mexico 1, Netherlands-Antilles 0
Canada 2, Bermuda 0

Argentina 7, Netherlands-Antilles 0
United States 3, Bermuda 0
Trinidad-Tobago 1, Jamaica 1 (tie)
Canada 2, Mexico 1

Argentina 6, Bermuda 0
United States 1, Jamaica 0
Canada 3, Netherlands-Antilles 0
Trinidad-Tobago 2, Mexico 1

Scores of Title Series

Semi-Final:
Argentina 1, United States 0
Trinidad-Tobago 2, Canada 0

Championship:
Argentina 5, Trinidad-Tobago 0
Third Place:
United States 1, Canada 0

Team Epee

1. USA (ANGER, PESTHY, RALPH SPINELLA, CARL BORACK) 16 wins 9 losses; 2. Brazil 12-13; 3. Venezuela 12-9; 4. Cuba 9-16. Other finalists Canada and Chile.

Individual Foil

1. Guillermo Saucedo, Argentina (5-0); 2. ALBERT AXELROD, USA (3-2, fewer hits against); 3. Orlando Nannini, Argentina (3-2); 4. ROBERT RUSSELL, USA (2-3); 5. Enrique Penabella Lugo, Cuba (1-4); 6. Leonardo Ferrer Ruiz, Cuba (1-4).

Team Foil

1. Argentina (Orlando Nannini, Guillermo Saucedo, Fernando Petrella, Avaristo Prendes); 2. USA (EDWIN RICHARDS, ROBERT RUSSELL, JEFFREY CHECKES, ALBERT AXELROD); 3. Cuba (Enrique Penabella Lugo, Victorio Ruiz, Dagoberto Borges, Luis Morales); 4. Canada.

Individual Sabre

1. ANTHONY KEANE, USA (5-0); 2. Roman Quinos, Argentina (3-2); 3. Les Samek, Canada (2-3); 4. WALTER FARBER, USA (1-4); 5. Alberto Lanteri, Argentina (2-3); 6. Pater Samek, Canada (2-3).

Team Sabre

1. USA (ANTHONY KEANE, WALTER FARBER, THOMAS BALL, CSABA GALL) 16-5; 2. Argentina 13-11; 3. Canada 9-14; 4. Cuba 9-17.

Women Individual Foil

1. Pilar Roldan, Mexico; 2. HARRIET KING, USA; 3. Pacita Wiedel, Canada. Other finalists: Margarita Rodriguez, Cuba; Olga Pareyon Moreno, Mexico; JANICE ROMARY, USA.

Women Team Foil

1. USA (HARRIET KING, JANICE ROMARY, MAXINE MITCHELL) 17-8; 2. Cuba 14-9; 3. Canada 11-14; 4. Argentina 8-17.

FIELD HOCKEY

A surprise third place finish by the men's field hockey team indicated a welcome development of United States talent in this sport and was the first such medal won by this nation in international competition. Eight nations participated in a preliminary round robin, the top four qualifying for a straight elimination title playoff series. The USA qualified behind Argentina, Canada, and Trinidad-Tobago, losing to these teams while winning four matches.

In the title playoffs, the United States was shut out by eventual champion Argentina, 1-0, while Trinidad-Tobago upset previously unbeaten, though tied, Canada, 2-0. Argentina won the final from Trinidad-Tobago,

3–0, and the United States nipped Canada, 1–0, on a goal by Francisco Noodt.

TEAM PERSONNEL

FIELD HOCKEY

E. Newbold Black IV, New York, N.Y.
Dudley E. Connors, Wilmington, Del.
Richard D. Gainer, New Hyde Park, N.Y.
Kulbir S. Issar, Old Bridge, N.J.
Jocelyn Kaligis, Allentown, Pa.
Michael Lichtenfeld, New York, N.Y.
Thomas A. Lingenfelter, Line Lexington, Pa.
W. P. Vance Luedeke, Greenwich, Conn.
Francisco Noodt, Middle Village, N.Y.
Juergen Schroeter, Englishtown, N.J.
Brendan Thompson, Phoenixville, Pa.
Frans Van Der Lee, Morrisville, Pa.
Herman Waetge, Whippany, N.J.
Christopher Waters, Larchmont, N.Y.
D. Lee Yoder, Ambler, Pa.
Hans Zucker, Pine Brook, N.J.

Staff Personnel

John Greer, Cos Cob, Conn. (Manager)
Andre Van Walleghem, Bloomfield, N.J. (Asst. Mgr.)

GYMNASTICS — MEN

Sparked by University of Wisconsin star Fred Roethlisberger, who won four gold medals, the USA male gymnasts took most of the honors in gymnastics. Fred won the all-around and horizontal bar championships, tied with Richard Loyd for first in the parallel bars, and was a member of the championship all-around team which included Mark Cohn, David Thor, Arno Lascari and Richard Loyd.

Cohn also won a gold in the side horse and tied for second with Roethlisberger in the still rings. The latter picked up his sixth medal, placing third in the long horse vault. Thor and Loyd were other frequent visitors to the victory stand, Loyd placing second in the side horse and floor exercise, while Thor was third in the all-around, the horizontal bar and the floor exercise. Another bronze medal was taken by Lascari in the parallel bars.

Loyd was the 1967 champion of the National Association of Intercollegiate Athletics (NAIA) while Thor, a University of Michigan student, was champion of the Big Ten conference.

TEAM PERSONNEL

GYMNASTICS — MEN

Mark Cohn, Philadelphia, Pa.
Robert Emery, Longmeadow, Mass.
Arno Lascari, Sacramento, Calif.
Richard Loyd, Winnsboro, La.
Fred Roethlisberger, Madison, Wis.
Dave Thor, Reseda, Calif.

Staff Personnel

Rudy Bachna, Kent, Ohio (Manager)
Fred Martinez, Natchitoches, La. (Coach)

OFFICIAL SUMMARIES

GYMNASTICS — MEN

Final Team Standings

1. USA 548.55 points (FRED ROETHLISBERGER, MARK COHN, DAVID THOR, RICHARD LOYD, ARNO LASCARI); 2. Cuba 536.55; 3. Mexico 529.40; 4. Canada 519.05; 5. Ecuador 402.45; 6. Argentina 210.75.

Final Individual Standings

All-Around — 1. FRED ROETHLISBERGER, USA 110.75; 2. Fernando Valles, Mexico 109.35; 3. DAVID THOR, USA 109.00; 4. Hector Ramirez, Cuba 108.75; 5. Octavio Suarez, Cuba 108.65; 6. RICHARD LOYD, USA 108.55.

Horizontal Bar — 1. ROETHLISBERGER, USA 18.85; 2. Armando Valles, Mexico 18.70; 3. THOR, USA 18.65; 4. Suarez, Cuba 18.40; 5. Ramirez, Cuba 18.30; 6. Jorge Rodriguez, Cuba 18.25.

Parallel Bars — 1. ROETHLISBERGER and LOYD, USA 18.95; 3. ARNO LASCARI, USA 18.90; 4. A. Valles, Mexico and MARK COHN, USA 18.85; 6. Roger Dion, Canada 18.50.

Pommel Horse (Side Horse) — 1. COHN, USA 19.15; 2. LOYD, USA 18.925; 3. THOR, USA 18.825; 4. A. Valles, Mexico 18.625; 5. ROBERT EMERY, USA 18.275; 6. Ramirez, Cuba 16.55.

Floor Exercises — 1. Ramirez, Cuba 18.450; 2. LOYD, USA 18.375; 3. THOR, USA and Armando Garcia, Mexico 18.325; 5. Rick Kinsmen, Canada and Jorge Rodriguez, Cuba 18.05.

Still Rings — 1. A. Valles, Mexico 18.90; 2. ROETHLISBERGER and COHN, USA 18.35; 4. Syd Jensen, Canada 18.10; 5. Roger Dion, Canada 17.60; 6. LASCARI, USA 11.60.

Long Horse Vault — 1. Rodriguez, Cuba 18.60; 2. Suarez, Cuba 18.40; 3. ROETHLISBERGER, USA, Dion, Canada and Rogelio Mendoza, Mexico 18.35; 6. Syd Jensen, Canada 18.15.

GYMNASTICS — WOMEN

Only Canadian Susan McDonnell's victory in the uneven parallel bars spoiled the United States' attempt to sweep all honors in women's gymnastics. She beat out the USA's Linda Metheny by .025 of a point, that slim margin preventing the latter from winning an unprecedented six gold medals!

Miss Metheny not only led the USA quintet (Marie Walther, Joyce Tanac, Deborah Bailey, Donna Schaenzer and herself) to the team title but she also took individual honors in the all-around, floor exercises, side horse vault,

(continued)

GYMNASTICS – MEN

M. Cohn   R. Emery   A. Lascari

R. Loyd   Roethlisberger   D. Thor

R. Bachna   F. Martinez

GYMNASTICS – WOMEN

D. Bailey   K. Gleason   C. Hacker

L. Metheny   D. Schaenzer   J. Tanac

M. Walther   R. Mulvihill   M. Grossfeld

B. Pascal

327

United States gymnast Linda Metheny won a spectacular five gold medals at Winnipeg.

and the balance beam. Twice the US athletes took all six places in an event, turning the trick in the individual all-around and in the floor exercises.

TEAM PERSONNEL

GYMNASTICS — WOMEN

Deborah Joan Bailey, Midwest City, Okla.
Kathy Gleason, Buffalo, N.Y.
Carolyn Hacker, Westport, Conn.
Linda Metheny, Tuscola, Ill.
Donna Schaenzer, Milwaukee, Wis.
Joyce Tanac, Seattle, Wash.
Marie Walther, Lakewood, Ohio

Staff Personnel

Richard J. Mulvihill, Champaign, Ill. (Manager)
Muriel Grossfeld, New Haven, Conn. (Coach)
Barbara Pascal, New Haven, Conn. (Pianist)

GYMNASTICS — WOMEN

Final Team Standings

1. USA 362.377 (MARIE WALTHER, JOYCE TANAC, DEBORAH BAILEY, DONNA SCHAENZER, LINDA METHENY); 2. Canada 336.75; 3. Cuba 334.526; 4. Mexico 289.130; 5. Brazil 112.231.

Final Individual Standings

All-Around — 1. LINDA METHENY, USA 74.03; 2. JOYCE TANAC, USA 72.99; 3. MARIE WALTHER, USA 71.61; 4. DONNA SCHAENZER, USA 71.61; 5. DEBORAH BAILEY, USA 70.86; 6. KATHY GLEASON, USA 70.28.

Floor Exercises — 1. MISS METHENY, USA 19.107; 2. MISS TANAC, USA 18.857; 3.

MISS SCHAENZER, USA 18.499; 4. MISS GLEASON, USA 18.275; 5. MISS WALTHER, USA 18.249; 6. MISS BAILEY, USA 18.133.

Side Horse Vault — 1. MISS METHENY, USA 18.500; 2. MISS SCHAENZER, USA 18.173; 3. MISS WALTHER, USA 18.016; 4. MISS TANAC, USA 17.841; 5. MISS GLEASON, USA 17.813; 6. Susan McDonnell, Canada 17.749.

Balance Beam — 1. MISS METHENY, USA 18.691; 2. MISS BAILEY, USA 18.566; 3. Zulima Bregado, Cuba 18.399; 4. MISS TANAC, USA 18.358; 5. MISS GLEASON, USA 18.162; 6. MISS WALTHER, USA 18.133.

Uneven Parallel Bars — 1. Susan McDonnell Canada 18.641; 2. MISS METHENY, USA 18.616; 3. MISS GLEASON, USA 18.608; 4. MISS TANAC, USA 18.308; 5. MISS WALTHER, USA 18.275; 6. Miss Bregado, Cuba 17.141.

JUDO

In the 1963 Games at Sao Paulo, the United States won three golds and one silver in the four weight divisions. This time in Winnipeg, with greatly improved competition extended to six weight divisions, the USA medal haul was just as successful, with all six entries winning medals, two golds, two silvers, and two bronzes.

The highlight of USA efforts was Allen Coage's defeat of Canada's strong Douglas Rogers in the heavyweight division. Rogers, who had been an

overwhelming favorite in the heavyweight class, also competed in the open division and won that.

Hayward Nishioka won the other gold medal for the USA, taking the middleweight crown. Silvers were won by lightweight Toshiyuke Seino and James Westbrook in the open class, while third place awards went to light heavyweight William Paul and featherweight Larry Fukuhara.

TEAM PERSONNEL

JUDO

Allen James Coage, St. Albans, N.Y. (heavyweight)
Larry Fukuhara, Long Beach, Calif. (lightweight)
Hayward Nishioka, Los Angeles, Calif. (middleweight)
William Paul, San Francisco, Calif. (light heavyweight)
Toshiyuki Seino, Gardena, Calif. (light middleweight)
James Westbrook, Oakland, Calif. (open class)

Staff Personnel

Thomas F. Dalton, Somerset, N.J. (Manager)
Kenneth K. Kuniyuki, Los Angeles, Calif. (Coach)

JUDO
(Third and Fourth Places each received Bronze Medals)

Open — 1. Douglas Rogers, Canada (won all four matches by a full point, "ippon," final

JUDO

A. Coage   L. Fukuhara   N. Nishioka

W. Paul   T. Seino   J. Westbrook

T. Dalton   K. Kuniyuki

total—0 penalty points); 2. JAMES WEST-BROOK, USA (3 penalty points, two victories by a full point, loss by a full point to Rogers); 3. Humberto Medina Gonzales, Cuba; 4. Kastriged Mehdi, Brazil.

Heavyweight — 1. ALLEN COAGE, USA; 2. Douglas Rogers, Canada; 3. Jose Luis Turietto, Argentina and Euladio Damasco Nicolaas, Netherlands-Antilles.

Light Heavyweight — 1. Michael Johnson, Canada (won three matches by a full point, lost a decision to silver medalist, final total, 2 penalty points); 2. Rodolfo Perez, Argentina; 3. WILLIAM PAUL, USA (4 penalty points); 4. Rolando Melendez Sanchez, Cuba.

Middleweight — 1. HAYWARD NISHIOKA, USA; 2. Lhosei Shiozawa, Brazil; 3. Gordon Buttle, Canada and Gabriel Goldschmied, Mexico.

Lightweight — 1. Takeshi Miura, Brazil (won five matches by a full point, won a decision in other, final total, 1 penalty point); 2. TOSHIYUKI SEINO, USA (won first four matches by a full point, lost by a full point to Miura, final total, 3 penalty points); 3. Ibrahim Torres Mayari, Cuba and Rene Arredondo Cepeda, Mexico.

Featherweight — 1. Akira Ono, Brazil (won three matches by a full point, won decision over bronze medalist, final total, 1 penalty point); 2. Patrick Bolger, Canada (5 penalty points); 3. LARRY FUKUHARA, USA (won one match by a full point, lost two decisions, final total, 4 penalty points; 4. Teodoro Luis

Gaston Castro, Cuba (final total, 5 penalty points).

ROWING

United States oarsmen improved greatly in their sport of rowing, taking firsts in all but one of the seven final races and placing second in that one, a showing virtually twice as good as that in 1963. The only gold medal to escape the USA clutches was taken by Argentina's single sculler, Alberto Demiddi, who beat off the challenge of USA's John Nunn.

The Vesper Boat Club of Philadelphia represented this nation in both the four-oars and the four-oars-with-coxswain events, winning both finals by convincing margins. The University of Pennsylvania supplied the winning pair-oars-with-coxswain combination, the Potomac Boat Club of Washington, D.C. made up the championship pair-oars tandem while James Dietz of the New York A.C. and James Storm of the San Diego Boat Club teamed to take first honors in the double sculls. Single sculler Nunn formerly rowed with Cornell University. Harvard Uni-

versity's vaunted crew, stroked by Ian H. Gardiner, easily regained the eight-oars-with-coxswain championship with a two-length victory over Canada's experienced crew.

Preliminary heats and repechages were staged only in the four-oars-with-coxswain, eight-oars-with coxswain, and pairs-with-coxswain events, limited entries in the four other classes permitting finals only.

TEAM PERSONNEL

ROWING

Lt. Robert Brayton, Beverly, N.J., USA (4-oars)
Gardner Cadwalader, Ambler, Pa. (2-oars with cox)
Curtis R. Canning, Salt Lake City, Utah (8-oars with cox)
Ens. Lee Demerest, Philadelphia, Pa., USN (4-oars)
James Dietz, New York, N.Y. (double sculls)
Arthur T. Evans, III, Cambridge, Mass. (spare)
Jacques P. Fiechter, Plymouth Meeting, Pa. (8-oars with cox)
Hugh Foley, Philadelphia, Pa. (4-oars with cox)
John J. Forster, Norristown, Pa. (spare)
Jay Fuhrman, Philadelphia, Pa. (2-oars with cox)
Ian H. Gardiner, Topsfield, Mass. (8-oars with cox)
Larry Gluckman, Philadelphia, Pa. (4-oars)
Mark Harrington, Litchfield, Conn. (spare coxswain)
Joseph Henwood, Philadelphia, Pa. (4-oars with cox)
David Higgins, Worcester, Mass. (8-oars with cox)
Franklin W. Hobbs, Concord, Mass. (8-oars with cox)
Paul Hoffman, St. Thomas, Virgin Islands (8-oars with cox)
Ens. Larry Hough, USN, Arlington, Va. (2-oars)
Anthony Johnson, Arlington, Va. (2-oars)
Clem Kopf, Springfield, Pa. (4-oars with cox)
Andrew B. Larkin, Kensington, Conn. (8-oars with cox)
J. Cleve Livingston, Carmichael, Calif. (8-oars with cox)
Perry Meek, Indianapolis, Ind. (2-oars with cox)
John Nunn, West Hollywood, Calif. (single sculls)
Paul Schlenker, Philadelphia, Pa. (spare)
Sean Shea, Philadelphia, Pa. (4-oars)
Eric Sigward, Cambridge, Mass. (spare)
Scott Steketee, Toledo, Ohio (8-oars with cox)
James Storm, San Diego, Calif. (double sculls)
William Stowe, Philadelphia, Pa. (4-oars with cox)
John Van Bloom, Long Beach, Calif. (spare)
Robert Zimonyi, Philadelphia, Pa. (4-oars with cox)

Staff Personnel

John Hutton, Akron, Ohio (Manager)
Conn Findlay, Belmont, Calif. (Asst. Mgr. & Asst. Coach)
Harry Parker, Cambridge, Mass. (Coach)
Dietrich Rose, Philadelphia, Pa. (Coach)
Campbell Balt, Cambridge, Mass. (Boatman)

America's Allen James Coage won the judo gold medal with quick throws like this.

ROWING

R. Brayton   Cadwalader   C. Canning

J. Livingston   P. Meek   J. Nunn

L. Demerest   J. Dietz   A. Evans

P. Schlenker   S. Shea   E. Sigward

J. Fiechter   H. Foley   J. Forster

S. Steketee   J. Storm   W. Stowe

J. Fuhrman   I. Gardiner   L. Gluckman

J. Van Bloom   R. Zimonyi   J. Hutton

M. Harrington   J. Henwood   D. Higgins

C. Findlay   H. Parker   D. Rose

F. Hobbs   P. Hoffman   L. Hough

C. Balt

A. Johnson   C. Kopf   A. Larkin

OFFICIAL SUMMARIES

ROWING

Eight Oars with Coxswain

Final — USA 6:30.86 (Harvard: IAN GARD-INER, stroke; CURTIS CANNING, no. 7; AN-DREW LARKIN, no. 6; SCOTT STEKETEE, no. 5; FRANKLIN HOBBS, no. 4; JACQUES FIECH-TER, no. 3; CLEVE LIVINGSTON, no. 2; DAVID HIGGINS, bow; PAUL HOFFMAN, coxswain); 2. Canada 6:37.53; 3. Cuba 6:51.41; 4. Argentina 6:53.51; 5. Mexico 7:06.27.

Repechage Heat — 1. Canada 6:04.11; 2. Argentina 6:17.06;; Mexico 6:25.90.

Heat No. 1 — 1. USA 6:18.99; 2. Canada 6:23.99; 3. Argentina 7:32.14.

Heat No. 2 — 1. Cuba 6:33.30; 2. Mexico 6:42.60; 3. Paraguay 6:57.55.

Four Oars with Coxswain

Final — 1. USA 6:47.91 (Vesper B.C. — WILLIAM STOWE, stroke; JOSEPH HENWOOD, no. 3; CLEM KOPF, no. 2; HUGH FOLEY, bow; ROBERT ZIMONYI, coxswain); 2. Argentina 6:50.04; 3. Cuba 6:59.51; 4. Canada; 5. Mexico.

Repechage Heat — 1. USA 6:36.06; 2. Cuba 6:47.02; 3. Mexico 6:58.26; 4. Peru 7:05.17; 5. Paraguay 7:17.47.

Heat No. 1 — 1. Canada 7:29.14; 2. Cuba 7:32.44 3. Mexico 7:49.23; 4. Peru 7:57.19.

Heat No. 2 — 1. Argentina 7:11.8; 2. USA 7:16.54; 3. Paraguay 7:58.55.

Four Oars without Coxswain

Final — 1. USA 6:46.99 (Vesper: Ens. LEE DEMAREST, USN, stroke; Lt. ROBERT BRAYTON, USAF, no. 3; LAWRENCE GLUCKMAN, no. 2; SEAN SHEA, bow); 2. Canada 6:50.14; 3. Mexico 7:18.01.

Pairs with Coxswain

Final — 1. USA 8:00.14 (Univ. of Penna.: PERRY MEEK, stroke; GARDNER CADWALADER, bow; JAMES FUHRMAN, coxswain); 2. Argentina 8:07.42; 3. Brazil 8:15.89; 4. Uruguay 8:27.61; 5. Peru 8:34.41.

Repechage Heat — 1. Brazil 7:46.32; 2. Argentina 7:50.15; 3. Peru 7:52.36; 4. Canada 7:55.61.

Heat No. 1 — 1. USA 8:09.1; 2. Argentina 8:25.27; 3. Brazil 8:38.23.

Heat No. 2 — 1. Uruguay 8:26.27; 2. Canada 8:31.73; 3. Peru 8:35.07.

Pairs without Coxswain

Final — 1. USA 7:20.24 (Potomac Boat Club: LAWRENCE HOUGH, stroke; PHILIP JOHNSON, bow); 2. Canada 7:46.68; 3. Mexico 7:57.54; 4. Argentina 8:08.83.

Double Sculls

Final — 1. USA 7:26.67 (JAMES DIETZ, New York A.C., stroke; JAMES STORM, San Diego B.C., bow); 2. Canada 7:40.41; 3. Argentina 7:50.08; 4. Brazil 8:00.55; 5. Mexico 8:08.75.

Single Sculls

Final — 1. Alberto Demiddi, Argentina 7:42.18; 2. JOHN NUNN, USA 7:52.59; 3. Otto Plettner, Mexico 8:08.03; 4. Claude Saunders, Canada 8:21.33.

SHOOTING

Canada's sharpshooting Alf Meyer, who scored a near perfect 598×600 to win the small bore rifle (50 meters) individual crown, was the only person who prevented a clean sweep of first places by United States marksmen. All told, the USA won team titles in the free pistol, small bore (50 meter) rifle, small bore rifle (three position), rapid fire pistol, center fire pistol, and skeet competitions, adding individual golds in five of these events, totalling 11 golds out of a possible dozen. In addition, USA shooters picked up three silvers and two bronzes.

A triple gold medal winner was M/Sgt. William Blankenship (USA) in the pistol events, while double gold medalists included Major William McMillan (USMC) in rapid fire pistol; S/Sgt. Hershel Anderson (USA) in free pistol; Gary Anderson in small bore rifle; Lt. Allen Morrison (USMC) in skeet shooting; Francis Higginson (USMC) in center fire pistol; and the first woman to win a championship, Lt. Margaret Thompson (USA), in small bore rifle three position.

Miss Thompson, on her way to the individual championship in the three position small bore rifle test, set a Pan-American record of 1152 points and tallied 391 in the kneeling division to tie the existing world mark.

TEAM PERSONNEL

SHOOTING

Gary L. Anderson, San Anselmo, Calif. (small bore rifle)
S/Sgt. Hershel Anderson, USA, Columbus, Ga. (free pistol)
M/Sgt. William Blankenship, USA, Columbus, Ga. (free, rapid fire, and center fire pistol)
W/O David I. Boyd II, USMC, Belleville, N.J. (rifle-alternate)
AOCS Allen F. Buntrock, USN, San Diego, Calif. (skeet)
T/Sgt. Robert Dueitt, USAF, San Antonio, Texas (pistol-alternate)
Maj. Franklin Green, USAF, San Antonio, Texas (free pistol)
ADR/1 Donald L. Hamilton, USN, Brookline, Mass. (center fire pistol)
Sgt. Bonnie Harmon, USA, Columbus, Ga. (center fire pistol)
S/Sgt. Francis Higginson, USMC, Quantico, Va. (center fire pistol)
Maj. William W. McMillan, USMC, Carlsbad, Calif. (rapid fire pistol)
Capt. Bruce A. Meredith, USA, Columbus, Ga. (small bore rifle)
Lt. Allen W. Morrison, USMC, Quantico, Va. (skeet)
Capt. Rhody L. Nornberg, USAF, San Antonio, Texas (small bore rifle)

A-2/C Robert Randle, USAF, Lackland AFB, Texas (rifle alternate)
Robert Rodale, Allentown, Pa. (skeet)
David Ross III, Philadelphia, Pa. (small bore rifle)
Robert Schuehle, Roselle, Ill. (skeet)
SFC Aubrey Smith, USA, Columbus, Ga. (rapid fire pistol)
S/Sgt. Edwin L. Teague, USA, San Antonio, Texas (rapid fire pistol)
Lt. Margaret Thompson, USA, Topeka, Kan. (small bore rifle)
M/Sgt. Ralph Thompson, USA, Columbus, Ga. (pistol alternate)
S/Sgt. Arnold Vitarbo, USAF, San Antonio, Texas (free pistol)
John Writer, Columbus, Ga. (small bore rifle)

Staff Personnel

Harry Reeves, Andrews, N.C. (Team Captain)
Lt. Col. Fred Keifer, USA, Columbus, Ga. (Team Adjutant)
Raymond Berthnay, USA, Columbus, Ga. (Rifle Armorer)
S/Sgt. David R. Breeding, USAF, San Antonio, Texas (Pistol Armorer)
E. Frank Coleman, USAF, San Antonio, Texas (Shotgun Armorer)

OFFICIAL SUMMARIES

SHOOTING

Free Pistol

Team — 1. USA 2171* (S/Sgt HERSHEL ANDERSON, USA 548, Major FRANKLIN GREEN, USAF 532, S/Sgt. ARNOLD VITARBO, USA 554, M/Sgt. WILLIAM BLANKENSHIP, USA 537); 2. Cuba 2127; 3. Mexico 2118; 4. Colombia 2097; 5. Peru 2091.

Individual — 1. S/Sgt. HERSHEL ANDERSON, USA 548; 2. Javier Peregrina, Mexico 545; 3. Edgar Espinoza, Venezuela 542; 4. Seguro Vita, Peru 538; 5. Hector Aspita, Argentina 538; 6. Leopoldo Martinez, Mexico 538.

Small Bore Rifle (50 Meters)

Team — 1. USA 2379*** (Capt. BRUCE MEREDITH, USA; GARY ANDERSON, Capt. RHODY NORNBERG, USAF; DAVE ROSS); 2. Canada 2363; 3. Mexico 2347; 4. Brazil 2332; 5. Cuba 2327; 6. Venezuela 2321.

Individual — 1. Alf Mayer, Canada 598****; 2. Capt. RHODY NORNBERG, USA 593; 3. Alegario Vazquez, Mexico 593; 4. Capt. BRUCE MEREDITH, USA 593; 5. Alfredo Luna, Argentina 592; 6. Gil Boa, Canada 589.

Rapid Fire Pistol (22 Rapid Fire Silhouette)

Team — 1. USA 2307 (Major WILLIAM McMILLAN, USMC, 581; SFC EDWIN TEAGUE, USA, 579; M/Sgt. WILLIAM BLANKENSHIP, USA, 564; SFC AUBREY SMITH, USA 583); 2. Venezuela 2283; 3. Mexico 2266; 4. Cuba 2258; 5. Argentina 2248; 6. Colombia 2241.

Individual — 1. Major WILLIAM McMILLAN, USMC, USA, 581; 2. Alirio Maya, Colombia 580; 3. Sgt./FC EDWIN TEAGUE, USA, 579; 4. F. De Castro, Venezuela 576; 5. Homero Laddaga, Mexico 574; 6. Victor Castellanos, Guatemala 572.

Small Bore Rifle (Prone, Kneeling, Standing)

Team — 1. USA 4571* (GARY ANDERSON 1139 Lt. MARGARET THOMPSON, USA 1152;

G. Anderson   H. Anderson   Blankenship

D. Boyd   A. Buntrock   R. Dueitt

F. Green   D. Hamilton   B. Harmon

F. Higginson   W. McMillan   B. Meredith

A. Morrison   R. Nornberg   R. Randle

R. Rodale   D. Ross   R. Schuehle

A. Smith   E. Teague   M. Thompson

SHOOTING

R. Thompson   A. Vitarbo   J. Writer

H. Reeves   F. Keifer   R. Berthnay

D. Breeding   F. Coleman

Capt. BRUCE MEREDITH, USA 1141; JOHN WRITER 1139; 2. Canada 4502; 3. Mexico 4465; 4. Cuba 4433; 5. Peru 4296; 6. Ecuador 4249.

Individual — 1. Lt. MARGARET THOMPSON, USA 1152*, tied world record for kneeling, 391; 2. Gerry Ouellette, Canada 1145; 3. GARY ANDERSON, USA 1139; 4. Bob Cheyne, Canada 1131; 5. Jesus Gonzalez, Mexico 1122; 6. Olagerio Vazquez, Mexico 1122.

Center Fire Pistol

Team — 1. USA 2342 (M/Sgt. WILLIAM BLANKENSHIP, USA 586; FRANCIS HIGGINSON, USMC 593; ADR 1 DONALD HAMILTON, USN 587; BONNIE HARMON, 586); 2. Canada 2280; 3. Venezuela 2264.

Individual — 1. FRANCIS HIGGINSON, USMC USA 593; 2. M/Sgt. WILLIAM BLANKENSHIP, USA 586; 3. Dr. Jules Sobrian, Canada 586.

Skeet Shooting

Team — 1. USA 379/400 (ROBERT RODALE 97; ROBERT SCHUEHLE 94; AOCS ALLEN BUNTROCK, USN 91; Lt. ALLEN MORRISON, USMC 97); 2. Cuba 376; 3. Chile 373; 4. Colombia 370; 5. Canada 362; 6. Mexico 347.

Individual — 1. Lt. ALLEN MORRISON, USMC, USA 195; 2. ROBERT SCHUEHLE, USA 193; 3. Delfin Gomez, Cuba, 188 plus 23 in shoot-off; 4. Amadeo Di Laura, Peru, 188 plus 22 in shoot-off; 5. Otto Javier Londono, Colombia, 188 plus 21 in shoot-off; 6. Eddie Tuvo, Canada and Don Sanderlin, Canada 187.

* Pan-American Games Record.
** Ties Pan-American Games Record.
*** Betters listed world record.
**** Ties listed world record.

SOCCER FOOTBALL

The United States soccer football team failed to qualify for the title playoff series, placing only third in the Group A match play. Its only victory was scored at the expense of Cuba, 2–1, while losses were to the eventual silver medalist, Bermuda, 7–3, and to fourth-place Canada, 2–1.

The first two places in each group advanced to the finals, with Mexico defeating Bermuda, 4–0, in an incredible overtime match, while Trinidad-Tobago whipped Canada for the bronze medal, 4–1.

Oddly enough, the USA team had already competed in regional Olympic tests months before the Pan-American Games, losing and tying Bermuda in a two-game test that eliminated United States hopes of advancing to a possible playing berth at Mexico City in 1968.

TEAM PERSONNEL

SOCCER FOOTBALL

Janos Benedek, Jr., Chicago, Ill.
Otto Brand, Philadelphia, Pa.
Gary J. DeLong, San Francisco, Calif.
Dieter W. Ficken, Brooklyn, N.Y.
Robert Gansler, Milwaukee, Wis.
Michael Ivanow, San Francisco, Calif.
Jack Kinealy, St. Louis, Mo.
Ned Kralj, East Chicago, Ind.
Patrick Jay Moore, St. Louis, Mo.
John Mueller, St. Louis, Mo.
Alex Roboostoff, Daly City, Calif.

Arpad K. Sipos, Middletown, Pa.
Neil J. Stam, Centereach, N.Y.
Horst Stemke, Milwaukee, Wis.
Ernest Tuchschecer, Chicago, Ill.
Eugene Ventriglia, New Paltz, N.Y.
Robert H. Watson, Philadelphia, Pa.
Myron Worobec, Irvington, N.J.

Staff Personnel

Walter Giesler, Clayton, Mo. (Manager)
Geza Henni, Houston, Texas (Coach)

SOCCER FOOTBALL

J. Benedek   O. Brand   G. De Long

D. Ficken   R. Gansler   M. Ivanow

J. Kinealy   N. Kralj   P. Moore

OFFICIAL SUMMARIES

SOCCER FOOTBALL

Final Rank	Nation	Group Matches W	L	T	PTS	Title series W	L	T	PTS	Overall total W	L	T	PTS
1	Mexico (B)	1	0	2	4	2	0	0	4	3	0	2	8
2	Bermuda (A)	1	0	2	4	1	1	0	2	2	1	2	6
3	Trinidad-Tobago (B)	2	0	1	5	1	1	0	2	3	1	1	7
4	Canada (A)	2	0	1	5	0	2	0	0	2	2	1	5
5	Argentina (B)	1	1	1	3	–	–	–	–	1	1	1	3
6	UNITED STATES (A)	1	2	0	2	–	–	–	–	1	2	0	2
7	Cuba (A)	0	2	1	1	–	–	–	–	0	2	1	1
8	Colombia (B)	0	3	0	0	–	–	–	–	0	3	0	0

Scores Group A Matches

Canada 2, Cuba 1
Bermuda 7, United States 3

Canada 2, United States 1
Bermuda 1, Cuba 1 (tie)

Canada 2, Bermuda 2 (tie)
United States 2, Cuba 1

Scores Group B Matches

Trinidad-Tobago 5, Colombia 2
Mexico 2, Argentina 2 (tie)

Trinidad-Tobago 1, Mexico 1 (tie)
Argentina 5, Colombia 0

Trinidad-Tobago 1, Argentina 0
Mexico 3, Colombia 0

Title Series Scores

Semi-Final Matches
Mexico 2, Canada 1
Bermuda 3, Trinidad-Tobago 1

Championship
Mexico 4, Bermuda 0 (overtime)
Third place playoff
Trinidad-Tobago 4, Canada 1

SOCCER FOOTBALL

J. Mueller   A. Roboostoff   A. Sipos

N. Stam   H. Stemke   Tuchscherer

E. Ventriglia   R. Watson   M. Worobec

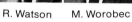

W. Giesler   G. Henni

SWIMMING — MEN

Monopoly was the name of the game in the swimming and diving events but while the United States repeatedly scored gold medal triumphs during the competitions, there were plenty of indications that, despite the obvious supremacy of the highly-trained USA natators, the opposition from the other entering nations was at an all-time high. Time and time again, although USA representatives were finishing 1–2, many of the next place winners were establishing new records for their respective national archives. In addition, the winning margins were narrow and the challenges strong. New Pan - American records were set in all 17 events as thousands packed the splendid facility constructed especially for the Games.

The USA male contingent of 25 competed in 17 championship events

(the program having been modeled after the expanded Olympic schedule), and scored firsts in all but three. Along with the 14 gold medals, nine silvers and six bronzes were picked up for an overall total of 29 awards.

Topping the USA list was a high school boy who had just completed his junior year. He was Mark Spitz of Santa Clara, California, who garnered five golds. He won both 100 and 200 meter butterfly races and competed on three winning relay teams. Donald Schollander, now classed an elder statesman in the upsurge of youthful USA contenders, picked up where he left off in the 1964 Olympic Games. The four-time Olympic gold medalist won the 200 meter freestyle and was a member of two winning relay quartets.

Other multiple gold medal winners were Doug Russell, Ken Walsh, Gregory Charlton, and Charles Hickcox, each taking two. Breaking the otherwise monotonous USA parade to the victory stand were a Canadian, Ralph Hutton, and a Brazilian, Jose Fiolo. Hutton convincingly defeated two USA favorites in the 200 meter backstroke, while Fiolo won both 100 and 200 meter breaststroke events in record-breaking style.

TEAM PERSONNEL

SWIMMING — MEN

Michael Burton, Carmichael, Calif. (400 & 1500 meter freestyle, 200 meter butterfly)
Gregory Charlton, Arcadia, Calif. (400 meter freestyle & 800 meter freestyle relay)
F. Michael Fitzmaurice, Greenwich, Conn. (200 meter freestyle)
Charles Goettsche, Wilmette, Ill. (200 meter backstroke)
Donald Havens, Granada Hills, Calif. (100 meter freestyle)
Fred Haywood, Santa Clara, Calif. (100 meter backstroke)
Charles Hickcox, Phoenix, Ariz. (100 & 200 meter backstroke and 800 meter freestyle relay)
Charles Knorr, Cincinnati, Ohio (platform diving)
Roger Lyon, Los Angeles, Calif. (freestyle alternate)
Kenneth Merten, Pacoima, Calif. (100 and 200 meter breaststroke)
Robert Momsen, San Jose, Calif. (200 meter breaststroke)
Douglas Russell, Midland, Texas (200 meter individual medley, 400 meter medley relay)
Keith Russel, Mesa, Ariz. (springboard diving)
Donald Schollander, Lake Oswego, Ore. (200 meter freestyle, 400 & 800 meter freestyle relay)
Mark Spitz, Santa Clara, Calif. (100 & 200 meter butterfly, 400 meter medley relay)

SWIMMING – MEN

M. Burton   G. Charlton   Fitzmaurice

C. Goettsche   D. Havens   F. Haywood

C. Hickcox   C. Knorr   R. Lyon

K. Merten   R. Momsen   D. Russell

K. Russell   Schollander   M. Spitz

A. Strenk   W. Utley   R. Wales

K. Walsh   R. Waples   K. Webb

333

R. Webb   B. Wrightson   W. Young

Z. Zorn   J. Bogert   D. Rivenes

A. Stager   J. Schleuter   R. O'Brien

Andrew Strenk, Fullerton, Calif.
  (1500 meter freestyle)
William Utley, St. Petersburg, Fla.
  (200 & 400 meter individual medley)
Ross Wales, Youngstown, Ohio
  (100 meter butterfly)
Kenneth Walsh, East Lansing, Mich.
  (400 meter freestyle & medley relay)
Robert Waples, Palo Alto, Calif.
  (freestyle alternate)
Kenneth Webb, Portland, Oregon
  (400 meter individual medley)
Russell Webb, Yorba Linda, Calif.
  (100 meter breaststroke & 400 meter
  medley relay)
Bernard Wrightson, Denver, Colo.
  (springboard diving)
Win Young, Bloomington, Ind.
  (platform diving)
Zachary Zorn, Buena Park, Calif.
  (100 meter freestyle)

Staff Personnel

Dr. John A. Bogert, Independence, Mo.
  (Manager)
David Rivenes, Miles City, Mont. (Asst. Mgr.)
Augustus Stager, Ann Arbor, Mich. (Coach)
J. Walter Schleuter, Scottsdale, Ariz.
  (Asst. Coach)
Ronald O'Brien, Columbus, Ohio
  (Diving coach)

OFFICIAL SUMMARIES

SWIMMING — MEN

100 Meter Freestyle — 1. DONALD HAVENS, USA 0:53.79* 2. ZACHARY ZORN, USA 0:53.97; 3. Sandy Gilchrist, Canada 0:54.85; 4. Bob Kasting, Canada 0:54.877 5. Ilson Pinto Asturiano, Brazil 0:54.879; 6. Alberto Nicolao, Argentina 0:55.30; 7. Salvador Ruiz de Chavez, Mexico 0:55.74; 8. Teodoro Capriles, Venezuela 0:56.00.
200 Meter Freestyle — 1. DONALD SCHOLLANDER, USA 1:56.01*; 2. Ralph Hutton, Canada 1:58.44; 3. Julio Arango, Colombia

2:01.77; 4. Alberto Nicolao, Argentina 2:01.96; 5. Ron Jacks, Canada 2:02.68; 6. Mario de Lucca, Argentina 2:02.80; 7. MIKE FITZMAURICE, USA 2:02.81; 8. Teodoro Capriles, Venezuela 2:06.41.
400 Meter Freestyle — 1. GREGORY CHARLTON, USA 4:10.23*; 2. Ralph Hutton, Canada 4:11.88; 3. MICHAEL BURTON, USA 4:15.74; 4. Julio Arango, Colombia 4:19.18; 5. Guillermo Echevarria, Mexico 4:21.43; 6. Mario de Lucca, Argentina 4:21.77; 7. Ron Jacks, Canada 4:23.23; 8. Celestino Perez, Puerto Rico 4:27.80.
1500 Meter Freestyle — 1. MICHAEL BURTON, USA 16:44:40*; 2. Ralph Hutton, Canada 16:51.81; 3. ANDREW STRENK, USA 17:03.43; 4. Guillermo Echevarria, Mexico 17:07.32; 5. Julio Arango, Colombia 17:18.1; 6. Sandy Gilchrist, Canada 17:45.12; 7. Fernando Gonzelez, Ecuador 17:54.14; 8. Thomas Becerra, Colombia 18:00.68.
100 Meter Backstroke — 1. CHARLES HICKCOX, USA 1:01.19*; 2. FRED HAYWOOD, USA 1:02.45; 3. Jim Shaw, Canada 1:02.87; 4. Vincente Capriles, Venezuela 1:03.21; 5. Carlos Vander Math, Argentina 1:03.73; 6. Edmundo Fossa Huergo, Argentina 1:03.99; 7. Bill Kennedy, Canada 1:04.16; 8. Waldur Ramos, Brazil 1:05.77.
200 Meter Backstroke — 1. Ralph Hutton, Canada 2:12.55*; 2. CHARLES HICKCOX, USA 2:13.05; 3. CHARLES GOETTSCHE, USA 2:15.94; 4. Jim Shaw, Canada 2:17.08; 5. Celesino Perez, Puerto Rico 2:22.13; 6. Alfonso Alvarez, Mexico 2:23,59; 7. Jorge Urreta, Mexico 2:33.85. Waldur Ramos, Brazil, disqualified.
100 Meter Breaststroke — 1. Jose Fiolo, Brazil 1:07.52*; 2. RUSSELL WEBB, USA 1:09.13; 3. KENNETH MERTEN, USA 1:09.32; 4. Bill Malhoney, Canada 1:10.76; 5. Paul Lottman, Canada 1:11.87; 6. Oswaldo Borretto, Argentina 1:12.02; 7. Felipe Munoz, Mexico 1:12.77; 8. Rafael Hernandez, Mexico 1:14.76.
200 Meter Breaststroke — 1. Jose Fiolo, Brazil 2:30.42*; 2. ROBERT MOMSEN, USA 2:31.01; 3. KENNETH MERTEN, USA 2:34.17; 4. Bill Mahoney, Canada 2:35.33; 5. Robert Stoddard, Canada 2:36.83; 6. Felipe Munoz, Mexico 2:38.88; 7. Oswaldo Borretto, Argentina 2:43.80; 8. Luis Angel Acosta, Mexico 2:44.50.
100 Meter Butterfly — 1. MARK SPITZ, USA 0:56.20*; 2. ROSS WALES, USA 0:57.04; 3. Alberto Nicolao, Argentina 0:58.63; 4. Ron Jacks, Canada 0:59.12; 5. Thomas Arusoo, Canada 0:59.53; 6. Jose Ferraioli, Puerto Rico 1:00.5; 7. Joao Costa Lima, Brazil 1:00.5; 8. Gary Goodner, Puerto Rico 1:00.65.
200 Meter Butterfly — 1. MARK SPITZ, USA 2:06.42*; 2. Thomas Arusoo, Canada 2:10.70; 3. MICHAEL BURTON, USA 2:13.26; 4. Gabriel Altamirano, Mexico 2:13.57; 5. Joao Costa Lima, Brazil 2:14.19; 6. Ron Jacks, Canada 2:15.57; 7. Juan Carranza, Argentina 2:17.01; 8. Jose Ferraioli, Puerto Rico 2:21.79.
200 Meter Individual Medley — 1. DOUGLAS RUSSELL, USA 2:13.22*; 2. WILLIAM UTLEY, USA 2:13.68; 3. Sandy Gilchrist, Canada 2:16.61; 4. Juan Carlos Bello, Puerto Rico 2:17.32; 5. George Smith, Canada 21:8.06; 6. Celestino Perez, Puerto Rico 2:21.75; 7. Teodoro Capriles, Venezuela 2:22.84; 8. Rafael Hernandez, Mexico 2:24.43.
400 Meter Individual Medley — 1. WILLIAM UTLEY, US 4:48.12*; 2. KENNETH WEBB, USA 4:50.89; 3. Sandy Gilchrist, Canada 4:55.60; 4. Juan Carlos Bello, Puerto Rico 4:58.54; 5. George Smith, Canada 5.01.66; 6. Hector Scerbo, Argentina 5:07.34; 7. Henry Chenaux, Puerto Rico 5:07.60; 8. Thomas Becerra, Colombia 5:12.59.
400 Meter Freestyle Relay — 1. USA (KEN WALSH, MIKE FITZMAURICE, MARK SPITZ,

DONALD SCHOLLANDER) 3:34.08*; 2. Canada (Ralph Hutton, Ron Jacks, Sandy Gilchrist, Bob Kasting) 3:40.82; 3. Argentina 3:45.50; 4. Puerto Rico 3:46.00; 5. Brazil 3:46.03; 6. Mexico 3:47.48; 7. Peru 3:53.04; 8. El Salvador 3:58.05.
800 Meter Freestyle Relay — 1. USA (DONALD SCHOLLANDER, CHARLES HICKCOX, GREGORY CHARLTON, MARK SPITZ) 8:00.46*; 2. Canada (Sandy Gilchrist, Ron Jacks, Bob Kasting, Ralph Hutton) 8:07.16; 3. Argentina 8:19.48; 4. Puerto Rico 8:23.65; 5. Mexico 8:27.15; 6. Brazil 8:35.46; 7. Peru 8:41.25; 8. El Salvador 8:54.99.
400 Meter Medley Relay — 1. USA (DOUGLAS RUSSELL, RUSSELL WEBB, MARK SPITZ, KEN WALSH) 3:59.31*; 2. Canada (Jim Shaw, Bill Mahoney, Ron Jacks, Sandy Gilchrist) 4:04.29; 3. Brazil 4:06.64; 4. Argentina 4:10.57; 5. Venezuela 4:15.23; 6. Mexico 4:16.04; 7. Puerto Rico 4:17.70; 8. Peru 4:42.71.
Springboard Diving — 1. BERNARD WRIGHTSON, USA; 2. KEITH RUSSELL, USA; 3. Paul Escobar, Colombia; 4. Luis Nino de Rivera, Mexico; 5. Jerry Anderson, Puerto Rico; 6. Peter Emond, Canada; 7. Jose Robinson, Mexico; 8. Luis Viere, Cuba.
Platform Diving — 1. WIN YOUNG, USA 774.65; 2. Luis Nino de Rivera, Mexico 706.95; 3. Henao Diego, Colombia 699.20; 4. Lawrence Folinsbee, Canada 668.70; 5. Alberto Moreno Yera, Cuba 667.85; 6. CHARLES KNORR, USA 649.70; 7. Jorge Telch, Mexico 635.04; 8. Robert Eaton, Canada 627.20.

SWIMMING — WOMEN

Like the USA men's team, the distaff division scored overwhelming triumphs. Only Canada's great Elaine Tanner broke through the USA ring, scoring victories in both backstroke races. Miss Tanner also won a silver in the 100 meter butterfly. The USA medal haul included 14 golds, nine silvers, and four bronzes for an overall total of 27 awards, two less that the men. As in the men's division, all Pan-American records were broken, and in some cases, existing world marks were bettered.

Claudia Kolb, 17-year-old Santa Clara high school student, scored three individual triumphs, winning both individual medley events and demonstrating her versatility by taking first in the 200 meter butterfly. She added a silver in the 200-meter breaststroke to lead her team in awards.

Catie Ball also picked up three golds, winning both breaststroke finals and swimming with the victorious 4 × 100 meter medley relay team. Double gold winners were Wendy Fordyce, Pamela Kruse, Eleanor Daniels, and 14-year-old Debbie Meyers. The latter broke world marks as well as Pan-Am standards in winning the gruelling 400 and 800 meter freestyle finals.

Miss Meyer, however, wasn't the youngest member of the USA team.

That honor was Susan Pedersen's. The 13-year-old from Sacramento, California, placed second in the 800-meter freestyle and both individual medley events for three silver medals.

TEAM PERSONNEL

SWIMMING — WOMEN

Catharine Ball, Jacksonville, Fla. (100 & 200 meter breaststroke, 400 meter medley relay)

Erika E. Bricker, Visalia, Calif. (100 meter freestyle)

Lesley Bush, Princeton, N. J. (platform diving)

Patty Caretto, Whittier, Calif. (freestyle alternate)

Pam Carpinelli, Santa Clara, Calif. (400 meter freestyle relay)

Eleanor Daniel, Elkins Park, Pa. (100 meter butterfly, 400 meter medley relay)

Lee Davis, Saratoga, Calif. (100 & 200 meter butterfly)

Cecilia Dougherty, Cornwells Heights, Pa. (backstroke alternate)

Cathy Jean Ferguson, Burbank, Calif. (200 meter backstroke)

Wendy Fordyce, Miami Springs, Fla. (400 meter medley relay)

Sue Gossick, Tarzana, Calif. (springboard diving)

Cynthia L. Goyette, Detroit, Mich. (100 meter breaststroke)

Linda L. Gustavson, Santa Cruz, Calif. (400 meter freestyle relay)

Peggy E. Hagwood, Falls Church, Va. (butterfly alternate)

Kaye M. Hall, Tacoma, Wash. (100 meter backstroke)

Catherine L. Jamison, Portland, Ore. (breaststroke alternate)

Lt. Micki King, USAF, Ann Arbor, Mich. (springboard diving)

Claudia Kolb, Santa Clara, Calif. (200 meter breaststroke, 200 meter butterfly, 200 & 400 meter individual medley)

Pamela J. Kruse, Pompano Beach, Fla. (200 & 400 meter freestyle, 400 meter freestyle relay)

Deborah Meyer, Sacramento, Calif. (400 & 800 meter freestyle)

Kendis Moore, Phoenix, Ariz. (100 & 200 meter backstroke, 400 meter medley relay)

Susan Pedersen, Sacramento, Calif. (800 meter freestyle)

Ann Peterson, Scottsdale, Ariz. (platform diving)

Nancy Ryan, Santa Clara, Calif. (freestyle alternate)

Kathleen Thomas, Springfield, Va. (individual medley alternate)

Lillian (Pokey) Watson, Portola Valley, Calif. (100 & 200 meter freestyle)

Staff Personnel

Phillip S. Hansel, Houston, Texas (Manager)
Mrs. Gloria Thompon, Richmond, Va. (Asst. Mgr.)
Mrs. Hazel M. Barr, Queens Village, N. Y. (Asst. Diving Coach & Chaperone)
Sherman Chavoor, Carmichael, Calif. (Coach)
Frank Elm, East Brunswick, N.J. (Asst. Coach)
Ward O'Connell, New Haven, Conn. (Diving Coach)

OFFICIAL SUMMARIES

SWIMMING — WOMEN
(*) Pan-American Games Record

Springboard Diving — 1. SUE GOSSICK, USA 752.05; 2. LT. MICKI KING, USAF, USA 736.70; 3. Kathy McDonald, Canada 712.00; 4. Nancy Robertson, Canada 634.75; 5. Bertha Baraldi, Mexico 559.85; 6. Dora Hilda Hernandes, Mexico 507.10; 7. Martha Manzano, Colombia 474.95.

Platform Diving — 1. LESLEY BUSH, USA 541.00; 2. Beverly Boys, Canada 515.45; 3. ANN PETERSON, USA 491.40; 4. Kathleen Rolo, Canada 455.75; 5. Bertha Baraldi, Mexico 376.00; 6. Dora Hilda Hernandes, Mexico 368.40.

100 Meter Freestyle — 1. ERIKA BRICKER, USA 1:00.89 (Miss Bricker set Pan-American Games record in heat, 0:59.93); 2. Marion Lay, Canada 1:01.02; 3. POKEY WATSON, USA 1:01.54; 4. Elaine Tanner, Canada 1:02.82; 5. Ann Lallande, Puerto Rico 1:04.60; 6. Materesa Ramirez, Mexico 1:05.22; 7. Rosario Vivanco, Peru 1:05.54; 8. Eliete Motta, Brazil 1:08.13.

200 Meter Freestyle — 1. PAMELA KRUSE USA 2:11.91*; 2. Marion Lay, Canada 2:14.68; 3. Angela Coughlan, Canada 2:15.66; 4. POKEY WATSON, USA 2:19.07; 5. Ann Lallande, Puerto Rico 2:20.40; 6. Carmen Ferracuti, El Salvador 2:20.95; 7. Materesa Ramirez, Mexico 2:21.60; Laura Baca, Mexico 2:24.75.

400 Meter Freestyle — 1. DEBORAH MEYER, USA 4:32.64*; 2. PAMELA KRUSE, USA 4:42.81; 3. Angela Coughlan, Canada 4:48.88; 4. Jane Hughes, Canada 4:51.09; 5. Ann Lallande, Puerto Rico 4:58.11; 6. Laura Baca, Mexico 4:58.69; 7. Kristina Moir, Puerto Rico 4:59.20; 8. Patricia Olano, Colombia 5:07.68.

800 Meter Freestyle — 1. DEBORAH MEYER, USA 9:22.86*; 2. SUSAN PEDERSEN, USA 9:38.37; 3. Angela Coughlan, Canada 9:48.56; 4. Jeanne Warren, Canada 9:50.50; 5. Laura Baca, Mexico 10:10.30; 6. Ann Lallande, Puerto Rico 10:25.58; 7. Patricia Olano, Colombia 10:26.88; 8. Carmen Ferracuti, El Salvador 10:28.35.

100 Meter Backstroke — 1. Elaine Tanner, Canada 1:07.32*; 2. KAYE HALL, USA 1:09.76; 3. Shirley Cazalet, Canada 1:11.33; 4. Patricia Sentous, Argentina 1:12.92; 5. Ann Cecilia Freire, Brazil 1:13.76; 6. Gloria Morales, Venezuela 1:13.06; 7. Susana Procopio, Argentina 1:14.22; 8. KENDIS MOORE, USA 1:15.12.

200 Meter Backstroke — 1. Elaine Tanner, Canada 2:24.55*; 2. KENDIS MOORE, USA 2:30.38; 3. CATHY FERGUSON, USA 2:32.48; 4. Jeanne Warren, Canada 2:35.44; 5. Patricia Sentous, Argentina 2:37.41; 6. Themis Trama, Uruguay 2:40.40; 7. Laura de Neef, Trinidad/Tobago 2:42.85; 8. Ann Lallande, Puerto Rico 2:43.22.

100 Meter Breaststroke — 1. CATHARINE BALL, USA 1:14.80*; 2. Ana Maria Norbis, Uruguay; 1:15.95; 3. CYNTHIA GOYETTE, USA 1:19.39; 4. Eliana Pereira, Brazil 1:22.05; 5. Tamara Oynick, Mexico 1:23.24; 6. Tamara Orejuela, Ecuador 1:23.27; 7. Marion Lay, Canada 1:24.58; 8. Nancy Thompson, Canada 1:25.41.

200 Meter Breaststroke — 1. CATHARINE BALL, USA 2:42.18*; 2. CLAUDIA KOLB, USA 2:48.93; 3. Ana Maria Norbis, Uruguay 2:52.11; 4. Tamara Oynick, Mexico 2:58.56; 5. Mary Pat Pumphrey, Canada 2:58.84; 6. Tamara Orejuela, Ecuador 2:59.78; 7. Donna Ross, Canada 2:59.78; 8. Victoria Casas, Mexico 3:07.08.

100 Meter Butterfly — 1. ELEANOR DANIEL, USA 1:05.24*; 2. Elaine Tanner, Canada 1:05.35; 3. Marilyn Corson, Canada 1:07.68; 4. LEE DAVIS, USA 1:07.83; 5. Materesa Ramirez, Mexico 1:12.75; 6. Adriana Comolli, Argentina 1:12.80; 7. Ruth Apt, Uruguay 1:12.91; 8. Ana Maria Monedero, El Salvador 1:15.48.

SWIMMING – WOMEN

C. Ball   E. Bricker   L. Bush

P. Caretto   P. Carpinelli   E. Daniel

L. Davis   C. Dougherty   C. Ferguson

W. Fordyce   S. Gossick   C. Goyette

L. Gustavson   P. Hagwood   K. Hall

C. Jamison   M. King   C. Kolb

P. Kruse   D. Meyer   K. Moore

SWIMMING – WOMEN

S. Pedersen   A. Peterson   N. Ryan

K. Thomas   L. Watson   P. Hansel

G. Thompson   H. Barr   S. Chavoor

F. Elm   W. O'Connell

200 Meter Butterfly — 1. CLAUDIA KOLB, USA 2:25.49*; 2. LEE DAVIS, USA 2:26.74; 3. Marilyn Corson, Canada 2:30.54; 4. Elaine Tanner, Canada 2:36.11; 5. Ann Lallande, Puerto Apt. 2:43.66; 6. Ruth Apt, Uruguay 2:44.15; 7. Kristina Moir, Puerto Rico 2:44.43; 8. Materesa Ramirez, Mexico 2:46.43.

200 Meter Individual Medley — 1. CLAUDIA KOLB, USA 2:26.06*; 2. SUSAN PEDERSEN, USA 2:30.91; 3. Sandra Dowler, Canada 2:36.18; 4. Kathy Tidey, Canada 2:38.64; 5. Carmen Ferracuti, El Salvador 2:40.83; 6. Kristina Moir, Puerto Rico 2:42.03; 8. Materesa Ramirez, Mexico 2:42.50; 8. Maria Moreno, El Salvador 2:46.45.

400 Meter Individual Medley — 1. CLAUDIA KOLB, USA 5:09.68*; 2. SUSAN PEDERSEN, USA 5:21.57; 3. Marilyn Carson, Canada 5:36.75; 4. Patricia Olano, Colombia 5:45.90; 5. Carmen Ferracuti, El Salvador 5:46.07; 6. Laura Baca, Mexico 5:47.46; 7. Maria Moreno, El Salvador 5:49.87; 8. Kristina Moir, Puerto Rico 6:00.10.

400 Meter Freestyle Relay — 1. USA (WENDY FORDYCE, PAM CARPINELLI, LINDA GUSTAVSON, PAMELA KRUSE) 4:04.57*; 2. Canada (Dowler, Tanner, Caughlan, Lay) 4:09.73; 3. Puerto Rico 4:26.56; 4. Mexico 4:26.87; 5. Peru 4:27.10; 6. Brazil 4:27.33; 7. El Salvador 4:28.67; 8. Venezuela 4:33.04.

400 Meter Medley Relay — 1. USA (KENDIS MOORE, CATHARINE BALL, ELEANOR DANIEL, WENDY FORDYCE) 4:30.0*; 2. Canada (Tanner, Ross, Corson, Lay) 4:40.88; 3. Uruguay 4:49.27; 4. Brazil 4:56.40; 5. Mexico 4:58.60; 6. Argentina 4:59.11; 7. Venezuela 5:05.93; 8. Puerto Rico 5:06.94.

TENNIS — MEN & WOMEN

The United States had its strongest entry since the 1955 Games and proved it with two gold medals, two silvers and two bronzes. Gold medals were taken by the women's double combo of Jane Albert and Patsy Rippy, the former also taking another first by teaming with Lt. Arthur Ashe (USA) to win the mixed doubles crown. Miss Rippy also placed second in the women's singles while Miss Albert, team captain and daughter of the famous Stanford football quarterback, Frankie Albert, placed third in the singles of her division.

Ashe, favored in the men's singles competition, was upset by the eventual champion, Tom Koch of Brazil, in the semi-finals but came back to win third place. Pfc. Herb Fitzgibbon (USA) placed second in the finals and teamed with Ashe to place fourth in the doubles, losing to Ecuador's Francisco Guzman and Miguel Olvera in the playoff.

TEAM PERSONNEL

TENNIS — MEN & WOMEN

Jane Albert, Pebble Beach, Calif.
2/Lt. Arthur Ashe, USA, Richmond, Va.
J/3C Bailey Brown, USN, Annapolis, Md.
Emilie Burrer, San Antonio, Texas
Pfc. Herbert Fitzgibbon, USA, West Point, N.Y.
Patsy Rippy, Shawnee, Okla.

Staff Personnel

Jack Roach, Minneapolis, Minn.
(Coach & Manager)

OFFICAL SUMMARIES

TENNIS — MEN

Singles

1. Thomas Koch, Brazil; 2. Pfc. HERB FITZGIBBON, USA; 3. Lt. ARTHUR ASHE, USA.

Final — Thomas Koch defeated Pfc. HERB FITZGIBBON, USA 5-7, 6-3, 6-3.

For Third Place — Lt. ARTHUR ASHE, USA defeated Edson Mandarino, Brazil 2-6, 7-5, 6-2, 6-0.

Semi-Finals — Koch, Brazil defeated ASHE, USA 3-6, 6-0, 7-5, 4-6, 6-3; FITZGIBBON, USA defeated Mandarino, Brazil 6-2, 3-6, 6-1, 6-2.

Quarter-Finals — Koch, Brazil def. Joaquin Loyo-Mayo, Mexico 6-2, 7-5, 7-5; FITZGIBBON, USA def. Patricio Cornejo, Chile 6-4, 6-2, 9-7; Lt. ASHE def. Ronald Barnes, Brazil 6-2, 4-6, 6-8, 6-4, 6-4; Mandarino, Brazil def. Marcello Lara, Mexico 6-3, 12-10, 6-4.

Second Round — Koch, Brazil def. Gewan Maharaj, Trin./Tobago 6-2, 6-1, 6-4; Loyo-Mayo, Mexico, def. BAILEY BROWN, USN, USA 7-5, 6-1, 6-3; FITZGIBBON, USA def. Luis Garcia, Mexico 6-4, 6-1; Cornejo, Chile def. Mike Belkin, Canada 6-2, 4-6, 7-5, 6-1; Lt. ASHE, USA def. Alfredo Acuna, Peru 6-0, 6-0, 6-4; Barnes, Brazil won by default over Lance Lumsden, Jamaica; Mandarino, Brazil def. Allan Simmons, Bermuda 6-0, 6-2, 6-0; Lara, Mexico def. Jaime Pinto, Chile 6-2, 6-3, 6-4.

First Round — Lt. ASHE, USA def. Patricio Rodriguez, Chile 4-6, 6-2, 6-3, 8-6; BROWN, USA won by default over Richard Russell, Jamaica; Pinto, Chile won by default over Eduardo Zuleta, Ecuador.

Doubles

1. Edson Mandarino & Thomas Koch, Brazil; 2. Marcello Lara & Joaquin Loyo-Mayo, Mexico; 3. Francisco Guzman & Miguel Olvera, Ecuador.

Final — Mandarino & Koch, Brazil def. Lara & Loyo-Mayo, Mexico 11-9, 6-2, 6-4.

For Third Place — Guzman & Olvera, Ecuador def. Lt. ASHE & FITZGIBBON, USA 6-2, 4-6, 10-8, 4-6, 6-3.

Semi-Finals — Mandarino & Koch, Brazil def. Lt. ASHE & FITZGIBBON, USA 6-1, 6-4, 6-3; Lara & Loyo-Mayo, Mexico def. Guzman & Olvera, Ecuador 6-8, 8-6, 7-5, 2-6, 6-3.

Quarter-Finals — Mandarino & Koch, Brazil def. Patricio Cornejo & Patricio Rodriguez, Chile 6-4, 6-3, 6-3; Lt. ASHE & FITZGIBBON won by default over Lance Lumsden & Richard Russel, Jamaica; Guzman & Olvera, Ecuador def. Allan Simmons and John Rihiluoma, Bermuda 6-0, 6-0, 6-0; Lara & Loyo Mayo Mexico def. Bob Bedard & Francois Godbout, Canada 6-3, 6-3, 6-2.

TENNIS — WOMEN

1. Elena Subirats, Mexico; 2. PATSY RIPPY, USA; 3. JANE ALBERT, USA.

Final — Elena Subirats, Mexico def. PATSY RIPPY, USA 6-3, 6-2.

For Third Place — JANE ALBERT, USA def. Faye Urban, Canada 6-3, 1-6, 6-1.

Semi-Finals — Subirats, Mexico def. ALBERT, USA 6-2, 6-8, 6-3; RIPPY, USA def. Urban, Canada 6-4, 5-7, 7-5.

Quarter-Finals — Subirats, Mexico def. Eugenia Guzman, Ecuador 6-3, 6-1; ALBERT, USA def. EMILIE BURRER, USA 6-3, 4-6, 6-4; Urban, Canada def. Patricio Montano, Mexico 6-3, 6-3; RIPPY, USA def. Vicki Berner, Canada 6-4, 6-3.

First Round — Subirats, Mexico def. Susan Butts, Canada 6-0, 6-3; Guzman, Ecuador def. Graciela Moran, Argentina 6-4, 6-1; ALBERT, USA def. Maria Holguin, Colombia 8-6, 6-1; BURRER, USA def. Virginia Caceres, Peru 6-3, 6-3; Urban, Canada def. Isabel Fernandez, Colombia 2-6, 6-2, 8-6; Montano, Mexico def. Ada DeCowan, Peru 6-3, 6-3; RIPPY, USA def. Anna Maria Icaza, Ecuador 6-3, 6-3; Berner, Canada def. Ria Chong-Ashing, Trin./Tobago 6-1, 6-3.

Preliminary Round — Montano, Mexico def. Anna Maria Bocjo, Argentina 4-6, 6-4, 6-1.

Doubles

1. JANE ALBERT & PATSY RIPPY, USA; 2. Eugenia Guzman & Anna Marie Icaza, Ecuador; 3. Vicki Berner & Faye Urban, Canada.

Final — JANE ALBERT & PATSY RIPPY, USA def. Eugenia Guzman & Anna Marie Icaza, Ecuador 6-1, 6-0.

For Third Place — Vicki Berner & Faye Urban, Canada def. Patricia Montano & Elena Subirats, Mexico 7-5, 6-1.

Semi-Finals — ALBERT & RIPPY, USA def. Montano & Subirats, Mexico 6-3, 5-7, 6-3; Guzman & Icaza, Ecuador def. Berner & Urban, Canada 1-6, 8-6, 7-5.

First Round — ALBERT & RIPPY, USA def. Maria Holguin & Isabel Fernandez, Colombia 6-2, 6-2; Montano & Subirats, Mexico def. Virginia Caceres & Ada De Cowan, Peru 6-0, 3-6, 7-5; Guzman & Icaza, Ecuador def. Graciela Moran & Anna Maria Bocio, Argentina 6-3, 6-2.

J. Albert   A. Ashe   B. Brown

E. Burrer   H. Fitzgibbon   P. Rippy

J. Roach

Mixed Doubles

1. JANE ALBERT & Lt. ARTHUR ASHE, USA; 2. Elena Subirats & Luis Garcia, Mexico; 3. Eugenia Guzman & Francisco Guzman, Ecuador.

Final — ALBERT & Lt. ASHE, USA def. Subirats & Carcia, Mexico 6-3, 6-8, 6-1.

For Third Place — Guzman & Guzman, Ecuador def. Vicki Berner & Bob Bedard, Canada 6-3, 6-3.

Semi-Finals — ALBERT & Lt. ASHE, USA def. Guzman & Guzman, Ecuador 6-3, 6-0; Subirats & Garcia, Mexico def. Berner & Bedard, Canada 6-4, 6-3.

Quarter-Finals — ALBERT & Lt. ASHE, USA def. Virginia Caceres & Alfredo Acuna, Peru 9-7, 6-4; Guzman & Guzman, Ecuador def. Faye Urban & Francois Godbout, Canada 7-5, 6-3; Berner & Bedard, Canada def. Anna Maria Icaza & Miguel Olivera, Ecuador 4-6, 6-2, 6-4; Subirats & Garcia, Mexico def. EMILIE BURRER & HERB FITZGIBBON, USA 6-4, 11-9.

First Round — Guzman & Guzman, Ecuador def. Patricia Montano & Joaquin Loyo-Mayo, Mexico 6-2, 6-2; Berner & Bedard, Canada def. PATSY RIPPY & BAILEY BROWN, USA 6-4, 6-1; Caceres & Acuna, Peru def. Ria Chong-Ashing & Gewan Maharaj, Trin./Tobago 6-0, 6-3.

VOLLEYBALL — MEN

The United States won its third volleyball championship in four Games, but not without a real struggle and the help of a tie-breaking formula. Winner in 1955 and 1959, then runner-up to Brazil in 1963, the USA wound up in a deadlock with Brazil and Cuba as the final standings were compiled. Each nation had a record of four wins against one loss but the final rating

OFFICIAL SUMMARIES

VOLLEYBALL — MEN

Final Rank	(Playoff Series) Nation	Matches W	L	Games W	L	OWN PTS	OPP PTS
1	*UNITED STATES	4	1	14	4	256	192
2	*Brazil	4	1	14	5	277	209
3	*Cuba	4	1	13	5	249	182
4	Mexico	2	3	6	11	184	216
5	Venezuela	1	4	5	12	163	223
6	Canada	0	5	0	15	112	225
	Other rankings						
7	Puerto Rico (1—3)						
8	Argentina (0—3)						
9	Bahamas (0—4)						

* final ranking determined on point spread in games involving the three nations who deadlocked in matches won and lost.

Scores of Playoff Series Matches

**United States 3, Cuba 1
**Brazil 3, Mexico 0

**United States 3, Venezuela 0
**Brazil 3, Canada 0

**Cuba 3, Venezuela 0
**Mexico 3, Canada 0

Brazil 3, United States 2
Cuba 3, Canada 0
Mexico 3, Venezuela 2

United States 3, Mexico 0
Venezuela 3, Canada 0
Cuba 3, Brazil 2

United States 3, Canada 0
Brazil 3, Venezuela 0
Cuba 3, Mexico 0

** matches won in group play carried on for credit in title series.

Standings Group A Play

	W	L
Brazil	4	0
Mexico	3	1
Canada	2	2
Puerto Rico	1	3
Bahamas	0	4

Standings Group B Play

	W	L
United States	3	0
Cuba	2	1
Venezuela	1	2
Argentina	0	3

was based on the point spread in games involving the three teams.

Competition first was held in two groups with the top three teams in each advancing to the final playoff series. In the playoff, a victory over a team in group play was counted. Consequently, the USA's 3 – 1 match win over Cuba in Group B play counted in the playoff series standings. However, Brazil defeated the United States, 3 – 2, but was in turn upset by Cuba, 3 – 2. Actual points scored in these games were tallied and the USA had the greatest spread, thus taking first place while Brazil and Cuba were ranked next in order for the medals.

Sparking the USA team were 1964 Olympian Pedro Velasco of Honolulu and Thomas Haine, a member of the 1959 Pan-American championship team.

TEAM PERSONNEL

VOLLEYBALL — MEN

John Kirby Alstrom, Fresno, Calif.
Robert William Clem, Los Angeles, Calif.
Winthrop Davenport, Jr., Los Angeles, Calif.
H. Smitty Duke, Irving, Texas.

VOLLEYBALL — MEN

J. Alstrom   R. Clem   W. Davenport

H. Duke   T. Haine   J. Henn

D. Patterson   L. Rundle   A. Scates

337

VOLLEYBALL – MEN

J. Stanley   R. Suwara   P. Velasco

J. Lowell   J. Coleman

VOLLEYBALL – WOMEN

A. Heck   F. Hopeau   N. Jorgensen

L. Lewis   M. McReavy   L. Murphy

N. Owen   M. Peppler   B. Perry

M. Perry   S. Peterson   J. Ward

A. Englert   H. Cohen

Thomas A. Haine, Honolulu, Hawaii.
John T. Henn, San Diego, Calif.
Daniel E. Patterson, Los Angeles, Calif.
Larry D. Rundle, Santa Monica, Calif.
Allen, E. Scates, Northridge, Calif.
Jon C. Stanley, Encinitas, Calif.
Rudy Suwara, Los Angeles, Calif.
Pedro Velasco, Jr., Honolulu, Hawaii.

Staff personnel

John Lowell, Laie, Hawaii (Manager)
James Coleman, Downers Grove, Ill. (Coach)

VOLLEYBALL — WOMEN

The United States women's volleyball team, highly conditioned and playing its best style, won all five of its matches by 3–0 scores and easily outdistanced the field for the gold medal. Captain Jane Ward, a 1964 Olympian as well as a member of the 1959 and 1963 Pan-American teams, paced the triumphs.

The championship was the USA's first, after having placed second three times, to Mexico in 1955 and to Brazil in 1959 and 1963.

TEAM PERSONNEL

VOLLEYBALL — WOMEN

Ann Heck, Ventura, Calif.
Fanny Hopeau, Honolulu, Calif.
Ninja Jorgensen, Los Angeles, Calif.
Laurie Ann Lewis, Los Angeles, Calif.
Marilyn McReavy, Big Lake, Texas.
Linda Murphy, Burbank, Calif.
Nancy Owen, Rolling Hills Estate, Calif.
Mary Jo Peppler, Rolling Hills Estate, Calif.
Barbara Perry, Honolulu, Hawaii
Mary Perry, Van Nuys, Calif.
Sharon Peterson, Honolulu, Hawaii
Jane Ward, Huntington Beach, Calif.

Staff personnel

Alice Englert, Burbank, Calif. (Manager)
Harlan S. Cohen, Los Angeles, Calif.
(Coach)

OFFICIAL SUMMARIES

VOLLEYBALL — WOMEN

Final Rank	(Round robin) Nation	Matches W	L	Games W	L	OWN PTS	OPP PTS
1	UNITED STATES	5	0	15	0	225	111
2	Peru	4	1	12	6	243	177
3	Cuba	3	2	10	9	242	220
4	Brazil	2	3	10	10	254	238
5	Mexico	1	4	5	12	153	222
6	Canada	0	5	0	15	76	225

Scores of Round Robin Schedule

United States 3, Brazil 0
Peru 3, Canada 0
Cuba 3, Mexico 1

United States 3, Cuba 0
Peru 3, Brazil 2
Mexico 3, Canada 0

United States 3, Mexico 0
Peru 3, Cuba 1
Brazil 3, Canada 0

United States 3, Peru 0
Cuba 3, Canada 0
Brazil 3, Mexico 1

United States 3, Canada 0
Peru 3, Mexico 0
Cuba 3, Brazil 2

Woman volleyballist Nancy Owen spikes the ball as the US takes a Pan-Am gold medal.

WATER POLO

D. Ashleigh

S. Barnett

W. Birch

S. Cole

G. Hing

G. Sheerer

J. Shores

A. Van Dorp

L. Willeford

Writzenberg

K. Nitzkowski

A. Lambert

R. Horn

OFFICIAL SUMMARIES

WATER POLO

Final Rank	Nation	Round Robin Schedule			
		W	L	Goals	Opp.
1	UNITED STATES	5	0	47	9
2	Brazil	4	1	36	18
3	Mexico	3	2	27	16
4	Cuba	2	3	29	21
5	Canada	1	4	13	45
6	Colombia	0	5	12	55

Scores of Games

United States 9, Cuba 3
Brazil 10, Canada 1
Mexico 10, Colombia 3

United States 4, Mexico 2
Brazil 11, Colombia 3
Cuba 7, Canada 0

United States 4, Brazil 3
Mexico 3, Cuba 2
Canada 8, Colombia 5

United States 16, Canada 1
Cuba 12, Colombia 1
Brazil 6, Mexico 5

United States 14, Colombia 0
Brazil 6, Cuba 5
Mexico 7, Canada 1

Three members of the 1964 Olympic team were on the gold medal team: Goalie Anton Van Dorp, Dean Willeford, and David Ashleigh. Van Dorp's defense of the goal was remarkable and all USA players indicated that the long development program was paying off handsomely.

TEAM PERSONNEL

WATER POLO

David M. Ashleigh, Pomona, Calif.
Steven W. Barnett, Campbell, Calif.
William H. Birch, Woodside, Calif.
Stanley C. Cole, Whittier, Calif.
Gregory W. Hing, Los Altos, Calif.
Gary P. Sheerer, Los Altos, Calif.
Jonathon W. Shores, Los Altos, Calif.
Anton Van Dorp, Camarillo, Calif.
Leslie Dean Willeford, Huntington Beach, Calif.
Charles Writzenberg, Los Altos, Calif.

Staff personnel

Kenneth Nitzkowski, Huntington Beach, Calif. (Manager)
Arthur F. Lambert, Los Altos, Calif. (Coach)
Robert Martin Horn, Manhattan Beach, Calif. (Asst. Coach)

WEIGHTLIFTING

This nation's weightlifters failed to equal their 1963 medal success but five gold medals in as many tries can't truly be faulted. Joseph Puleo, light heavyweight; Phillip Grippaldi, middle heavyweight; Russell Knipp, middleweight;

Joe Dube presses 424½ pounds on way to heavyweight gold medal.

and Joseph Dube, heavyweight, each set Pan-American records for overall totals, as well as new marks in the three lift categories. The other gold medalist was Walter Imahara, featherweight, who set a Pan-American record in the military press.

Bob Bednarski, another USA heavyweight entry, was injured during the competition and had to withdraw. The USA did not enter the bantamweight and lightweight divisions.

WATER POLO

The superbly conditioned and trained US water polo team had no difficulty at all, winning all five of its matches to take its second Pan-American championship. Winner in 1959, third in 1951, and second in 1955 and 1959, the USA foiled defending champion Brazil's bid with a 4–3 setback, leading all the way in that match. Other wins were recorded over Cuba, Mexico, Canada, and Colombia in the round-robin schedule.

WEIGHTLIFTING

R. Bednarski   J. Dube   A. Garcy

P. Grippaldi   W. Imahara   R. Knipp

J. Puleo   R. Hise   D. Mayor

TEAM PERSONNEL

WEIGHTLIFTING

Robert Bednarski, York, Pa. (heavyweight)
Joseph Dube, Jacksonville, Fla. (heavyweight)
Anthony Garcy, York, Pa. (middleweight)
Philip Grippaldi, Belleville, N. J. (middle heavyweight)
Walter M. Imahara, Baton Rouge, La. (featherweight)
Russell Knipp, Pittsburg, Pa. (middleweight)
Joseph Puleo, Detroit, Mich. (light heavyweight).

Staff personnel

Robert Hise, Los Angeles, Calif. (Manager)
David Mayor, Philadelphia, Pa. (Coach)

OFFICIAL SUMMARIES

WEIGHTLIFTING

Bantamweight (123.5 lbs.) — 1. Fernando Baez, Puerto Rico 735½ pounds (342½ kilos)* 258½* press; 291½* clean and jerk, 203½ snatch; 2. Anthony Phillips, Barbados 704 lbs. 3. Martin Diaz, Guyana 682 lbs.; 4. R. F. Linderborg, Netherlands-Antilles 671 lbs.; 5. C. H. Chan, Canada 654½ lbs.; 6. G. Boyd Mora, Panama 649 lbs.

Featherweight (123.3 lbs.) — 1. WALTER IMAHARA, USA 777 pounds (352.5 kilos), 247.5* press; 231 snatch; 297 clean & jerk; 2. Manuel Mateos de Larosa, Mexico 775 lbs., 247.5* press; 3. Idelfonzo Lee Valdez, Panama 749½ lbs.; 4. P. Serrano, Puerto Rico 737 lbs.; 5. N. Pagan, Puerto Rico 710 lbs.; 6. R. Urrutia, Guatemala 583 lbs.

Lightweight (148.8 lbs.) — 1. Pastor Rodriguez, Cuba 848 pounds (385 kilos)*, press 275½*, 325* clean and jerk, 247½** snatch; 2. Hugo Gittens, Trinidad/Tobago 809 lbs.; 3. Arnaldo Munoz Herrera, Cuba 787 lbs.

Middleweight (165.4 lbs.) — 1. RUSSELL KNIPP, USA 948 pounds (430 kilos)*, press 341.7*, 253 snatch, 353** clean and jerk. In an extra lift in the press new world record 346 lbs. (157 kilos); 2. Koji Michi, Brazil 882 lbs. (400 kilos); 3. Luis Gonzaga De Almeida, Brazil 882 lbs. (400 kilos); 4. Jose Figueroa, Puerto Rico, 876.5 lbs.; 5. Aldo Roy, Canada 837.9 lbs.; 6. Rene Gomez, Cuba 832 lbs.

Light Heavyweight (181.9 lbs.) — 1. JOSEPH PULEO, USA 992 lbs. (450 kilos)*, press 319½*, snatch 297½*, clean and jerk 375**; 2. Angel Pagan, Puerto Rico 942½ lbs.; 3. Pierre St. Jean, Canada 931½ lbs.; 4. F. T. Rijna, Netherlands-Antilles 913 lbs.; 5. A. Salorzano, Venezuela 902 lbs.; 6. H. Springer, Barbados 880 lbs.

Middle Heavyweight (Up to 198.4 lbs.) — 1. PHILIP GRIPPALDI, USA 1047 lbs. (475 kilos)*, press 353, snatch 303**, clean and jerk 391*; 2. Paul Bjarnason, Canada 931½ lbs.; 3. Andres Martinez, Cuba 920½ lbs.; 4. Fernando Torres, Puerto Rico 904 lbs.; 5. Roland Roosberg, Netherlands-Antilles 871 lbs.; 6. Tamer Chaim, Brazil 860 lbs.

Heavyweight (Over 198.4 lbs.) — 1. JOSEPH DUBE, USA, 1163 lbs. (572½ kilos)*, press 424¼*; 2. Ernesto Varona, Cuba 1040¼ lbs.; 3. Brandon Bailey, Trinidad/Tobago, 1014¼ lbs.; 4. Price Morris, Canada 964¾ lbs.; 5. Juan Bryce-Coates Munoz, Peru 937 lbs.; 6. Antonio Ochoa, Colombia 870 lbs. Note: BOB BEDNARSKI, USA, injured during the competition and had to withdraw.

*New Pan-American Games record.
**Ties Pan-American Games record.

WRESTLING

For the third successive Games, USA wrestlers completely dominated the competition, winning all eight gold medals as they did in 1959 and 1963. Furthermore, as the matches progressed in each weight division, not a lost decision or a draw was chalked up against the United States grapplers; the record totalled 33 victories.

Larry Kristoff, heavyweight, and a runnerup for world championship honors in 1966, exemplified the USA strength. He pinned Orlando Ochoa of Peru in 26 seconds of his first bout, decisioned Bob Chambreault of Canada, then polished off Cuba's Javier Campostena in 52 seconds to win the gold medal.

TEAM PERSONNEL

WRESTLING

Lt. R. Wayne Baughman, USAF, Oklahoma City, Okla. (middleweight)
Gerald R. Bell, Cortland, N.Y. (lightweight)
Harry Houska, Parma, Ohio (light heavyweight)
Patrick J. Kelly, Waukegan, Ill. (welterweight)
Larry D. Kristoff, Carbondale, Ill. (heavyweight)
Richard Sanders, Portland, Oregon (bantamweight)
Richard Sofman, West Orange, N.J. (flyweight)
Michael Young, Provo, Utah (featherweight)

Staff personnel

Thomas M. Lumly, Tulsa, Okla. (Manager)
Eric J. Miller, Ithaca, N.Y. (Coach)

OFFICIAL SUMMARIES

WRESTLING

Flyweight (114.5 pounds) — 1. RICHARD SOFMAN, USA; 2. Wanelge Castillo, Panama; 3. Florentino Martinez, Mexico.

SOFMAN won gold medal by decisioning Castillo. Previously he had pinned Geredo Leon, Colombia (2:43); decisioned Martinez, Mexico; pinned Peter Michienzi, Canada; and decisioned Miguel Tachin, Cuba in his first bout.

Bantamweight (125.7 pounds) — 1. RICHARD SANDERS, USA; 2. Moises Lopez, Mexico; 3. Jose Ramos, Cuba.

SANDERS won gold medal by decisioning Ramos. Previously he had decisioned Charles Nixon, Canada; won by default due to injury to Octavio Velez, Colombia, and decisioned Lopez in his first bout.

Featherweight (138.9 pounds) — 1. MIKE YOUNG, USA; 2. Roberto Wallejo, Mexico; 3. Francisco Ramos, Cuba.

The Pan-Am gold medal in heavyweight wrestling went to America's Larry Kristoff, shown here decisioning Canada's Bob Chambreault, the only opponent he failed to pin.

WRESTLING

R. Baughman | G. Bell | H. Houska

P. Kelly | L. Kristoff | R. Sanders

R. Sofman | M. Young | T. Lumly

E. Miller

YOUNG won gold medal by decisioning Wallejo. Previously he had decisioned Ramos in the round-robin; decisioned Luis Rodriguez, Argentina; decisioned Fenelon Diaz, Venezuela and decisioned Patrick Bolger in his first bout.

Lightweight (154.3 pounds) — 1. GERALD BELL, USA; 2. Ray Lougheed, Canada; 3. Severino Aquilar, Panama.

BELL won gold medal by pinning Aquilar (1:33). Previously he had decisioned Lougheed in the round-robin; pinned Silvio Michel, Cuba (5:22; pinned Jose Echecary, Peru (1:53); and opened by decisioning Jose Palomino, Colombia.

Welterweight (171.9 pounds) — 1. PATRICK KELLY, USA; 2. Alejandro Guevara, Venezuela; 3. Nick Schori, Canada.

KELLY won gold medal by pinning Guevara (5:18). Previously he had decisioned Schori; pinned Lupe Lara, Cuba (8:42) and pinned Raul Lupez, Mexico (6:55) in his first bout.

Middleweight (191.3 pounds) — 1. Lt. WAYNE BAUGHMAN, USAF, USA; 2. Julio Graffigna, Argentina; 3. Castor Gomez, Cuba.

BAUGHMAN won gold medal by pinning Ed Millard, Canada (8:40). Previously he had pinned Gomez (2:09); and decisioned Julio Traffigna, Argentina in his first bout.

Light Heavyweight (Up to 213.9 pounds) — 1. HARRY HOUSKA, USA; 2. Juan Ortiz Caballero, Cuba; 3. Victor Vernik, Argentina.

HOUSKA won gold medal by pinning Ortiz (2:45) and Vernik (1:25) in the round-robin after he had drawn a bye, pinned Luis Rengel

Reyes, Venezuela (1:53) and pinned Ruben Gotti, Panama (0:26) in the first bout.

Heavyweight (Over 213.9 pounds) — 1. LARRY KRISTOFF, USA; 2. Bob Chambreault, Canada; 3. Javier Campostena, Cuba.

KRISTOFF won gold medal by pinning Compostena (0:52) and decisioning Chambreault in the round-robin after he had drawn a bye and pinned Orlando Ochoa, Peru (0.26) in his first bout.

YACHTING

United States skippers finished with two gold medals and two silvers in the four yachting classes of competition held on Lake Winnipeg. Not included on the program were the Dragon and Star classes in which the USA had placed third and first respectively in 1963.

The husband and wife team of Bruce and Pamela Goldsmith won five races to take the gold in the Lightning class, while Harry C. Melges, Jr. and William B. Bentsen combined as crew of the first place Flying Dutchman entry. Carl Van Duyne, in the Finn class, and the brothers Alan and Harry Levinson in the Snipe class, were silver medalists.

Van Duyne figured in one of the most dramatic incidents ever recorded in this competition. During one of the races he turned about to pick up an opponent whose craft had capsized in the heavy seas, delivered him to the judge's boat, then resumed the race to win.

TEAM PERSONNEL

YACHTING

Thomas G. Allen, Buffalo, N.Y. (alternate)
William B. Bentsen, Beloit, Wis. (Flying Dutchman)
Bruce Goldsmith, Northfield, Ill. (Lightning)
Pamela Goldsmith, Northfield, Ill. (Lightning)
Alan C. Levinson, Indianapolis, Ind. (Snipe)
Harry N. Levinson, Indianapolis, Ind. (Snipe)
H. Carey Long, Chicago Heights, Ill. (Lightning)
Harry C. Melges, Jr., Zenda, Wis. (Flying Dutchman)
Carl I. Van Duyne, Short Hills, N.J. (Finn)

Staff personnel

Paul H. Smart, Darien, Conn. (Manager)
Capt. Richard L. Tillman, USAF, Elkhart, Ind. (boatman).

OFFICAL SUMMARIES

YACHTING

Lightning Class

1. USA (BRUCE GOLDSMITH, helmsman; MRS. PAMELA DEXTER GOLDSMITH and HUGO LONG, crew) 3.0; 2. Brazil (A. Damatta, helmsman) 20.4; 3. Argentina (B. Belada, helmsman) 37.4; 4. Canada (D. Allen, helmsman) 45.4; 5. Colombia (M. Jacobs, helmsman) 62.4; 6. Trinidad/Tobago (R. Mayers, helmsman) 65.4.

YACHTING

T. Allen | W. Bentsen | B. Goldsmith

P. Goldsmith | A. Levinson | H. Levinson

H. Long | H. Melges, Jr. | C. Van Duyne

P. Smart | R. Tillman

Final placings are determined on the best 6 out of 7 races. USA, on this basis, won five of the six races counted in the final placings, winning all but the 5th race among those which were counted.

Flying Dutchman

1. USA (HARRY C. MELGES, JR., helmsman; WILLIAM B. BENTSEN, crew) 3.0; 2. Brazil (R. Conrad) 22.0; 3. Canada (P. Byrne) 41.8; 4. Jamaica (E. Brimo) 51.7; 5. Mexico (E. Ochoa) 60.4; 6. Virgin Islands (J. Hamber) 62.1.

USA won five out of the six races counted in the final placing, winning all but the 3rd race among those which were counted.

Finn Class

1. Brazil (J. Bruder) 9.0; 2. USA (CARL VAN DUYNE) 17.4; 3. Canada (J. Clarke) 36.7; 4. Bermuda (J. Hopper) 43.7; 5. Argentina (A. Obarrio) 45.8; 6. Cuba (L. Del Rosario) 70.4.

USA, on the basis of counting Van Duyne's six highest placings, had two 1sts, two 2nds, and two 3rds.

Snipe Class

1. Brazil (C. Delorenzi) 11.7; 2. USA (ALAN LEVINSON, helmsman, HARRY LEVINSON, crew) 28.4; 3. Bermuda (R. Belvin) 32.0; 4. Puerto Rico (J. Hoyt) 42.5; 5. Argentina (F. Sanjuro) 65.4; 6. Bahamas (D. Kelly) 70.0.

USA, on the basis of counting Levinson's six highest placings, had two 1sts, one 2nd, two 3rds, and one 8th.

341

(Unless specifically designated as 1967 Pan-American Games (A), 1968 Olympic Winter Games (B) or Games of the XIX Olympiad (C), the following served in their respective capacities at all three competitions.)

J. Abraham   J. Altott   D. Ball

R. Beeten   E. Byrne   C. Campbell   J. Conboy

D. Cooper   L. Crane   D. Crowl   A. Dodd

B. Drury   R. Dunham   G. Ellison   J. Emmerich

Greifenstein   G. Greiner   R. Gunn   A. Gwynne

USOC OFFICERS

Douglas F. Roby, Detroit, Mich., President
Franklin L. Orth, Washington, D.C., 1st Vice President
Dr. Merritt H. Stiles, Spokane, Wash., 2nd Vice President
Robert J. Kane, Ithaca, N.Y., Secretary
Julian K. Roosevelt, Oyster Bay, N.Y., Treasurer
Patrick H. Sullivan, New York, N.Y., Counselor

EXECUTIVE STAFF

Miguel A. de Capriles, New York, N.Y., Chief of Mission
Arthur G. Lentz, New York, N.Y., Executive Director
William J. Bachert, Montclair, N.J., Assistant Treasurer
Asa S. Bushnell, Princeton, N.J., Assistant Secretary (C)

GAMES PLANNING DIRECTORS
Administration

Albert F. Wheltle, Baltimore, Md., chairman (A & C)
Clifford H. Buck, Denver, Colo., co-chairman
Wilson T. Hobson, Jr., Wayne, Pa., co-chairman

Food and Housing

Hermann C. Rusch, White Sulphur Springs, W.Va., chairman
Philip O. Krumm, Kenosha, Wis., vice-chairman

Medical and Training Services

**Dr. Merritt H. Stiles, Spokane, Wash., chairman
Dr. Allen Ryan, Madison, Wisconsin, vice-chairman (A & C)

Supplies and Equipment

Al O. Duer, Kansas City, Mo., chairman
**Marion H. Miller, New York, N.Y., vice-chairman

V. Haigh	D. Hanley	W. Harris	J. Henson
S. Hicks	D. Hopp	H. Hussnatter	N. Jackson
R. Johnson	A. Landon	E. Lane	MacAusland
McClughan	McLaughlin	A. Martin	R. Mathias
C. Medlar	W. Meives	D. Messner	C. Meyer
D. Miller	M. Miller	W. Mills	L. Morgan
G. Nagabods	J. Owens	C. Paul	T. Pederson

Transportation

*Everett C. Barnes, Hamilton, N.Y., chairman
**Richard S. Dunham, New York, N.Y., vice-chairman
*served as acting executive director at Mexico City during leave
of absence for Mr. Arthur G. Lentz
**also listed in another capacity

ARMED FORCES REPRESENTATIVES

Col. Donald Miller, USA, Washington, D.C. (A & C)
Col. George McClughan, USAF, Randolph AFB, Texas (A)
Col. A. M. Dodd, USAF, Randolph AFB, Texas (B)
Col. Claude Campbell, USAF, Randolph AFB, Texas (C)
Col. Gerald Russell, USMC, Washington, D.C. (C)
Major G. Vernon Ellison, USMC, Washington, D.C. (A)
Capt. Josiah Henson, USN, Washington, D.C. (A & C)

USOC STAFF PERSONNEL

**Marion H. Miller, New York, administrative assistant
**Richard S. Dunham, New York, N.Y., administrative
assistant
C. Robert Paul, Merion, Pa., administrative
assistant and press officer
H. Jamison Swarts, Philadelphia, Pa., housing supervisor
Mrs. Alice Lord Landon, Lynbrook, N.Y., head chaperone
Mrs. Frances Zito, New York, N.Y., staff secretary
Helen Greifenstein, New York, N.Y., staff secretary (A & C)
Mrs. Marion Thomas, New York, N.Y., staff secretary (A)
Maurice Schulman, New York, N.Y., staff assistant (A & C)
Herman Hussnatter, Saddlebrook, N.J. staff assistant (A)
Vera Haigh, New York, N.Y., staff secretary (C)
Catherine D. Meyer, Glen Rock, N.J., housing
assistant (A & C)
Edward Rosenblum, Washington, D.C., housing assistant (C)
Chris von Saltza, Berkeley, Calif., asst. chaperone (C)
Lucile Wilson, Chicago, Ill., asst. chaperone (C)
Karen Denis Saloomey, Providence, R.I., asst.
chaperone (B)
William T. Harris, Jr., St. Paul, Minn., press officer (A)
William McLaughlin, New York, N.Y., staff
assistant (A & C)
Walter J. Meives, Madison, Wis., photographer
Milton Stark, Baltimore, Md., photographer
Duane Hopp, Madison, Wis., photographer (A)
Dean S. Ball, Jr., Madison, Wis., photographer (C)
James Emmerich, Brookings, S.D., equipment (A & C)
Dr. William Plummer, Walnut, Calif., medical research (C)

MEDICAL AND TRAINING SERVICES

Dr. Daniel F. Hanley, Brunswick, Maine, chief team physician

J. Persson   E. Pillings   W. Plummer   J. Price

W. Riehl   G. Robinson   R. Rose   Rosenblum

H. Rusch   G. Russell   A. Russo   A. Ryan

Sabasteanski   K. Saloomey   A. Savastano   J. Sayre

M. Schulman   F. Sheridan   M. Stark   H. Swarts

B. Taylor   M. Thomas   C. von Saltza   R. White

D. Wike   L. Wilson   E. Zanfrini   F. Zito

Pan American Games

Dr. George Greiner, Kent, Conn., physician
Dr. A. A. Savastano, Providence, R.I., physician
June Persson, Denver, Colo., nurse
Mrs. Barbara Sabasteanski, Brunswick, Maine, nurse
Robert H. Gunn, Beaumont, Texas, head trainer
Edward Byrne, Moraga, Calif., trainer
James Conboy, Colorado Springs, Colo., trainer
Laurence Morgan, Manhattan, Kan., trainer
Edward Pillings, West Point, N.Y., trainer
James Price, Columbia, S.C., trainer
Gayle Robinson, Lansing, Mich., trainer
Francis Sheridan, Phillipsburg, N.J., trainer
Blanche Drury, Mail Valley, Calif., trainer
Ann Martin, Rochester, Minn., trainer

Olympic Winter Games

Dr. Lawrence Crane, Portland, Maine, physician
Dr. Duane Messner, Denver, Colo., physician
Dr. George Nagabods, Minneapolis, Minn.,
physician (ice hockey)
Edward A. Zanfrini, Princeton, N.J., head trainer
Joseph Altott, Williamstown, Mass., trainer
Robert Beeten, Pocatello, Idaho, trainer
Tage Pedersen, Aspen, Colo., trainer (alpine ski)
Richard Rose, Minneapolis, Minn., trainer (ice hockey)
Lt. Shirlee C. Hicks, USN, St. Albans, N.Y., trainer

Olympic Summer Games

Dr. Donald Cooper, Stillwater, Okla., physician
Dr. William MacAusland, Boston, Mass., physician
Dr. Winston Riehl, New Orleans, La., physician
***June Persson, Denver, Colo., nurse
***Mrs. Barbara Sabasteanski, Brunswick, Maine, nurse
Charles Medlar, University Park, Pa., head trainer
Joseph Abraham, Geneva, N.Y., trainer
Lewis Crowl, Sacramento, Calif., trainer
A. C. Gwynne, Morgantown, W.Va., trainer
Edward Lane, Dallas, Texas, trainer
***Ann Martin, Rochester, Minn., trainer
Anthony Russo, Glendora, Calif., trainer
Buddy Taylor, Nashville, Tenn., trainer
Robert White, Detroit, Mich., trainer
David Wike, Miami, Fla., trainer
*** served at Pan-American Games

BOARD OF CONSULTANTS — MEXICO CITY

Jesse Owens, Chicago, Ill., chairman
Dr. Nell Jackson, Urbana, Ill.
Robert Mathias, Washington, D.C.
William Mills, San Diego, Calif.
John Sayre, Armonk, N.Y.
Rafer Johnson, Los Angeles, Calif.

RESULTS

Ahletics (Track and Field), Men

Although every sporting activity of man which has found a form of official recognition is represented at the Olympic Games, it is the track and field events which, rightly or wrongly, are the heart of this *Festival of Sport.* They command the greatest interest because they undoubtedly provide the greatest thrills. Mexico City was no different.

In fact, more exciting races were run, more astonishing performances were seen—for instance in the men's jumping events—and more currently recognized world records broken than ever before. And, most important, it was not only a few extraordinary athletes who extended the barriers of what was hitherto believed possible into new regions, but it was the number of new Olympic records, bettering former standards in both the heats and finals, which was quite staggering.

Mexico City's high altitude and thin air, of course, contributed to these record-shattering performances in the sprint races, while the adverse effect of these atmospheric conditions influenced the long distance runners—but this is only part of the story.

Progress, greater knowledge of the workings of the human body and the ever-widening area from which sportsmen and sportswomen are being drawn (including the emergence of the new African nations) are some of the factors which contributed to this avalanche of record performances. Not only the spectators in the bowl of Mexico City's magnificent stadium were given a continuous feast, but also the American public had the added pleasure of witnessing on their television screens the USA's unchallenged supremacy in the track and field events, clearly shown by the USA men and women harvesting 15 gold medals.

The **100 meters** race for man is perhaps the most "concentrated" in thrills of all events: drama, highest tension and total effort from start to finish, packed into less than ten seconds. And this time the race equalled the fastest ever run anywhere in the world.

The heats hinted what was to come. The time of 10.2 seconds in the semi-finals was too slow to qualify for the final: Small wonder, therefore, that the final turned out to be equal to the fastest ever run anywhere and a new Olympic record performance. Jim Hines, 22, USA, was the winner in 9.9 seconds. One should not be surprised if in the not too distant future, one or two tenths of a second will be clipped off the current record.

Lennox Miller of Jamaica and Charlie Greene, USA, took a silver and a bronze medal, respectively, both being clocked in 10 seconds flat. The rest of the field was only a tenth of a second slower, except Ravelomanantsoa of Madagascar, last in 10.2 seconds.

Statistics: 66 participants from 42 nations; 9 heats, 4 second-round races, 2 semi-finals. Recognized world record 10.0 sec. held by six men. Olympic record: Hayes (USA) 10.0, 1964. The Olympic record and recognized world record were beaten once and equalled six times. New Olympic record: Hines (USA) 9.9 sec.

Final	Time		Time
1. Jim Hines, USA	9.9	5. Roger Bambuck, France	10.1
2. Lennox Miller, Jamaica	10.0	6. Mel Pender, USA	10.1
3. Charlie Greene, USA	10.0	7. Harry Jerome, Canada	10.1
4. Pablo Mentes, Cuba	10.1	8. Jean Ravelomanantsoa, Mdgr.	10.2

The **200 meters** race brought a repeat USA winning performance, with Tommie Smith, holder of the recognized world record, setting another Olympic record. Smith ran a beautifully calculated race. Coming up from behind, his victory was never in doubt after about two-thirds of the race, least of all to himself. He passed the field in a jubilant gesture of triumph, possibly also rejoicing over the fact that he had been a doubtful starter after having pulled a leg muscle slightly in the semi-final.

Statistics: 49 participants from 37 countries; 7 heats, 4 second-round races, 2 semi-finals. Recognized world record: Smith (USA) 20.0 sec., 1966. Olympic record: Carr (USA) 20.3 sec., 1964. The recognized world record was beaten eight times and equalled three times. New Olympic record: Smith (USA) 19.8 sec.

Final	Time		Time
1. Tommie Smith, USA	19.8	5. Roger Bambuck, France	20.5
2. Peter Norman, Australia	20.0	6. Larry Questad, USA	20.6
3. John Carlos, USA	20.0	7. Mike Fray, Jamaica	20.6
4. Edwin Roberts, Trinidad	20.3	8. Joachim Eigenherr, W. Germany	20.6

The **400 meters** was also a USA affair with its runners winning gold, silver and bronze medals as all three bettered the recognized world record in the final. Things like this don't happen often, not even at the Olympic Games. LEE EVANS, LARRY JAMES and RON FREEMAN reached the tape first, in that order, with three runners from African nations trailing. The times are past when European runners dominated the field in the classic 400 meters distance. EVANS' time of 43.8 seconds can only be called fabulous; it equals only a fraction more than a succession of four 100-meter races of 10.9 seconds each.

Statistics: 54 participants from 36 countries; 8 heats, 4 second-round races, 2 semi-finals. Recognized world record: SMITH (USA) 44.5 sec., 1967. Olympic record: OTIS DAVIS (USA) and Kaufman (Germany) 44.9 sec., 1960. The recognized world record was broken three times and the Olympic record was broken four times and equalled twice. New Olympic record: EVANS (USA) 43.8 sec.

Final	Time		Time
1. LEE EVANS, USA	43.8	5. Martin Jellinghaus, W. Germany ..	45.3
2. LARRY JAMES, USA	43.9	6. Tegegne Bezabeh, Ethiopia	45.4
3. RON FREEMAN, USA	44.4	7. Andrzej Badenski, Poland	45.4
4. Amadou Gakou, Senegal	45.0	8. Amos Omolo, Uganda	47.6

The **800 meters** race was won by Australia's Ralph Doubell, 23, who before the start of the race was counted on as a clear outsider. Wilson Kiprugut of Kenya, 30, the favorite, was 0.2 seconds slower than the winner. Who can tell whether the result would not have been reversed if Kiprugut had employed different tactics? It is possible that he became the victim of his own methods. He covered the first 400 meters in the very fast time of 51 seconds. His lead was not sufficient to shake off the very confident Doubell, who at this stage was running behind Cayenne of Trinidad and Eastern Germany's Fromm. After about 600 meters, Doubell moved up into second place, but Kiprugut accelerated as well; however, Kiprugut was too spent to stop Doubell from overtaking him at the tape. Doubell's time equals Peter Snell's world record time of 1:44.3.

Statistics: 41 participants from 32 countrires; 6 heats, 2 semi-final races. World record: Snell (New Zealand) 1:44.3, 1962. Olympic record: Snell, 1:45.1, 1964. The world record was equalled and the Olympic record beaten twice. New Olympic record: Doubell (Australia) 1:44.3, equals world record.

Final	Time		Time
1. Ralph Doubell, Australia	1:44.3	5. Josef Plachy, Czechoslovakia	1:45.9
2. Wilson Kiprugut, Kenya	1:44.5	6. Dieter Fromm, E. Germany	1:46.2
3. TOM FARRELL, USA	1:45.4	7. Thomas Saisi, Kenya	1:47.5
4. Walter Adams, W. Germany	1:45.8	8. Benedict Cayenne, Trinidad	1:54.3

The **1,500 meters** race at first looked like an All-Kenyan affair. Ben Jipcho and Kipchoge Keino raced ahead from the start as if the rest of the field didn't count. At the start, JIM RYUN, USA world record-holder at this distance, was next to last. At 400 meters Jipcho began to fall back, but his job as pace-maker for Keino had been done. But then the whole stadium's concentration shifted to RYUN who pushed forward, overtook the two Germans, Tummler and Norpoth, and in a great sprint captured second. Keino, 28 years old, was 25 yards in front of RYUN at the finish.

Statistics: 54 participants from 37 countries; 5 heats, 2 semi-finals. World record: RYUN (USA) 3:33.1, 1967. Olympic record: Elliott (Australia) 3:35.6, 1960. The Olympic record was beaten only once. New Olympic record: Keino (Kenya) 3:34.9.

Final	Time		Time
1. Kipchoge Keino, Kenya	3:34.9	5. John Whetton, Britain	3:43.8
2. JIM RYUN, USA	3:37.8	6. Jacques Boxberger, France	3:46.6
3. Bodo Tummler, W. Germany ...	3:39.0	7. Henryk Szordykowski, Poland ...	3:46.6
4. Harald Norpoth, W. Germany ...	3:42.5	8. Josef Odlozil, Czechoslovakia ...	3:48.6

The **5,000 meters** race, like the 10,000 meters on the opening day of track and field, became an African event. Or, perhaps more accurately, was an event for high altitude countries as the athletes from the lowlands seemed to be affected by the lack of oxygen. (Mexico's Martinez came in fourth in both the 5,000 and 10,000 meters because his body was better adapted to the atmospheric conditions.) The race was characterized by a continuous changing of positions of the runners and a different man was in the lead after each thousand meters. Around the 4,000-meter mark the field was reduced to a select group of runners in which world record holder Ron Clarke, 31, of Australia tried to hold his own against the Africans. It became clear in the final laps that Gammoudi, 29, Tunisia, had the biggest reserve, but only after shaking off Keino in a tremendously exciting "sprinters' finish." The margin between the winner of the gold and silver medals was about two yards.

Statistics: 37 participants from 26 countries; 3 heats. World record: Clarke (Australia) 13:16.1, 1966. Olympic record: Kuts (USSR) 13:39.6, 1956.

Final	Time		Time
1. Mohamed Gammoudi, Tunisia ..	14:05.0	5. Ron Clarke, Australia	14:12.4
2. Kipchoge Keino, Kenya	14:05.2	6. Wohib Masresha, Ethiopia	14:17.6
3. Naftali Temu, Kenya	14:06.4	7. Nikolai Sviridov, USSR	14:18.4
4. Juan Martinez, Mexico	14:10.8	8. Fikru Deguefu, Ethiopia	14:19.0

The **10,000 meters** proved almost too much of a test for those not adjusted to the thin air. Many competitors broke down and it wasn't a beautiful sight. At the end, doctors were kept busy. Ron Clarke, Australia's magnificent runner, now 31, collapsed at the finish. Temu, only 23 years old, ran a perfectly paced race to defeat Wolde, two years his senior.

Statistics: 37 participants from 23 countries. World record: Clarke (Australia) 27:39.4, 1965. Olympic Record: MILLS (USA) 28:24.4, 1964.

Final	Time		Time
1. Naftali Temu, Kenya	29:27.4	5. Nikolai Sviridov, USSR	29:43.2
2. Mamo Wolde, Ethiopia	29:28.0	6. Ron Clarke, Australia	29:44.8
3. Mohamed Gammoudi, Tunisia ..	29:34.2	7. Ron Hill, Britain	29:53.2
4. Juan Martinez, Mexico	29:35.0	8. Wohib Masresha, Ethiopia	29:57.0

The **marathon** race fortunately did not turn into the expected torturer in spite of the unbearable heat. Most of the competitors completed the 26 miles 385 yards, sticking to the green lane at the edge of the road which showed them the way through Mexico City.

Among those who dropped out of the race was Abebe Bikila, 37, Ethiopia, winner in 1960 and 1964. He gave up after 15 kilometers, suffering from stomach cramps and a heavy cold. His fellow-countryman, Mamo Wolde, was the winner and still had enough reserve energy to run an additional lap in the Estadio Olimpico in celebration of his victory. Wolde, silver medalist in the 10,000 meters, is 12 years younger than Bikila.

Statistics: 72 participants from 44 countries, 57 participants finished the race. Olympic Games' best performance: Abebe Bikila (Ethiopia) 2:12:11.2, 1964.

Final	Time		Time
1. Mamo Wolde, Ethiopia	2:20:26.4	5. William Adcocks, Britain	2:25:33.0
2. Kenji Kimihara, Japan	2:23:31.0	6. Merawi Gebru, Ethiopia	2:27:16.8
3. Mike Ryan, New Zealand	2:23:45.0	7. Derek Clayton, Australia	2:27:23.8
4. Ismail Akcay, Turkey	2:25:18.8	8. Tim Johnston, Britain	2:28:04.0

The **110-meter hurdles** was won, as was expected, by the USA's WILLIE DAVENPORT, 25. ERVIN HALL, USA, gained second, but this nation's superiority was strongly challenged by the Europeans. The Italian Ottoz ran an especially beautiful race, clocking the same time as HALL and leaving COLEMAN, USA, in fourth.

Statistics: 33 participants from 24 countries; 5 heats, 2 semi-finals. World record: Lauer (West Germany) 1959; CALHOUN (USA) 1960; McCULLOUCH (USA) 13.2 sec. Olympic record: CALHOUN and DAVIS (USA) 13.5, 1956. The Olympic record was broken four times and equalled five times. New Olympic Record: DAVENPORT (USA) and HALL (USA) 13.3 sec. HALL made his record in the semi-finals.

Final	Time		Time
1. WILLIE DAVENPORT, USA	13.3	5. Werner Trzmiel, W. Germany	13.6
2. ERVIN HALL, USA	13.4	6. Bo Forssander, Sweden	13.7
3. Eddy Ottoz, Italy	13.4	7. Marcel Duriez, France	13.7
4. LEON COLEMAN, USA	13.6	8. Pierre Schoebel, France	14.0

The **400-meter hurdles** turned out to be one of the great races of the Games of the XIX Olympiad as far as style, speed, technique and thrills are concerned. The result of the race was also something very rare—a triumph to be shared between Great Britain and the USA. David Hemery, 22, who won in the fantastic world record time of 48.1 seconds is a Briton who has resided in the USA for many years and is a product of American training methods and facilities. He is also NCAA champion over this distance.

Hemery started the race at a pace which nobody in the Estadio Olimpico thought he could maintain. But the people were proved wrong. Hemery's victory was never in doubt from the moment he overtook VANDERSTOCK, the USA favorite. The latter had to be satisfied with fourth place behind West Germany's Hennige and Sherwood of Great Britain.

Statistics: 30 participants from 24 countries; 4 heats, 2 semi-finals. World record: CAWLEY (USA) 49.1, 1964. Olympic record: DAVIS (USA) 49.3 sec., 1960. The world record was broken five times and equalled three times. New Olympic and world records: Hemery (Great Britain) 48.1 sec.

Final	Time		Time
1. Dave Hemery, Britain	48.1	5. Viach. Skomarokhov, USSR	49.1
2. Gerhard Hennige, W. Germany	49.0	6. RON WHITNEY, USA	49.2
3. John Sherwood, Britain	49.0	7. Rainer Schubert, W. Germany	49.2
4. GEOFF VANDERSTOCK, USA	49.0	8. Roberto Frinolli, Italy	50.1

The **3,000-meter steeplechase** was won by Amos Biwott, only 21 in September, of Kenya who displayed the most extraordinary, crowd-pleasing, and exciting style taking the water jump ever witnessed anywhere in this event. Kudinsky of the Soviet Union, the pre-race favorite, was injured and collapsed during the 12-man final.

In the final 400 meters, Australia's Kevin O'Brien, and GEORGE YOUNG, 31-year-old USA steeplechaser, battled stride for stride for third place, as Kogo of Kenya earned the silver medal. Roelants, 1964 Olympic champion, faltered after leading at the 2,000-meter mark. In the end it was a convincing triumph for Kenya, finishing 1–2. But Mexico's altitude had greater effect on the time performances of the athletes than any other Olympic track event.

Statistics: 37 participants from 26 countries; 3 heats. World record: Roelants (Belgium) 8:26.4, 1965· Olympic record: Roelants (Belgium) 8:30.8, 1964.

Final	Time		Time
1. Amos Biwott, Kenya	8:51.0	5. Aleksandr Morozov, USSR	8:55.8
2. Benjamin Kogo, Kenya..........	8:51.6	6. Jelev Mihail, Bulgaria	8:58.4
3. GEORGE YOUNG, USA	8:51.8	7. Gaston Roelants, Belgium	8:59,4
4. Kevin O'Brien, Australia	8:52.0	8. Arne Risa, Norway	9:09.0

The **20,000-meter race walk** through Mexico City's suburbs proved not only a fight between the various race walkers, but also a battle against the closely-observing jury of judges which was watching closely for those who in their opinion crossed the imaginary line separating race walking from trotting. Many walkers were disqualified.

José Pedraza of Mexico, fearing to be one of those disqualified when one of the judges approached him, lost his bearing and possibly also the gold medal. But Pedraza finished second behind the veteran Golubnichy, 32, victor in this event at Rome eight years earlier. RUDY HALUZA, 37, USA, gave his country its highest finish ever in this event by gaining fourth place.

Statistics: 41 participants from 21 countries with 29 finishing the race. Olympic best performance: Matthews (Great Britain) 1:29:34.0, 1964.

Final	Time		Time
1. Vladimir Golubnichy, USSR .	1:33:58.4	5. Gerhard Sperling, E. Germany	1:35:27.2
2. José Pedraza, Mexico	1:34:00.0	6. Otto Barch, USSR	1:36:16.8
3. Nikolai Smaga, USSR	1:34:03.4	7. Hans Reimann, E. Germany ..	1:36:31.4
4. RUDY HALUZA, USA	1:35:00.2	8. Stefan Ingvarsson, Sweden ...	1:36:43.4

The **50,000-meter race walk** proved again that long distance race walking is a European sport. Except for YOUNG, USA, in third place and Mexico's Pedraza in eighth place, Europeans picked up the other six places among the first eight. Hohne, 27, of East Germany, dominated the race and was in first place at the end of each five kilometers of the race over the distance of 31.25 miles.

In gaining the bronze medal, LARRY YOUNG, one of the ten youngest walkers in the race at 25, brought the USA its first medal in this event.

Statistics: 40 participants from 21 countries with 28 finishing the race. Olympic best performance: Pamich (Italy) 4:11:12.4, 1964.

Final	Time		Time
1. Christoph Hohne, E.Germany	4:20:13.6	3. LARRY YOUNG, USA	4:31:55.4
2. Antal Kiss, Hungary	4:30:17.0	4. Peter Selzer, E. Germany	4:33:09.8

5. Stig Lindberg, Sweden	4:34:05.0		7. Bryan Eley, Britain	4:37:32.2
6. Vittorio Visini, Italy	4:36:33.2		8. José Pedraza, Mexico	4:37:51.4

The **4×100-meter relay** final reversed the results of the heats. After the Jamaican team had bettered the recognized world record in the heats, the USA foursome earned the gold medals and a world record with a fastest ever performance of 38.2 seconds on a sensational anchor leg by sprint champion JIM HINES. Only the next Olympic Games in Munich will show whether these are freak times or not because of Mexico's special atmospheric conditions.

Statistics: 19 teams from 19 countries; 3 heats, 2 semi-finals. Recognized world record: USA (McCULLOUCH, KULLER, SIMPSON, L. MILLER) 38.5 sec., 1967. Olympic record: USA (DRAYTON, ASHWORTH, STEBBINS, HAYES) 39.0 sec., 1964. The recognized world record was broken five times and equalled four times. The Olympic record was broken eighteen times and equalled twice. New Olympic record and world record: USA 38.2 sec.

Final	Time			Time
1. USA (CHARLIE GREENE, MEL PENDER, RONALD RAY SMITH, JIM HINES)	38.2	5. East Germany (Erbstoesser, Scheiter, Haase, Eggers)	38.6
2. Cuba (Ramirez, Morales, Montes, Figuerola)	38.3	6. West Germany (Schmidtke, Metz, Wucherer, Eigenherr)	38.7
3. France (Fenouil, Delecour, Piquemal, Bambuck)	38.4	7. Italy (Ottolina, Preatoni, Sguazzero, Berruti)	39.2
4. Jamaica (Stewart, Fray, Forbes, L. Miller)	38.4	8. Poland (Maniak, Pomanowski, Nowosz, Dudziak)	39.2

The **4×400-meter relay** saw the USA win by 30 yards over a surprising Kenyan foursome after the latter team's lead-off man Daniel Rudisha handed off to Munyoro Nyamu in first place. However, the USA had at its disposal for the last three legs the three medal winners of the 400-meter race. A new world record was to be expected and was duly delivered in the fantastic time of 2:56.1, without any real opposition after RON FREEMAN put the USA into a long lead on the second leg.

Statistics: 16 teams from 16 countries. World record: USA (FREY, EVANS, T. SMITH, LEWIS) 2:59.0, 1966. Olympic record: USA (CASSELL, LARRABEE, WILLIAMS, CARR) 3:00.7, 1964. The recognized world record was broken once and equalled once. The Olympic record was broken four times and equalled once. New Olympic record and world record: USA (MATTHEWS, FREEMAN, JAMES, EVANS) 2:56.1.

Final	Time			Time
1. USA (VINCENT MATTHEWS, RON FREEMAN, LARRY JAMES, LEE EVANS)	2:56.1	5. Great Britain (Winbolt-Lewis, Campbell, Hemery, Sherwood) ...	3:01.2
2. Kenya (Rudisha, Nyamu, Bon, Asati)	2:59.6	6. Trinidad (Simon, Bobb, Cayenne, Roberts)	3:04.5
3. West Germany (Mueller, Kinder, Hennige, Jellinghaus)	3:00.5	7. Italy (Ottolina, Puosi, Fusi, Bello)	3:04.5
4. Poland (Gredezinski, Balachowski, Werner, Badenski)	3:00.5	8. France (Nallet, Carette, Bertould, Boccardo)	3:07.5

The **long jump** was not so much a competition as an exhibition. For, with his opening jump—the opening jump of the final round of the competition—BOB BEAMON, 22, USA, seemed not to jump but rather to fly through Mexico City's rarified atmosphere. When he landed 29–2½ (8. 90 m) later, the world and Olympic records were smashed beyond comprehension and the competition was over. All RALPH BOSTON, USA, Igor Ter-Ovanesyan, USSR, and Lynn Davies, Great Britain, could hope for was the runner-up position. However, Klaus Beer, East Germany, with only one jump over 26 feet, edged out Boston for the silver medal.

"Beamon's Bombshell," as it is now known, had flattened everyone—competitors and spectators alike. It will be a long time before people stop discussing it, or anyone else matches it. The consensus of those attending the Olympic Games considered it the most spectacular single event of the men's track and field competition.

Statistics: 35 participants from 23 countries; 17 competitors qualified for the final by jumping more than 24 feet 9 inches. World record: RALPH BOSTON (USA) 1965 and Igor Ter-Ovanesyan (USSR) 1967, 27-4¾. Olympic record: BOSTON (USA) 26-7¾ (8.12 m), 1960. The world record was broken once. The Olympic record was broken five times and equalled once. New Olympic and world record: BEAMON (USA) 29-2½ (8.90 m).

Final	Distance		Distance
1. BOB BEAMON, USA ..... 29-2½ (8.90 m)		5. Tonu Lepik, USSR ..... 26-6½ (8.09 m)
2. Klaus Beer, E. Germany . 26-10½ (8.19 m)		6. Allen Crawley, Australia . 26-3¾ (8.02 m)
3. RALPH BOSTON, USA ... 26-9¼ (8.16 m)		7. Jack Pani, France .... 26-1¾ (7.97 m)
4. Igor Ter-Ovanesyan, USSR 26-7¾ (8.12 m)		8. Andrzej Stalmach, Poland. 26-0½ (7.94 m)

The **triple jump** showed how world standards in sports are still improving. In this contest the recognized world record was broken nine times before the winner could be established. Prior to the Games of the XIX Olympiad the 56-foot mark was considered the decisive line to cross. Now six jumpers managed to go beyond (including fourth place ART WALKER, USA, who set a new American record in the event) and the former record holder and Olympic champion, Jozef Schmidt, was relegated to seventh place in the greatest triple jump competition ever seen. This is ample evidence that "better" jumping was more of a factor than the rarified atmosphere.

Statistics: 34 competitors from 24 countries; 12 contestants reached the qualifying distance of 52-6 (16.10 m) and the best six competed in the final three jumps. Recognized world record: Schmidt (Poland) 55-10½ (17.03 m), 1960. Olympic record: Schmidt (Poland) 55-3¼ (16.85 m), 1964. The world record was broken nine times and the Olympic record twelve times. New Olympic and world record: Saneev (USSR) 57-¾ (17.39 m).

Final	Distance		Distance
1. Victor Saneev, USSR ... 57-0¾ (17.39 m)		5. Nikolai Dudkin, USSR . 56-0¾ (17.09 m)
2. Nelson Prudencio, Braz.. 56-8 (17.27 m)		6. Philip May, Australia .. 55-10 (17.02 m)
3. Guiseppe Gentile, Italy .. 56-6 (17.22 m)		7. Jozef Schmidt, Poland . 55-5 (16.89 m)
4. ART WALKER, USA .... 56-2 (17.12 m)		8. Mamadou Dia, Senegal . 54-10¾ (16.73 m)

The **pole vault** competition demanded good nerves of both those who took part and those who watched it. The battle of gamesmanship at the vaulting pits lasted seven and a half hours. After nightfall descended on the Estadio Olimpico, the final decision was reached under the floodlights.

JOHN PENNEL, USA, first man ever to scale the 17-foot height and a two-year world record holder, after clearing 17-8½ (5.40 m) was eliminated when his pole "passed" unter the cross-bar, a technical fault which will become legal in May, 1969, under a new IAAF rule.

The three top competitors, including BOB SEAGREN, just turned 22, USA, cleared 17-8½. However, when none of them was successful in three tries at a new world record height of 17-10½ (5.45 m), the final placings for the medals was decided on total misses at earlier heights, SEAGREN winning the gold medal by virtue of only two misses to three for West Germany's Claus Schiprowski.

Statistics: 23 participants from 16 countries; 15 competitors cleared the height of 13-6 (4.90 m). World record: WILSON (USA) 17-8 (5.38 m), 1967; Olympic record: HANSEN (USA) 16-9 (5.10 m), 1964. The world record was broken three times and the Olympic record twenty-eight times and equalled five times. New Olympic and world record: SEAGREN (USA), Schiprowski (West Germany), Nordwig (East Germany) 17-8½ (5.40 m).

Final	Height		Height
1. BOB SEAGREN, USA ..... 17-8½ (5.40 m)		5. JOHN PENNEL, USA ..... 17-6¾ (5.35 m)
2. Claus Schiprowski, West Germany .... 17-8½ (5.40 m)		6. Gennady Blitznetsov, USSR .... 17-4¾ (5.30 m)
3. Wolfgang Nordwig, East Germany .... 17-8½ (5.40 m)		7. Herve d'Encausse, France 17-2¾ (5.25 m)
4. Chris Papanicolaou, Gr. .. 17-6¾ (5.35 m)		8. Heinfried Engel, W. Germany .... 17-0¾ (5.20 m)

The **high jump** provided a sensation of a special and a totally-unexpected kind. DICK FOSBURY, 21, USA, showed an astonished world a brand-new way to jump better and higher. He invented and perfected it himself and there's an indication that many jumpers (novices and world class alike), will begin to copy what has been named the "Fosbury Flop." It isn't easy to describe in words, one has to see it in action. It consists of a very fast sprint up, followed by a jumping action in which the body sails over the bar head first. FOSBURY's new Olympic record 7-4¼ (2.24 m) speaks a clear language: This flop is no flop and it enabled the USA to win the high jump title for the first time since 1956.

Statistics: 39 participants from 27 countries; six competitors cleared the qualifying height of 7-0¼ (2.14 m), seven other participants were admitted to the final round of 13 under Olympic rules for the top 12 and ties. World record: Brumel (USSR) 7-5¾ (2.28 m), 1963; Olympic record: Brumel (USSR) 7-1¾ (2.18 m), 1964. The Olympic record was broken six times and equalled twice. New Olympic record: FOSBURY (USA) 7-4¼ (2.24 m).

Final

	Height			Height
1. DICK FOSBURY, USA	7-4¼ (2.24 m)	6. Giacomo Crosa, Italy	7-0¼	(2.14 m)
2. ED CARUTHERS, USA	7-3½ (2.22 m)	7. Gunther Spielvogel,		
3. Valentin Gavrilov, USSR .	7-2¾ (2.20 m)	W. Germany	7-0¼	(2.14 m)
4. Valery Skvortsov, USSR .	7-1 (2.16 m)	8. Laurie Peckham, Australia	6-11½	(2.12 m)
5. REYNALDO BROWN, USA .	7-0¼ (2.14 m)			

The **shot put** event accounted for an additional gold and silver medal for the USA. RANDY MATSON, 23, the favorite, actually had his best throw in the qualifying preliminary round 67-10½ (20.68 m) and then won the whole event with his first put of 67-4¾ (20.54 m) in the final. GEORGE WOODS, 25, largest member of the USA team at 6-2, 295 pounds, sewed up the silver with his first toss also, 66-0¼ (20.12 m). The third USA member, DAVE MAGGARD, was sub-par physically and could do no better than fifth, 3–6 under his best throw in the Olympic selection trials.

Statistics: 19 competitors (smallest number of entries for an individual event) from 14 countries with 12 of them attaining the qualifying distance of 60-4¼ (18.90 m) and eight reaching the final three puts. World record: MATSON (USA) 71-5½ (21.78 m), 1967. Olympic record: DALLAS LONG (USA) 66-8¼ (20.33 m), 1964. MATSON bettered LONG's record twice. New Olympic record: MATSON (USA) 67-10½ (20.68 m) in the qualifying round.

Final

	Distance		Distance
1. RANDY MATSON, USA ..	67-4¾ (20.54 m)	6. Wladyslaw Komar,	
2. GEORGE WOODS, USA ..	66-0¼ (20.12 m)	Poland 64-3	(19.28 m)
3. Eduard Guschin, USSR .	65-11 (20.09 m)	7. Uwe Grabe, E. Germany . 62-5¼	(19.03 m)
4. Dieter Hoffmann,		8. Heinfried Birlenbach,	
E. Germany	65-7½ (20.00 m)	W. Germany 61-8¼	(18.80 m)
5. DAVE MAGGARD, USA .	63-9 (19.43 m)		

The **javelin throw** proceeded exactly as expected. The Soviet Union's Janis Lusis, 29, is in a class of his own in this sport and there was no doubt that he would also win in Mexico. Victory had been denied him at Tokyo. The top three finishers all bettered the Norwegian Danielsen's 12-year old Olympic record.

Never a real power in this event, the highest placed member of the USA team, MARK MURRO at ninth, finished two places higher than the top USA thrower at Tokyo. The defending champion, Finland's Pauli Nevala, failed to advance past the preliminary round.

Statistics: 27 participants from 18 countries; the qualifying distance of 263-0 (80.00 m) was attained by 11 men, one more was admitted to the final in conformance with the rules of the competition. World record: Pedersen (Norway) 300-11 (91.72 m), 1964. Olympic record: Danielsen (Norway) 281-2¼ (85.71 m), 1956. The Olympic record was bettered a total of seven times by the four top throwers. New Olympic record: Lusis (USSR) 295-7 (90.10 m).

Final

	Distance		Distance
1. Janis Lusis, USSR ...	295-7 (90.10 m)	5. Manfred Stolle,	
2. Jorma Kinnunen,		E. Germany 276-11½	(84.42 m)
Finland	290-7½ (88.58 m)	6. Karl-Ake Nilsson,	
3. Gergely Kulcsar,		Sweden 273-10½	(83.48 m)
Hungary	285-7½ (87.06 m)	7. Janusz Sidlo, Poland . 264-4½	(80.58 m)
4. Wladyslav Nikicluk,		8. Urs von Wartburg,	
Poland	281-2 (85.70 m)	Switzerland 264-3½	(80.56 m)

The **discus throw** was won by AL OERTER, USA, for the fourth straight time. The tall, 32-year-old American has therefore performed the unique feat in Olympic track and field of collecting four gold medals in four consecutive Olympic Games in the same event. No other athlete can boast of such a feat. And looking at OERTER's 212-6½ (64.78 m) toss, which was about five and a half feet better than runner-up Milde of East Germany, one cannot exclude the possibility that OERTER might even collect a fifth gold medal at the next Games in Munich.

Spectators in the Estadio Olimpico could plainly see that the opposition collapsed immediately after OERTER's winning throw, his third of six in the final. On his next to last throw he was a scant two inches (.04 m) away from his winning throw.

In the qualifying preliminary JAY SILVESTER, USA, broke the Olympic record with a throw of 207-9½ (63.34 m), his only try. However, in the final SILVESTER could do no better than fifth with 202-8 (61.78 m), made before OERTER's Olympic record throw. Danek, the world record holder, finished third.

Statistics: 27 participants from 19 countries of which 12 attained the qualifying standard of 190-3 (58.00 m) and eight competed in the final three throws. Recognized world record: Danek (Czechoslovakia) 214-0 (65.22 m), 1965. Olympic record: OERTER (USA) 200-1½ (61.00 m), 1964. The Olympic record was broken fifteen times in the qualifying preliminary and competition proper by five men (on all five fair throws by OERTER in the final). New Olympic record: OERTER (USA) 212-6½ (64.78 m).

Final

	Distance			Distance
1. AL OERTER, USA 212-6½	(64.78 m)		5. JAY SILVESTER, USA .. 202-8	(61.78 m)
2. Lothar Milde, E. Germany 206-11½	(63.08 m)		6. GARY CARLSEN, USA . 195-1	(59.46 m)
3. Ludvik Danek, Czechoslovakia 206-5	(62.92 m)		7. Edmund Piatkowski, Poland 194-10½	(59.40 m)
4. Manfred Losch, E. Germany 203-9½	(62.12 m)		8. Rick Bruch, Sweden .. 194-6	(59.28 m)

The **hammer throw** was won *this time* by Zsivotzky of Hungary; the defending champion (Klim, USSR) was left in second place. We say "this time" because these two have turned this event into a private duel on innumerable occasions. In Tokyo, the order of finish was reversed.

The USA dropped out of the top six for the first time as ED BURKE placed eleventh, 215-7½ (65.72 m), and was the only USA hammer thrower to enter the final round. Former Olympic champion HAROLD CONNOLLY fouled two of three throws; his best was 213-0 (65.00 m), and AL HALL, USA, could do no better than 215-6 (65.70 m).

Statistics: 22 participants from 12 countries and 12 attained the qualifying distance of 209-11 (66.00 m); the eight best competed in the final three throws. Recognized world record: Zsivotzky (Hungary) 241-11 (73.74 m), 1965. Olympic record: Klim (USSR) 228-9½ (69.74 m), 1964. The Olympic record was broken thirteen times by four hammer throwers (including five times each by Zsivotzky and Klim in the final). New Olympic record: Zsivotzky (Hungary) 240-8 (73.26 m).

Final

	Distance			Distance
1. Gyula Zsivotzky, Hungary 240-8	(73.36 m)		5. S. Eckschmidet, Hungary 227-10½	(69.46 m)
2. Romuald Klim, USSR 240-5	(73.28 m)		6. G. Kondrashov, USSR 226-7½	(69.08 m)
3. Lazar Lovasz, Hungary 228-11	(69.78 m)		7. Reinhard Thelmer, E. Germany 225-10	(68.84 m)
4. Takeo Sugawara, Japan 228-11	(69.78 m)		8. Helmut Baumann, E. Germany 223-11¼	(68.26 m)

The **decathlon** was won by BILL TOOMEY, a 29-year-old schoolteacher from Laguna Beach, Calif. But he had to fight hard for his victory, mainly against two long-time foes from West Germany, Walde, 26, and Bendlin, 25. What made TOOMEY's victory possible was his tremendous performance in the short events (including a 45.6 in the 400 meters in a torrential rainstorm), his surprising strength in the throwing event, and a recovery in the pole vault after missing twice at the opening height.

When it came to the tenth and final event, the 1,500 meters, he had secured a firm hold on the competition, but it would still have been possible for the two Germans to beat him with better than their best efforts. TOOMEY, running in a dank, heavy mist, won a smart tactical race, keeping the situation well in hand at every post, and led his closest rivals across the finish line. This tactical race at the end of twenty hours of the most concentrated and varied competition known in the athletic world provided the spectators with an added thrill. Toomey more than passed the test, a test as much of nerves as of physical strength and endurance. He won this most coveted of all gold medals with the new Olympic record of 8,193 points. And TOOMEY is the oldest decathlon champion ever crowned in the Olympic Games.

Statistics: 33 competitors from 20 countries, 20 of whom finished the competition (including the three from the USA in 1st, 6th and 7th places). World record: Bendlin (West Germany) 8,318 points, 1967. Olympic record: JOHNSON (USA) 8,001 points, 1960. (This record was broken by the top three finishers.) New Olympic record: TOOMEY (USA) 8,193 points.

Decathlon Results	Points		Points
1. BILL TOOMEY, USA	8,193	5. Joachim Kirst, E. Germany	7,861
2. Hans-Joachim Walde, W. Germany	8,111	6. Dr. TOM WADDELL, USA	7,720
3. Kurt Bendlin, W. Germany	8,064	7. RICK SLOAN, USA	7,692
4. Nikolai Avilov, USSR	7,909	8. Steen Smidt-Jensen, Denmark	7,648

TOOMEY's Performances.

First Day: 100 meters 10.4 sec. (959 points), Long Jump 25-9¾ (994); Shot Put 45-1¼ (712); High Jump 6-4¾ (813); 400 meters 45.6 sec. (1,021).

Second Day: 110-meter Hurdles 14.9 sec. (859); Discus Throw 143-3½ (757); Pole Vault 13-9½ (859); Javelin Throw 206-0½ (795); 1,500 meters 4:57.1 (424).

Athletics (Track and Field), Women

The women's track and field results present the same overall picture as that of the men's — improved performances all along the way with many new Olympic records.

People have asked themselves, in view of the astonishing results, where the limits in performances will finally be. Actually, today the women now run as fast and jump as far or as high (to mention nothing about the performances in other sports) as the men used to do a few years ago.

And at Mexico City's Games of the XIX Olympiad there was ample evidence that women had proceeded one more step toward a near-equality of the sexes. What the ladies are accomplishing in everyday life, they also intend to do in sport. This was the overall impression of the highly-charged ladies' contests which provided spectators in the Estadio Olimpico with plenty of thrills.

The USA girls continued to display their superiority in the sprints, and produced a surprising winner in the 800 meters. Otherwise, the successes in ladies' track and field were distributed widely among the competing nations.

Whereas the men's events attracted 856 athletes from 91 nations, 257 women athletes from 41 nations entered the Games of the XIX Olympiad.

The **100 meters** was, of course, an American affair. Nobody really expected that WYOMIA TYUS, 23, could be beaten. She won in 11 seconds "flat," thus adding to her Tokyo gold medal and becoming the first woman in Olympic Games' history to defend her sprint laurels successfully. People with longer memories compared her to the unforgettable WILMA RUDOLPH whose true successor she is. In the finals, only one tenth of a second separated her from her teammate, BARBARA FERRELL, 21. Poland's lanky Irena Kirszenstein Szewinska, clocked in the same time as Barbara, and came in third.

Statistics: 41 participants from 21 countries; 6 heats, 4 second-round races and 2 semi-finals. World record: Irena Kirszenstein (Poland) and WYOMIA TYUS and BARBARA FERRELL, both USA, 11.1 sec. Olympic record: WYOMIA TYUS (USA) 11.2 sec., 1964. The recognized world record was broken twice and equalled 5 times; the Olympic record was broken seven times and equalled five times. New Olympic record: WYOMIA TYUS (USA) 11.0 sec.

Final	Time		Time
1. WYOMIA TYUS, USA	11.0	5. MARGARET BAILES, USA	11.3
2. BARBARA FERRELL, USA	11.1	6. Dianne Burge, Australia	11.4
3. Irena Kirszenstein, Poland	11.1	7. Chi Cheng, Taiwan	11.5
4. Raelene Boyle, Australia	11.1	8. Miguelina Cobian, Cuba	11.6

The **200 meters** did not belong to Wyomia. Something may have gone wrong for her in this race—the final was the seventh race for all three USA sprinters within a five-day period. Miss TYUS led early but was overtaken down the homestretch and finished sixth while Miss FERRELL just failed to land the bronze medal, losing out in a driving finish to Miss Lamy of Australia.

Mrs. Kirszenstein Szewinska, 22, Poland, proved to be the fastest with a 22.5 sec. performance, bettering her own recognized world record. Four years ago she had run second to EDITH McGUIRE, USA.

Statistics: 36 participants from 22 countries; 5 heats, 2 semi-final races. World record: Irena Kirszenstein (Poland) 22.5 sec., 1965. Oylmpic record: EDITH McGUIRE (USA) 23.0 sec., 1964. The recognized world record was broken once and equalled once while the Olympic record was broken nine times and equalled four times. New Olympic record: Irena Kirszenstein Szewinska (Poland) 22.5 sec.

Final	Time		Time
1. Irena Kirszenstein, Poland	22.5	5. Nicole Montandon, France	23.0
2. Raelene Boyle, Australia	22.7	6. WYOMIA TYUS, USA	23.0
3. Jennifer Lamy, Australia	22.8	7. MARGARET BAILES, USA	23.1
4. BARBARA FERRELL, USA	22.9	8. Jutta Stock, W. Germany	23.2

The **400 meters** brought a minor sensation and a surprise among Europeans. France's lissom Colette Besson, 22, scored a narrow victory over the pre-race favorite among the Europeans, Lilian Board, Great Britain. While Miss Board had been installed as the favorite by newspapers, radio and TV, Miss Besson hardly rated among the top six in the pre-race prognostications. The final was an exciting affair and Miss Besson's margin of victory was two yards at the tape.
Miss JARVIS SCOTT, USA, never fully recovered from leg miseries resulting from altitude training. She had to be content with a sixth-place finish.

Statistics: 29 participants from 21 countries; 4 heats, 2 semi-finals. Recognized world record: Shin Geum Dan (No. Korea) 51.9 sec., 1962. Olympic record: Betty Cuthbert (Australia) 52.0 sec., 1964. The Olympic record was equalled by Miss Besson in the final.

Final	Time		Time
1. Colette Besson, France	52.0	6. JARVIS SCOTT, USA	52.7
2. Lilian Board, Britain	52.1	7. Helga Henning, W. Germany	52.8
3. Natalia Pechenkina, USSR	52.2	8. Hermina van der Hoeven,	
4. Janet Simpson, Britain	52.5	Netherlands	53.0
5. Aurelia Penton, Cuba	52.7		

The **800 meters** commanded more interest, perhaps, from those who did not compete in the race, rather than those who did. The final race was overshadowed by a most startling incident in the semifinal when Vera Nikolic of Yugoslavia, suddenly and without apparent reason, simply "gave up" and stopped racing. She was neither unfit or suffering from lack of oxygen, being well acclimatized after racing and winning in Mexico in the III International Sports Competition of 1967. Perhaps the excitement of the Olympic Games was just too much for her.
MADELINE MANNING, 20, completely ignoring the absence of Vera, ran the most magnificent race of her career, coming down the homestretch almost 20 yards in front of her nearest competitor in bettering the recognized world record. Mrs. BROWN, USA, was fifth.

Statistics: 24 participants from 17 countries; 4 heats, 2 semi-finals. Recognized world record and Olympic record: Ann Packer (Great Britain) 2:01.1, 1964. New Olympic record: MADELINE MANNING (USA) 2:00.9.

Final	Time		Time
1. MADELINE MANNING, USA	2:00.9	5. DORIS BROWN, USA	2:03.9
2. Ilona Silai, Rumania	2:02.5	6. Patricia Lowe, Britain	2:04.2
3. Maria Gommers, Netherlands	2:02.6	7. Abby Hoffman, Canada	2:06.8
4. Sheila Taylor, Britain	2:03.8	8. Marie Dupureur, France	2:08.2

The **80-meter hurdles** saw Australia gain both first and second places, followed by Chi Cheng of Taiwan, a 24-year-old college student who has been residing in California for more than five years. The defending champion, East Germany's Karin Balzer, couldn't do better than finish fifth.

Statistics: 32 participants from 23 countries; 5 heats, 2 semi-finals. World record: Irina Press (USSR) 10.3 sec., 1965. Olympic record: 10.5 sec. shared among Karin Balzer (East Germany), Teresa Ciepla (Poland) and Pamela Kilborn (Australia) all 1964. The world record was equalled. The Olympic record was broken six times and equalled five times. New Olympic record: Maureen Caird (Australia) 10.3 sec.

Final	Time		Time
1. Maureen Caird, Australia	10.3	5. Karin Balzer, E. Germany	10.6
2. Pam Kilborn, Australia	10.4	6. Danuta Straszynska, Poland	10.6
3. Chi Cheng, Taiwan	10.4	7. Elzbieta Zebrowska, Poland	10.7
4. PAT VAN WOLVELAERE, USA	10.5	8. Tatiana Talisheva, USSR	10.6

The **4×100-meter relay** race was extremely fast. What has happened since the Tokyo Games is not only that the girls run faster, but also that many more are able to do so. The West German team, sixth in the final, nonetheless, was three tenths of a second faster than the world record time set by the USA at Tokyo. The USA team in 1968 won, as expected. The girls of Cuba and the USSR fought for second place in a thrilling photo finish, Cuba being awarded the silver medal. The anchor leg by Miss Tyus was responsible for the five-yard margin of victory for the USA.

Statistics: 14 relay teams from 14 countries; 2 heats. Olympic and world record: USA (Willye White, Wyomia Tyus, Marilyn White, Edith McGuire) 43.9 sec., 1964. The Olympic and world records were broken eleven times and equalled once by eight different teams. New Olympic and world records: USA (Barbara Ferrell, Margaret Bailes, Mildrette Netter, Wyomia Tyus) 42.8 sec.

Final	Time		Time
1. USA (Barbara Ferrell, Margaret Bailes, Mildrette Netter, Wyomia Tyus) 42.8		4. The Netherlands (Wilhelmina Van Den Berg, Mieka Sterk, Geertruide Hennipman, Cornelia Bakker) 43.4	
2. Cuba (Marienne Elejarde, Fulgencia Romay, Violete Queseda, Miguelina Cobian) 43.3		5. Australia (Jennifer Lamy, Joyce Bennett, Raelene Boyle, Dianne Burge) .. 43.4	
3. USSR (Ludmila Zharkova, Galina Bukharina, Vera Popova, Ludmila Samotesova) 43.4		6. West Germany (Renate Meyer, Jutta Stoeck, Rita Jahn, Ingrid Becker) 43.6	

The **long jump** was won by an outsider from Rumania—29-year-old Viorica Viscopoleanu. The deciding jump, exactly as the case with Bob Beamon in the men's long jump, was her first leap. She had five excellent jumps, all better than her effort in the qualifying preliminary when she led the field with 21-3 (6.48 m). The winning effort of 22-4½ (6.82 m) recorded on the scoreboard at the Estadio Olimpico was another world record. Prior to the Olympic Games Mrs. Irena Kirszenstein Szewinska, Poland, had recorded the longest jump of the year. She failed to survive the preliminary qualifying round.

Statistics: 27 participants from 19 countries; 9 participants reached the qualifying distance of 20-10 (6.35 m) and five additional athletes were admitted to the competition proper. Olympic and world records: Mary Rand (Great Britain) 22-2 (6.76 m), 1964. The Olympic and world records were broken by Miss Viscopoleanu. New Olympic and world records: Viorica Viscopoleanu (Rumania) 22-4½ (6.82 m).

Final	Distance			Distance	
1. V. Viscopoleanu, Rumania ..... 22-4½ (6.82 m)			5. Miroslawa Sarna, Poland	21-2¾	(6.47 m)
2. Sheila Sherwood, Britain	21-11	(6.68 m)	6. Ingrid Becker, W. Germany 21-1¼		(6.43 m)
3. Tatiana Talisheva, USSR	21-10¼	(6.66 m)	7. Berit Berthelsen, Norway	21-0	(6.40 m)
4. Burghild Wiesczorek, E. Germany 21-3¼		(6.48 m)	8. H. Rosendahl, W. Germany 21-0		(6.40 m)

The **high jump** was essentially a competition among girls from Eastern Europe. Whatever connection there may be between the women's high jump and socialist regimen the fact has to be recorded that the first seven in this competition all came from Communist countries. The contest was won by the 18-year-old Czechoslovakian girl, Miloslava Rezkova. Her victory over the Soviet champion, Antonina Okorokova, was warmly applauded by the spectators.

Statistics: 24 participants from 14 countries, 15 girls reached the qualifying height of 5-8½ (1.74 m) for the competition proper. World record: Iolanda Balas (Rumania) 6-3 (1.91 m), 1961. Olympic record: Iolanda Balas 6-2¾ (1.90 m), 1964.

Final	Height			Height	
1. Miloslava Rezkova, Czechoslovakia ..... 5-11¾ (1.82 m)			5. Rita Schmidt, E. Germany	5-10	(1.78 m)
2. Antonina Okorokova, USSR	5-11	(1.80 m)	6. Maria Falthova, Czechoslovakia 5-10		(1.78 m)
3. Valentina Kozyr, USSR ..	5-11	(1.80 m)	7. Karin Schulze, E. Germany	5-9¼	(1.76 m)
4. Jaroslava Valentova, Czechoslovakia 5-10		(1.78 m)	8. Maria Gusenbauer, Austria 5-9¼		(1.76 m)

The **discus throw** event took place in a pouring rainstorm which affected the performances. The throwing circle was as slippery as the discus. Lia Manoliu, Rumania, won the gold medal on her first throw. It was the fifth Olympic Games for the 36-year-old athlete who entered the competition with the fourth best throw of the year, behind West Germany's Liesel Westermann who finished second in the final Olympic Games' placing. Mrs. OLGA CONNOLLY, USA, gold medalist in 1956, finished sixth.

Statistics: 15 participants from 8 countries. All participants entered the competition proper, eight qualifying for the final three throws. Recognized world record: Liesel Westermann (West Germany) 205-2 (62.54 m), 1968. Olympic record: Tamara Press (USSR) 187-10¾ (57.27 m), 1964. The Olympic record was broken by the first two place winners. New Olympic record: Lia Manoliu (Rumania) 191-2½ (58.28 m).

Final	Distance		Distance
1. Lia Manoliu, Rumania . 191-2½	(58.28 m)	6. OLGA CONNOLLY, USA . 173-9	(52.96 m)
2. Liesel Westermann,		7. Christine Spielberg,	
W. Germany 189-6	(57.76 m)	E. Germany 173-5	(52.86 m)
3. Jolan Kleiber, Hungary 180-1½	(54.90 m)	8. Brigitte Berendonk,	
4. Anita Otto, E. Germany 178-5½	(54.40 m)	W. Germany 173-2½	(52.80 m)
5. Antonina Popova, USSR 175-3	(53.42 m)		

The **javelin throw** event was more or less a duel between Angela Nemeth, 22, Hungary, and the defending Olympic champion, Mihaela Penes, 21, Rumania. Miss Nemeth's winning throw on her second toss eclipsed Miss Penes whose best throw came on her initial effort of the competition. The top USA entrants, BARBARA FRIEDRICH and RANAE BAIR finished ninth and eleventh, respectively.

Statistics: 16 participants from 11 countries, all of whom were admitted to the competition proper and the eight best qualified for the final three throws. Olympic and world records: Elena Gorchakova (USSR) 204-8¾, 1964.

Final	Distance		Distance
1. Angela Nemeth,		5. Daniela Jaworska,	
Hungary 198-0½	(60.36 m)	Poland 183-11	(56.06 m)
2. Mihaela Penes,		6. Natasa Urbancic,	
Rumania 196-7	(59.92 m)	Yugoslavia 181-10	(55.42 m)
3. Eva Janko, Austria 190-5	(58.04 m)	7. Ameli Koloska,	
4. Marta Rudas, Hungary 184-11½	(56.38 m)	W. Germany 181-1	(55.20 m)
		8. Kaisa Launela, Finland 177-0½	(53.96 m)

The **shot put** event turned out to be hotly-contested. Two girls from East Germany, Margitta Gummel, 27, and Marita Lange, 25, finally emerged as the most powerful performers; but they had anxious moments watching Nadezhda Chizova of the Soviet Union. The winning throw came on Miss Gummel's next to last put when she broke all existing records with a toss of the 4-kilogram ball 64-4 (19.61 m).

Statistics: 14 participants from 10 countries with all athletes being admitted to the competition proper and the eight best selected for the final three puts. Recognized world record: Tamara Press (USSR) 61-0 (18.59 m), 1965. The world record was broken three times and equalled once by the first two place winners. The Olympic record: Tamara Press (USSR) 59-6 (18.14 m), 1964, was broken eleven times by the three top place winners. New Olympic and world records: Margitta Gummel (East Germany) 64-4 (19.61 m).

Final	Distance		Distance
1. Margitta Gummel,		5. Renate Boy, E. Germany 58-1¾	(17.72 m)
E. Germany 64-4	(19.61 m)	6. Ivanka Christova,	
2. Marita Lange,		Bulgaria 56-7¼	(17.25 m)
E. Germany 61-7½	(18.78 m)	7. Marlene Fuchs,	
3. Nadezhda Chizova, USSR 59-8¼	(18.19 m)	W. Germany 56-1¾	(17.11 m)
4. Judith B. Lendval,		8. Elsemia Van Nooduyn,	
Hungary 58-4	(17.78 m)	Netherlands 53-3	(16.23 m)

The **pentathlon** result might probably have turned out differently if Heide Rosendahl, West Germany, had not pulled a muscle a few minutes before the start of the opening event while doing her warm-up exercises. On the basis of performances prior to the Olympic Games, the 21-year-old Heide had scored the highest number of points for the five-event competition. Even so, West Germany had the satisfaction that another member of its team, Ingrid Becker, 26, proved a good "replacement" for Heide Rosendahl. She even managed to surpass a total of 5,000 points which is the dream of all pentathletes. She was first or tied for first in four of the five events.

Miss Becker's top opponent was Austria's Liese Prokop, 27, who scored heavily in the shot put, the second event. But Ingrid's sprinting times and her jumping efforts (long jump and high jump) were so much better than those of the Austrian that she emerged as the clear winner.

Statistics: 33 participants from 24 countries of which 27 completed all five events. Olympic and world records: Irina Press, (USSR,) 5,246 points, 1964.

Final Standings	Points		Points
1. Ingrid Becker, W. Germany	5,098	5. Manon Bornholdt, W. Germany ..	4,890
2. Liese Prokop, Austria	4,966	6. Pat Winslow, USA	4,877
3. Annamaria Toth, Hungary	4,959	7. Ingeborg Bauer, E. Germany	4,849
4. Valentina Tikhomirova, USSR	4,927	8. Meta Antenen, Switzerland	4,848

Miss Becker's Performances.
First Day: 80-meter Hurdles 10.9 sec. (1,061); Shot Put 37-8 (819).

Second Day: High Jump 5-7½ (1,067); Long Jump 21-1 (1,084); 200 meters 23.5 sec. (1,077). Total 5,098 points.

Basketball

This was a highly-successful tournament, both from the point of view of the overall excitement in the games and the largest crowds ever to watch the 72-game round-robin competition.

The *Palacio de los Deportes* was packed every day (morning, afternoon and evening) during the fortnight the tournament lasted. The crowds of 25,000 persons at each session were somewhat disappointed at the Mexican team's failure to end up in the top three teams. A medal victory for Mexico might have surprised the experts, but not the home rooters, who had been led to expect a finish among the top three as a result of an aggressive, well-developed "crash" program to get this team ready for the competition.

Before the opening of the Games, one heard rumors that the USA team would perhaps not come up to expectations this time. But in the end, it was evident that any expectation of another team dominating play proved to be a serious miscalculation.

The USA, winner in all six Olympic Games' tournaments and unbeaten during that period, again won the gold medal. It was the general feeling among those close to the international picture, either as administrative officials or official chroniclers of Olympic Games competitions, that the USA team had been decimated by losing several players to the professional camp; and by absences of certain outstanding college players who did not desire to make a try for the squad. Lew Alcindor was one of the stars missed.

Yet the loss of Alcindor and the others mattered little. Coach Henry Iba, in a four-week training course, moulded a great team. Joseph White of Kansas University, Captain Mike Silliman of the US Army and, of course, the bearded 19-year-old Negro, Spencer Haywood from Detroit, are worthy successors to previous USA Olympic champions. They are giants in the metaphorical as well as in the physical meaning of the word—although there were at least four other teams with taller personnel.

The "tall" teams showed that height by itself is not a guarantee for success in basketball; yet to be of only medium height is a tremendous handicap in this game. In this respect, nations with players below the average height of those of the Western World, such as the Philippines and Morocco, were at a distinct disadvantage.

A final game between the USA and the Soviet Union—which most were certain would decide first and second places—never took place. The Soviet Union lost a one-point game to Yugoslavia in the "Eastern European" semifinal, while the USA handily whipped Brazil in the other game of the penultimate round.

With four seconds to play in the USSR–Yugoslavia game, the Soviets enjoyed an uncomfortable 62–61 lead, but a personal foul against Captain Ivo Daneu of the Yugoslav team gave him two free throws. He converted both tosses to put the Yugoslavs into the finals. It is doubtful if any basketball team in the history of the Olympic Games so unabashedly "enjoyed" their triumph in front of 25,000 stunned spectators as much as did the Yugoslavs.

In the regular group round-robin play the USA had won over the Yugoslavs by 15 points, 73–58. In the gold medal game the USA again defeated Yugoslavia, 65–50, winning the game with a tightly-drawn defense, the hallmark of every team coached by Henry P. Iba.

The first half was close, as the USA led, 32–39, aided by a last-second field goal by reserve GLYNN SAULTERS. But the USA team really let go in the second half. In the space of seven minutes, SPENCER HAYWOOD and JO JO WHITE made a shambles of the game with their deft shooting and overpowering defensive strength, as the USA outscored the Yugoslavs, 17–3.

It was not only the scores of the games that convinced most of the journalists that the USA still has no serious challenger from any quarter. It was the manner in which the USA accomplished its basket-ball mission. The USA team showed distinct tactical superiority as well as technical skills unapproached by any of the other teams.

But to the foreign correspondent who seldom has an opportunity to watch American basketball, its most impressive feature is the individual artistic wizardry of the players, whom the USA seems to produce on a conveyor belt. For example, eight years ago it was OSCAR ROBERTSON who dominated the Olympic Games' tournament; in Tokyo, it was BILL BRADLEY; at Mexico it was SPENCER HAYWOOD, touted as the youngest USA player ever selected for its Olympic team.

As long as the USA can carry on with fresh new faces at each Olympic Games, one cannot see how this nation can be removed from the basketball pinnacle.

Statistics: 16 teams from 16 countries. The best teams from the 1964 Tokyo Olympic Games are included, as well as the first 2 teams from the 1967 Pan-American, European, African, and Asian elimination tournaments. Finally, there are 2 more teams included for their success in the Pre-Olympic Qualifying Games which were held in Monterray, as well as a team from the host country. The Olympic tournament consists of a qualifying round in 2 groups (A and B) of 8 teams each, a semi-final round, and the final.

Group A Eliminations	W.	L.
1. USA	7	0
2. Yugoslavia	6	1
3. Italy	5	2
4. Spain	4	3
5. Puerto Rico	3	4
6. Panama	2	5
7. Philippines	1	6
8. Senegal	0	7

Group B Eliminations	W.	L.
1. Soviet Union	7	0
2. Brazil	6	1
3. Mexico	5	2
4. Poland	4	3
5. Bulgaria	3	4
6. Cuba	2	5
7. South Korea	1	6
8. Morocco	0	7

The Scores

USA defeated Puerto Rico 61–56. Italy 100–61. Panama 95–60, Yugoslavia 74–58, Philippines 96–75, Senegal 93–36 and Spain 81–46.

Yugoslavia defeated Puerto Rico 93–72, Italy 80–69, Panama 96–85. Philippines 89–68, Senegal 84–68 and Spain 92–79.

Italy defeated Puerto Rico 68–65, Panama 94–87, Philippines 91–66, Senegal 81–55 and Spain 98–86.

Spain defeated Puerto Rico 86–62, Panama 88–82, Philippines 108–79 and Senegal 64–54.

Puerto Rico defeated Panama 80–69, Philippines 89–65 and Senegal 69–26.

Panama defeated Philippines 95–92 and Senegal 94–79.

Philippines defeated Senegal 80–68.

The Scores

Soviet Union defeated Brazil 76–65, Mexico 82–62. Cuba 100–66, Bulgaria 81–56, South Korea 89–58, Morocco 123–51 and Poland 91–50.

Brazil defeated Mexico 60–53, Cuba 81–68, Bulgaria 75–59, South Korea 91–59, Morocco 98–52 and Poland 88–51.

Mexico defeated Cuba 76–75, Bulgaria 73–63, South Korea 75–62, Morocco 86–38 and Poland 68–63.

Poland defeated Cuba 78–75, Bulgaria 69–67, South Korea 77–67 and Morocco 85–48.

Bulgaria defeated Cuba 70–61, South Korea 64–60 and Morocco 77–59.

Cuba defeated South Korea 80–71 and Morocco 89–53.

South Korea defeated Morocco 76–54.

Playoffs

1st–4th Places
Semi-final—USA 75, Brazil 63.
Semi-final—Yugoslavia 63, Soviet Union 62.
1st—USA 65, Yugoslavia 50.
3d—Soviet Union 70, Brazil 53.

5th–8th Places
Semi-final—Mexico 73, Spain 72.
Semi-final—Poland 66, Italy 52.
5th—Mexico 75, Poland 65.
7th—Spain 88, Italy 72.

Semi-final—Puerto Rico 71, Cuba 65.
Semi-final—Bulgaria 83, Panama 79.
9th—Puerto Rico 67, Bulgaria 57.
11th—Cuba 91, Panama 88.

Semi-final—Philippines 86, Morocco 57.
Semi-final—South Korea 76, Senegal 59.
13th—Philippines 66, South Korea 53.
15th—Senegal 42, Morocco 38.

Final Placings

1. USA	5. Mexico	9. Puerto Rico	13. Philippines
2. Yugoslavia	6. Poland	10. Bulgaria	14. South Korea
3. Soviet Union	7. Spain	11. Cuba	15. Senegal
4. Brazil	8. Italy	12. Panama	16. Morocco

Box Score of USA–Yugoslav Final

USA (65)	G.	F.	P.	Yugoslavia (50)	G.	F.	P.
JOHN CLAWSON	0	0–0	0	Korac	0	1–4	1
KEN SPAIN	0	1–2	1	Maroevic	1	0–0	2
JO JO WHITE	6	2–2	14	Rajkovic	2	0–0	4
MIKE BARRETT	3	0–0	6	Cvetkovic	0	3–4	3
SPENCER HAYWOOD	10	1–2	21	Raznatovic	1	0–0	2
CHARLIE SCOTT	2	1–2	5	Daneu	6	4–4	16
BILL HOSKET	1	1–2	3	Cosic	1	2–2	4
CALVIN FOWLER	2	0–0	4	Solman	1	3–4	5
MIKE SILLIMAN	3	0–0	6	Cermak	4	0–0	8
GLYNN SAULTERS	2	0–0	4	Skansi	2	1–2	5
JIM KING	0	1–2	1	Total	18	14–20	50
DON DEE	0	0–0	0				
Total	29	7–12	65				

Half-time score—USA 33, Yugoslavia 32.

Boxing

The boxing tournament was certainly the biggest tournament of its kind ever staged (312 boxers from 67 nations). To call it the best tournament would be a wild exaggeration, yet to criticize it does not mean that one was not satisfied with the boxing standards.

The problem was what went on outside the ring.

The atmosphere was charged with passion and prejudice and the refereeing reflected these charges. One has become accustomed to bad decisions in boxing, but in this respect certainly a world record was established in Mexico (a heinous one at that) which won't be broken for a long time.

Favoritism and disagreement were so rampant that 32 judges and referees were themselves disqualified and dismissed on short notice. And to top it all, the boxing bouts were often extended to the spectators themselves.

One of the victims of these strange proceedings was ALBERT ROBINSON, USA, featherweight, whom the Russian referee, Zybalov, disqualified in the second round of the final bout for the gold medal for allegedly butting his Mexican opponent, Roldan, and drawing blood from an old wound, sustained in the semi-final bout. Disqualification was not enough. Under the international boxing rules, boxers disqualified in the finals also forfeit their prizes, in this case a coveted silver medal. After an American protest to the International Amateur Boxing Association officials, in a surprising about-face, the AIBA executive committee "awarded" the silver medal to ROBINSON, although the gold one, in all logic, was due him on the basis of his performance up to the time he was disqualified for "butting" (which never showed up in the fight films).

Although the Soviet Union boxers were the most successful in the "quality" of medals won at the Games of the XIX Olympiad, the USA was the most successful "quantitatively." Among eleven Soviet boxers, they collected three gold, two silver and a bronze. The US fighters earned two gold, one silver and four bronze.

Mexico celebrated some highly acclaimed victories (two gold medals in the first four finals bouts) and there were significant successes by a number of African nations. The "dark continent" has now also arrived in boxing and one will certainly soon hear more about its performers in the ring.

The **lightweight** division final bout was decided when RONNIE HARRIS, USA, was given a unanimous decision over wily Josef Grudzien, the 29-year-old Polish boxer who won the gold medal in Tokyo. No judge possibly could have been of a different opinion as HARRIS outpointed his ring-wise foe with speed and crisp punching.

The **light middleweight** final saw Lagutin, USSR, square off against the Cuban Garbey. The Soviet boxer at 30 years of age was ten years older than his foe. Lagutin won an extremely ugly bout which had little to do with boxing. It all ended with "booing" and cat calls while the Korean referee was the target for a barrage of poorly aimed coins and other small missiles.

The **middleweight** crown was won by Great Britain's Chris Finnegan. Three of the five judges decided he had collected more points in the final with Alexi Kiselev, USSR. The public was obviously of a different opinion and Finnegan was roundly booed. There can be no doubt that the Briton was extremely lucky in these Games. Whether he was favored by the officials cannot be proven. But amendments were perhaps made in his case (both in the semi-final and final) for the outrageous and ill-treatment accorded other British boxers by the referees and judges.

The **heavyweight** fight ended before the second round was over. Chepulis, USSR, simply had no adequate answer to any of the blows he received from hard-hitting GEORGE FOREMAN, USA, all of which seemingly found their target in and around the Soviet boxer's eyes, nose and mouth. The claret was flowing freer than wine at a post-Olympic Games wetting down party when the referee mercifully stepped between the two fighters and awarded FOREMAN a knockout in lieu of permitting continued mayhem in the squared circle.

Statistics: 312 participants from 70 nations. 11 weight classes (until 1964, only 10 weight classes. New class: Light flyweight, up to 48 kg). Each defeated boxer eliminated from the tournament. There were no bouts for the 3rd and 4th places. The two losers of the semi-finals shared the 3rd place and both got a bronze medal.

Light Flyweight
Up to 48 kg weight. 24 entries from 24 nations. Semi-finals—Francisco Rodriguez, Venezuela, outpointed HARLAND MARBLEY, USA; Yong Ju Lee, South Korea, outpointed Hubert Skrzypczak, Poland.
Final—Rodriguez outpointed Yong.

Flyweight
Up to 51 kg weight. 26 entries from 26 nations. Semi-finals—Ricardo Delgado, Mexico, outpointed Ser-Villio de Oliveira, Brazil; Arthur Olech, Poland, outpointed Leo Rwabwogo, Uganda.
Final—Delgado outpointed Olech.

Bantamweight
Up to 54 kg weight. 39 entries from 39 nations. Semi-finals—Valery Sokolov, USSR, outpointed Eiji Morioka, Japan; Eridari Mukwanga, Uganda, outpointed Soon Kill Chang, South Korea.
Final—Sokolov knocked out Mukwanga, second round.

Featherweight
Up to 57 kg weight. 32 entries from 32 nations. Semi-finals—Antonio Roldan, Mexico, outpointed Philip Waruingi, Kenya; ALFRED ROBINSON, USA, outpointed Ivan Michailov, Bulgaria.
Final—Roldan defeated ROBINSON by disqualification, second round.

Lightweight
Up to 60 kg weight. 37 entries from 37 nations. Semi-finals—RONNIE HARRIS, USA, outpointed Calistrat Cutov, Rumania; Josef Grudzien, Poland, outpointed Zvonimir Vulin, Yugoslavia.
Final—HARRIS outpointed Grudzien.

Light Welterweight
Up to 63.5 kg weight. 36 entries from 36 nations. Semi-finals—Jerzy Kulei, Poland, outpointed Arto Nilsson, Finland; Enrique Regueiferos, Cuba, outpointed JIM WALLINGTON, USA.
Final—Kulei outpointed Regueiferos.

Welterweight
Up to 67 kg weight. 34 entries from 34 nations. Semi-finals—Manfred Wolke, E. Germany, outpointed Vladimir Musalimov, USSR; Joseph Bessala, Cameroun, outpointed Mario Guilloti, Argentina.
Final—Wolke outpointed Bessala.

Light Middleweight
Up to 71 kg weight. 27 entries from 27 nations. Semi-finals—Boris Lagutin, USSR, outpointed Gunter Meier, W. Germany; Rolando Garbey, Cuba, outpointed JOHN BALDWIN, USA.
Final—Lagutin outpointed Garbey.

Middleweight

Up to 75 kg weight. 23 entries from 23 nations. Semi-finals—Christopher Finnegan, Great Britain, outpointed ALFRED JONES, USA; Aleksei Kiselev, USSR, knocked out Agustin Zaragoza, Mexico, first round.

Final—Finnegan outpointed Kiselev.

Light Heavyweight

Up to 81 kg weight. 18 entries from 18 nations. Semi-finals—Dan Pozdniak, USSR, outpointed Gueorgui Stankov, Bulgaria; Ion Monea, Rumania, outpointed Stanislav Dragan, Poland.

Final—Pozdniak won by default from Monea.

Heavyweight

Over 81 kg weight. 16 entries from 16 nations. Semi-finals—GEORGE FOREMAN, USA, knocked out Giorgio Bambini, Italy, second round; Ionis Chepulis, USSR, knocked out Joaquin Rocha, Mexico, second round.

Final—FOREMAN knocked out Chepulis, second round.

Canoeing – Men and Women

Canoeing is now considered a European sport. Eastern Europe and Germany have ascended the heights as the Scandinavians have slipped from the canoeing pinnacle—after sweeping the men's kayak races in 1960 and 1964. But, the Soviet's A. Shaparenko, after finishing second in the kayak singles, joined V. Morozov to score a clean-cut triumph over Hungary and Austria duos.

In the women's kayaking competition, West Germany's *pairs* combination of Roswitha Esser and Annemarie Zimmermann returned as victors and became the only 1964 Olympic champions in canoeing and kayaking to retain their championship.

In the **500 meters women's kayak singles**, Anna Pfeffer, Hungary, in trying to overtake Ludmila Pinaeva, USSR, spun over in her kayak and was eliminated from the race. The Soviet paddler won. Only minutes later Anna Pfeffer was racing again in the Kayak pairs. This time Anna and her partner caught the Soviet pairs (including Ludmila) and paddled their way to a silver medal, while the Soviet duo of Pinaeva and Seredina earned the bronze medal, behind the winning pairs from West Germany.

Men's Canoe Singles

12 boats from 12 countries.

	min.		min.
1. Tibor Tatai, Hungary	4:36.14	6. Ole Emanuelsson, Sweden	4:45.80
2. Detlef Lewe, W. Germany	4:38.31	7. Ivan Patzaichin, Rumania	4:49.32
3. Vitaly Kalkov, USSR	4:40.42	8. ANDRES WEIGAND, USA	4:50.42
4. Jiri Ctvrtecka, Czechoslovakia	4:40.74	9. Christopher Hook, Canada	4:55.88
5. Boris Lubenov, Bulgaria	4:43.43		

Men's Kayak Singles

22 boats from 22 countries.

	min.		min.
1. Mihaly Hesz, Hungary	4:02.63	6. Vaclav Mara, Czechoslovakia	4:09.35
2. A. Shaparenko, USSR	4:03.58	7. Andrei Contolenco, Rumania	4:09.96
3. Erik Hansen, Denmark	4:04.39	8. Wolfgang Lange, E. Germany	4:10.03
4. Wladyslaw Szuszkiewicz, Poland	4:06.36	9. Paul Hoekstra, Netherlands	4:13.28
5. Rolf Peterson, Sweden	4:07.86		

Women's Kayak Singles

13 boats from 13 countries.

	min.		min.
1. Ludmilla Pinaeva, USSR	2:11.09	4. MARCIA JONES SMOKE, USA	2:14.68
2. Renate Breuer, W. Germany	2:12.71	5. Iva Vavrova, Czechoslovakia	2:14.78
3. Viorica Dumitru, Rumania	2:13.22	6. Anita Nussner, E. Germany	2:16.02

Men's Canoe Pairs

13 boats from 13 countries.

		min.
1. Rumania	Patzaichin, Covaliov	4:07.18
2. Hungary	Wichmann, Petrikovics	4:08.77
3. USSR	Prokupets, Zamotin	4:11.30
4. Mexico	Martinez, Altamirano	4:15.24
5. Sweden	Lindelof, Zeidlitz	4:16.60
6. East Germany	Harpke, Wagner	4:22.53
7. West Germany	Kapf, Lewandowski	4:26.36

Men's Kayak Pairs
20 boats from 20 countries.

		min.
1. USSR	Shaparenko, Morozov	3:37.54
2. Hungary	Giczi, Timar	3:38.44
3. Austria	Seibold, Pfaff	3:40.71
4. Netherlands	Hoekstra, Geurts	3:41.36
5. Sweden	Anderson, Utterberg	3:41.99
6. Rumania	Sciotnic, Vernescu	3:45.18

Men's Kayak Fours
19 boats from 19 countries.

		min.
1. Norway	Amundsen, Berger, Soby, Johansen	3:14.38
2. Rumania	Calenic, Ivanov, Ivanov, Turcas	3:14.81
3. Hungary	Giczi, Szollosi, Timar, Csizmadia	3:15.10
4. Sweden	Larsson, Sahlen, Nilsson, Sandin	3:16.68
5. Finland	Von Alfthan, Lehtosalo, Makela, Nummisto	3:17.28
6. East Germany	Wenzke, Riedrich, Will, Ebeling	3:18.03

Women's Kayak Pairs
11 boats from 11 countries.

		min.
1. West Germany	Zimmermann, Esser	1:56.44
2. Hungary	Pfeffer, Sagi/Rozsnyoi	1:58.60
3. USSR	Pinaeva, Seredina	1:58.61
4. Rumania	Serghei, Dumitru	1:59.17
5. East Germany	Kobuss, Haftenberger	2:00.18
6. Netherlands	Jaapies, Bergers-Duif	2:02.02

Cycling

The Mexican Games were unable to resuscitate cycling's waning popularity as a competitive sport. Professional cycling, once tremendously popular on the European continent, in now in the doldrums; and those who expected the amateurs in Mexico City to take over and revive the public's interest were greatly disappointed. Perhaps it was because there was no dominant colorful personality on view; perhaps the atmospheric conditions of Mexico City, combined with a merciless sun blazing down on the cyclists, added to the lack of excitement; and the disqualification of the West German team because of a silly offense resulted in some scenes which looked like they came right out of the *Opera Comique*, with the officials, the jury of appeals and the representatives of the nations involved taking the parts of soloists and chorus.

The velodrome—the wooden indoor track constructed by the Mexicans—was magnificent. It produced very fast times, as expected by those who had watched the pre-Olympic trials. Most appreciative of the facilities were the French, who collected four of the five gold medals won indoors in replacing the Italians as overall team champions. Leading the French was Pierre Trentin, who collected two gold medals and one bronze, and Daniel Rebillard, a 20-year-old Lyonnese, who took first place in the *4,000 meter individual pursuit*. Trentin set a new world record in winning the *1,000 meters*, then combined with Daniel Morelon to win the *tandem sprint*. Morelon also won the *scratch sprint*.

West Germany's disqualification came in the *4,000 meter team pursuit*, after Juergen Kissner pushed forward the bike of a lagging teammate. After they had won the race the Germans admitted the rules violation, but felt that they were still entitled to the silver medal; the officials disagreed and no second-place medal was awarded at Mexico. (The Germans have since collected their silver.)

1,000 Meter Individual Time Trial

Statistics: 32 participants from 32 nations. World record: Sartori (Italy) 1:04.61 min. Olympic record: Gaiardoni (Italy) 1:07.27 min. (Rome 1960). New Olympic and world records set by Trentin (France) 1:03.91 min.

Final

	min.		min.
1. Pierre Trentin, France	1:03.91	5. Roger Gibbon, Trinidad	1:04.66
2. Niels Fredborg, Denmark	1:04.61	6. Leijn Loevesijn, Netherlands	1:04.84
3. Janusz Kierzkowski, Poland	1:04.63	12. JACK SIMES 3d, USA	1:05.67
4. Gianni Sartori, Italy	1:04.65		

Scratch Sprint

Statistics: 51 participants from 30 nations. 17 heats, 12 repechages. Eighth-finals: 10 heats, 8 repechages. Quarter-finals: 4 heats. Semi-finals: 2 heats. Final: 2 heats.

Final

	sec.		sec.
1. Daniel Morelon, France	10.68	4. Omar Pkhakadze, USSR	—
2. Giordano Turrini, Italy	—	Jack Simes 3d and Tim Mountford, USA,	
3. Pierre Trentin, France	10.92	eliminated in repechage finals of eighth-finals.	

2,000 Meter Tandem

Statistics: 28 participants from 14 nations. 7 heats, 4 repechages. Quarter-finals: 4 heats. Semi-finals: 2 heats. Final: 2 heats.

Final

	sec.		sec.
1. Morelon-Trentin, France	9.83	4. Gorini-Borghetti, Italy	—
2. Jansen-Loevesijn, Netherlands ...	—	USA (Jack Disney-Charles Pranke) elimi-	
3. Goens-van Lancker, Belgium	11.20	nated in repechage.	

4,000 Meter Individual Pursuit

Statistics: 28 participants from 28 nations. 14 elimination heats, 4 second-round heats. Semi-finals: 2 heats. Final: 2 heats. World record: Daler (Czechoslovakia) 4:45.94 min. Olympic record: Ursi (Italy) 4:56.07 min. (Tokyo 1964). New Olympic and world records: Mogens Jensen (Denmark) 4:37.54 min. (in second-round).

Final

	min.		min.
1. Daniel Rebillard, France	4:41.71	4. John Bylsma, Australia	4:41.60
2. Mogens Jensen, Denmark	4:42.43	David Brink, USA (4:55.40), placed 18th in	
3. Xaver Kurmann, Switzerland ...	4:39.42	qualifying round.	

4,000 Meter Team Pursuit

Statistics: 22 teams from 22 nations. 11 qualifying rounds, 4 second-rounds. Semi-finals: 2 rounds. Final: 2 rounds. World record: West Germany, 4:19.8 min. Olympic record: Italy, 4:30.90 min. (Rome 1960). New Olympic and world records: West Germany, 4:15.76 min. in semi-finals.

Final

	min.	
1. Denmark	4:22.44	*West Germany won final from Denmark but
2. West Germany*	4:18.94	was disqualified.
3. Italy	4:18.35	USA (4:32.87) placed 15th in qualifying round.
4. Soviet Union	4:33.39	

Individual Road Race

Statistics: 144 participants from 47 nations; 64 completed the race. Length of course: 196.2 kilometers.

Results

	h.		h.
1. Pierfranco Vianelli, Italy	4:41:25.24	6. Jean Monsere, Belgium	4:43:51.77
2. Lief Mortensen, Denmark ...	4:42:49.71	44. John Howard, USA	4:52:45.80
3. Gosta Pettersson, Sweden ...	4:43:15.24	Dan Butler, USA	unplaced
4. Stephen Abrahamian, France .	4:43:36.54	David Chauner, USA	unplaced
5. Marinus Pijnen, Netherlands .	4:43:36.81	Walter Wessberg, USA ...	unplaced

Team Time Trial

Statistics: 30 four-man teams from 30 nations. Length of course: 104 kilometers.

Results

	h.		h.
1. Netherlands	2:07:49.06	5. Mexico	2:14:08.44
2. Sweden	2:09:26.60	6. Norway	2:14:32.85
3. Italy	2:10:18.74	20. USA	2:24:13.50
4. Denmark	2:12:41.41		

The **three-day event** took place in Avandaro, a resort located some 120 miles west of the capital. The trials were held on and around the local golf course, and the facilities for both horses and riders could not have been better. But the Mexicans had not bargained on one thing—a torrential rain which fell each day of the competition. This unfortunate turn of events was not without its tragic elements, for it turned the cross-country ride into a nightmare. Riding over a brook or even what only a few minutes before had been a stream assumed the proportions of a deadly risk. Raging torrents appeared which swept away horses and riders alike, often resulting in multiple injuries.

The horses fared worse than their riders; one Irish horse had to be shot after sustaining a broken leg, and a Russian mount was swept under a bridge and drowned. Most of these unfortunate accidents could have been avoided had the events been re-scheduled to start earlier in the day, for the rains usually began around two o'clock in the afternoon.

The course was divided into two parts: one leading over open terrain in a steep climb to a steeple-chase course, the other a cross-country race with obstacles. Most of the accidents occurred on the latter part, with ten of the 48 entrants failing to even finish. The Russians tried to cope with the difficulties by placing observers along the cross-country course, communicating with their riders by walkie-talkie and helping them avoid major pitfalls. Told that this was a violation of Olympic rules, the Russians pleaded ignorance.

Although the USSR held a comfortable lead after the first two days of competition, the gold medal was taken by Great Britain, which was led by 54-year-old Major Derek Allhusen, oldest participant in the three-day event. The USA finished second and Australia, third, with the Russians far down the line because one of their riders was disqualified for jumping the obstacles out of order.

The **individual event** was won by Jean-Jacques Guyon of France. The USA's JAMES WOFFORD seemed a sure silver medalist, but a late fall dropped him into sixth. Britain's Allhusen took second place, with MICHAEL PAGE of the USA placing third.

Statistics: 49 riders from 13 nations, competing for individual and team awards. Each team consisted of 4 riders, with the 3 highest scores being recorded. There were 3 scoring sections: dressage, cross country and jumping.

Individual	Horse	Dressage	Cross-Country	Jumping	Total
1. Jean-Jacques Guyon, France	Pitou	− 73.01	44.4	− 10.25	− 38.86
2. Derek Allhusen, Britain ...	Lochinvar	− 85.01	44.4	0.00	− 41.61
3. MICHAEL PAGE, USA	Foster	− 107.51	59.2	− 4.00	− 52.31
4. Richard Meade, Britain	Cornishman V	− 97.01	54.8	− 22.25	− 64.46
5. Ben Jones, Britain	The Poacher	− 68.51	4.4	− 5.75	− 69.86
6. JAMES WOFFORD, USA	Kilkenny	− 101.51	71.20	− 43.75	− 74.06

Team		Horse	Dressage	Cross-Country	Jumping	Total
1. Great Britain	Derek Allhusen	Lochinvar	− 85.01	44.4	0.0	− 41.61
	Richard Meade	Cornishman V	− 97.01	54.8	− 22.25	− 64.46
	Reuben S. Jones	The Poacher	− 68.51	4.4	− 5.75	− 69.86
						− 175.93
2. USA	JAMES WOFFORD	Kilkenny	− 101.51	71.2	− 43.50	− 74.06
	MICHAEL PAGE	Foster	− 107.51	59.2	− 4.00	− 52.31
	MICHAEL PLUMB	Plain Sailing	− 63.00	− 54.0	− 2.50	− 119.50
						− 245.87
3. Australia	B. Cobcroft	Depeche	− 115.01	22.0	− 15.75	− 108.76
	Wayne Roycroft	Zhivago	− 103.50	21.3	− 12.75	− 94.95
	W. Roycroft	Warrathoola	− 84.00	− 40.8	− 2.75	− 127.55
						− 331.26
4. France	A. le Goupil	Olivette B	− 83.01	− 14.0	− 10.25	− 107.26
	J. J. Guyon	Pitou	− 73.01	44.4	− 10.25	− 38.86
	J. Sarrazin	Joburg	− 80.51	− 279.2	0.0	− 359.71
						− 505.83

5. West Germany	K. Wagner	Abdulla	– 102.00	– 99.6	– 14.25	– 215.85
	J. Mehrdorf	Lapislazuli	– 68.01	– 108.2	– 23.00	– 199.41
	H. Karsten	Adagio	– 74.01	– 39.2	– 5.75	– 102.96
						– 518.22
6. Mexico	E. Del Castillo	Codicioso	– 117.00	– 19.6	– 34.00	– 170.60
	R. Mejia	Centinela	– 112.50	– 60.4	– 10.00	– 182.90
	E. Avalos	Ludmilla II	– 98.01	– 148.8	– 31.25	– 278.06
						– 631.56

The **team dressage grand prix** was staged on the grass of the *Campo Marte* polo ground in Chapultepec Park. The favored West Germans won their second straight gold medal, but not without a strong fight from the USSR. Leading the Soviets was Ivan Kozomov, who took the gold medal in the **individual dressage** by compiling an incredible 664 points during a jump-off on the second day of competition. West Germany's Josef Neckermann, a 56-year-old Olympic veteran, was unable to correct two glaring faults by his mount, and had to settle for the silver medal, with teammate Dr. Reiner Klimke taking the bronze.

Statistics: 26 riders from 9 nations, including 8 national teams of 3 riders each. For individual placings, a jump-off between the first 7 finishers was held.

Individual	Horse	First Attempt	Final	Total
1. Ivan Kozomov, USSR	Ijor	908	664	1,572
2. Josef Neckermann, W. Germany	Mariano	948	598	1,546
3. Reiner Klimke, W. Germany	Dux	896	641	1,537
4. Ivan Kalita, USSR	Absent	879	640	1,519
5. Horst Köhler, E. Germany	Neuschnee	875	600	1,475
6. Elena Petuchkova, USSR	Pepel	870	601	1,471

Team		Horse	Points
1. West Germany	Josef Neckermann	Mariano	948
	Liselott Linsenhoff	Piaff	855
	Reiner Klimke	Dux	896
			2,699
2. Soviet Union	E. Petuchkova	Pepel	870
	I. Kozomov	Ijor	908
	I. Kalita	Absent	879
			2,657
3. Switzerland	H. Chammartin	Wolfdietrich	845
	M. Gossweiler	Stephan	836
	G. Fischer	Wald	866
			2,547
4. East Germany	W. Müller	Marios	693
	G. Brockmüller	Tristan	789
	H. Köhler	Neuschnee	875
			2,357
5. Great Britain	H. Johnstone	El Guapo	777
	I. Hall	Conversano Caprice	762
	D. Lawrence	San Fernando	793
			2,332
6. Chile	G. Squella	Colchaguino	693
	P. Escudero	Prete	650
	A. Piraino	Ciclon	672
			2,015

In the **Grand Prix jumping** the **individual** competition preceded the **Grand Prix des Nations** and was held in the *Campo Marte*. The course was one of the toughest ever seen in Olympic competition, with extremely high fences, tricky turns and short distances between obstacles. The career of an equestrian lasts much longer than that of, say, a runner; thus all of the top riders over the past 10 to 15 years were competing in Mexico City: France's d'Oriola, who won the gold medal in 1952, Germany's Winkler, the USA's BILL STEINKRAUS, Italy's D'Inzeo, and many others.

The course was kept secret from the riders and the public, even the press, until one hour before starting time. What they saw then was a Round 1 course of 8,202 yards (750 meters) with 14 obstacles, such as walls, ditches, fences, a triple bar, even a park gate with bar. Each contestant was allowed 112 seconds for the round. Only two came clear without a penalty point: Great Britain's Marion Coakes and STEINKRAUS of the USA.

Sixteen riders joined these two in the final round, with STEINKRAUS going last. Miss Coakes compiled eight penalty points on the six-obstacle course, so STEINKRAUS knew that she was the one to beat. He cleared the first four obstacles beautifully, then on the next to last jump knocked down the vertical bar. A miss on the final jump would lose first place for him, but he went over cleanly to cinch the gold. Miss Coakes was awarded the silver, and the bronze went to Great Britain's David Broome —who tied three others in penalty points—on the basis of time.

Because it was to be the final event of the 1968 Summer Games, the **Grand Prix des Nations** was held in the *Stadio Olympico* before a roaring crowd of 100,000 spectators. The USA and Great Britain were favored, but injuries to the mounts of both Mr. STEINKRAUS and Miss Coakes dimmed their countries' chances. Most felt that the French had the best chance at taking the gold, particularly with M. d'Oriola riding last for them. But he gave a disappointing performance, leaving the door open for Canada to take first place after magnificent rides by Jim Elder. France finished second and West Germany, third, beating out the USA for the bronze by just one-quarter of a penalty point.

Individual

Statistics: 42 riders from 15 countries. The first 18 finishers of Round 1 qualified for Round 2. The final placing is based upon the fewest penalty points earned.

	Horse	First round	Second round	Time	Total Penalties
1. WILLIAM STEINKRAUS, USA	Snow Bound	0.00	4.00	—	4.00
2. Marion Coakes, Great Britain	Stroller	0.00	8.00	—	8.00
3. David Broome, Great Britain	Mr. Softee	4.00	8.00	35.3	12.00
4. FRANK CHAPOT, USA	San Lucas	4.00	8.00	36.8	12.00
5. Hans Winkler, West Germany	Enigk	8.00	4.00	37.5	12.00
6. Jim Elder, Canada	The Immigrant	8.00	4.00	39.2	12.00

Team

		Round 1			Round 2			Total Penalties
		Obstacle Penalties	Time	Time Penalties	O.P.	T.	T.P.	
1. Canada	Tom Gayford (Big Dee)	20	104.1	2.25	16	100.3	1.25	39.50
	Jim Day (Canadian Club)	16	103.9	2.00	16	103.2	2.00	36.00
	Jim Elder (The Immigrant)	8	100.8	1.25	16	103.2	2.00	27.25
								102.75
2. France	J. Rozier (Quo Vadis)	20	101.6	1.50	12	96.0	—	33.50
	J. Lefèvre (Rocket)	16	100.3	1.25	12	97.6	0.50	29.75
	P. D'Oriola (Nagir)	16	102.5	1.75	28	101.1	1.25	47.25
								110.50
3. West Germany	H. Schridde (Dozent)	32	102.8	1.75	36	97.9	0.50	70.25
	A. Schockemöhle (Donald Rex)	12	99.7	1.00	4	102.9	1.75	18.75
	H. Winkler (Enigk)	8	109.8	3.50	12	114.9	4.75	28.25
								117.25

Rank	Country	Rider (Horse)							
4.	USA	Mrs. Frank Chapot (White Lightning)	24	107.9	3.00	20	99.3	1.00	48.00
		Kathy Kusner (Untouchable)	20	116.0	5.00	16	109.7	3.50	44.50
		Frank Chapot (San Lucas)	8	107.5	3.00	12	103.7	2.00	25.00
									117.50
5.	Italy	G. Mancinelli (Doneraile)	20	109.6	3.50	32	103.2	2.00	57.50
		R. D'Inzeo (Bellevue)	12	95.0	—	12	96.8	0.25	24.25
		P. D'Inzeo (Fidux)	24	113.4	4.50	16	107.6	3.00	47.50
									129.25
6.	Switzerland	Blickenstorfer (Marianka)	20	102.4	1.75	28	98.4	0.75	50.50
		M. Bachmann (Erbach)	15	127.5	8.00	24	105.9	2.50	49.50
		P. Weier (Satan)	19	113.2	4.50	12	100.1	1.25	36.75
									136.75

Fencing

What was once the knight's way of defending his kings or his own honor with foil, épée or sabre has now become the sport in which the State "amateurs" of Eastern Europe are excelling. This impression was gained in Tokyo and further supported by the success of the Eastern Europeans at Mexico. The Soviet Union, Hungary, Poland and Rumania are gobbling up a large majority of the medals, with only France and Italy from the West getting a "look see" on an occasional basis.

But while France and Italy continue a very old tradition and try to perpetuate its art and finer points, the Easterners treat fencing simply as a sport — as an efficient all-around ploy of attack, supported by fitness and stamina. The traditionalist may regret this development but there can be no doubt, that this approach is the one which brings home the gold and silver medals. The USA relied pretty much on the same fencers seen in recent and past Olympic Games and world championships and were simply not in the same class with the nations approaching the sport in a serious vein. The USA fencers are most capable week-end fencers.

Men's Events

Foil — Individual

Statistics: 64 participants from 25 nations. 1st round (12 groups), and 2nd round (8 groups), to provide the last 32 fencers. Direct elimination to obtain last 4. In addition there were 2 competitors from the play-off rounds.

Results	W–L	*TR	**TG
1. Ian Drimbu, Rumania	4–1	15	22
2. Jeno Kamuti, Hungary	3–2	14	19
3. Daniel Revenu, France	3–2	17	22
4. Christian Noel, France	2–3	18	14
5. Jean Magnan, France	2–3	22	18
6. Mihai Tiu, Rumania	1–4	23	14
Fence-Off			
2. J. Kamuti, Hungary	1–0	4	5
3. D. Revenue, France	0–1	5	4

* TR Touches received   ** TG Touches given

Epee — Individual

Statistics: 73 participants from 28 nations. 1st round (12 pools) and 2nd round (8 pools) to obtain last 32 fencers. Direct elimination for the last 4. In addition there were 2 more competitors from the play-off rounds.

Results	W–L	TR	TG
1. Gyozo Kulcsar, Hungary	4–1	14	24
2. Grigory Kriss, USSR	4–1	19	25
3. Gianluigi Saccaro, Italy	4–1	19	21
4. Viktor Mondzolevski, USSR	2–3	23	20

		W–L	TR	TG
5. Herbert Polzhuber, Austria		1–4	24	17
6. Jean Allmand, France		0–5	25	17

Fence-Off
1. G. Kulcsar, Hungary
2. G. Kriss, USSR
3. G. Saccaro, Italy

Sabre — Individual

Statistics: 41 participants from 18 nations. 1st round (6 pools) and 2nd round (4 pools) to obtain the last 16 fencers. Direct elimination to obtain the last 4. In addition there were 2 more competitors from the play-off rounds.

Results		W–L	TR	TG
1. Jerzy Pawlowski, Poland		4–1	18	22
2. Mark Rakita, USSR		4–1	16	22
3. Tibor Pezsa, Hungary		3–2	16	20
4. Vladimir Nazlimov, USSR		3–2	17	21
5. Rolando Rigoli, Italy		1–4	21	11
6. Josef Nowara, Poland		0–5	25	15

Fence-Off

		W–L	TR	TG
1. J. Pawlowski, Poland		1–0	4	5
2. M. Rakita, USSR		0–1	5	4

Foil — Teams

Statistics: 17 teams from 17 nations. 1st round (5 pools) to obtain the last 8 teams. 2nd round (direct elimination) to obtain last 4. Additional round for 5th and 6th place.

Results		W–L
1. France (9)	Revenu	3–1
	Berolatti	3–1
	Noel	2–2
	Magnan	1–2
2. USSR (6)	Sveshnikov	3–1
	Sharov	2–2
	Stankovich	1–2
	Putiatin	0–3
3. Poland (9)	Woyda	3–2
	Skrudlik	2–1
	Parulski	2–1
	Franke	2–1
4. Rumania (3)	Drimba	2–1
	Tiu	1–2
	Haukler	0–2
	Muresan	0–2
5. Hungary (9)	Szabo	4–0
	Kamuti	3–0
	Furedi	1–2
	Kamuti	1–2
6. West Germany	Theuerkauff	2–2
	Gerresheim	1–2
	Wessel	1–2
	Brecht	0–3

Epee — Teams

Statistics: 20 teams from 20 nations. 1st round (5 pools) with an additional round of the least successful 4 to obtain the last 8 teams. 2nd round, direct elimination, to obtain the last 4. Additional round for 5th and 6th place.

Results		W–L
1. Hungary (1)	Fenyvesi	3–1
	Nemere	3–1
	Schmitt	1–2
	Kulcsar	0–3

2. Soviet Union (4)	Kriss	2–2
	Vitebsky	1–2
	Nikanchikov	1–3
	Smoliakov	0–3
3. Poland (9)	Andrzejewski	3–1
	Butkiewicz	3–1
	Gonsior	2–2
	Nielaba	1–2
4. West Germany (6)	Jung	3–1
	Rompza	1–2
	Zimmermann	1–3
	Geuter	1–3
5. East Germany (9)	Uhlig	3–1
	Dumke	2–1
	Schulze	2–2
	Fiedler	2–2
6. Italy (6)	Paolucci	3–1
	Francesconi	2–2
	Breda	1–2
	Saccaro	0–4

Sabre — Teams

Statistics: 12 teams from 12 nations. 1st round (4 pools) to obtain the last 8 teams. 2nd round (direct elimination) to obtain the last 4. Additional round to decide 5th and 6th place.

Results		W–L
1. USSR (9)	Nazlymov	4–0
	Sidiak	2–2
	Vinokurov	2–2
	Rakito	1–3
2. Italy (7)	Calarese	3–1
	Maffei	2–2
	Salvadori	2–2
	Chicca	0–4
3. Hungary (9)	Kovacs	3–1
	Kalmar	2–1
	Bakonyi	2–1
	Meszena	2–2
4. France (5)	Parent	2–1
	Arabo	2–2
	Vallee	1–2
	Panizzo	0–4
5. Poland (9)	Pawlowski	3–1
	Nowara,	3–1
	Sobczak	2–1
	Kawecki	1–2
6. USA	ORBAN, A.	2–1
	MORALES, A.	1–2
	BLUM, R.	1–3
	KEANE, A.	1–3

Women's Events

Foil — Individual

Statistics: 38 participants from 16 nations. 1st round (6 pools), and 2 round (4 pools) in order to provide the 16 best fencers. Direct eliminations until the last 4 were reached. In addition there were 2 more competitors from the play-off rounds.

Results	W–L	TR	TG
1. Elena Novikova, USSR	4–1	11	19
2. Pilar Roldan, Mexico	3–2	14	17
3. Ildiko Rejto, Hungary	3–2	16	14

4. Brigitte Gapais, France	2–3	15	15
5. Kerstin Palm, Sweden	2–3	17	17
6. Galina Gorokhova, USSR	1–4	19	10

Foil — Teams

Statistics: 10 teams from 10 nations. 1st round (3 pools) to provide best 6 teams. Direct eliminations in 2nd round to reach last 4. Additional round to decide 5th and 6th place.

Results		W–L
1. USSR (9)	Zabelina	3–0
	Samusenko	2–1
	Novikova	2–1
	Gorokhova	2–1
2. Hungary (3)	Sakovics	1–2
	Bobis	1–2
	Rejto	1–2
	Gutacsi	0–3
3. Rumania (8)	Iencic	4–0
	Drimba	2–2
	Vicol	1–3
	Szabo	1–3
4. France (8)	Ceretti	3–1
	Gapais	2–2
	Depetris	2–2
	Herbster	1–3
5. West Germany (8)	Schmid	3–1
	Koch	2–1
	Theuerkauff	2–2
	Pulch	1–3
6. Italy (7)	Ragno	3–1
	Lorenzoni	2–2
	Colombetti	1–2
	Masciotta	1–3

Field Hockey

The tournament's main surprise was the eclipse of India as the world's leading hockey nation. The winners of seven gold medals at previous Olympics failed for the first time in forty years to reach the final. Australia, on the other hand, improved its Tokyo-position, from bronze to silver. They defeated the Indians, and, but for the methodically-trained Pakistanis who have developed a marvellous blend of Asian technique and European tactics, they might even have carried off the gold medal. Pakistan, of course, had the advantage of having trained and played at altitudes similar to that of Mexico City. But one musn't therefore minimize Pakistan's success: their stick-work was as pleasant to watch as it was efficient; they played an attacking game without neglecting their iron defense; and they had in Abdul Rashid a player of outstanding quality. Their grand total: nine games played, all of them won, 26 goals scored and only 5 conceded. They are a true world champion team. Generally speaking, one noted a development that was thought to be confined to professional soccer: packed defenses, close covering of each player, very little room left for manœuvering and individual skills, a tendency towards well-drilled uniformity, and alas, very tough, ruthless, physical play. What one saw in the *Magdalena Mixhuca* was certainly not the dainty game played by school girls—and here we are not even thinking of the sensational scandal when the entire Japanese team walked off the field during a game against India, in protest against British umpire Young's awarding India a penalty stroke. A thing like this had never happened before in an Olympic competition.

But what were formerly games are now treated in deadly earnest; and one must admit that some umpiring has not adjusted itself to this development. While the players get younger, those who have to sort out the rights and wrongs are getting older; and they seem to be umpiring according to the gentleman's hockey that was played in their younger days. This obviously won't do in the future.

The semi-final match between India and Australia brought the tournament's most exciting moments. India was defeated 2–1, in the last minute of extra time on a goal scored by Australia's fullback Glencross. The long reign of India was over. The other match, Pakistan against Germany, was just as close. The only goal of the game came near the end, with Pakistan's Mahmood the scorer. These final scores perhaps illustrate best the defensive tactics that now dominate hockey and have robbed it of much of its appeal. Winning is everything—but *not losing* seems even more important.

Statistics: 16 teams from 16 countries, divided into two 8-team groups (A and B).

Group A Eliminations	W.	T.	L.	Pts.
1. India	6	0	1	12
2. West Germany	5	1	1	11
3. New Zealand	3	4	0	10
4. Spain	2	3	2	7
5. Belgium	3	1	3	7
6. East Germany	2	2	3	6
7. Japan	1	1	5	3
8. Mexico	0	0	7	0

Group B Eliminations	W.	T.	L.	Pts.
1. Pakistan	7	0	0	14
2. Australia	4	1	2	9
3. Kenya	4	1	2	9
4. Netherlands	4	0	3	8
5. France	2	1	4	5
6. Great Britain	2	1	4	5
7. Argentina	1	1	5	3
8. Malaysia	0	3	4	3

The Scores
India defeated West Germany 2–1, East Germany 1–0, Belgium 2–1, Spain 1–0, Japan 5–0 and Mexico 8–0.
West Germany defeated East Germany 3–2, Belgium 2–0, Spain 2–0, Japan 2–0 and Mexico 5–1 and tied New Zealand 0–0.
New Zealand defeated India 2–1, Japan 1–0 and Mexico 2–0 and tied West Germany 0–0, East Germany 1–1, Belgium 1–1 and Spain 1–1.
Spain defeated Belgium 2–0 and Mexico 3–0 and tied East Germany 1–1 and Japan 0–0.
Belgium defeated East Germany 4–0, Japan 4–2 and Mexico 4–0.
East Germany defeated Japan 1–0 and Mexico 2–0.
Japan defeated Mexico 2–1.

The Scores
Pakistan defeated Argentina 5–0, Australia 3–2, France 1–0, Britain 2–1, Netherlands 6–0, Kenya 2–1 and Malaysia 4–0.
Australia defeated Argentina 3–1, Netherlands 2–0, Kenya 2–0 and Malaysia 2–0 and tied Britain 0–0.
Kenya defeated Argentina 2–1, France 2–0, Britain 3–0 and Netherlands 2–0 and tied Malaysia 1–1.
Netherlands defeated Argentina 7–0, France 1–0, Britain 2–1 and Malaysia 1–0.
France defeated Australia 1–0 and Britain 1–0 and tied Malaysia 0–0.
Britain defeated Argentina 2–0 and Malaysia 2–0. Argentina defeated France 1–0 and tied Malaysia 1–1.

Playoffs

1st–4th Places
Semi-final—Pakistan 1, West Germany 0.
Semi-final—Australia 2, India 1.
1st—Pakistan 2, Australia 1.
3d—India 2, West Germany 1.
9th Place
Belgium 3, France 0.
13th Place
Japan 2, Argentina 0.

5th–8th Places
Semi-final—Netherlands 3, New Zealand 1.
Semi-final—Spain 2, Kenya 1.
5th—Netherlands 1, Spain 0.
7th—New Zealand 2, Kenya 0.
11th Place
East Germany 2, Britain 1.
15th Place
Malaysia 1, Mexico 0.

Final Placings

1. Pakistan	5. Netherlands	9. Belgium	13. Japan
2. Australia	6. Spain	10. France	14. Argentina
3. India	7. New Zealand	11. East Germany	15. Malaysia
4. West Germany	8. Kenya	12. Britain	16. Mexico

Gymnastics – Men

The men's gymnastics competition established beyond doubt Japan's supremacy. Her team victory over the robot-like Soviets was a victory of art, individuality and imagination over machine-like precision in which the Soviet gymnasts avoided taking unnecessary risks in performing their well-rehearsed routines. Mikhail Voronin, the Soviet world champion, saved face for the USSR team. He took seven (including two gold, four silver and one bronze) of 13 medals earned by the USSR, as only two other members of the team accounted for medals in the individual competition. Five of the Soviet medals came in second place finishes behind Japan.
The other competing nations had *no* say in this Japan–USSR duel, with the solitary exception of Cerar of Yugoslavia, who came in ninth in the floor exercises and retained his gold medal on the

pommelled horse, or side horse. If the world does not begin to catch up soon, men's gymnastics could cease being a true international competition. After Japan and the USSR skimmed the cream of the medal crop, only Yugoslavia and Finland won a single individual medal each, the gold and silver medals in the side horse.

Team Competition

Statistics: 16 teams of 6 competitors each from 16 countries. The best individual totals constitute the team total. One compulsory and one voluntary exercise each on parallel bars, the horizontal bar, the pommelled horse, the rings and a compulsory and a voluntary vault on the long horse.

		Floor Exercises	Side Horse	Rings	Horse Vault	Parallel Bars	Horizon- tal Bar	Total Points
1. Japan (Yukid Endo,	C	48.00	46.90	48.35	47.00	48.20	47.95	286.40
Sawao Kato, Tasheki	V	48.80	47.30	48.40	47.75	48.50	48.75	289.50
Kato, Eiko Kenmotsu,	T	96.80	94.20	96.75	94.75	96.70	96.70	575.90
Akinori Nakayama)								
2. USSR	C	47.35	47.35	47.60	47.15	48.00	47.70	285.15
	V	47.70	47.50	47.35	47.30	47.85	48.25	285.95
	T	95.06	94.85	94.95	94.45	95.85	95.95	571.10
3. East Germany	C	45.30	45.70	45.60	46.20	47.05	47.65	277.50
	V	46.70	44.60	46.70	46.75	47.10	47.80	279.65
	T	92.00	90.30	92.30	92.95	94.15	95.45	557.15
4. Czechoslovakia	C	46.40	45.60	45.35	46.10	47.00	46.05	276.50
	V	46.70	46.80	45.95	46.50	47.60	47.05	280.60
	T	93.10	92.40	91.30	92.60	94.60	93.10	557.10
5. Poland	C	45.45	45.90	45.55	45.65	46.45	46.15	275.15
	V	46.00	46.66	46.30	46.55	47.40	47.35	280.25
	T	91.45	92.55	91.85	92.20	93.85	93.50	555.40

Individual Awards

Statistics: 138 participants from 31 countries. The individual awards are made on the points scored during the progress of the team competition.

		Floor Exercises	Side Horse	Rings	Horse Vault	Parallel Bars	Horizon- tal Bar	Total Points
1. Sawao Kato, Japan	C	9.75	9.45	9.70	9.35	9.65	9.60	57.50
	V	9.90	9.55	9.85	9.55	9.70	9.85	58.40
	T	19.65	19.00	19.55	18.90	19.35	19.45	115.90
2. Mikhail Voronin, USSR	C	9.55	9.70	9.75	9.45	9.75	9.70	57.90
	V	9.70	9.50	9.70	9.55	9.70	9.80	57.95
	T	19.25	19.20	19.45	19.00	19.45	19.50	115.85
3. Akinori Nakayama, Jap.	C	9.60	9.40	9.75	9.45	9.70	9.70	57.60
	V	9.80	9.45	9.75	9.40	9.85	9.80	58.05
	T	19.40	18.85	19.50	18.85	19.55	19.50	115.65
4. Eiko Kenmotsu, Japan	C	9.55	9.45	9.55	9.40	9.60	9.55	57.10
	V	9.70	9.65	9.45	9.55	9.65	9.80	57.80
	T	19.25	19.10	19.00	18.95	19.25	19.35	114.90
5. Tasheki Kato, Japan ..	C	9.60	9.20	9.70	9.45	9.60	9.55	57.10
	V	9.75	9.45	9.70	9.60	9.70	9.55	57.75
	T	19.35	18.65	19.40	19.05	19.30	19.10	114.85
6. Sergei Diomidov, USSR	C	9.50	9.50	9.60	9.45	9.45	9.60	57.10
	V	9.45	9.50	9.45	9.45	9.45	9.70	57.00
	T	18.95	19.00	19.05	18.90	18.90	19.30	114.10

Apparatus Individual Awards

The 6 best on each apparatus, as established during the team competition, competed for the final title of the best on each apparatus (a voluntary exercise). The results of the team competition were counted as semi-final performance by halving the total of compulsory and voluntary exercises.

374

			Average	Final	Total Points
Floor Exercises	1. Sawao Kato, Japan	....	9.825	9.650	19.475
	2. Akinori Nakayama, Japan	....	9.700	9.700	19.400
	3. Tasheki Kato, Japan	....	9.675	9.600	19.275
	4. Mitsuko Tsukahara, Japan.	....	9.559	9.500	19.050
	5. Valery Karasev, USSR	....	9.550	9.400	18.950
	6. Eiko Kenmotsu, Japan	....	9.625	9.300	18.925
Side Horse	1. Miroslav Cerar, Yugoslavia	....	9.675	9.650	19.325
	2. Olli Laiho, Finland	....	9.575	9.650	19.225
	3. Mikhail Voronin, USSR	....	9.600	9.600	19.200
	4. Wilhelm Kubica, Poland	....	9.550	9.600	19.150
	5. Eiko Kenmotsu, Japan	....	9.550	9.500	19.050
	6. Vladimir Klimenko, USSR	....	9.550	9.400	18.950
Rings	1. Akinori Nakayama, Japan	....	9.750	9.700	19.450
	2. Mikhail Voronin, USSR	....	9.725	9.600	19.325
	3. Sawao Kato, Japan	....	9.775	9.450	19.225
	4. Mitsuko Tsukahara, Japan	....	9.625	9.500	19.125
	5. Tasheki Kato, Japan	....	9.700	9.350	19.050
	6. Sergei Diomidov, USSR	....	9.525	9.450	18.975
Horse Vault	1. Mikhail Voronin, USSR	....	9.500	9.500	19.000
	2. Yukio Endo, Japan	....	9.500	9.450	18.950
	3. Sergei Diomidov, USSR	....	9.450	9.475	18.925
	4. Tasheki Kato, Japan	....	9.525	9.250	18.775
	5. Akinori Nakayama, Japan	....	9.425	9.300	18.725
	6. Eiko Kenmotsu, Japan	....	9.475	9.175	18.650
Parallel Bars	1. Akinori Nakayama, Japan	....	9.775	9.700	19.475
	2. Mikhail Voronin, USSR	....	9.725	9.700	19.425
	3. Vladimir Klimenko, USSR	....	9.625	9.600	19.225
	4. Tasheki Kato, Japan	....	9.650	9.550	19.200
	5. Eiko Kenmotsu, Japan	....	9.625	9.550	19.175
	6. Wilhelm Kubica, Poland	....	9.600	9.350	18.950
Horizontal Bar	1. Mikhail Voronin, USSR	....	9.750	9.800	19.550
	1. Akinori Nakayama, Japan	....	9.750	9.800	19.550
	3. Eiko Kenmotsu, Japan	....	9.675	9.700	19.375
	4. Klaus Koste, E. Germany	....	9.725	9.500	19.225
	5. Sergei Diomidov, USSR	....	9.650	9.500	19.150
	6. Yukio Endo, Japan	....	9.625	9.400	19.025

Gymnastics - Women

If the men's gymnastics competition was a battle between the Soviet Union and Japan, the women's competition was between Czechoslovakia's queen of gymnastics, Vera Caslavska, and the Soviet women's team. The USSR won more medals, nine, to six for Miss Caslavska. But the real winner was Miss Caslavska.

The Czechoslovakian beauty must be recognized not only for her stupendous feat of gaining four gold and two silver medals; not only for her grace and artistry; not only for endearing herself to the Mexican people for choosing a Mexican song for her last floor routine and for doing the Mexican Hat Dance; not only for sentimental-political reasons or for the fact that she married her teammate, Josef Odlozil (track and field) in an Olympic village ceremony on the night before closing, but also because she is a personality who possesses a unique blend of grace and attack, feminity and concentrated will-power, poise and acrobatic artistry.

In talking about Miss Caslavska the person, the athlete and world champion (she is the current world champion in the all-around, and defended her 1964 Olympic diadem), one might add additional words without overstating the impact of this one person on her 6,000 fellow athletes as she takes to the floor for exercises or routines.

The competition was not without its tension. On the balance beam the judges took an eternity to make up its mind about the final point scores for Vera, finally upgrading the Czechoslovakian in her direct confrontation with Natalia Kuchinskaya of the Soviet Union. However, whatever emotions were displayed by the competitors and public alike, all ended in a great triumph for Vera Caslavska. Rarely has there been a more popular winner than this young Czechoslovakian who has established new standards for others to seek out in the years to come.

The USA made its greatest stride in the gymnastics competition, with the girls finishing sixth as a team to earn a coveted Olympic Games diploma. They were within striking distance of fourth. Also, LINDA METHENY in finishing fourth in the exciting balance beam competition became the first USA women's gymnast ever to qualify for a final event.

Statistics: 14 teams of 6 competitors from 14 countries. The best five individual totals constitute the team total. One compulsory and one voluntary exercise each on uneven parallel bars, a floor exercise and 1 compulsory and 1 voluntary vault each on horse sideways, without pommels.

		Floor Exercises	Uneven Parallel Bars	Balance Beam	Horse Vault	Total Points
1. Soviet Union (Ljurov Burda, Olga Khar-	C	48.45	47.10	47.50	48.10	191.15
lova Karaseva, Natalia Kuchinskaya,	V	47.70	47.95	47.45	48.60	191.70
Larisa Petrik, Zinaida Voronina)	T	96.15	95.05	94.95	96.70	382.85
2. Czechoslovakia	C	48.55	46.80	47.20	47.65	190.20
	V	48.00	48.65	47.30	48.05	192.00
	T	96.55	95.45	94.50	95.70	382.20
3. East Germany	C	48.25	47.10	47.05	47.00	189.40
	V	48.05	47.70	47.00	46.95	189.70
	T	96.30	94.80	94.05	93.95	379.10
4. Japan	C	47.35	45.95	46.90	46.90	187.10
	V	47.15	47.55	46.55	47.10	188.35
	T	94.50	93.50	93.45	94.00	375.45
5. Hungary	C	46.65	44.65	46.90	46.55	184.75
	V	46.20	46.75	45.90	46.20	185.05
	T	92.85	91.40	92.40	92.75	369.80

Individual Awards

Statistics: 113 participants from 24 countries. The individual awards are made on the points scored during the progress of the team competition.

		Floor Exercises	Uneven Parallel Bars	Balance Beam	Horse Vault	Total Points
1. Vera Caslavska, Czechoslovakia	C	9.90	9.60	9.65	9.70	38.85
	V	9.85	9.90	9.80	9.85	39.40
	T	19.75	19.50	19.45	19.55	78.25
2. Zinaida Voronina, USSR	C	9.75	9.55	9.40	9.65	38.35
	V	9.65	9.70	9.40	9.75	38.50
	T	19.40	19.25	18.80	19.40	76.85
3. Natalia Kuchinskaya, USSR	C	9.75	8.45	9.80	9.75	37.75
	V	9.70	9.65	9.80	9.85	39.00
	T	19.45	18.10	19.60	19.60	76.75
4. Larisa Petrik, USSR	C	9.70	9.45	9.50	9.70	38.35
	V	9.50	9.50	9.50	9.85	38.35
	T	19.20	18.95	19.00	19.55	76.70
4. Erika Zuchold, E. Germany	C	9.80	9.45	9.45	9.50	38.20
	V	9.85	9.60	9.55	9.50	38.50
	T	19.65	19.05	19.00	19.00	76.70
6. Karin Janz, E. Germany	C	9.70	9.60	9.45	9.50	38.25
	V	9.50	9.70	9.60	9.50	38.30
	T	19.20	19.30	19.05	19.00	76.55

Apparatus Individual Awards

The 6 best on each apparatus, as established during the team competition competed after the event for the title of the best on each apparatus (a voluntary exercise). The results of the team competition were counted as a semi-final performance, by taking half of the sum of the compulsory and voluntary exercises.

		Average	Final	Total Points
Floor Exercise	1. Vera Caslavska, Czechoslovakia	9.775	9.900	19.675
	1. Larisa Petrik, USSR	9.775	9.900	19.675
	3. Natalia Kuchinskaya, USSR	9.800	9.850	19.650
	4. Zinaida Voronina, USSR	9.700	9.850	19.550
	5. Olga Karaseva, USSR	9.575	9.750	19.325
	5. Bohumila Rimnacova, Czechoslovakia	9.575	9.750	19.325
Side Horse	1. Vera Caslavska, Czechoslovakia	9.875	9.900	19.775
	2. Erika Zuchold, E. Germany	9.825	9.800	19.625
	3. Zinaida Voronina, USSR	9.700	9.800	19.500
	4. Mariana Krajcirova, Czechoslovakia	9.725	9.750	19.475
	5. Natalia Kuchinskaya, USSR	9.725	9.650	19.375
	6. Miroslava Sklenickova, Czechoslovakia	9.675	9.650	19.325
Uneven Parallel Bars	1. Vera Caslavska, Czechoslovakia	9.750	9.900	19.650
	2. Karin Janz, E. Germany	9.650	9.850	19.500
	3. Zinaida Voronina, USSR	9.625	9.800	19.425
	4. Bohumila Rimnacova, Czechoslovakia	9.650	9.700	19.350
	5. Erika Zuchold, E. Germany	9.525	9.800	19.325
	6. Miroslava Sklenickova, Czechoslovakia	9.550	8.650	18.200
Balance Beam	1. Natalia Kuchinskaya, USSR	9.800	9.850	19.650
	2. Vera Caslavska, Czechoslovakia	9.725	9.850	19.575
	3. Larisa Petrik, USSR	9.500	9.750	19.250
	4. LINDA METHENY, USA	9.575	9.650	19.225
	4. Karin Janz, E. Germany	9.525	9.700	19.225
	6. Erika Zuchold, E. Germany	9.500	9.650	19.150

Modern Pentathlon

This contest in the equestrian arts, fencing, shooting, swimming and athletics is doubtless one of the tougher competitions of the Games, if not *the* toughest. The gruelling five-event program not only requires all-round abilities in each sport, but is also a very strenuous endurance test for the body and for the nerves, particularly at Mexico City. Its high altitude made special demands on those not acclimated to it; the terrain mapped out for the cross country running was extremely difficult, while the riders were given horses who excelled in a truly 'individual' Mexican temper of their own, which often proved stronger than the will of their riders. Collapsing from exhaustion and being given oxygen, as in the gruelling cross country race, became the rule rather than the exception.

This modern pentathlon will also be remembered for the fact that Sweden's Hans Liljenvall was disqualified for having had a fraction above the allowed alcohol limit in his blood. This was the only disqualification on such grounds of the whole Games, and the first one in seventy-two years for a similar offense. It had consequences, for it cost Sweden the bronze medal in the team placings. The French—who certainly didn't deserve the bronze medal on the strength of their performance—were the lucky ones who obtained it. Yet Sweden had the satisfaction of winning the individual gold medal through Bjorn Ferm, a 25-year-old student from Norkopping (which lies by the sea, and can therefore not be said to have helped Ferm to his high altitude-victory).

What is also interesting about Ferm's performance is that he didn't finish first in any of the five events. What made him the overall winner was the fact that he kept steadily among the high finishers, while the contributions of the other contestants were of a wildly-fluctuating nature. Torok and Mona of Hungary—who together with Balczo eventually won the team event—were superb in the fencing, but disastrous in the horse riding. The Russians were excellent in the cross country 4,000 meter race; and they did better in the 300 meter swimming contest than the Hungarians, where Torok, who had won this event in Tokyo, surprisingly failed—a victim of Mexico's air. The USA had no top individual placings, but finished fourth in the team placing.

The Games in Mexico failed again to provide a clear-cut answer to the question of which type of sport should be the basis around which to develop the successful modern pentathlon athlete. The Soviet Union, and Sweden as well, seem to feel that the athlete who is a naturally good runner and swimmer can be developed into a reasonably good fencer, horseman and marksman. The Hungarians, who also won the team gold medal in Tokyo, have a long tradition in fencing, riding, and shooting. These factors seem to have been decisive, for Hungary won the contest despite her unexpected failure in the 300 meters. The very character of the pentathlon, with its emphasis on diverse military, or (if one prefers to so call it), gentlemanly sports makes it a rather unglamorous competition which fails to attract the all-round athlete of the West. He is much more drawn by the decathlon, and one cannot blame him.

Statistics: 48 participants from 18 countries, among them 15 national teams, consisting of 3 competitors each. Individual and team competition in each event. The team result was reached by adding together of the individual results of the team-members. 1,000 points scoring.

Individual	Equestrian	Fencing	Shooting	Swimming	Cross Country	Total
1. Bjorn Ferm, Sweden	1,100	885	934	1,075	970	4,964
2. Andras Balczo, Hungary	1,010	931	934	1,054	1,024	4,953
3. Pavel Lednev, USSR	1,070	839	934	1,060	892	4,795
4. Karl Kutschke, E. Germany	1,070	632	846	1,126	1,090	4,764
5. Boris Onishchenco, USSR	995	885	912	1,054	910	4,756
6. Raoul Gueguen, France	1,040	954	912	1,000	850	4,756

Team						
1. Hungary (Balczo, Mona, Torok)	2,940	3,130	2,714	2,877	2,664	14,325
2. USSR (Lednev, Onishchenco, Shaparnis)	3,135	2,558	2,648	3,141	2,766	14,248
3. France (Gueguen, Giudicelli, Guiguet)	2,855	2,168	2,626	2,931	2,709	13,280
4. USA (BECK, MOORE, LOUGH)	3,030	2,324	2,670	2,844	2,412	13,280
5. Finland (Hotanen, Ketela, Ano)	2,890	2,558	2,384	2,799	2,607	13,238
6. E. Germany (Tscherner, Luderitz, Kutschke)	2,485	2,194	2,626	3,093	2,769	13,167

Note: Sweden compiled 14,188 points for a third-place finish, but was disqualified because one competitor was found to have too high a percentage of alcohol in his blood during the competition.

Rowing

Rowing was conducted at Xochimilco, the magnificent basin the Mexicans constructed in the suburbs. It was beautiful to look at but the oarsmen complained that the waters reflected the sunshine of mid-day. Apparently the combination of the bright sun mixed with the enervating effects of high altitude added to the state of exhaustion, breathlessness and a run of bronchial trouble that had failed to wipe out a single other sport. As a result the final standings in many of the events reflected the success of those crews which had overcome the levelling effects of sunshine and high altitude.

The two most significant races were the single sculls and the eights with coxswain. The **single sculls** races looked as if nothing and nobody could stop West Germany's Jochen Meissner. He was the highest-stroking sculler off the mark, built up a two-and-a-half length lead in the first 1,000 meters and then challenged Jan Wienese of the Netherlands to catch him. Jan came alongside him at 1,200 meters and had open water at the 1,500 meter mark before sprinting for home as Meissner faded. The **eights with coxswain** is the crown race of rowing. The final was a breath-taking race for oarsmen and spectators alike. West Germany and New Zealand had been the most impressive in the heats. The USA, represented by the Harvard eight, qualified for the final by placing second to Czechoslovakia in a repechage or second chance race.

New Zealand got away fast and built up a lead of one-half a boat length over West Germany in the first 1,000 meters. At this point the USA was third and less than a length behind New Zealand. Things happened in the next 500 meters. The West Germans continued to row at the same steady pace, New Zealand faded to second and the USA yielded third place to the Soviet Union.

As the smooth-stroking shells raced past a crowd estimated at 40,000, West Germany maintained its lead as Australia put on a driving finish to come within one quarter of a length of catching the winning West German crew. It was in this final 500 meters that the USA faded to sixth and last, two lengths behind the gold medalists.

Statistics: 7 events with 350 oars from 30 countries with 102 boats. Heats and repechages in all events. Final from 1st to 6th place.

Single Sculls 17 boats from 17 countries.

		min.			min.
1. Jan Wienese, Netherlands		7:47.80	4. JOHN VAN BLOM, USA		8:00.51
2. Jochen Meissner, W. Germany ..		7:52.00	5. Achim Hill, E. Germany		8:06.09
3. Albert Demiddi, Argentina		7:57.19	6. Ken Dwan, Great Britain		8:13.76

Pair Oars With Coxswain 18 boats from 18 countries.

		min.
1. Italy	Baran, Sambo, Cipolla	8:04.81
2. Netherlands	Suselbeek, Vannes, Rijnders	8:06.80
3. Denmark	Krab, Jorgensen, Krab	8:08.07
4. East Germany	Wollmann, Gunkel, Neubert	8:08.22
5. USA	WILLIAM HOBBS, RICHARDS EDMUNDS, STEWART MACDONALD	8:12.60
6. West Germany	Hiesinger, Hartung, Benter	8:41.51

Double Sculls 13 boats from 13 countries.

		min.
1. USSR	Sass, Timoshinin	6:51.82
2. Netherlands	Droog, Van Dis	6:52.80
3. USA	JOHN NUNN, WILLIAM MAHER	6:54.21
4. Bulgaria	Jelev, Valtchev	6:58.48
5. East Germany	Schmied, Haake	7:04.92
6. West Germany	Hild, Glock	7:12.20

Pair Oars Without Coxswain 18 boats from 18 countries.

		min.
1. East Germany ...	Lucke, Bothe	7:26.56
2. USA	LAWRENCE HOUGH, ANTHONY JOHNSON	7:26.71
3. Denmark.......	Christiansen, Larsen	7:31.84
4. Austria	Ebner, Losert	7:41.86
5. Switzerland	Russli, Swimpfer	7:46.79
6. Netherlands.....	Luynenburg, Stokvis	no time

Four Oars With Coxswain 13 boats from 13 countries.

		min.
1. New Zealand	Joyce, Storey, Collinge, Cole, Dickie	6:45.62
2. East Germany	Kremtz, Gohler, Gelpke, Jacob, Semetzky	6:48.20
3. Switzerland	Oswald, Waser, Bolliger, Grob, Frohlich	6:49.04
4. Italy	Sgheiz, Trivini, Galante, Sgheiz, Gottifredi	6:49.54
5. USA	LUTHER JONES, WILLIAM PURDY, ANTHONY MARTIN, GARDNER CADWALADER, JOHN HARTIGAN	6:51.41
6. USSR	Nemtyrev, Surov, Mishin, Kudinov, Mikheev	7:00.00

Four Oars Without Coxswain 11 boats from 11 countries

		min.
1. East Germany	Forberger, Ruhle, Grahn, Schubert	6:39.18
2. Hungary	Melis, Csermely, Sarlos, Melis	6:41.64
3. Italy	Bosatta, Contimanzini, Baraglia, Albini	6:44.01
4. Switzerland	Rentsch, Meister, Gobet, Altenburger	6:45.78
5. USA	PETER RAYMOND, CHARLES HAMBLIN, RAYMOND WRIGHT, LAWRENCE TERRY	6:47.70
6. West Germany	Hitzbleck, Buchter, Weinreich, Heck	7:08.22

Eights 12 boats from 12 countries.

			min.
1. West Germany	Meyer, Henning, Hottenrott, Siebert, Thiersch, Schreyer, Ulbricht, Hirschfelder, Bose		6:07.00
2. Australia	Duval, Fazio, Doublas, Pearce, Grover, Morgan, Dickson, Ranch, Shirlaw		6:07.98
3. USSR	Jukna, Sterlik, Matryshkin, Kravchuck, Lorentsson, Bagdonavichus, Yagelavichus, Briedis, Suslin		6:09.11
4. New Zealand	Webster, Dryden, Brownlee, Just, Page, Veldman, Hunter, Gibbons, Cawood		6:10.43
5. Czechoslovakia	Janos, Svojanovsky, Svojanovsky, Marecek Ptak, Kuba, Kolesa, Wallisch, Cermak		6:12.17
6. USA	STEPHEN BROOKS, ANDREW LARKIN, FRANZ HOBBS, CLEVE LIVINGSTON, PAUL HOFFMAN, CURTIS CANNING, SCOTT STEKETEE, JACQUES FIECHTER, DAVID HIGGINS		6:14.34

Shooting

The *Poligono Olimpico*, where the shooting contests were held, provided an ideal setting. No previous Olympics could boast of such marvellous facilities, whether for the spectators, the organizing and administrative staff, or for the press; and the ranges themselves, although fitted into a comparatively narrow confine within the spacious grounds, were laid out to enable the simultaneous staging of various competitions.

In the overall analysis, the American team proved a disappointment. In Tokyo, it had won seven out of eighteen medals to lead all competitors. In the *Poligono* it had to be satisfied with coming in second to the Soviet Union. Supremacy in shooting has gone, at least for the time being, to Eastern Europe. Some amends were made for America by divinity student GARY ANDERSON in the **free rifle** event. The seven-times world champion and Tokyo gold medal winner broke his own world record in placing first—ahead of Kornev, USSR, beating him by six points.

Altogether the majority of the more successful marksmen in the Games were members of the Armed Forces. One notable exception was Great Britain's Bob Braithwaite, a veterinary surgeon and a true amateur. He won a gold medal in the **clay-pigeon shooting;** it was the United Kingdom's first victory in this sport in sixty years.

The **small bore rifle, three positions** contest was the most thrilling of all the shooting competitions. After a program of 120 shots that lasted six hours, it was anyone's guess whether Bernd Klingner, Germany, or JOHN WRITER, USA, had the higher score. It took the judges two hours to establish that the German finished ahead of the American by one point! In the process he also established a new world record for the kneeling position.

Czechoslovakia's Jan Kurka won the gold medal for the **small bore rifle, prone,** Russian Evgeny Petrov for the **skeet,** his fellow countryman Gregory Kosykh for the **free pistol,** and Poland's Jozef Zapedzki for the **rapid fire pistol.** But to get the full picture one has to take the silver and bronze medals into consideration as well, since only negligible margins often separated win from place. The 21 medals that were distributed went to no less than twelve nations. In this light, the superiority of the Soviet Union and of the Eastern bloc looks somewhat less impregnable.

Small Bore Rifle, Prone

Statistics: 86 participants from 46 nations. 60 shots in six 10-shot series. World record: BOYD (USA) 598 points (1966). Olympic record: Hammerl (Hungary) 597 points (Tokyo 1964). New Olympic record: Kurka (Czechoslovakia) and Hammerl (Hungary) 598 points. World record was equalled twice.

	Points		Points
1. Jan Kurka, Czechoslovakia	598	4. Nicolae Rotaru, Rumania	597
2. Laszlo Hammerl, Hungary	598	5. John Palin, Britain	596
3. Ian Ballinger, New Zealand	597	6. Jean Loret, France	596

Small Bore Rifle, 3 Positions

Statistics: 62 participants from 35 nations. 120 shots, 40 each in the 3 positions, prone, kneel, stand. World and Olympic record: WIGGER (USA) 1,164 points (Tokyo 1964).

	Points		Points
1. Bernd Klingner, W. Germany	1,157	4. JOHN FOSTER, USA	1,153
2. JOHN WRITER, USA	1,156	5. Jose Gonzalez, Mexico	1,152
3. Vitaly Parkhinovich, USSR	1,154	6. Gerald Ouellette, Canada	1,151

Free Rifle

Statistics: 30 participants from 16 nations. 120 shots in 3 series of 40 shots. World record: ANDERSON (USA) 1,156 points (1966). Olympic record: ANDERSON (USA) 1,153 points (Tokyo 1964). Both the world and Olympic records were broken once. New Olympic and world record: ANDERSON (USA) 1,157 points.

	Points			Points
1. GARY ANDERSON, USA	1,157		4. Shota Kveliashvili, USSR	1,142
2. Valentin Kornev, USSR	1,151		5. Erwin Vogt, Switzerland	1,140
3. Kurt Müller, Switzerland	1,148		6. Hartmut Sommer, E. Germany	1,140
			7. JOHN FOSTER, USA	1,140

Rapid Fire Pistol

Statistics: 56 participants from 35 nations. 60 shots in two 30-shot series. World record: Atanasiu (Rumania) 596 points (1966). Olympic record: Linnosvuo (Finland) 592 points (Tokyo 1964). New Olympic record: Zapedzki (Poland) 593 points.

	Points			Points
1. Josef Zapedzki, Poland	593		5. Erich Masurat, W. Germany	590
2. Marcel Rosca, Rumania	591		6. Gerhard Dommrich, E. Germany	589
3. Renart Suleimanov, USSR	591		17. WILLIAM McMILLAN, USA	584
4. Christian Düring, E. Germany	591		25. JAMES McNALLY, USA	580

Free Pistol

Statistics: 69 participants from 43 nations. 60 shots in six 10-shot series. World record: Jassinsky (USSR) 566 points (1955). Olympic record: Gustchin (USSR) 560 points (Rome 1960), and Markkanen (Finland) (Tokyo 1964). New Olympic record: Kosykh (USSR) and Mertel (W. Germany) 562 points.

	Points			Points
1. Grigory Kosykh, USSR	562		5. Pawel Malek, Poland	556
2. Heinz Mertel, W. Germany	562		6. Helmut Artelt, E. Germany	555
3. Harald Vollmar, E. Germany	560		16. DON HAMILTON, USA	549
4. ARNOLD VITARBO, USA	559			

Clay Pigeon - Skeet

Statistics: First Olympic staging. 52 participants from 30 countries. Best world performance: Durnev (USSR) 200 points. Best Olympic performance: Petrov (USSR) 198 points.

	Points			Points
1. Yevgeny Petrov, USSR	198		5. Pedro Gianella, Peru	194
2. Romano Garagnani, Italy	198		6. Nicolai Atalah, Chile	194
3. Konrad Wirnhier, W. Germany	198		16. EARL HERRING, USA	190
4. Yury Tsuranov, USSR	196		19. ROBERT RODALE, USA	189

Clay Pigeon - Trap

Statistics: 59 participants from 34 nations. 200 shots in 8 series of 25 shots each. Best world and Olympic performances: Mattarelli (Italy) 198 points (Tokyo 1964). Both records were equalled.

	Points			Points
1. John Braithwaite, Britain	198		5. Pierre Candelo, France	195
2. THOMAS GARRIGUS, USA	196		6. Adam Smelczynski, Poland	195
3. Kurt Czekalla, E. Germany	196		26. LARRY STAFFORD, USA	189
4. Pavel Senichev, USSR	196			

Soccer This tournament became the setting for more brawls, cushions thrown by spectators, disqualifications and sendings-off, downright bad officiating and tumultuous scenes in the stands than any previous Games has ever seen—and soccer football has never been known as one of the quieter Olympic sports. The game is by its very nature a spectacular and dramatic one, always involving the spectators to such a degree that it is impossible for them to remain neutral. And if, on top of all this, the "home team" is in the thick of the fight, with a good chance of winning honors, things are bound to get out of hand. Add to that the divergence of the various national teams, each having its own ideas of how to interpret the rules; the language difficulties facing the referees; and the Latin temperament of the Mexican crowd which so badly wanted the host eleven to win—and you get an idea of what happened in Mexico City.

Those who expected the Mexican eleven to play in the final match were disappointed, for they were defeated by the Bulgarians in the semi-finals by a score of 3–2. Actually, it could well have been Israel facing the Mexicans in that contest, for the choice rested on the toss of a coin between the two, after they tied 1–1 in the quarter-finals. Bulgaria won, and the Israelis were out.

After losing to Bulgaria, Mexico still had a shot at a bronze medal, but this too eluded them. It was won by, of all countries, Japan, which in placing third announced to the world its intention of becoming a world power in football. Europe and Latin America will have to be particularly wary in the future, for apart from the astonishing success of Japan in Mexico City, the emerging African nations also showed great improvement on past performances. Although it was the brawls and disqualifications which made the headlines, it should not be overlooked that much good soccer was played in the matches between teams who still play for the love of the game, and the state-financed players from Eastern Europe didn't always have things their own way. But in the end, Hungary proved its superiority by giving up only three goals in its impressive sweep to the gold, while silver-medalist Bulgaria gave up only one more.

Statistics: 16 teams from 16 nations. The Olympic tournament consists of a qualifying round in four groups (A–D) of 4 teams each. The first 2 teams in each group continued in the tournament quarter-finals.

Group A Eliminations	W.	L.	T.	Pts.
1. France	2	1	0	4
2. Mexico	2	1	0	4
3. Colombia	1	2	0	2
4. Guinea	1	2	0	2

The Scores
France defeated Mexico 4–1 and Guinea 3–1.
Mexico defeated Colombia 1–9 and Guinea 4–0.
Colombia defeated France 2–1.
Guinea defeated Colombia 3–2.

Group B Eliminations	W.	L.	T.	Pts.
1. Spain	2	0	1	5
2. Japan	1	0	2	4
3. Brazil	0	1	2	2
4. Nigeria	0	2	1	1

The Scores
Spain defeated Brazil 1–0 and Nigeria 3–0 and tied Japan 0–0.
Japan defeated Nigeria 3–1 and tied Brazil 1–1.
Brazil tied Nigeria 3–3.

Group C Eliminations	W.	L.	T.	Pts.
1. Hungary	2	0	1	5
2. Israel	2	1	0	4
3. Ghana	0	1	2	2
4. El Salvador	0	2	1	1

The Scores
Hungary defeated Israel 2–0 and El Salvador 4–0 and tied Ghana 2–2.
Israel defeated Ghana 5–3 and El Salvador 3–1.
Ghana tied El Salvador 1–1.

Group D Eliminations	W.	L.	T.	Pts.
1. Bulgaria	2	0	1	5
2. Guatemala	2	1	0	4
3. Czechoslovakia ...	1	1	1	3
4. Thailand	0	3	0	0

The Scores
Bulgaria defeated Guatemala 2–1 and Thailand 7–0 and tied Czechoslovakia 2–2.
Guatemala defeated Czechoslovakia 1–0 and Thailand 4–1.
Czechoslovakia defeated Thailand 8–0.

Playoffs

Quarter-final Round
Hungary 1, Guatemala 0.
Bulgaria 1, Israel 1.
Mexico 2, Spain 0.
Japan 3, France 1.

Semi-final Round
Bulgaria 3, Mexico 2.
Hungary 5, Japan 0.

Final Round
Hungary 4, Bulgaria 1.

Third Place
Japan 2, Mexico 0.

The Olympic Swimming and Diving events were held in the Alberca. It was supposedly built in world record time and the Mexicans deserve a number of medals for its facilities and its size (14,000 spectators jampacked the seats and aisles on several occasions), as well as for its functional yet beautifully-simple design outside and inside.

The superiority of the USA men's and women's swimming and diving teams over the rest of the world manifested itself clearly. One has become used to this USA superiority in swimming and diving

Swimming – Men

since 1960. Among Olympic spectators it has become a moot point whether the USA is a nation whose greatest strength is in track and field or in swimming.

Taking as a guide the harvest of 23 gold, 15 silver and 20 bronze medals reaped by the USA swimming and diving team, one is almost forced to conclude that the USA does better in the water. To win an overall total of 73 medals out of a possible 104 (which includes a total of 20 medals in five relays) and to be represented among the first three finishers in every swimming and diving event, as well as winning all relay events, these are attainments which speak for themselves.

Even so, perhaps there were some inglorious disappointments among the performances of the US swimmers. Those who had expected a spate of new world records also may have been disappointed. But the atmospheric conditions found at Mexico City's altitude held world record performances to a minimum. New Olympic records, nevertheless, were written into the books in 12 of the 18 events included on the 1964 program.

The surge of the USA was slowed by the new found strength of the young Australian team and the increasing strength of all other nations. It can be remarked that the margin between the USA and the rest of the world gets smaller, which is a desirable turn of events, indeed. This development will enliven the coming international competitions leading up to the 1972 Olympic Games, while spurring the nations of the New World to new efforts.

Using swimming as an example or a guide, it was shown that in sport no one nation is "safe."

The **100 meter freestyle** illustrates the previous point well. Before the start of the swimming events, many of the experts figured that the elite US sprinters—ZACHARY ZORN, KEN WALSH and MARK SPITZ—would fight it out among themselves. Yet all three were beaten by the 18-year-old Mike Wenden of Australia, who established an amazing new world record over the distance. The stop watches recorded 52.2 seconds, which is four-tenths of a second faster than the previous world record which ZORN had equaled in the US Olympic Trials. While WALSH captured the silver and SPITZ the bronze medal, ZORN—without complaining of illness which had felled him for almost a week—came home a puzzling (to the spectators) eighth and last, after tying for second-fastest time of the heats and winning his semi-final race.

Statistics: 67 participants from 37 countries. 9 heats, 3 semi-finals. World record: WALSH (USA) 52.6 sec. (1967). Olympic record: SCHOLLANDER (USA) 53.4 sec. (Tokyo 1964). World record broken once, Olympic record broken four times and equalled once. New Olympic and world record: Wenden (Australia) 52.2 sec.

Final	sec.		sec.
1. Michael Wenden, Australia	52.2	5. Leonid Ilychev, USSR	53.8
2. KEN WALSH, USA	52.8	6. Georgy Kulikov, USSR	53.8
3. MARK SPITZ, USA	53.0	7. Luis Nicolao Yanuzzi, Argentina ...	53.9
4. Bobby McGregor, Great Britain ...	53.5	8. ZACHARY ZORN, USA	53.9

The **200 meter freestyle,** in the expectation of a large percentage of the swimming fans, was to be the grand climax of DON SCHOLLANDER's glittering career as certainly the greatest swimmer thus far in the second half of the century. He set out to add another gold medal in an individual event to the four he had won at Tokyo (two individual and two relays) and the gold for anchoring the winning US 4×200 meter relay team earlier in the Mexico City Olympic Games. This was to be his last individual race in international competition. But it did not turn out quite as expected—as was forecast by the stopwatch clockings during the 4×200 freestyle relay, Wenden 1:54.3 vs. SCHOLLANDER 1:54.6, and in the heats, Wenden 1:59.3 and SCHOLLANDER 2:00.0.

Wenden, four years younger than the Yale student, was simply faster and proved it convincingly in the final. At 150 meters, SCHOLLANDER made a mighty effort to catch the young Australian, but continued to lose ground during the last 50 meters as Wenden set a new Olympic record in an event that was on the program for the first time since the Games of the II Olympiad in 1900.

Statistics: Event last staged in Paris (1900). 57 participants from 30 countries. 9 heats. World record: SCHOLLANDER (USA) 1:54.3 min. (1968). Olympic record: Lane (Australia) 2:25.2 min. (Paris 1900). New Olympic record: Wenden (Australia) 1:55.2 min.

Final	min.		min.
1. Michael Wenden, Australia	1:55.2	5. Alain Mosconi, France	1:59.1
2. DON SCHOLLANDER, USA	1:55.8	6. Robert Windle, Australia	2:00.9
3. JOHN NELSON, USA	1:58.1	7. S. Belits-Geiman, USSR	2:01.5
4. Ralph Hutton, Canada	1:58,6	8. STEVE RERYCH, USA	non-starter

The **400 meter freestyle** was considered a four-cornered competition involving Canada's Ralph Hutton, the world record holder; MIKE BURTON, the US distance freestyle ruler; Alain Mosconi of France and Guillermo Echevarria of the host nation. The Mexican champion, by having the 11th fastest time in the heats, failed to qualify for the final.

The final was distinctly a race between Hutton and BURTON with the Canadian turning after the first 100 meters a couple of strokes in front. But BURTON cut down this margin with dispatch and had a clear lead after 200 meters, which margin he tripled in the second half of the race to win handily.

Statistics: 36 participants from 20 countries. 6 heats. World record: Hutton (Canada) 4:06.5 min. (1968). Olympic record: SCHOLLANDER (USA) 4:12.2 min. (Tokyo 1964). Olympic record broken twice. New Olympic record: BURTON (USA) 4:09.0 min.

Final

	min.		min.
1. MIKE BURTON, USA	4:09.0	5. Graham White, Australia	4:16.7
2. Ralph Hutton, Canada	4:11.7	6. JOHN NELSON, USA	4:17.2
3. Alain Mosconi, France	4:13.3	7. Hans Fassnacht, W. Germany	4:18.1
4. Gregory Brough, Australia	4:15.9	8. BRENT BERK, USA	4:26.0

The **1,500 meter freestyle** was Echevarria's last stand, and he turned in a stunning 17:11.0 in the heats to be the second-fastest in an overall field of 21. He had broken the world record only a few weeks before the Games and he was "at home," even if BURTON had climaxed the US Olympic Trials with a fantastic record of 16:08.5 clocking to rock the world. In fact, because of the problems of altitude, Guillermo was unconcerned that both BURTON and his young teammate, JOHN KINSELLA, had bettered Echevarria's best—the US swimmers had done it at sea level.

But Mexico's dream of a second gold medal in swimming was not to come true. Guillermo led BURTON for the first 200 meters before the 21-year-old UCLA swimmer took over the lead for keeps. By the half-way mark JOHN KINSELLA had battled his way from fourth, to third to second which place he held, trailing BURTON by more than 18 seconds at the finish.

Statistics: 21 participants from 16 countries. 3 heats. World record: BURTON (USA) 16:08.5 min. (1968). Olympic record: Windle (Australia) 17:01.7 min. (Tokyo 1964). Olympic record: broken twice. New Olympic record: BURTON (USA) 16:38.9 min.

Final

	min.		min.
1. MIKE BURTON, USA	16:38.9	5. Ralph Hutton, Canada	17:15.6
2. JOHN KINSELLA, USA	16:57.3	6. Guillermo Echevarria, Mexico	17:36.4
3. Gregory Brough, Australia	17:04.7	7. Juan Alanis, Mexico	17:46.6
4. Graham White, Australia	17:08.0	8. JOHN NELSON, USA	18:05.1

The **100 meter breaststroke** was won by DONALD McKENZIE, USA, in Olympic record time. It marked the USA ascendancy in a style in which they have not felt really at home in the water. Thus far the USSR men and women swimmers had been the breaststroke specialists of the world, but no longer does this hold true. The Soviets had to be content with second, third and fifth places, as the winner was the only US breaststroker to qualify for the final.

Statistics: First time staged in the Olympic Games. 41 participants from 25 countries. 6 first round heats, 3 semi-finals. World record: Pankin (USSR) 1:06.2 min. (1968). First Olympic record: McKENZIE (USA) 1:07.7 min.

Final

	min.		min.
1. DON McKENZIE, USA	1:07.7	5. Yevgeny Mikhailov, USSR	1:08.4
2. Vladimir Kosinsky, USSR	1:08.0	6. Ian O'Brien, Australia	1:08.6
3. Nikolai Pankin, USSR	1:08.0	7. Alberto Forelli Lopez, Argentina	1:08.7
4. José Fiolo, Brazil	1:08.1	8. Egon Henninger, E. Germany	1:09.7

The **200 meter breaststroke** noise-wise was the highlight of the magnificent 33-event program in swimming and diving. The champion is Felipe Muñoz, Mexico's 17-year-old *wunderkind*. And what had been until then a sedate celebration of the Olympic Games now became a wonderful and glorious Mexican fiesta. Mexico had its first gold medal winner and all hell broke loose. It was a dramatic climax to this Festival of Sport, with Muñoz becoming a local legend in his own lifetime. In the last 50 meters he pulled away from Kosinsky of the Soviet Union and JOB of the USA, gliding through the water with graceful yet powerful strokes.

Statistics: 36 participants from 24 countries. 5 heats. World record: Kosinsky (USSR) 2:27.4 (1968). Olympic record: O'Brien (Australia) 2:27.8 min. (Tokyo 1964).

Final

	min.			min.
1. Felipe Muñoz, Mexico	2:28.7		5. Yevgeny Mikhailov, USSR	2:32.8
2. Vladimir Kosinsky, USSR	2:29.2		6. Egon Henninger, E. Germany ...	2:33.2
3. BRIAN JOB, USA	2:29.9		7. PHIL LONG, USA	2:33.6
4. Nikolai Pankin, USSR	2:30.3		8. Osamu Tsurumine, Japan	2:34.9

The **100 meter backstroke** proved that no one in the world is equal to Roland Matthes, 17-year-old East German and world record holder. Matthes seemed completely in control and is undoubtedly capable of even faster times if and when challenged.

Statistics: Last staged in Rome (1960). 37 participants from 26 countries. 6 first round heats, 2 semi-finals. World record: Matthes (E. Germany) 58.4 sec. (1967). Olympic record: Theile (Australia) 1:01.9 min. (Rome 1960). New Olympic record: Matthes (East Germany) 58.0 sec. (as swimmer of first leg of 4×100 metres medley).

Final

	min.			min.
1. Roland Matthes, E. Germany	0:58.7		5. Jim Shaw, Canada	1:01.4
2. CHARLES HICKCOX, USA	1:00.2		6. Bob Schoutsen, Holland	1:01.8
3. RONNIE MILLES, USA	1:00.5		7. Reinhard Blechert, W. Germany .	1:01.9
4. LARRY BARBIERE, USA	1:01.1		8. Franco del Campo, Italy	1:02.0

The **200 meter backstroke** witnessed Matthes winning his second gold medal, after posting the second best time to MITCHELL IVEY, USA, in the heats. In the final, IVEY and JACK HORSLEY, also USA, touched simultaneously at 100 meters, five yards ahead of Matthes. But the eventual winner turned on the speed in the final 50 meters to outrace IVEY and HORSLEY, who trailed in that order, with GARY HALL, USA, fourth.

Statistics: 30 participants from 21 countries. 5 heats. World record: Matthes (East Germany) 2:07.5 min. (1968). Olympic record: GRAEF (USA) 2:10.3 min. New Olympic record: Matthes (East Germany) 2:09.6 min.

Final

	min.			min.
1. Roland Matthes, E. Germany	2:09.6		5. Santiago Esteva, Spain	2:12.9
2. MITCHELL IVEY, USA	2:10.6		6. Leonid Dobroskokin, USSR	2:15.4
3. JACK HORSLEY, USA...........	2:10.9		7. Joachim Rother, E. Germany	2:15.8
4. GARY HALL, USA	2:12.6		8. Franco del Campo, Italy	2:16.5

The **100 meter butterfly** was a complete triumph for the USA, and, at the same time, a bitter pill for MARK SPITZ who—instead of the hoped-for gold—had to be satisfied with the silver medal. Those close to the US team had made it known that the magnificent Texan, DOUG RUSSELL, who nipped SPITZ at the tape, had been turning in fantastic times during the period of altitude training prior to the Olympic Games.

Statistics: First time event staged in the Olympic Games. 47 participants from 27 countries. 7 heats, 3 semi-finals. World record: SPITZ (USA) 55.6 sec. (1968). First Olympic record: RUSSELL (USA) 55.9 sec.

Final

	sec.			sec.
1. DOUG RUSSELL, USA	55.9		5. Satoshi Maruya, Japan	58.6
2. MARK SPITZ, USA	56.4		6. Yury Suzdaltsev, USSR	58.8
3. ROSS WALES, USA	57.2		7. Lutz Stocklasa, W. Germany	58.9
4. Vladimir Nemshilov, USSR	58.1		8. Robert Cusack, Australia	59.8

The **200 meter butterfly** which is SPITZ' real speciality (he is the world record holder in both 'fly events) showed conclusively that the 18-year-old swimmer was away off the form he had been expected to show in Mexico, where originally he was to have had an opportunity to win three individual gold medals and three more gold on winning US relay teams. In this race, SPITZ trailed the field as CARL ROBIE, US silver medalist at Tokyo, forged into an early lead and refused to relinquish his position at the head of the pack of eight swimmers. ROBIE, tied for fifth in the heats, was confident of his speed over the final 100 meters. Wanting to stay close to the pack at the end of two laps, he surprisingly found himself in the van and by the end of the race made up for his keen disappointment at finishing second in Tokyo. SPITZ faded to last.

Statistics: 29 participants from 18 countries. 5 heats. World record: SPITZ (USA) 2:05.7 min. (1967). Olympic record: Berry (Australia) 2:06.6 min. (Tokyo 1964).

Final	min.		min.
1. CARL ROBIE, USA	2:08.7	5. Lars Feil, Sweden	2:10.9
2. Martyn Woodroffe, Great Britain	2:09.0	6. Volkert Meeuw, W. Germany ...	2:11.5
3. JOHN FERRIS, USA	2:09.3	7. Viktor Sharygin, USSR	2:11.9
4. Valentin Kuzmin, USSR	2:10.6	8. MARK SPITZ, USA	2:13.5

The **200 meter individual medley** enriched the US medal tally by three, in order of value: HICK-COX, BUCKINGHAM and FERRIS. HICKCOX trailed his two teammates in qualifying times, but that didn't tell the story. The winner excelled in the backstroke and freestyle to clinch the gold in a race which saw FERRIS make his bid in the butterfly and then barely hold on until the finish, as BUCKING-HAM turned it on during the breaststroke.

Statistics: First time staged in the Olympic Games. 46 participants from 27 countries. 7 heats. World record: HICKCOX (USA) 2:10.6 min. (1968). First Olympic record: HICKCOX (USA) 2:12.0 min.

Final	min.		min.
1. CHARLES HICKCOX, USA	2:12.0	5. George Smith, Canada	2:15.9
2. GREG BUCKINGHAM, USA	2:13.0	6. Sandy Gilchrist, Canada	2:16.6
3. JOHN FERRIS, USA	2:13.3	7. Michael Holthaus, W. Germany ..	2:16.8
4. Juan Bello, Peru	2:13.7	8. Peter Lazar, Hungary	2:18.3

The **400 meter individual medley** provided the setting for a repeat performance by HICKCOX, aided and abetted by GARY HALL, another of the inexhaustible pool of US world-class swimmers. It was a stirring two-way battle with HALL holding a distinct lead after the backstroke leg, only to lose it during the breaststroke. Holthaus, West Germany, had the satisfaction of touching the finish line a fraction of a second ahead of BUCKINGHAM, USA, to prevent a second US sweep in the individual medley.

Statistics: 34 participants from 21 countries. 5 heats. World record: HICKCOX (USA) 4:39.0 min. (1968). Olympic record: ROTH (USA) 4:45.4 min. (Tokyo 1964).

Final	min.		min.
1. CHARLES HICKCOX, USA	4:48.4	5. Sandy Gilchrist, Canada	4:56.7
2. GARY HALL, USA	4:48.7	6. Reinhard Merkel, W. Germany ...	4:59.8
3. Michael Holthaus, W. Germany ..	4:51.4	7. Andrei Dunajev, USSR	5:00.3
4. GREG BUCKINGHAM, USA	4:51.4	8. Rafael Hernandez, Mexico	5:04.3

The **4x100 meter freestyle relay** was so clearly a US event that the race almost need not have taken place; the issue was never in doubt. The USA foursome was simply unbeatable in setting another world record in winning.

Statistics: 16 teams from 16 countries. 2 heats. World record: USA (ZORN, RERYCH, WALSH, SCHOLLANDER) 3:32.5 min. (1968). Olympic record: USA (CLARK, AUSTIN, ILMAN, SCHOLLANDER) 3:33.2 min. (Tokyo 1964). New world and Olympic record: USA (ZORN, RERYCH, SPITZ, WALSH) 3:31.7 min.

Final	min.		min.
1. USA (ZACHARY ZORN, STEVE RERYCH, KEN WALSH, MARK SPITZ)	3:31.7	5. East Germany	3:38.8
		6. West Germany	3:39.0
2. USSR	3:34.2	7. Canada	3:39.2
3. Australia	3:34.7	8. Japan	3:41.5
4. Great Britain	3:38.4		

The **4x200 meter freestyle relay** saw another US victory. The *connoisseurs* of fine swimming relished the fact that SPITZ was swimming third and SCHOLLANDER last. STEVE RERYCH gave SPITZ a solid 2.5-second lead over Australia's Windle (1964 Olympic Champion at 1,500 meters). Windle shaved the lead slightly but not frighteningly and SCHOLLANDER held off Mike Wenden, although the Australian swam two-tenths of a second faster in his quest for gold.

Statistics: 16 teams from 16 countries. 3 heats. Olympic and world record: USA (CLARK, SAARI, ILMAN, SCHOLLANDER) 7:52.1 min. (Tokyo 1964).

Final	min.		min.
1. USA (JOHN NELSON, STEVE RERYCH, MARK SPITZ, DON SCHOLLANDER)	7:52.3	4. Canada	8:03.2
		5. France	8:03.7
		6. West Germany................	8:04.3
2. Australia	7:53.7	7. East Germany	8:06.0
3. USSR	8:01.6	8. Sweden	8:12.1

The **4 x 100 meter medley relay** was swum and won by the US team of HICKCOX, MCKENZIE, RUSSELL and WALSH (the four best US 100-meter men in each of the strokes based on their performances in Mexico), in world-record time, upsetting the same East Germans who had set the world record the previous year. Matthes and Henninger in the backstroke and breaststroke gave the East Germans a lead at 200 meters, but it was wiped out by DOUG RUSSELL's splendid 55-second butterfly leg.

Statistics: 18 teams from 18 countries. 3 heats. World record: East Germany (Matthes, Henninger, Gregor, Wiegand) 3:56.5 min. (1967). Olympic record: USA (MANN, CRAIG, SCHMIDT, CLARK) 3:58.4 min. (Tokyo 1964). New Olympic and world record: USA (HICKCOX, MCKENZIE, RUSSELL, WALSH) 3:54.9 min.

Final

	min.			min.
1. USA (CHARLES HICKCOX, DON MCKENZIE, DOUG RUSSELL, KEN WALSH)	3:54.9		4. Australia	4:00.8
			5. Japan	4:01.8
			6. West Germany	4:05.4
2. East Germany	3:57.5		7. Canada	4:07.3
3. USSR	4:00.7		8. Spain	4:08.8

The **springboard diving** was distinguished by beautiful performances as BERNARD WRIGHTSON, USA, and Italy's Klaus Dibiasi dominated the large field. Although the latter led at the end of the preliminaries, WRIGHTSON, a 24-year-old enlisted man in the Navy, more than made up the difference on the second day as he excelled in his three voluntary dives to wipe out the early lead of his worthy opponent.

Statistics: 28 participants from 16 countries. The 12 competitors with the highest points in the first round heat qualified for the final.

Final

	1st round points	Total points
1. BERNIE WRIGHTSON, USA	102.95	170.15
2. Klaus Dibiasi, Italy	104.68	159.74
3. JIM HENRY, USA	105.47	158.09
4. Luis Niño de Rivera, Mexico	99.13	155.71
5. Franco Cagnotto, Italy	95.92	155.70
6. KEITH RUSSELL, USA	100.61	151.75

In the **platform diving** off the ten-meter tower, Italy's Dibiasi is without a peer. WIN YOUNG, USA, impressed everyone but the international judges who consistently scored Alvaro Gaxiola, Mexico, higher and the Mexican won the silver.

Statistics: 35 participants from 17 countries. The 12 competitors with the highest points in the first round heat qualified for the final.

Final

	1st round points	Total points
1. Klaus Dibiasi, Italy	108.04	164.18
2. Alvaro Gaxiola, Mexico	103.33	154.49
3. WIN YOUNG, USA	99.98	153.93
4. KEITH RUSSELL, USA	101.38	152.34
5. José Robinson, Mexico	91.16	143.62
6. Lothar Matthes, E. Germany	92.19	141.75

*Swimming -
Women*

The women's freestyle events were all won by US girls; and they won all four silver medals as well. Only twice in the bronze category did "foreigners" intrude—one Australian and one Mexican. The US mermaids seemed to be a race apart. It is true that the four-year-old world record of Dawn Fraser, Australia, in the 100 meters (58.9 sec.) remained intact. But it is rather doubtful whether the great Australian would have established the record in Mexico City! After 36 years of waiting the USA won a gold medal in the **100 meter freestyle** as JAN HENNE, 21, was clocked in exactly one minute, trailed by teammates SUE PEDERSEN and LINDA GUSTAVSON in an impressive USA sweep.

Statistics: 56 participants from 27 countries. 8 first round heats, 3 semi-finals. World record: Dawn Fraser (Australia) 58.9 sec. (1964). Olympic record: Dawn Fraser (Australia) 59.5 sec. (Tokyo 1964).

Final

	min.		min.
1. Jan Henne, USA	1:00.0	5. Martina Grunert, E. Germany ...	1:01.0
2. Susan Pedersen, USA	1:00.3	6. Alexandra Jackson, Great Britain .	1:01.0
3. Linda Gustavson, USA	1:00.3	7. Mirjana Segrt, Yugoslavia	1:01.5
4. Marion Lay, Canada	1:00.5	8. Judit Turoczy, Hungary	1:01.6

The **200, 400, 800, meter freestyle** could almost have been staged as a US championship race, except for the talented Karen Moras of Australia, and strong Maria Teresa Ramirez of Mexico. If Debbie Meyer caused raised eyebrows by failing to break her own world records, she caught the fancy of the real *cognoscenti* on the day she won the 200 meters after setting a brisk pace in the 800 meters heats in the morning following a fretful night beset with a horrible gastroenteritis attack that would have felled a less-dedicated swimmer. The bronze medal for Miss Ramirez in the 800 meters caused such excitement and enthusiasm among the knowledgeable Mexican swimming fans that visitors to the *Alberca* might have thought Maria Teresa finished first.

200 meter freestyle
Statistics: This is the first time this event has been held in the Olympics. 39 participants from 23 countries. 6 heats. World record: Debbie Meyer (USA) 2:06.7 min. (1968). First Olympic record: Debbie Meyer (USA) 2:10.5 min.

Final

	min.		min.
1. Debbie Meyer, USA	2:10.5	5. Mirjana Segrt, Yugoslavia	2:13.3
2. Jan Henne, USA	2:11.0	6. Claude Mandonnaud, France	2:14.9
3. Jane Barkman, USA	2:11.2	7. Lynnette Bell, Australia	2:15.1
4. Gabriele Wetzko, E. Germany ...	2:12.3	8. Olga Kozicova, Czechoslovakia ..	2:16.0

400 meter freestyle
Statistics: 30 participants from 17 countries. 6 heats. World record: Debbie Meyer (USA) 4:24.5 min. Olympic record: Virginia Duenkel (USA) 4:43.3 min. (Tokyo 1964). The Olympic record was broken nine times. New Olympic record: Debbie Meyer (USA) 4:31.8 min.

Final

	min.		min.
1. Debbie Meyer, USA	4:31.8	5. Gabriele Wetzko, E. Germany ...	4:40.2
2. Linda Gustavson, USA	4:35.5	6. Maria Teresa Ramirez, Mexico ...	4:42.2
3. Karen Moras, Australia	4:37.0	7. Angela Coughlaw, Canada	4:51.9
4. Pam Kruse, USA	4:37.2	8. Ingrid Morris, Sweden	4:53.8

800 meter freestyle
Statistics: First time staged in Olympic Games. 25 participants from 16 countries. 5 heats. World record: Debbie Meyer (USA) 9:10.4 min. (1968). First Olympic record: Debbie Meyer (USA) 9:24.0 min.

Final

	min.		min.
1. Debbie Meyer, USA	9:24.0	5. Patty Caretto, USA	9:51.3
2. Pamela Kruse, USA	9:35.7	6. Ann Coughlaw, Canada	9:56.4
3. Teresa Ramirez, Mexico	9:38.5	7. Denise Langford, Australia	9:56.7
4. Karen Moras, Australia	9:38.6	8. Laura Vaca, Mexico	10:02.5

The **100 and 200 meter backstroke** were consigned by many to Canada's "Mighty Mouse" and Pan-American Games' Champion, Elaine Tanner, in the absence of Karen Muir of South Africa, prevented from competing because her country was excluded from the Games.
Previous reputations mean little in Olympic competition. Kaye Hall, USA, chased Elaine to a world record in the 100 meters semi-final, then came back in the finals to whip her Canadian arch foe for the first time. This time the race was for gold and Kaye won all the way.

Statistics: 40 participants from 23 countries. 6 heats, 2 semi-finals. World record: Karen Muir (S. Africa) 1:06.4 min. (1968). Olympic record: Cathy Ferguson (USA) 1:07.7 min. (Tokyo 1964). World record broken once and Olympic record (including the results of the first swimmers in the 4×100 meters medley) was broken five times. New world and Olympic record: Kaye Hall (USA) 1:06.2 min.

Final

	min.		min.
1. Kaye Hall, USA	1:06.2	5. Andrea Gyarmati, Hungary	1:09.1
2. Elaine Tanner, Canada	1:06.7	6. Lynette Watson, Australia	1:09.1
3. Jane Swagerty, USA	1:08.1	7. Sylvie Canet, France	1:09.8
4. Kendis Moore, USA	1:08.3	8. Glenda Stirling, N. Zealand	1:10.6

The 200 meters was perhaps a surprise to everyone but the US coaches. POKEY WATSON, four years older than when she won a gold medal at 14 as a member of a winning free style relay team, was the top US entrant in the longer backstroke event. She had staked her claim by turning in the fastest time in the heats. However, in the final Elaine Tanner struck out fast, led at 100 meters but was overtaken by the powerfully stroking Pokey before the final turn. The winning time of Miss WATSON was within five-tenths of a second of her winning time in the sea-level US Olympic Trials.

200 meter backstroke
Statistics: First time event staged in the Olympic Games. 30 participants from 19 countries. 5 heats. World record: Karen Muir (South Africa) 2:23.8 min. (1968). First Olympic record: POKEY WATSON (USA) 2:24.8 min.

Final	min.		min.
1. POKEY WATSON, USA	2:24.8	5. Wendy Burrell, Great Britain	2:32.3
2. Elaine Tanner, Canada	2:27.4	6. Zdenka Gasparak, Yugoslavia	2:33.5
3. KAYE HALL, USA	2:28.9	7. Maria Corominas, Spain	2:33.9
4. Lynette Watson, Australia	2:29.5	8. Benedicte Duprez, France	2:36.6

The **100 and 200 meter breaststroke** produced the most surprising results in the women's competition. Djurdjica Bjedov, 21-year-old Yugoslavian swimmer, upset all pre-race prognostications by outswimming the Soviet's monumentally-built champion and former world record holder, Galina Prozumenshikova. The US world record holder, CATIE BALL, installed as the favorite on the basis of a fine comeback had only the seventh fastest time in the heats, was placed second to the Uruguayan champion and record holder, Ana Maria Norbis, in the semi-finals and then slumped to fifth place in the final. Miss BALL withdrew from the 200 meter breaststroke.

100 meter breaststroke
Statistics: First time event staged in the Olympic Games. 33 participants from 20 countries. 5 heats, 2 semi-finals. World record: CATIE BALL (USA) 1:14.2 min. (1968). First Olympic record: Djurdjica Bjedov (Yugoslavia) 1:15.8 min.

Final	min.		min.
1. Djurdjica Bjedov, Yugoslavia	1:15.8	5. CATIE BALL, USA	1:16.7
2. Galina Prozumenshikova, USSR	1:15.9	6. Kiyoe Nakagawa, Japan	1:17.0
3. SHARON WICHMAN, USA	1:16.1	7. Svetlana Babanina, USSR	1:17.2
4. Uta Frommater, W. Germany	1:16.2	8. Ana Maria Norbis, Uruguay	1:17.3

Drama was packed into the final of the **200 meter breaststroke** which looked like a rematch of the 100 meters — Bjedov, Prozumenshikova and the 16-year-old US entry, SHARON WICHMAN. At the end of the first 100 meters the Soviet champion held a slight lead over Miss WICHMAN, with the Yugoslav third. It was on the second 100 meters that Galina slumped and was three seconds slower than Miss WICHMAN, fading to third, as WICHMAN erased two full seconds from Miss Prozumenshikova's Olympic record at Tokyo. Galina was totally exhausted at the end of the race and oxygen was administered by a fast-thinking medical doctor in attendance.

200 meter breaststroke
Statistics: 30 participants from 19 countries. 5 heats. World record: CATIE BALL (USA) 2:38.5 min. (1968). Olympic record: Galina Prozumenshikova (USSR) 2:46.4 min. Olympic record once broken, once equalled. New Olympic record: SHARON WICHMAN (USA) 2:44.4 min.

Final	min.		min.
1. SHARON WICHMAN, USA	2:44.4	5. CATHY JAMISON, USA	2:48.4
2. Djurdjica Bjedov, Yugoslavia	2:46.4	6. Svetlana Babanina, USSR	2:48.4
3. Galina Prozumenshikova, USSR	2:47.0	7. Chieno Shibata, Japan	2:51.5
4. Alla Grebennikova, USSR	2:47.1	8. Ana Maria Norbis, Uruguay	2:51.9

The **100 and 200 meter butterfly** events predictably would pit the world record holder Miss Ada Kok of the Netherlands against ELEANOR DANIEL, USA. However, in the 100 meters Lynn McClements, Australia, swam home first as Miss DANIEL and others duelled Miss Kok oblivious of Lynn. Ellie won a silver and Ada was relegated to fourth.

100 meter butterfly
Statistics: 28 participants from 21 countries, 5 heats, 2 semi-finals. World record: Ada Kok (Netherlands) 1:04.5 min. (1965). Olympic record: SHARON STOUDER (USA) 1:04.7 min. (Tokyo 1964).

Final		min.			min.
1. Lynette McClements, Australia ...		1:05.5	5. Andrea Gyarmati, Hungary		1:06.8
2. ELLIE DANIEL, USA		1:05.8	6. Heike Hustede, W. Germany		1:06.9
3. SUSIE SHIELDS, USA		1:06.2	7. TONI HEWITT, USA		1:07.5
4. Ada Kok, Netherlands		1:06.2	8. Helga Lindner, E. Germany......		1:07.6

But in the longer butterfly event the Dutch secretary proved without a doubt she is entitled to her laurels. Helga Lindner, East Germany, was a surprise silver medalist—swimming in second place the entire race while the others jockeyed back and forth before Miss Kok exerted her superiority.

200 meter butterfly
Statistics: First time event staged in the Olympic Games. 21 participants from 16 countries. 4 heats. World record: Ada Kok (Netherlands) 2:21.0 min. (1967). First Olympic record: Ada Kok 2:24.7min.

Final		min.			min.
1. Ada Kok, Netherlands		2:24.7	5. Heike Hustede, W. Germany		2:27.9
2. Helga Lindner, E. Germany		2:24.8	6. DIANE GIEBEL, USA		2:31.7
3. ELLIE DANIEL, USA		2:25.9	7. Margaret Auton, Great Britain ...		2:33.2
4. TONI HEWITT, USA		2:26.2	8. Yasuko Fujii, Japan		2:34.3

The **200 and 400 meter individual medley** races were both won by CLAUDIA KOLB, USA. For no one can contest her towering supremacy as the world's best all-around women's swimmer. For the last three years she has been the world's most versatile swimmer and the logical successor to DONNA DE VARONA, 1964 Olympic champion at 200 meters. Claudia is supreme in all four strokes and in the longer race demonstrates her strength and power which leaves all opponents trailing far behind in her wake. The USA took five of the six medals in these two races with Sabine Steinbach, East Germany, edging out SUE PEDERSEN for the bronze medal in the longer race.

200 meter medley
Statistics: First time staged in the Olympic Games. 38 participants from 26 countries. 6 heats. World record: CLAUDIA KOLB (USA) 2:23.5 min. (1968). First Olympic record: CLAUDIA KOLB (USA) 2:24.7 min.

Final		min.			min.
1. CLAUDIA KOLB, USA		2:24.7	5. Yoshimi Nishigawa, Japan		2:33.7
2. SUSAN PEDERSEN, USA		2:28.8	6. Marianne Seydel, E. Germany ...		2:33.7
3. JAN HENNE, USA		2:31.4	7. Larisa Zakharova, USSR		2:37.0
4. Sabine Steinbach, E. Germany ...		2:31.4	8. Shelagh Ratcliffe, Great Britain		disqualified

400 meter medley
Statistics: 27 participants from 17 countries. 5 heats. World record: CLAUDIA KOLB (USA) 5:04.7 min. (1968). Olympic record: DONNA DE VARONA (USA) 5:18.7 min. (Tokyo 1964). Olympic record broken twice. New Olympic record: CLAUDIA KOLB (USA) 5:08.5 min.

Final		min.			min.
1. CLAUDIA KOLB, USA		5:08.5	5. Shelagh Ratcliffe, Great Britain ..		5:30.5
2. LYNN VIDALI, USA		5:22.2	6. Marianne Seydel, E. Germany ...		5:32.0
3. Sabine Steinbach, E. Germany ...		5:25.3	7. Tui Shipston, N. Zealand		5:34.6
4. SUE PEDERSEN, USA		5:25.8	8. Laura Vaca, Mexico		5:35.7

The **4 x 100 freestyle relay** and **4 x 100 medley relay** were both won by the USA. Somewhat surprising was the foursome in the freestyle relay failing to eclipse the listed world mark set by the Santa Clara Swim Club, USA, in 1968. However, on the opening day of the swimming competition, the medley relay foursome of KAYE HALL, CATIE BALL, ELLIE DANIEL and SUE PEDERSEN (the latter had celebrated her 15th birthday the previous day) were pushed to a world record to defeat Australia, although the US swimmers enjoyed only a small lead at the end of each leg of the relay.

4 x 100 meter freestyle
Statistics: 15 teams from 15 countries. 3 heats. World record: USA (JAN HENNE, SUE CARPINELLI, POKEY WATSON, LINDA GUSTAVSON) 4:01.0 min. (1968). Olympic record: USA (SHARON STOUDER, DONNA DE VARONA, POKEY WATSON, KATHLEEN ELLIS) 4:03.8 min. (Tokyo 1964). Olympic record broken once. New Olympic record: USA (JANE BARKMAN, LINDA GUSTAVSON, SUSAN PEDERSEN, JAN HENNE) 4:02.5 min.

	min.			min.
1. USA (JANE BARKMAN, LINDA GUSTAVSON, SUSAN PEDERSEN, JAN HENNE)	4:02.5		4. Australia	4:08.7
			5. Hungary	4:11.0
			6. Japan	4:13.6
2. East Germany	4:05.7		7. Great Britain	4:18.0
3. Canada	4:07.2		France	disqualified

4×100 meter medley

Statistics: 16 teams from 16 countries. 2 heats. World record: USA 4:30.0 min. (1967). Olympic record: USA (CATHY FERGUSON, CYNTHIA GOYETTE, SHARON STOUDER, KLENA BIMDT) 4:33.9 min. (Tokyo 1964). New Olympic and world record: USA (KAYE HALL, CATIE BALL, ELLIE DANIEL, SUE PEDERSEN) 4:28.3 min.

Final

	min.			min.
1. USA (KAYE HALL, CATIE BALL, ELLIE DANIEL, SUE PEDERSEN)	4:28.3		5. East Germany	4:38.0
2. Australia	4:30.0		6. Great Britain	4:38.3
3. West Germany	4:36.4		7. Netherlands	4:38.7
4. USSR	4:37.0		8. Hungary	4:42.8

The **springboard** contest produced the highest quality of diving ever seen in the Olympic Games. SUE GOSSICK and her two USA teammates finished in the top four. Miss GOSSICK, fourth at Tokyo, performed at her very best as an experienced and confident internationalist. She fully deserved the plaudits of the spectators and the high scores from the judges. The young Hawaiian, KEALA O'SULLIVAN, enthralled the spectators with the sheer beauty of her diving, and placed third.

Statistics: 22 participants from 15 countries. The 12 with the highest points qualified for the final.

	1st round points	Total points
1. SUE GOSSICK, USA	97.32	150.77
2. Tamara Pogozheva, USSR	97.50	145.30
3. KEALA O'SULLIVAN, USA	95.58	145.23
4. MICKI KING, USA	98.17	137.38
5. Ingrid Kramer-Gulbin, E. Germany	90.56	135.82
6. Vera Baklanova, USSR	88.89	132.31

The **platform diving** had in the 17-year-old Czechoslovakian girl, Milena Duchkova, a very popular winner. Whatever she attempted, she succeeded. Presenting a striking appearance on the 30-foot tower in her bold patterned swim suit, Milena appeared to be in a class by herself. A miscue on the first dive of the preliminary round all but eliminated defending champion. LESLEY BUSH, USA, who never fully recovered and failed to make the cut-off for the finals. ANN PETERSON and BARBARA TALMADGE failed to display the same exciting dives exhibited in the Olympic Trials and Ann was relegated to third place, trailing Miss Duchkova and Natalia Lobanova, USSR.

Statistics: 24 participants from 15 countries. The 12 with the highest points qualified for the final.

	1st round points	Total points
1. Milena Duchkova, Czechoslovakia	55.25	109.59
2. Natalia Lobanova, USSR	55.24	105.14
3. ANN PETERSON, USA	54.06	101.11
4. Beverley Boys, Canada	53.20	97.97
5. Boguslawa Pietkiewicz, Poland	49.76	95.28
6. Regina Krause, W. Germany	49.70	93.08
6. Keiko Ohsaki, Japan	47.77	93.08

Volleyball

Invented in 1895 by William G. Morgan, a YMCA physical education instructor in Holyoke, Massachusetts, volleyball did not become an Olympic sport until 1964. Seldom has a "new" game been accepted so readily, and in Mexico City, the tournament hall was always packed by enthusiastic crowds.

That the Soviet Union and Japan possess the world's strongest teams was well-known before the 1968 Games began, and Mexico City certainly confirmed this fact. The Russian team was considerably older than the Japanese, but this proved to be more of an advantage than a hindrance. Experience and physical strength seem to count more in this sport than youthful agility. However, the margin between the two nations was slim, and their positions may well become reversed in the near future.

The greatest upset in the tournament was the USA's totally unexpected victory over Russia by a score of two sets to one. It jolted the Soviet team out of any complacency they might have harbored; after that, they were always on their toes, they tightened up their defense and intensified their interchanging attack. They lost no more matches. But the USA's remarkable victory over the world's No. 1 team will serve as a filip for the future. If they continue to intensify their efforts, there is no reason why the USA shouldn't be able to become a power in the sport. As it was, they finished seventh, after Russia and Japan and four Eastern European teams. As for the ladies' competition, the USSR and Japan again dominated, with Peru breaking the Eastern monopoly by finishing fourth.

Men

Statistics: 10 teams from 10 nations. The participants qualified from the results of the 1964 Tokyo Olympic Games and the 1967 world championship, as well as continental elimination rounds. The final placing was established on the round-robin system, with each team playing every other team 1 time.

Final Standing	Games		Sets		Total		Games		Sets		Total
	W.	L.	W.	L.	Pts.		W.	L.	W.	L.	Pts.
1. Soviet Union	8	1	26	8	17	6. Bulgaria	4	5	16	17	13
2. Japan	7	2	24	6	16	7. USA	4	5	15	18	13
3. Czechoslovakia ..	7	2	22	15	16	8. Belgium	2	7	6	24	11
4. East Germany ...	6	3	22	12	15	9. Brazil	1	8	8	25	10
5. Poland	6	3	18	11	15	10. Mexico	0	9	5	21	9

Scores

Soviet Union defeated East Germany 3–2, Belgium 3–0, Brazil 3–1, Bulgaria 3–0, Czechoslovakia 3–0, Japan 3–1, Mexico 3–1 and Poland 3–0.

Japan defeated East Germany 3–0, Belgium 3–0, Brazil 3–0, Bulgaria 3–0, USA 3–0, Mexico 3–0 and Poland 3–0.

Czechoslovakia defeated East Germany 3–2, Belgium 3–0, Bulgaria 3–2, USA 3–1, Brazil 3–2, Japan 3–2 and Mexico 3–0.

East Germany defeated Belgium 3–0, Brazil 3–1, Bulgaria 3–2, USA 3–0, Mexico 3–0 and Poland 3–0.

Poland defeated Belgium 3–0, Brazil 3–0, Bulgaria 3–0, Czechoslovakia 3–1, USA 3–0 and Mexico 3–1.

Bulgaria defeated Belgium 3–0, Brazil 3–0, USA 3–2 and Mexico 3–0.

USA defeated Belgium 3–0, Brazil 3–0, Mexico 3–1 and Soviet Union 3–2.

Belgium defeated Brazil 3–1 and Mexico 3–2.

Brazil defeated Mexico 3–1.

Women

Statistics: 8 teams from 8 nations. The participants qualified from the results of the 1964 Tokyo Olympic Games and the 1967 world championship, as well as continental elimination rounds. The final placing was established on the round-robin system, with each team playing every other team 1 time.

Final Standing	Games		Sets		Total		Games		Sets		Total
	W.	L.	W.	L.	Pts.		W.	L.	W.	L.	Pts.
1. Soviet Union	7	0	21	3	14	5. South Korea	3	4	11	14	10
2. Japan	6	1	19	3	13	6. Czechoslovakia ..	3	4	11	15	10
3. Poland	5	2	15	11	12	7. Mexico	1	6	7	18	8
4. Peru	3	4	12	15	10	8. USA	0	7	3	21	7

Scores

Soviet Union defeated South Korea 3–0, Czechoslovakia 3–1, USA 3–1, Japan 3–1, Mexico 3–0, Peru 3–0 and Poland 3–0.

Japan defeated South Korea 3–0, Czechoslovakia 3–0, USA 3–0, Mexico 3–0, Peru 3–0 and Poland 3–0.

Poland defeated South Korea 3–2, Czechoslovakia 3–0, USA 3–0, Mexico 3–2 and Peru 3–1.

Peru defeated South Korea 3–0, USA 3–1 and Mexico 3–2.

South Korea defeated Czechoslovakia 3–1, USA 3–1 and Mexico 3–0.

Czechoslovakia defeated USA 3–1, Mexico 3–0 and Peru 3–2.

Mexico defeated USA 3–0.

Water Polo

This tournament may not have been one of the spectacles attracting large crowds during its 72 games, but those who understand the sport can attest that the Olympic Games have never had more thrilling games, nor a more stirring finish than when Yugoslavia won the gold medal by defeating the Soviet Union in overtime. Hungary, the defending champion, grabbed off the bronze with a victory over Italy.

It has been reported many times that the games were marked by continuous calls of rules infractions, some of them justified and others perhaps imaginary or illusory, and too many of the goals were the direct result of penalty throws. These factors may have detracted from the overall attractiveness of a burgeoning sport which is dominated by Eastern Europe.

The USA moved up from the second division four years ago to earn fifth place among 16 nations. A team that had been playing together for two years and had won the Pan-American Games titles the previous year, beyond any question, was the finest team ever to represent the USA in the Olympic Games.

After tying Cuba for third place, the USA moved into a play-off for fifth place against the Netherlands, scoring a narrow 6–5 triumph and advancing to meet East Germany. After a close first half, the USA forged ahead on two goals by BARRY WEIZENBERG and won the contest 6–4 to clinch fifth place.

The deciding game for the title will long be remembered. Barkalov of the Soviet Union scored seven of his team's 11 goals in regulation time. However in the over-time Marovic scored two quick goals against the Soviets and nothing came within the purview of referee Abe Fuchs of Belgium (the most authoritative among the international arbiters) to cause any radical change in the scoring patterns with penalty throws. The final score was 13–11, Yugoslavia.

Statistics: 15 teams from 16 countries. First round: 2 groups (A–7, B–8). The 2 teams that came 1st and 2nd qualified for the semi-final, the winners then qualified for the final; the losers competed against one another to decide 3rd and 4th places.

Group A Eliminations	W.	L.	T.	Pts.	Group B Eliminations	W.	L.	T.	Pts.
1. Hungary	6	0	0	12	1. Italy	6	0	1	13
2. Soviet Union	5	1	0	10	2. Yugoslavia	5	1	1	11
3. USA	3	2	1	7	3. East Germany	5	1	1	11
4. Cuba	3	2	1	7	4. Netherlands	4	2	1	9
5. West Germany	2	4	0	4	5. Japan	3	4	0	6
6. Spain	0	5	1	1	6. Mexico	1	5	1	3
7. Brazil	0	5	1	1	7. Greece	1	6	0	2
					8. U.A.R.	0	6	1	1

Playoffs

1st–4th Places
Semi-final—Yugoslavia 8, Hungary 6.
Semi-final—Soviet Union 8, Italy 5.
1st—Yugoslavia 13, USSR 11.
3rd—Hungary 9, Italy 4.

5th–8th Places
Semi-final—USA 6, Netherlands 3.
Semi-final—East Germany 8, Cuba 2.
5th—USA 6, East Germany 4.
7th—Netherlands 8, Cuba 5.

9th–12th Places
Semi-final—Spain 5, Japan 0.
Semi-final—West Germany 6, Mexico 3.
9th—Spain 7, West Germany 5.
11th—Mexico 5, Japan 4.

13th–15th Places
Semi-final—Brazil 5, U.A.R. 3.
13th—Brazil 5, Greece 2.

Final Placings

1. Yugoslavia	5. USA	9. Spain	13. Brazil
2. Soviet Union	6. East Germany	10. West Germany	14. Greece
3. Hungary	7. Netherlands	11. Mexico	15. U.A.R.
4. Italy	8. Cuba	12. Japan	

In the weightlifting competition, conducted in the picturesque but inadequately small (1,200 capacity) "Teatro de los Insurgentes," it is doubtful if the colorful outside Riviera mural was as colorful as the lifters in the competition inside the theatre. Olympic records were established in five of the seven classes.

The Soviet Union continued to dominate the lifting by capturing three gold and three silver medals none the less "embarrassing" those persons who had predicted medals for all seven Soviet lifters selected for the competition. The exception occurred when the world record holding bantamweight finished fourth. The remaining gold medals were captured by Poland, Finland, Iran and Japan—one each. The bantamweight class on opening day set the pattern for the remaining six days of competition. Gennady Chetin, USSR, the world record holder, fell behind his foes in the press and never caught up as the battle was between Imre Foldi, Hungary, silver medalist at Tokyo, and Mohammad Nassiri, Iran. Foldi took a 22-pound lead in the press, held Nassiri even in the snatch and then the Iranian bounced back in the clean and jerk by lifting 22 pounds more than Foldi to equalize the total lift. However when they stepped on the scales to resolve the contest, Foldi was the lighter of the two and under international rules was awarded the gold medal.

The only lifters to repeat their successes at Tokyo were: Yoshinobu Miyake, Japan, bantamweight; Waldemar Baszanowski, Poland, lightweight; and the Soviet's parade standard bearer in 1964 and 1968, Leonid Zhabotinsky. The huge heavyweight was not pressed during his competition and didn't reach his 1964 winning total of 1,272.5 pounds, but still maintained a 38.5-pound edge over silver medalist Serge Reding, Belgium.

In the heavyweight class, where the battle was strictly for second place, JOE DUBE, USA, actually tied Reding for second, but DUBE weighed well over 300 pounds and yielded the silver medal on the scales. Perhaps the best competition in the seven days of lifting resulted from the head-to-head confrontation of a pair of Soviet athletes, Vladimir Belyaev and Boris Selitsky. Vladimir had a 5.5-pound edge in the press, the two had the same lift in the snatch, while Selitsky came through with a 5.5-pound better lift in the clean and jerk to deadlock Belyaev for total weight. On the scales, Selitsky weighed eight ounces less and captured the gold medal accordingly.

Statistics: 160 competitors from 54 nations. 7 weight classes: Bantam up to 56 kg. Feather up to 60 kg· Light up to 67.5 kg. Middle up to 75 kg. Light-heavy up to 82.5 kg. Middle-heavy up to 90 kg· Heavy over 90 kg. In all weight-classes: three disciplines, consisting of the press, snatch and jerk, each one with both hands. Where the same total was reached, the competitor's weight decided the order of placings.

Bantamweight

Statistics: 20 competitors from 19 nations. World record: Chetin (USSR) 367.5 kg (1968). Olympic record: Vakkonin (USSR) 357.5 kg (Tokyo 1964). The Olympic record was twice broken. New Olympic record: Nassiri (Iran) and Foldi (Hungary) 367.5 kg.

Results	Press	Snatch	Jerk	Total lbs.	kg
1. Mohammad Nassiri, Iran*	247.5	231.0	330.0	808.5	(367.5)
2. Imre Foldi, Hungary	269.5	231.0	308.0	808.5	(367.5)
3. Henryk Trebicki, Poland	253.0	236.5	297.0	786.5	(357.5)
4. G. Chetin, USSR	242.0	225.5	308.0	775.5	(352.5)
5. Shiro Ichinoseki, Japan	242.0	236.5	291.5	770.0	(350.0)
6. Fernando Baez, Puerto Rico	264.0	203.5	291.5	759.0	(345.0)

*Nassiri won first place because he weighed less than Foldi, 122.5 pounds to 123.2.

Featherweight

Statistics: 28 competitors from 22 nations. World record: Yoshinobu Miyake (Japan) 397.5 kg (1964). Olympic record: Yoshinobu Miyake (Japan) 397.5 kg (Tokyo 1964).

Results	Press	Snatch	Jerk	Total lbs.	kg
1. Yoshinobu Miyake, Japan	269.5	258.5	335.5	863.5	(392.5)
2. Dito Shanidze, USSR	264.0	258.5	330.0	852.5	(387.5)
3. Yoshiyuki Miyake, Japan	269.5	253.0	324.5	847.0	(385.0)
4. Jan Wojnowski, Poland	258.5	253.0	330.0	841.5	(382.5)
5. Mieczyslaw Nowak, Poland	258.5	253.0	324.5	825.0	(375.0)
6. Nasrolla Dehnavi, Iran	258.5	236.5	308.0	803.0	(365.0)

Lightweight

Statistics: 20 competitors from 17 nations. World record: Baszanowski (Poland) 440 kg. (1967). Olympic record: Baszanowski (Poland) and Kaplunov (USSR) 432.5 kg (Tokyo 1964). The Olympic record was once broken. New Olympic record: Baszanowski (Poland) 437.5 kg.

Results	Press	Snatch	Jerk	Total lbs.	kg
1. Waldemar Baszanowski, Poland	297.0	297.0	368.5	962.5	(437.5)
2. Parviz Jalayer, Iran	275.0	291.5	363.0	929.5	(422.5)
3. Marian Zielinski, Poland	297.0	275.0	352.0	924.0	(420.0)
4. Nobuyuki Hatta, Japan	297.0	280.0	341.0	918.5	(417.5)
5. Shin Hee Won, South Korea	280.5	275.0	357.5	913.0	(415.0)
6. Janos Bagocs, Hungary	291.5	269.5	346.5	907.5	(412.5)

Middleweight

Statistics: 20 competitors from 17 nations. World record: Kurentsov (USSR) 482.5 kg (1968). Olympic record: Zdrazila (Czechoslovakia) 445.0 kg (Tokyo 1964). The Olympic record was twice broken. New Olympic record: Kurentsov (USSR) 475.0 kg.

Results	Press	Snatch	Jerk	Total lbs.	kg
1. Viktor Kurentsov, USSR	335.5	297.0	412.5	1,045.0	(475.0)
2. Masashi Ohuchi, Japan	308.0	308.0	385.0	1,001.0	(455.0)
3. Karoly Bakos, Hungary	302.5	291.5	374.0	968.0	(440.0)
4. RUSSELL KNIPP, USA	324.5	269.5	368.5	962.5	(437.5)
5. Chun Lee, South Korea	308.0	291.5	363.0	962.5	(437.5)
6. Werner Dittrich, E. Germany	308.0	286.0	363.0	957.0	(435.0)

Light-Heavyweight

Statistics: 26 competitors from 22 nations. World record: Belyaev (USSR) 485.0 kg (1966); Olympic record: Plyukfelder (USSR) 474.0 kg (Tokyo 1964). The Olympic record was twice broken. New Olympic record: Selitsky and Belyaev (USSR) 485.0 kg.

Results	Press	Snatch	Jerk	Total lbs.	kg
1. Boris Selitsky, USSR*	330.0	324.5	412.5	1,067.0	(485.0)
2. Vladimir Belyaev, USSR	335.5	324.5	407.0	1,067.0	(485.0)
3. Norbert Ozimek, Poland	330.0	308.0	401.5	1,039.5	(472.5)
4. Gyozo Veres, Hungary	330.0	308.0	401.5	1,039.5	(472.5)
5. Karl Arnold, E. Germany	341.0	302.5	385.0	1,028.5	(467.5)
6. Hans Zdrazila, Czechoslovakia	297.0	324.5	396.0	1,017.5	(462.5)

*Selitsky won first place because he weighed less than Belyaev, 179.3 pounds to 180.

Middle-Heavyweight

Statistics: 29 competitors from 21 nations. World record: Kangasniemi (Finland) 522.5 kg (1968). Olympic record: Golovanov (USSR) 487.5 kg (Tokyo 1964). The Olympic record was broken four times. New Olympic record: Kangasniemi (Finland) 517.5 kg.

Results	Press	Snatch	Jerk	Total lbs.	kg
1. Kaarlo Kangasniemi, Finland	379.5	347.5	412.5	1,138.5	(517.5)
2. Jan Talts, USSR	352.0	330.0	434.5	1,116.5	(507.5)
3. Narek Golab, Poland	363.0	319.0	407.0	1,089.0	(495.0)
4. Bo Johansson, Sweden	363.0	319.0	401.5	1,083.5	(492.5)
5. Jaakko Kailajarvi, Finland	319.0	330.0	418.0	1,067.0	(485.0)
6. Arpad Nemessany, Hungary	330.0	319.0	412.5	1,061.5	(482.5)

Heavyweight

Statistics: 17 competitors from 14 nations. World record: Zhabotinsky (USSR) 590.0 kg (1967). Olympic record: Zhabotinsky (USSR) 572.5 kg (Tokyo 1964).

Results	Press	Snatch	Jerk	Total lbs.	kg
1. Leonid Zhabotinsky, USSR	440.0	374.0	445.5	1,259.5	(572.5)
2. Serge Reding, Belgium	429.0	324.5	467.5	1,221.0	(555.0)
3. JOE DUBE, USA	440.0	319.0	462.0	1,221.0	(555.0)
4. Manfred Rieger, E. Germany	385.0	341.0	445.5	1,171.5	(532.5)
5. Rudolf Mang, W. Germany	390.5	335.5	429.0	1,155.0	(525.0)
6. Mauno Lindroos, Finland	346.5	319.0	423.5	1,089.0	(495.0)

The Free-Style and Greco-Roman tournaments were held in the Pista de Hielo, Mexico City's Ice Skating Rink. A quick look at the overall results points up clearly that wrestling is dominated by the Eastern grapplers, only four of 24 medal winners in the Free-Style belonging to the West.

It seems that Japan truly established itself in Mexico City (after success in the lighter weights at the Tokyo Olympic Games) as the world's Number One wrestling nation with gold medals in the three lightest weight classes.

At Mexico the wrestlers from Mongolia proved the biggest surprise. Their invasion of the West was successful, attested to by four medals in Free-Style. The world clearly will hear more about them in the future. As for the Turks, formerly the world specialists in wrestling, their decline (begun in Tokyo) continued. This time one can fairly talk of an eclipse since they didn't win a single medal in Greco-Roman and only posted two champions among the eight winners in the Free-Style.

The single earth-moving match of the Free-Style appeared to be the fifth round heavyweight match bringing together Aleksandr Medved, USSR (light heavyweight champion in 1964) and West Germany's Wilfried Dietrich (1960 heavyweight champion). In a matter of seconds it was all over. Dietrich suffered a recurrence of a leg injury, the referee stopped the bout. Dietrich was out of the tournament, and Medved had no more worlds to conquer. In winning the gold medal Medved accumulated one "black mark," a decision victory over Bulgaria's Douraliev (eventually the silver medalist), which marred his offensive wrestling record of felling every opponent.

The USA won two silver medals: DICK SANDERS, flyweight, and DONALD BEHM, bantamweight.

Statistics: In the Free-Style Wrestling: 164 competitors from 38 nations. In the Greco-Roman Wrestling: 179 competitors from 37 nations. In both types: 8 weight class divisions: Flyweight up to 52 kg; Bantam up to 57 kg; Feather up to 63 kg; Light up to 70 kg; Welter up to 78 kg; Middle up to 87 kg; Lightheavy up to 97 kg; Heavy 97 kg or over. In each round wrestlers with 6 bad points or more were eliminated. Victory by fall – 0 bad points. Decision on points – 1 bad point. Draw – 2 bad points. Defeat on points – 3 bad points. Fall – 4 bad points.

Free-Style Wrestling

Flyweight   23 competitors from 23 nations.

1. Shigeo Nakata, Japan
2. RICHARD SANDERS, USA
3. Surenjan Sukhbaatar, Mongolia
4. Nazar Albarian, USSR
5. Vincenzo Grassi, Italy
6. Sudesh Kumar, India

Bantamweight   21 competitors from 21 nations.

1. Yojiro Uetake, Japan
2. DONALD BEHM, USA
3. Abutaleb Gorgoni, Iran
4. Ali Aliev, USSR
5. Ivan Chavov, Bulgaria
6. Zbigniew Zedzicki, Poland

Featherweight   27 competitors from 27 nations.

1. Masaaki Kaneko, Japan
2. Enio Todorov, Bulgaria
3. Shamseddin Abassy, Iran
4. Nikolaos Karypidis, Greece
5. Petre Coman, Rumania
6. Elkan Tedeev, USSR

Lightweight   26 competitors from 26 nations.

1. Abdollah Movahed, Iran
2. Enio Valtchev, Bulgaria
3. Sereeter Danzandarjaa, Mongolia
4. WAYNE WELLS, USA
5. Zarbeg Beriashvili, USSR
6. Udev Chand, India

Welterweight   19 competitors from 19 nations.

1. Mahmud Atalay, Turkey
2. Daniel Robin, France
3. Dagvasuren Purev, Mongolia
4. Ali-Mohammed Momeni, Iran
5. Tatsuo Sasaki, Japan
6. Yury Shakhmuradov, USSR

Middleweight   22 competitors from 22 nations.

1. Boris Gurevitch, USSR
2. Munkhbat Jigjid, Mongolia
3. Prodane Gardjev, Bulgaria
4. THOMAS PECKHAM, USA
5. Huseyin Gursoy, Turkey
6. Peter Döring, E. Germany

Light-Heavyweight 16 competitors from 16 nations.

1. Ahmet Ayuk, Turkey
2. Shota Lomidze, USSR
3. Joszef Csatari, Hungary
4. Said Moustafov, Bulgaria
5. Bayanmunk Khorloogyn, Mongolia
6. JESS LEWIS, USA

Heavyweight 14 competitors from 14 nations.

1. Aleksandr Medved, USSR
2. Osman Douraliev, Bulgaria
3. Wilfried Dietrich, W. Germany
4. Stefan Stingu, Rumania
5. LARRY KRISTOFF, USA
6. Abolfazi Anvari, Iran

Greco-Roman Wrestling

Flyweight 25 competitors from 25 nations.

1. Petar Kirov, Bulgaria
2. Vladimir Bakulin, USSR
3. Miroslav Zeman, Czechoslovakia
4. Imre Alker, Hungary
5. Rolf Lacour, W. Germany
6. Jussi Vesterinen, Finland

Bantamweight 27 competitors from 27 nations.

1. Janos Varga, Hungary
2. Ion Baciu, Rumania
3. Ivan Kochergin, USSR
4. Othon Moschidis, Greece
5. Kouji Sakurama, Japan
6. Ibrahim el Sayed, UAR

Featherweight 24 competitors from 23 nations.

1. Roman Rurua, USSR
2. Hideo Fujimoto, Japan
3. Simion Popescu, Rumania
4. Ditimar Gualintchev, Bulgaria
5. Hizir Alakoc, Turkey
6. Martti Laakso, Finland

Lightweight 28 competitors from 28 nations.

1. Muneji Munemura, Japan
2. Stevan Horvat, Yugoslavia
3. Petros Galaktopoulos, Greece
4. Klaus Rost, W. Germany
5. Ero Tapio, Finland
6. WERNER HOLZER, USA
6. Gennady Sapunov, USSR

Welterweight 21 competitors from 21 nations.

1. Rudolf Vesper, E. Germany
2. Daniel Robin, France
3. Karoly Bajko, Hungary
4. Metodi Zarev, Bulgaria
5. Ion Taranu, Rumania
6. Jan Karstrom, Sweden

Middleweight 21 competitors from 21 nations.

1. Lothar Metz, E. Germany
2. Valentin Olenik, USSR
3. Branislav Simic, Yugoslavia
4. Nicolae Negue, Rumania
5. WAYNE BAUGHMAN, USA
6. Petar Kroumov, Bulgaria

Light-Heavyweight 17 competitors from 17 nations.

1. Boyan Radev, Bulgaria
2. Nikolai Yakovenko, USSR
3. Nicolae Martinescu, Rumania
4. Per Oskar Svensson, Sweden
5. Tore Hem, Norway
6. Caj Malmberg, Finland
6. Peter Jutzeler, Switzerland
6. Waclaw Orlowski, Poland

Heavyweight 16 competitors from 16 nations.

1. Istvan Kozma, Hungary
2. Anatoly Roshin, USSR
3. Petr Kment, Czechoslovakia
4. Ragnar Sten Svensson, Sweden
5. Constantin Busoi, Rumania
6. Stefane Petrov, Bulgaria

The races were held in Acapulco, Mexico's famous yachting resort and playground for millionaires. Humidity in the air, burning heat, and special meteorological and oceanic conditions—these were some of the problems the competitors had to face. They were lost without the right meteorological expert advice, and those who made best use of the tricky currents under ever-changing wind conditions fared best. The United States won two gold medals, and Great Britain, Sweden and the USSR, one gold medal each.

The **5.5 meter class** was won by the three Sundelin brothers of Sweden, Ulf, Joergen and Peter. They displayed their well-known exuberant and youthful manner, which again paid dividends. Their win was hardly ever in doubt, but there were thrills in the fight for third place. It looked like Harmstorf, Germany, and his crew would win the bronze. But Great Britain's Robin Aisher, lying well behind, decided on a gamble by breaking away and out to sea, in search of more favorable conditions of current and wind. The gamble paid dividends. The British crew won the bronze medal.
Note: In yachting, scoring is done by taking the best six of seven finish places. After each man's name in parentheses are listed his six best finish places and the total number of penalty points assessed.

Statistics: 14 entries from 14 nations, one per nation. All finished the competition.

1. Sweden, Ulf Sundelin, helmsman   (4, 1, 1, 1, 1, 1– 8.0 points)
2. Switzerland   (1, 5, 2, 2, 4, 4–32.0 points)
3. Great Britain   (6, 2, 4, 3, 3, 3–39.8 points)
4. West Germany   (2, 3, 5, 3, 9, 4–47.4 points)
5. Italy   (3, 7, 3, 1, 6, 9–51.1 points)
6. Canada   (9, 12, 7, 2, 2, 10–68.0 points)
8. USA, J. GARDNER COX, helmsman   (7, 8, 8, 4, 8, 6–74.7 points)

The **Dragon class** was most convincingly won by America's GEORGE "BUDDY" FRIEDRICHS (with BARTON JAHNCKE and GERALD SCHRECK in his boat). He had already proven before, when competing in 1966 in Oresund, Denmark, that he could beat Europe's finest; and this time he underlined the fact with the amazing total of four wins and two second places in the six best individual races which were taken into account in the marking. European honor was saved by Aage Birch, Denmark, who won the silver medal.

Statistics: 23 entries from 23 nations. All finished the competition.

1. USA, GEORGE FRIEDRICHS, helmsman and BARTON W. B. JAHNCKE and
     G. CLICK SCHRECK, crew   (2, 1, 1, 2, 1, 1– 6.0 points)
2. Denmark   (6, 1, 2, 3, 2, 2–26.4 points)
3. East Germany   (1, 2, 3, 4, 4, 4–32.7 points)
4. Canada   (3, 8, 6, 7, 7, 3–64.1 points)
5. Australia   (8, 4, 9, 2, 5, 9–65.0 points)
6. Sweden   (7, 5, 9, 6, 5, 6–71.4 points)

In the **Flying Dutchman class** Britain's Rodney Pattisson, sailing with Ian Macdonald Smith, were classes ahead of all other yachtsmen who competed. They had in Superdoccious a boat which was fitted with the latest technical developments, among them an electronic wind indicator. They were disqualified in the first of the seven races for an irregular start; their win came to nothing, and they lost 39 points. But from then on, they were more careful, and there was nothing to stop them from winning easily.

Statistics: 30 entries from 30 nations. All finished the competition.

1. Great Britain, Rodney Pattisson, helmsman   (1, 1, 1, 1, 1, 2– 3.0 points)
2. West Germany   (1, 3, 2, 2, 13, 7–43.7 points)
3. Brazil   (7, 4, 3, 3, 10, 1–48.4 points)
4. Australia   (3, 5, 3, 8, 4, 3–49.1 points)
5. Norway   (2, 2, 7, 6, 6, 5–52.4 points)
6. France   (5, 4, 9, 4, 2, 18–68.0 points)
10. USA, ROBERT JAMES, helmsman   (9, 14, 18, 15, 3, 6–97.4 points)

In the **Star class** race America added one more gold medal to its Olympic tally. LOWELL NORTH, sailing with PETER BARRETT, took revenge on Paul Elvstrom, Sweden, who had beaten him at two previous world championships. Elvstrom ended fourth. The silver medal was won surprisingly by Pede Lunde, Norway, the Flying Dutchman gold medal winner of 1960.

Yachting

1. USA, LOWELL NORTH, helmsman, PETER BARRETT, crew
            (1, 3, 3, 1, 2, 1–14.4 points)
2. Norway   (2, 1, 6, 7, 7, 2–43.7 points)
3. Italy   (2, 4, 8, 1, 4, 6–44.7 points)
4. Denmark   (3, 6, 7, 5, 1, 5–50.4 points)
5. Bahamas   (6, 2, 3, 4, 9, 14–63.4 points)
6. Australia   (4, 7, 5, 12, 6, 4–68.7 points)

The **Finn class** race was characterized by the eclipse of all those one had expected to celebrate victory or a medal. Russia's Valentin Mankin was the surprise winner and deservedly so, for his was a carefully organized and concentrated effort.

Statistics: 36 entries from 36 nations. All finished the competition.

1. USSR, Valentin Mankin, helmsman   (3, 1, 1, 2, 1, 1–11.7 points)
2. Austria   (3, 3, 4, 4, 4, 12–53.4 points)
3. Italy   (16, 7, 2, 3, 3, 3–55.1 points)
4. Australia   (4, 1, 7, 15, 16, 2–67.0 points)
5. Great Britain   (15, 12, 8, 5, 1, 4–71.0 points)
6. Finland   (8, 8, 8, 5, 5, 5–72.0 points)
13. USA, CARL VAN DUYNE, helmsman
           (Disq. – 11, 3, 10, 14, 11–117.7 points)

GRENOBLE

To call the Tenth Olympic Winter Games the "Games of Grenoble" is not a very exact statement, for most of the events were staged in the Alpine territory extending over a wide area surrounding the town. But the Games were unquestionably the "Games of France," perhaps even more than the Summer Games were those of Mexico. This is true not so much because of France's many victories and the overwhelming popularity of its great national hero, Jean-Claude Killy, but because of the entire organization of the spectacle.

These Games were meant to reflect France's regained *gloire*, and the world was duly impressed by the magnificent show the host nation staged in Grenoble. Despite the dense fogs and low clouds which played havoc with many of the competitions, and some disqualifications for breaching the Olympic competitive regulations, it was the "sport" that truly mattered, and it was the "sport" that made Grenoble magnificent. It was the young men and women on their skis and skates and those riding the bobsleds and tobbogans who stamped these Games with the mark of their skills, their courage and strength, and of course, with the imprint of their personalities. It was this that made Grenoble truly great.

Biathlon

The **biathlon** is a comparatively new Olympic sport that demands of the long distance skier that he also be an excellent marksman. It is a contest best-suited for the military and for frontier police in mountainous countries. As expected, the race was a duel between the Scandinavians and the Soviet Union, with Norway's Magnar Solberg winning the gold medal and Russia's Alexander Tikhonov, the silver. The Russian actually was the better skier, but he twice missed targets; this cost him first place.

Individual Race

Statistics: 60 participants from 16 countries. Start and finish in stadium west of Autrans. 20 kilometers race with 4 shooting exercises of 5 shots each; 1 miss = 1 minute time penalty. Highest point 1,135 meters, lowest point 1,010 meters, gradient differential 125 meters. February 12, 1968.

Results	Total time hours
1. Magnar Solberg, Norway	
2. in 1:13:45.9 hrs., no penalty	1:13:45.9
2. Aleksandre Tikhonov, USSR	
1. in 1:12:40.0 hrs. 2 min. penalty	1:14:40.0

3. Vladimir Groundartsev, USSR
   5. in 1:16:27.4 hrs. 2 min. penalty 1:18:27.4
4. Stanislaus Szczepaniak, Poland
   10. in 1:17:56.8 hrs. 1 min. penalty 1:18:56.8
5. Arve Kinnari, Finland
   8. in 1:17:47.9 hrs. 2 min. penalty 1:19:47.9
6. Nikolai Pousanov, USSR
   7. in 1:17:14.5 hrs. 3 min. penalty 1:20:14.5

In the **biathlon relay,** the situation was reversed, with the Russians taking the gold. The Swedish, however, were the better shooters. One of the early surprises was the fine performance of the American team, but imprecise shooting later on dropped them to eighth place in the end.

Relay Race

Statistics: The first time this event has been held in the Olympic Games. 14 teams from 14 countries. Autrans. Start and finish: Biathlon stadium. Every competitor lapped a 2.5 km course 3 times and there were 2 shooting exercises of 8 shots at 5 targets. The competitor had to go back 200 meters for each target he did not hit.

Results		Targets not hit	Individual times min.	Total time hours
1. USSR	Tikhonov	1	33:28.9	
	Pousanov	1	34:07.2	
	Mamatov	0	32:53.2	
	Groundartsev	0	32:33.1	2:13:02.4
2. Norway	Waerhavg	1	35:12.1	
	Jordet	2	34:06.8	
	Solberg	0	32:26.4	
	Istad	2	33:04.9	2:14:50.2
3. Sweden	Arwidson	0	34:13.3	
	Eriksson	0	35:03.8	
	Petrusson	0	35:00.0	
	Olsson	0	33:09.2	2:17:26.3
4. Poland	Rozak	2	36:46.3	
	Fiedor	1	36:40.6	
	Lukaszczyk	1	34:01.9	
	Szczepaniak	0	32:50.8	2:20:19.6
5. Finland	Suutarinen	3	38:05.0	
	Floejt	1	35:57.3	
	Vaehaekylae	0	32:52.3	
	Kinnari	1	33:47.2	2:20:41.8
6. East Germany	Kluge	1	36:48.1	
	Jahn	1	36:22.5	
	Koscha	0	35:22.7	
	Speer	2	33:21.2	2:21:54.5

Bobsled

The bobsled competition took place in the Alpe d'Huez, more than 90 minutes by car from Grenoble. The organizers took great pains and did not spare costs to improve the track by artificial means. But although parts of it were additionally frozen and also rebuilt, this alone did not suffice to make the program a success. The races were scheduled to take place in the evening. But what the organizers had not bargained for was the fact that the wind blowing from the Mediterranean kept shifting the snow onto the track, making it unusable, so that starts had to be delayed time and time again. Then, after some runs, the track would be impossible for 50 more bobs to use it; the days had been warm, and the sun had softened the surface. As a result the runs in the evenings had to be abandoned and were raced in the later stages of the competition at the unusual hour of five in the morning. It was pitch-dark and 160 searchlights along the 1,641 yard track showed the bobsledders the way.

The story of the **two-man event** became the story of Italians Eugenio Monti and Luciano de Paolis, his brakeman. Monti had his share of nine different world championship titles, but had never won an Olympic gold medal. Another favorite was the German, Horst Floth, a hotelier by profession. He was supported by his brakeman, Pepi Bader. Further serious challengers for the title were the Rumanian pair of Panturu and Neagoe, the Austrian pair Thaler and Durnthaler, and Britain's former world champions, Tony Nash and Robin Dixon.

But back to Monti. First he went into the lead. Then Floth managed in his run to be a tenth-of-a-second faster than Monti. Now it was Monti's turn to better Floth's performance and in the process to establish a new record of 1:10.05. But this was his last attempt, and Floth still had one to go. You can guess what happened: his time was 1:10.15. Now the times of all four runs were added together and what was the total? Equal time for Monti and Floth. A close competition indeed. But it wasn't the end of the story. Someone remembered that there was a special ruling for such a situation. The book of rules was consulted, and the answer gave Monti his gold medal since his team had the fastest time in the first heat.

Technical details of the Alpe d'Huez Bob run: Length of run 1,500 meters. Gradient differential 140 meters. Start 2,030 meters. Finish 1,890 meters. 6 hairpin bends, 1 labyrinth, 6 bends.

Final result obtained by addition of the times of each run.

Two-Man-Bob

Statistics: 22 bobs from 11 nations. 4 runs for each bob. February 11, 1968.

Results		1st Run min.	2nd Run min.	3rd Run min.	4th Run min.	Total min.
1. Italy I	Monti, De Paolis	1:10.13	1:10.72	1:10.64	1:10.05	*4:41.54
2. Germany I	Floth, Bader	1:10.76	1:10.43	1:10.20	1:10.15	*4:41.54
3. Rumania I	Panturu, Neagoe	1:10.20	1:11.62	1:11.31	1:11.33	4:44.46
4. Austria I	Thaler, Durnthaler	1:11.27	1:11.26	1:10.72	1:11.88	4:45.13
5. Great Britain	Nash, Dixon	1:10.57	1:11.60	1:11.77	1:11.22	4:45.16
6. USA	LAMEY, HUSCHER	1:11.30	1:11.54	1:11.04	1:12.15	4:46.03

* In the case of equal times, placing was based on fastest single run.

The **four-man bobsled** race took place on an icy and very fast track as the temperature had dropped considerably. There was a danger of a sudden thaw and the officials did not want to submit the track to a risk of collapsing, so contestants were limited to two runs. This fear was unwarranted, as it later proved, but by then the contest was already over. We shall never know what the result would have been if all four runs had been taken. At any rate, Monti and his crew won themselves a second gold medal and nobody begrudged the popular Italian his second win. There has never been a more likeable sportsman.

Four-Man-Bob

Statistics: 19 bobs from 11 nations. 2 out of four proposed runs only took place. February 17, 1968.

Results		1st Run min.	2nd Run min.	Total min.
1. Italy I	Monti, De Paolis, Zandonella, Armano	1:09.84	1:07.55	2:17.39
2. Austria I	Thaler, Durnthaler, Gruber, Eder	1:10.08	1:07.40	2:17.48
3. Switzerland I	Wicki, Candrian, Hofmann, Graf	1:10.65	1:07.39	2:18.04
4. Rumania	Panturu, Neagoe, Hristovici, Maftei	1:10.59	1:07.55	2:18.14
5. Germany I	Floth, Bader, Schäfer, Lange	1:10.49	1:07.84	2:18.33
6. Italy II	Gaspari, Cavallini, Rescigno, Clemente	1:10.24	1:08.12	2:18.36

Figure Skating

This highly popular competition was staged in the beautiful Stade de Glace in mid-town Grenoble, which was specially built for this occasion. What the spectators saw was skating of an extremely high standard. Many skaters demonstrated movements which broke completely with the traditional pattern, and extended at the same time the technical limits to a degree one would not have believed possible. It was as if this sport of grace and skill, of physical accomplishment and the art of dancing had sought for itself a new language. There might be some purists who regret this development, which would seem to be influenced by television and the prospects of rewarding professional careers in the ice revues. They may claim that these skaters have in mind first to please the crowd and only second the judges. Well, they obviously did both!

All this applies mostly to Oleg Protopopov and his wife Ludmila, who of course were fêted winners in the **pairs figure skating.** They added new laurels to their Olympic triumphs of Innsbruck and the world championships of 1963 and 1966. Seeing the Protopopovs in action, one has the impression that they are technically so highly developed that they don't need the world of gimmicks and bathos.

The 16 other pairs who competed against them must have realized that they stood no chance while trying to beat the Protopopovs in their own style. Thus, the very opposite approach of exuberant attack and a whole firework's display of new kinds of flips, jumps and pirouettes was displayed which in its scope not only enlarged the existing repertory, but also enriched it by an athletic virtuosity that set new standards for the future. Such bravura applies foremost to the USSR's Tamara Moskvina and Alexei Michine, whose free skating contained some themes and variations more complex than one would have believed possible. Still, they gained only fifth place. Tatiana Joukchesternava and Aleksandr Gorelik won the silver medal. Numbers three and four belonged to two German pairs, Margot Glockshuber and Wolfgang Danne from West Germany, and to Heidemarie Steiner and Heinz-Ulrich Walter from East Germany.

Statistics: 18 pairs from 9 nations. Grenoble, February 14, 1968.

Results	Ordinals	Total Points
1. Ludmila Beloussova/Oleg Protopopov, USSR	10	315.2
2. Tatiana Joukchesternava/Aleksandr Gorelik, USSR	17	312.3
3. Margot Glockshuber/Wolfgang Danne, W. Germany	30	304.4
4. Heidemarie Steiner/Heinz-Ulrich Walter, E. Germany	37	303.1
5. Tamara Moskvina/Aleksei Michine, USSR	44	300.3
6. CYNTHIA KAUFFMANN/RONALD KAUFFMANN, USA	58	297.0

Twenty-eight competed in the **men's figure skating,** among them such gifted and artistically endowed performers as the Austrian Emmerich Danzer, his fellow countryman Wolfgang Schwarz, the Frenchman Patrick Pera, and last but not least, the American TIMOTHY WOOD. While the first three looked like they reached their peak in Grenoble, WOOD still seems to be improving. His potential looks bigger than what he showed in the ice stadium, technically and artistically. Seeing WOOD gracefully gliding over the ice, a Pavlova or a Fonteyn come to mind, for he too is maturing slowly and steadily.

In Grenoble WOOD was, according to the judges, only good enough for the silver medal. We don't intend to take issue with them over their appraisal. But we know, on the other hand, that the system under which they had to work is open to criticism. To give higher marks to the compulsory than to the free skating is schoolmarmishly ridiculous, for it is surely just as important to show what one *can* do as well as what one *has* to do.

The above mentioned Schwarz owes his surprise-victory to this anomaly. And Danzer, who, like WOOD, did badly in the compulsory, owed his fourth place to it. He did not even win the bronze medal, which was awarded to the Frenchman Pera—a decision which to many spectators seemed somewhat bizarre. TIMOTHY WOOD was runner-up to Schwarz. Altogether, it was one of those results that happen at competitions...

Statistics: 28 participants from 14 nations. 5 compulsory figures and free-skating. The finishing order is decided on the place marks of the majority of the judges. Grenoble, February 16, 1968.

Results	Ordinals	Total Points
1. Wolfgang Schwarz, Austria	13	1904.1
2. TIM WOOD, USA	17	1891.6
3. Patrick Pera, France	31*	1864.5
4. Emmerich Danzer, Austria	29*	1873.0
5. GARY VISCONTI, USA	52	1810.2
6. JOHN MISCHA PETKEVICH, USA	56	1806.2

* The highest number of place marks gets 3rd place.

The **ladies' figure skating** had in America's PEGGY FLEMING by far the most accomplished skater. And the most popular. The way the marks were awarded showed how impressed the judges were by her performance. Yet she didn't pander to sentimental effects and didn't dance herself "into the heart" of the public. It was her very own personality, naturally expressed through her great technical command on the ice and the graceful movements of a ballerina, that won for her. What impresses most is that Peggy is a truly bewitching little person on the ice; and as her technical ability enables her to project this fully, the results are endearing and utterly convincing. Scores of other girls tried by their own means to contest Peggy's superiority—but there was never any doubt in the stadium that

PEGGY FLEMING was the reigning Queen on the ice. Her long and painstaking efforts to reach the top have at last paid dividends. She stood on the prize winners rostrum flanked by Gabriele Seyfert, East Germany (silver) and Hana Maskova, Czechoslovakia (bronze).

Statistics: 31 participants from 15 nations. 5 compulsory figures and free-skating. The finishing order is decided on the place marks of the majority of the judges. Grenoble, February 11, 1968.

Results	Ordinals	Total Points
1. PEGGY FLEMING, USA	9	1970.5
2. Gabriele Seyfert, E. Germany	18	1882.3
3. Hana Maskova, Czechoslovakia	31	1828.8
4. ALBERTINA NOYES, USA	40	1797.3
5. Beatrix Schuba, Austria	51	1773.2
6. Zsussa Almassy, Hungary	57	1757.0

Ice Hockey

The *ice hockey* competition provided one of the most exciting tournaments in memory. No dramatist could have plotted a bigger climax. Coming up to the final matches, three teams were still in the running for the gold medal: Russia, Czechoslovakia and Canada.

What made it even more exciting was that the final standings did not only depend upon how one match ended, but also on the result of another match. And all of this after the tournament's great sensation had already occurred when the Czechs upset the Russians, 5–4, in the most memorable Olympic Game in years. It was more than an ordinary athletic victory; it was a release of emotions for the Czechs, who last conquered the Soviets seven years ago.

The next day, the Czechs had what many thought would be a relatively easy match against Sweden, only to come away with a 2–2 draw, a natural letdown after their titanic effort the day before. Suddenly, the Russians had the way open and they took advantage of it by crushing the Canadians in the final, 5–0. Their teamwork was the key, although their speed and stickwork were almost equally impressive. There was little the Canadians could do.

Statistics: 14 teams from 14 countries. The tournament was held in 2 groups (A = 1–8, B = 9–14)

Results of elimination heats

West Germany – Rumania	7–0
Finland – Yugoslavia	11–2
East Germany – Norway	3–1

Results

1. USSR — Alexandrov, Blinov, Davydov, Firsov, Jonov, Konovalenko, Kouzine, Maiorov, Michakov, Moisseev, Poloupanov, Ragouline, Romichevskii, Starchinov, Vykoulov, Zaitsev, Zimine, Zinger

2. Czechoslovakia — Cerny, Dzurila, Golonka, Havel, Hejma, Holik, Hoesovsky, Hrbaty, Jirik, Klapac, Kochta, Machac, Masopust, Nadrchal, Nedomansky, Pospichil, Sevcik, Suchy

3. Canada — Bourbonnais, Broderick, Cadieux, Conlin, Dineen, Glennie, Hargreaves, Huck, Johnston, Mackenzie, Macmillan, Monteith, Mott, O'Malley, O'Shea, G. Pinder, H. Pinder, Stephenson

4. Sweden — Bengtsson, Carlsson, Dahlloef, Granholm, Hedlund, Henriksson, Holmovist, Johansson, Lundstrom, Nilsson, Nordlander, Oeberg, Olsson, Palmovist, Sjoberg, Stoltz, Svedberg, Wickberg

5. Finland — Harju, Keninonen, Ketola, Koskela, Kuusisto, Leimu, Lindstroem, Johansson, Wahlsten, Oksanen, Partinen, E. Peltonen, J. Peltonen, Rantasila, Revnamaki, Tikkonen, Ylonen

6. USA — BROOKS, CUNNIFF, DALE FALKMAN, GAUDREAU, P. HURLEY, T. HURLEY, LILYHOLM, LOGUE, MORRISON, NANNE, PARADISE, PLEAU, RIUTTA, ROSS, RUPP, STORDAHL, VOLMAR

Results of games in group A

	USSR	Czech.	Can.	Sw.	Fin.	USA	W. Ger.	E. Ger.
1. USSR	—	4–5	5–0	3–2	8–0	10–2	9–1	9–0
2. Czechoslovakia	5–4	—	2–3	2–2	4–3	5–1	5–1	10–3
3. Canada	0–5	3–2	—	3–0	2–5	3–2	6–1	11–0
4. Sweden	2–3	2–2	0–3	—	5–1	4–3	5–4	5–2
5. Finland	0–8	3–4	5–2	1–5	—	1–1	4–1	3–2
6. USA	2–10	1–5	2–3	3–4	1–1	—	8–1	6–4
7. West Germany	1–9	1–5	1–6	4–5	1–4	1–8	—	4–2
8. East Germany	0–9	3–10	0–11	2–5	2–3	4–6	2–4	—

Results of games in group B

	Yugo.	Jap.	Nor.	Rum.	Aus.	Fr.
9. Yugoslavia	—	5–1	3–2	9–5	6–0	10–1
10. Japan	1–5	—	4–0	5–4	11–1	6–2
11. Norway	2–3	0–4	—	4–3	5–4	4–1
12. Rumania	5–9	4–5	3–4	—	3–2	7–3
13. Austria	0–6	1–11	4–5	2–3	—	5–2
14. France	1–10	2–6	1–4	3–7	2–5	—

Luge

This sport is really only popular in the Alpine countries. It has only been included in the previous Olympic Games of Innsbruck, and no competitor from a non-European country has ever been in the top list of performers. The tobogganing was decided in Villard de Lans, which is about 28 miles from Grenoble. The ice *piste* was 1,094 yards long and had a vertical drop of 109 yards. The weather was far from favorable and the start had to be postponed several times.

Technical details of the run in Villard de Lans: length of run 1,000 meters. Start 1,110 meters. Finish 1,000 meters. 5 bends, 6 hairpin bends, and 1 labyrinth.
Final result obtained by addition of the times of each run.

In the **men's singles** the decision lay between competitors from Austria and the two Germanies, with a solitary Pole thrown in. The ice was thawing and that made for slow times. Schmid, Austria, won the gold medal; the two East Germans won the silver and the bronze. The Pole, Zbigniew Gawior, came fourth.

Statistics: 50 toboggans from 14 nations. 3 out of 4 proposed runs only took place. February 15, 1968.

Results	1st Run sec.	2nd Run sec.	3rd Run sec.	Total min.
1. Schmid, Austria	57.16	57.73	57.59	2:52.48
2. Köhler, E. Germany	57.68	57.47	57.51	2:52.66
3. Bonsack, E. Germany	57.90	57.63	57.80	2:53.33
4. Gawior, Poland	57.55	58.35	57.61	2:53.51
5. Feistmantl, Austria	57.78	58.06	57.73	2:53.57
6. Plenk, W. Germany	57.30	58.37	58.00	2:53.67

In the **two-man event,** which was held after everybody from countries outside Europe had already left, Klaus Bonsack and Thomas Köhler of East Germany won the gold medal; an Austrian pair the silver, and another East German pair took the bronze.

Statistics: 14 toboggans from 8 nations. February 18, 1968.

Results	1st Run sec.	2nd Run sec.	Total min.
1. Bonsack/Köhler, E. Germany	47.88	47.97	1:35.85
2. Schmid/Walch, Austria	48.16	48.18	1:36.34
3. Winkler/Nachmann, W. Germany	48.58	48.71	1:37.29
4. Plenk/Aschauer, W. Germany	48.70	48.91	1:37.61
5. Hoernlein/Bredow, E. Germany	48.80	49.01	1:37.81
6. Z. Gawior/R. Gawior, Poland	49.01	48.84	1:37.85

At last the **ladies' event** got under way, long before dawn, and was won by Ortrun Enderlein of East Germany. Places number two and four were also taken by females from beyond the Berlin Wall, while the bronze medal placing went to Erica Lechner of Italy. But the final official placing looked different, for the East German girls were all disqualified. It was alleged that they had heated their runners before the race. This makes the sleds move faster, but it is also illegal. A first-class scandal blew up, the air became thick with protests and accusations using a vocabulary that is more appropriate to the General Assembly of the United Nations then to Olympic Games. The one who benefited was Italy's Erica Lechner, who was awarded the gold medal.

Statistics: 26 toboggans from 10 nations. 3 out of 4 proposed runs only took place. February 15, 1968.

Results	1st Run sec.	2nd Run sec.	3rd Run sec.	Total min.
1. Erica Lechner, Italy	48.76	49.39	50.51	2:28.66
2. Christa Schmuck, W. Germany	49.15	49.84	50.38	2:29.37
3. Angelika Duenhaupt, W. Germany	49.34	49.88	50.34	2:29.56
4. Helena Macher, Poland	49.55	50.02	50.48	2:30.05
5. Jadwiga Damse, Poland	49.64	50.43	50.08	2:30.15
6. Dana Beldova, Czechoslovakia	49.22	50.36	50.77	2:30.35

Angela Knoesel, Anna-Maria Müller and Ortrun Enderlein (all of East Germany) were disqualified.

Skiing - Alpine - Men

The *Alpine skiing* was set in Chamrousse, the small resort known to the world from the 1967 pre-Olympic trials when three national teams left abruptly because they didn't like the accommodations. Chamrousse is about 20 miles from Grenoble and a little less than one mile higher above sea level. Although the facilities there had been considerably improved since 1967, there is still some doubt as to whether it was the best site for the Alpine events. Visibility on the mountains was quite poor, and the strong gales which swept over the snow presented serious difficulties in the downhill and slalom competitions.

The **men's downhill** course was one mile, 1,400 yards long, with a vertical drop of 831 yards. It started at the *Croix de Chamrousse* and finished in Chamrousse, along the northwest slope of the mountain. Its gradient, with a 65 percent maximum and 29 percent average, made tremendous demands on the skiers' physical and mental resources. There was only one flat section, past the extremely tricky *Col de la Balme* bump. It provided a brief respite for 500 yards; there was no other. The obligatory non-stop run (a sort of warm-up before the race) took place under a cloudless sky. The times, of course, were not recorded, but unofficial timings showed that France's Jean-Claude Killy, Austria's Gerhard Nenning, and Edmund Bruggmann of Switzerland were the fastest men on the run. There was one unfortunate accident, when BILLY KIDD of the USA fell and injured his ankle. KIDD seems to be cursed with bad luck, for he had broken his leg in training for the world championships in Portillo in 1966. But this time his injury was not serious enough to prevent him from competing in the downhill two days later.

Yes, it was two days later, because the race—scheduled for the following day—had to be postponed one day because of the fog conditions. Guy Perillat of France was the first skier over the course. He raced in great style, taking the "S" bend magnificently and finishing with a time of 1:59.93. A very good performance by the French veteran but how good, nobody could tell, for lack of comparison. Soon one could tell, for none of the next 11 skiers managed to cover the course in under two minutes. Daetwyler of Switzerland was close, at 2:00.32, while BILLY KIDD, the 12th man down, had to favor his ankle and gave no serious challenge to Perillat's time. But after him came three Frenchmen, including Killy. The *piste* was quite hard, and his skis needed re-waxing, yet there was no time. But Killy rose to the occasion, and skiing in his inimitable manner finished eight-hundredths-of-a-second ahead of Perillat. No one could challenge this time, thus Killy added the Olympic gold medal in the downhill to his world championship, with Perillat taking the silver, and Daetwyler, the bronze.

Statistics: 88 participants from 29 countries. Chamrousse, Casserousse course. Start 2,252 meters. Finish 1,412 meters. Length of course 2,890 meters. February 9, 1968.

Results	min.		min.
1. Jean-Claude Killy, France	1:59.85	4. Heinrich Messner, Austria	2:01.03
2. Guy Perillat, France	1:59.93	5. Karl Schranz, Austria	2:01.89
3. Daniel Daetwyler, Switzerland	2:00.32	6. Ivo Mahlknecht, Italy	2:02.00

The **giant slalom** was taken in two legs, on successive days, with the total time giving the results. The first *piste* was 1,970 yards long, with a 492-yard drop, the second was 23 yards shorter and had 57 gates, 13 fewer than the first. The first day was blessed with ideal conditions, but the second was practically ruined by thick snowfall and fog. Once again it was Killy ahead of the field after the first day's run, and although he was beaten by KIDD the second day, he had built such a lead that the gold medal was his easily. KIDD makes a habit of concentrating on his final runs and had a fantastic race, particularly in view of the inconsistent nature of the course and his own bandaged ankle. But his first day's performance dropped him to fifth in the final standings. After Killy came Willy Favre of Switzerland and Heini Messner of Austria, both of whom just barely edged past Perillat.

Statistics: 102 participants from 33 countries. For the first time there were two courses; first course, Simond course. Start 2,090 meters. Finish 1,650 meters. Length of course 1,800 meters. 70 gates. Second course, Piste des Vallons. The start and finish were the same as in the first course. Length of course 1,780 meters, 57 gates. February 12, 1968.

Results	First Run min.	Second Run min.	Total min.
1. Jean-Claude Killy, France	1:42.74	1:46.54	3:29.28
2. Willy Favre, Switzerland	1:43.94	1:47.56	3:31.50
3. Heinrich Messner, Austria	1:45.16	1:46.67	3:31.83
4. Guy Perillat, France	1:44.78	1:47.28	3:32.06
5. BILLY KIDD, USA	1:45.91	1:46.46	3:32.37
6. Karl Schranz, Austria	1:45.28	1:47.80	3:33.08

The **slalom** eventually turned into a comedy of errors, but for Jean-Claude Killy—who else?—it had a happy ending. He had the gods on his side and gained his third gold medal, thus emulating Toni Sailor's feat at the 1956 Games in Cortina. The first error was committed by those who insisted that the slalom be staged as an elimination race; this proved to be too tiring and cumbersome. But the participants erred too, by going on strike just before the placing race deciding the starting order for the final run. As it turned out, the placing race was abandoned anyway because of heavy fog.

The organizers retreated before the alliance of skiers and weather, reverting to the old Fédération Internationale de Ski system of assessing the slalom result on the basis of points. But just as the race began, the weather became even worse than it had been earlier, and instead of postponing the whole affair until the sun shone through again, the cardinal error was committed by allowing the race to continue. Thus the slalom was turned into an eerie show of fleeting shadows appearing and disappearing in the murky mist.

Ironically enough, the sun did make one appearance—during Killy's first run. And shine it did on France's great champion, for he came away with his third first-place medal. But even that was accompanied by more errors, this time on the part of two competitors: Haakon Mjoen of Norway and Karl Schranz of Austria. Both of them beat Killy's time, only to find out that they had missed two gates high on the course. Schranz's case was particularly strange: he told officials that he had to skid to a halt in order to avoid an observer who had suddenly crossed his path at gate 22. The officials accepted this and allowed Schranz to start over. He beat Killy's time, but was then disqualified for having missed gates 17 and 18 in the first run, before he was forced to stop at gate 22. But was the interloper responsible for his missing the gates? Why was Schranz allowed the extra run, if he missed gates before the intrusion occurred? Once he was allowed the extra run, should it have counted? These are questions too difficult for humans to answer. Austrians claimed first place for Schranz, but he was disqualified. Killy had won his third.

Statistics: 100 participants from 33 countries. Chamrousse, February 14, 1968. On two courses elimination heats were held in 8 and 9 groups respectively, in each group there were 6 competitors (4 competitors in one group). Those in 1st and 2nd place reached the final. Other elimination heats were held for the remaining competitors in which the courses were changed. The winners of each group also reached the final.

In the final of the Slalom there were 51 participants. Chamrousse, Slalom stadium. Start 1,827 meters. Finish 1,650 meters. Length of the stretch 520 meters. First run 62 gates, second run 69 gates. February 17, 1968.

Results	First Run sec.	Second Run sec.	Total min.
1. Jean-Claude Killy, France	49.37	50.36	1:39.73
2. Herbert Huber, Austria	50.06	49.76	1:39.82
3. Alfred Matt, Austria	49.68	50.41	1:40.09

4. Dumeng Giovanoli, Switzerland .	49.89	50.33	1:40.22
5. VLADIMIR SABICH, USA	49.75	50.74	1:40.49
6. Andrzei Bachleda Curus, Poland	49.88	50.73	1:40.61

Skiing - Alpine - Women

In the **women's downhill** the weather was fine and there were no scandals, disqualifications, protests, or any of the things that marred the men's events. There was only the happiness of the winners and the disappointment of the losers.

With a course 2,363 yards long and a vertical drop of 953 yards, the downhill had its start in *Croix de la Chamrousse* and its finish in the Skiing Stadium of Recoin. The event was won by a 20-year-old Austrian girl, Olga Pall. She was $^{46}/_{100}$-of-a-second faster than France's petite Isabelle Mir from the Pyrenees. Christl Haas, Austria, collected the bronze medal. The ladies' downhill used to be a purely Austrian affair, hence the delight of the French in Isabelle's success.

Statistics: 41 participants from 14 countries. The Olympic course in Chamrousse. Start 2,525 meters. Finish 1,650 meters. Length of course 2,160 meters. February 10, 1968.

Results	min.		min.
1. Olga Pall, Austria	1:40.87	4. Brigitte Seiwald, Austria	1:41.82
2. Isabelle Mir, France	1:41.33	5. Annie Famose, France	1:42.15
3. Christl Haas, Austria	1:41.41	6. Felicity Field, Great Britain	1:42.79

The women's **giant slalom** was won by Canada's Nancy Greene. Her performance was 2.64 seconds better than that of France's Annie Famose. She packed an incredible amount of attack and energy into her run, and was, in her own words, "fighting all the way." The extremely long course—1,761 yards with a 492 yard vertical drop—demanded stamina, technical skill and a good deal of courage. Nancy, a 24-year-old student at Notre Dame University, British Columbia, had all of these qualities in large measure. She was a highly popular winner.

Statistics: 49 participants from 18 countries. Gaboureaux course in Chamrousse. Start 2,101 meters. Finish 1,650 meters. Length of course 1,610 meters. 68 gates. February 15, 1968.

Results	min.		min.
1. Nancy Greene, Canada	1:51.97	4. Florence Steurer, France	1:54.75
2. Annie Famose, France	1:54.61	5. Olga Pall, Austria	1:55.61
3. Fernande Bochatay, Switzerland .	1:54.74	6. Isabelle Mir, France	1:56.07

The **slalom** was a battle between Nancy Greene, Marielle Goitschel of France, and Annie Famose, the other French slalom champion. (Marielle had won the gold medal in Innsbruck, Annie in Portillo); but at first it looked, to everyone's surprise, as if the American foursome of KIKI CUTTER, ROSIE FORTNA, WENDY ALLEN and JUDY NAGEL would spring a huge surprise for they had, in the first leg, the four fastest runs—that is before the official results were known. Then the picture changed radically: Kiki, Rosie and Wendy were all disqualified, victims of their own dashing dare-devil tempestuousness. The knowledge that she was the only American girl left must have thrown Judy's well-known excitable nature completely out of balance, for she took gate 10, and then for no obvious reason at all behaved as if she had reached the finish. She didn't know why she left the track, nor could she explain it after the race. Nancy Greene had the fastest time in the second run, but it wasn't fast enough to catch Marielle Goitschel, whose 40.27 seconds in the first leg was, on the icy *piste*, an exceptionally good performance. Annie Famose won the bronze medal.

Statistics: 49 participants from 18 countries. Chamrousse, slalom stadium. Start 1,806 meters. Finish 1,650 meters. Length of courses 425 meters; first course 56 gates, second course 57 gates. February 13, 1968.

Results	First Run	Second Run	Total
	sec.	sec.	min.
1. Marielle Goitschel, France	40.27	45.49	1:25.86
2. Nancy Greene, Canada	41.45	44.70	1:26.15
3. Annie Famose, France	42.21	45.68	1:27.89
4. Gina Hathorn, Great Britain	41.84	46.08	1:27.92
5. Isabelle Mir, France	42.14	46.08	1:28.22
6. Burgl Färbinger, W. Germany ..	42.70	46.20	1:28.90

The **500 meter race** consisted of 48 skaters racing in 24 pairs. Among them were the most illustrious names in this event —TERRY McDERMOTT of the USA, Yevgeny Grishin of the USSR, both of whom had won gold medals at previous Winter Games, and Germany's Erhard Keller, who then held the world record. In addition there were 11 other men who had at one time or other clocked under 40 seconds in the event. Therefore it was no surprise that it turned out to be a furious fight for the medals.

Keller's early time of 40.3 looked too good to be bettered by the later skaters, mainly because the rising temperatures of the sunny day caused the surface of the course to soften considerably. Last year's winner, American TERRY McDERMOTT, was last in the field of 14 pairs, with almost no chance of overcoming the conditions. He had a tremendous epening burst, covering the first 100 meters in 10.2 seconds, but he simply couldn't maintain such a torrid pace. He finished in 40.5, good enough for a tie with Norway's Magne Thomassen for second place. Grishin finished fourth.

Statistics: 48 participants from 17 nations. Olympic record: McDERMOTT (USA), 40.1 sec. (1964, Innsbruck). World record: Keller (Germany), 39.2 sec. (1968). Temp. +7.2°C, ice temp.— 4°C. Grenoble, February 14, 1968.

Results	sec.		sec.
1. Erhard Keller, Germany	40.3	5. Arne Herjuaunet, Norway	40.7
2. Magne Thomassen, Norway	40.5	5. JOHN WURSTER, USA	40.7
2. TERRY McDERMOTT, USA	40.5	5. NEIL BLATCHFORD, USA	40.7
4. Yevgeny Grishin, USSR	40.6		

The **5,000 meters** was the next contest instead of the scheduled 1,500 meters. The organizers had decided that the sprinters should get a day of respite after their 500 meters exertions. Fred Anton Maier, the 29-year-old Norwegian world champion saw his world record performance of 7:26.2 minutes bettered by Kees Verkerk, Netherlands, who reduced it by three seconds — only to beat Verkerk's fresh world record 20 minutes later by nine-tenths of a second. The Dutchman Nottet won the bronze medal, 2.3 seconds slower than Verkerk. Yet his time was — by seven-tenths of a second— faster than Maier's old world record. The limits have not nearly been reached in speed skating. As this sport gets more popular, one can look forward to a completely new set of standards.

Statistics: 38 participants from 17 countries. Olympic record: Johannesen (Norway), 7:38.4 min. (1964, Innsbruck). World record: F. A. Maier (Norway), 7:26.2 min. (1968). New Olympic record (at the same time a new world record): F.A. Maier (Norway), 7:22.4 min. Temp. +6.5°C., ice temp. —5.0°C. Grenoble, February 15, 1968.

Results	min.		min.
1. Fred Maier, Norway	7:22.4	4. Willy Guttormsen, Norway	7:27.8
2. Kees Verkerk, Netherlands	7:23.2	5. Johnny Hoeglin, Sweden	7:32.7
3. Petrus Nottet, Netherlands	7:25.5	6. Perjen Sandler, Sweden	7:32.8

The **1,500 meters** was won by Verkerk. Second best was Schenk, his fellow countryman, ahead of Eriksen, Norway.

Statistics: 53 participants from 17 nations. Olympic record: Grishin (USSR), 2:08.6 min. (1956, Cortina). World record: Thomassen (Norway), 2:02.5 min. (1968). New Olympic record: Verkerk (Netherlands), 2:03.4 min. Temp. +6.2°C, ice temp. —4.2°C. Grenoble, February 16, 1968.

Results	min.		min.
1. Kees Verkerk, Netherlands	2:03.4	4. Magne Thomassen, Norway	2:05.1
2. Ard Schenk, Netherlands	2:05.0	5. Bjoern Tveter, Norway	2:05.2
3. Ivar Eriksen, Norway	2:05.0	5. Johnny Hoeglin, Sweden	2:05.2

The **10,000 meters**, the last event of the competition, was skated unter heavy wind conditions which were a great nuisance to the skaters. Maier, the world record holder, blamed the weather for not having bettered his own best time. But this was before Sweden's Hoeglin had his chance. He didn't break Maier's record, but beat him into second place. Rarely has one seen better skating than the Swede's, marvellously spaced and sustained over the long distance. Altogether Hoeglin provided the big sensation in the men's speed skating. All the Innsbruck gold medalists failed to repeat their successes. Only McDERMOTT won at least a silver medal.

Statistics: 28 participants from 13 nations. Olympic record: Johannesen (Norway), 15:46.6 min. (1960, Squaw Valley). World record: F.A. Maier (Norway), 15:20.3 min. (1968). New Olympic record: Hoeglin (Sweden), 15:23.6 min. Temp. +2.6°C., ice temp. —4.3°C. Grenoble, February 17, 1968.

Results	min.		min.
1. Johnny Hoeglin, Sweden	15:23.6	4. Willy Guttormsen, Norway	15:32.6
2. Fred Maier, Norway	15:23.9	5. Kees Verkerk, Netherlands	15:33.9
3. Perjen Sandler, Sweden	15:31.8	6. Johnny Nilsson, Sweden	15:39.6

Speed-Skating -
Women

The **500 meter race** looked like an American victory at first. MARY MEYERS covered the distance in the fast time of 46.3 seconds. Things looked very good for the St. Paul, Minnesota, teenager, since Lydia Skoblikova of Russia was not competing this year. (Miss Skoblikova had won six of the possible eight gold medals in women's speed-skating since the events were added to the Olympic program in 1960.)

But then came another Russian, Ludmila Titova, who decided the issue by bettering Miss MEYERS' mark by two-tenths of a second. Then, in one of the Olympic Games most startling developments, two other American girls — DIANNE HOLUM and JENNIFER FISH — posted the same time as Miss MYERS, thus sharing the silver medal.

Statistics: 28 participants from 11 nations. Olympic record: Lidia Skoblikova (USSR), 45.0 sec. (1964, Innsbruck). World record: Tatiana Sidorova (USSR), 44.7 sec. (1968). Temp. +6°C., ice temp. —5°C. Grenoble, February 9, 1968.

Results	sec.		sec.
1. Ludmila Titova, USSR	46.1	2. JENNIFER FISH, USA	46.3
2. MARY MEYERS, USA	46.3	5. Elisabeth van den Brom, Holland ..	46.6
2. DIANNE HOLUM, USA	46.3	6. Sigrid Sundby, Norway	46.7

In the **1,000 meter race** Ludmila Titova gained only the silver medal, the gold being won by Carolina Geijssen, Netherlands. DIANNE HOLUM was third, but this time she collected the bronze by herself.

Statistics: 29 participants from 12 nations. Olympic record: Lidia Skoblikova (USSR), 1:33.2 min. (1964, Innsbruck). World record: Lidia Skoblikova (USSR), 1:31.8 min. (1963). New Olympic record: Carolina Geijssen (Netherlands), 1:32.6 min. Temp. +4.5°C., ice temp. —4°C. Grenoble, February 11, 1968.

Results	min.		min.
1. Carolina Geijssen, Netherlands ...	1:32.6	4. Kaija Mustonen, Finland	1:33.6
2. Ludmila Titova, USSR	1:32.9	5. Irina Egorova, USSR	1:34.4
3. DIANNE HOLUM, USA	1:33.4	6. Sigrid Sundby, Norway	1:34.5

The **1,500 meters** was won by Kaija Mustonen, Finland. Two Dutch girls took second and third place. Lidia Skoblikova, who had won this event in 1960 and 1964, was unable to do better than 11th place.

Statistics: 30 participants from 12 nations. Olympic record: Lidia Skoblikova (USSR), 2:22.6 min. (1964, Innsbruck). World record: Inga Woronina (USSR), 2:19.0 min. (1962). New Olympic record: Kaija Mustonen (Finland), 2:22.4 min. Temp. +5.5°C., ice temp. —4.0°C. Grenoble, February 10, 1968.

Results	min.		min.
1. Kaija Mustonen, Finland	2:22.4	4. Sigrid Sundby, Norway	2:25.2
2. Carolina Geijssen, Netherlands ...	2:22.7	5. Lasma Kaouniste, USSR	2:25.4
3. Christina Kaiser, Netherlands	2:24.5	6. Kaija-L. Keskivitikka, Finland ...	2:25.8

The **3,000 meters** reversed the previous Finland-Netherlands order. In this longest and last of the ladies' events, Netherlands (Johanna Schut) got the gold medal, and Kaija Mustonen the silver. Christina Kaiser of Netherlands won the bronze medal, just as she had done in the 1,500 meters. It is possible that if it hadn't rained so badly all through the race, Christina—or Stein, as she is called—would have done much better. The world record holder over the 3,000 meters certainly showed her class, but she was unlucky. The ice was already very bad when her turn came with the twelfth pair, and she also fell a victim to a bad lapse of concentration, causing her momentarily to lose her rhythm shortly before the end.

Statistics: 26 participants from 12 nations. Olympic record: Lidia Skoblikova (USSR), 5:14.3 min. (1960, Squaw Valley). World record: Christina Kaiser (Netherlands), 4:54.6 min. (1968). New Olympic record: Johanna Schut (Netherlands), 4:56.2 min. Temp. +3.8°C., ice temp. —4.5°C. Grenoble, February 12, 1968.

Results	min.		min.
1. Johanna Schut, Netherlands	4:56.2	4. Kaija-L. Keskivitikka, Finland ...	5:03.9
2. Kaija Mustonen, Finland	5:01.0	5. Wilhelmina Burgmeijer, Netherlands	5:05.1
3. Christina Kaiser, Netherlands	5:01.3	6. Lidia Skoblikova, USSR	5:08.0

The long-distance ski races, which originated in the Scandinavian mountains (and which the Nordic skiers have made their monopoly), were contested for in a 15 square mile area of the Vercors group of mountains which the French organizers named, with some imagination, "the Norway of the Alps." The little village of Autrans became the center of the Olympic interest; the competitors were housed there, and the events had their organization headquarters near by.

The **15,000 meter cross-country** posed a number of problems for the competitors. Dense fog in parts of the course, a rising temperature which had its effects on the snow, and the abnormally high degree of humidity in the air were some of them. The first three-fifths of the course were generally uphill, while the final part was downhill. Harald Groenningen, the 33-year-old Norwegian who won the event, was lucky in having a low starting number. He was fifth to start, and had no difficulty in overtaking the first four, thus having the clear track for himself. Eero Maentyranta, Finland, who gave Groenningen the expected duel, was less lucky: he had to start twenty-ninth. The outcome of the race was very close: only 1.9 seconds separated the victorious Groenningen from the Finn, thus reversing the order of four years earlier. No one outside Scandinavia was among the first eight.

Statistics: 75 participants from 25 countries. Autrans. Start and finish: Ski-stadium. Highest point 1,304 meters. Lowest point 1,056 meters. Gradient differential 248 meters. February 10, 1968.

Results	5 km min.	10 km min.	Finish min.
1. Harold Groenningen, Norway ..	16:57.1	35:06.5	47:54.2
2. Eero Maentyranta, Finland	17:06.4	34:56.9	47:56.1
3. Gunnar Larsson, Sweden	17:25.5	35:30.1	48:33.7
4. Kalevi Laurila, Finland	17:12.3	35:11.8	48:37.6
5. Jan Halvarsson, Sweden	17:26.0	35:46.9	48:39.1
6. Bjarne Andersson, Sweden	17:20.3	35:29.0	48:41.1

The **30,000 meter cross-country** provided a huge sensation. It was won by Franco Nones, the 27-year-old customs official from the Fieme Valley in the Dolomites; for the very first time, a gold medal in a Nordic event was won by a non-Scandinavian. And to prove that Italy's success was no fluke, it also had in fifth-place finisher Guilio de Florian another skier in the race who finished well ahead of many Scandinavians.

The race proceeded under ideal conditions, which suited Nones very well. He was in top condition and had undergone extensive training preparation for this distance to which the Scandinavians are not overdevoted. But this should in no way diminish the magnitude of the Italian's breakthrough. Nones began the race at a pace which nobody believed he could keep up. Events like these are always decided in the last few miles and this seemed to apply more than ever, for the course was very tough, especially in its uphill section after the first eight miles. Yet Nones forged ahead and so did Eero Maentyranta, who was generally "tipped" to win the race. He kept making up time and before the halfway stage he was clocked only some two seconds slower than Nones. But from then on, the course sloped into its down hill section, and the Italian coasted home.

Statistics: 66 participants from 22 countries. Autrans. The 30 km course consists of 2 legs of 10 and 20 km respectively. Start and finish: Ski-stadium. Highest point 1,331 meters. Lowest point 1,056 meters. Gradient differential 275 meters. February 7, 1968.

Results	20 km hours	Finish hours
1. Franco Nones, Italy	1:07:40.4	1:35:39.2
2. Odd Martinsen, Norway	1:08:12.7	1:36:28.9
3. Eero Maentyranta, Finland	1:07:44.6	1:36:55.3
4. Vladimir Voronkov, USSR	1:08:35.4	1:37:10.8
5. Giulio de Florian, Italy	1:08:48.7	1:37:12.9
6. Kalevi Laurila, Finland	1:08:18.1	1:37:29.8

The **50,000 meter cross-country** was distinguished by the fact that there was only one Scandinavian among the first three finishers; Nordic honor was preserved by Ole Ellefsaeter of Norway, who won the gold medal. Vedenine of the USSR took the silver, and Haas of Switzerland the bronze. The expected victory by Maentyranta, who started as clear favorite did not take place. It was obvious that the exertions of the previous races had not left him with sufficient reserves of strength for this marathon. It is true that the winners of the men's Nordic events were mainly in a mature age group—

around 30 is obviously the best age suited for the long distance —but the Finn was clearly a little too old to repeat those feats he had been capable of only a few years earlier. It was sad to see this great long distance skier, one of the greatest the world has ever seen, finish 15th.

The race consisted of covering the 25 kilometer circuit twice. Ole Ellefsaeter was already in a commanding position after the first leg. As the race continued, the time margin between the Norwegian and Vedenine became less and less, but the Russian had started too late; the Norwegian was already home and dry before he could better him. Haas' third place is a more significant indication for the future; it serves notice that skiers from Alpine countries can also play their part in the long distances.

Statistics: 51 participants from 18 countries. Autrans. The course consists of one 25 km leg which was lapped twice. Start and finish: Ski-stadium. Highest point 1,304 meters. Lowest point 1,056 meters. Gradient differential 248 meters. February 17, 1968.

Results	25 km hours	40 km hours	Finish hours
1. Ole Ellefsaeter, Norway ..	1:11:39.5	2:03:11.3	2:28:45.8
2. Viatchos Vedenine, USSR .	1:13:30.8	2:04:11.3	2:29:02.5
3. Josef Haas, Switzerland ...	1:13:28.1	2:04:28.0	2:29:14.8
4. Paal Tyldum, Norway	1:13:33.8	2:03:40.6	2:29:26.7
5. Melcher Risberg, Sweden .	1:12:23.4	2:04:21.2	2:29:37.0
6. Gunnar Larsson, Sweden .	1:12:50.2	2:04:14.3	2:29:73.2

The **4×10,000 meter relay** gave Norway another gold medal—for the first time ever in this event. Each one of its team, Odd Martinsen, Paal Tyldum, Harald Groenningen and Ole Ellefsaeter, clocked the fastest time over his distance. Their victory was never in doubt. The Swedish team came second, the Finnish third. But Finland owes its success only to Maentyranta's marvellous run. As last man in his team he overtook Vedenine in the last stages of the race for third place.

Statistics: 15 teams from 15 countries. Autrans. Start and finish: Ski-stadium. Highest point 1,230 meters. Lowest point 1,056 meters. Gradient differential 248 meters. February 14, 1968.

Results		Individual time min.	Total time hours
1. Norway	Martinsen	31:57.3	
	Tyldum	32:13.8	
	Groenningen	32:05.2	
	Ellefsaeter	32:17.2	2:08:33.5
2. Sweden	Halvarsson	32:37.0	
	Andersson	32:26.4	
	Larsson	32:24.4	
	Roennlund	32:45.4	2:10:13.2
3. Finland	Oikarainen	33:00.7	
	Taipale	33:16.0	
	Laurila	32:16.3	
	Maentyranta	32:23.7	2:10:56.7
4. USSR	Voronkov	32:38.4	
	Akentiev	32:32.5	
	Tarakanov	32:56.4	
	Vedenine	32:49.9	2:10:57.0
5. Switzerland	Hishier	34:27.1	
	Haas	33:02.2	
	Koch	33:45.9	
	Kaelin	34:17.2	2:15:32.4
6. Italy	De Florian	34:58.4	
	Nones	33:55.6	
	Serafin	34:09.9	
	Stella	33:28.3	2:16:32.2

Both the **women's 5,000** and **10,000 meters** were won by Toini Gustafsson, the 29-year-old sports teacher from Sweden. Considering that the women's $3 \times 5,000$ meter race was won by the Norwegian team, one can say in fairness that the superiority of the Russian girls in this field is declining. In the 5,000 meters, Toini was certainly having luck. Galina Koulakova, USSR, broke her ski and Marjatta Kajosmaa, Finland, had a bad fall in the last downhill section—but the Swedish girl showed her true and great qualities in the following 10,000 meters race, when she had to cope with quite tricky snow conditions. The way she waxed her skis was as correct as her racing was immaculate. Berit Moerdre of Norway (silver) and Inger Aufles, also Norway (bronze), were not in her class.

5 kilometers Cross-country

Statistics: 34 participants from 11 countries. Autrans. Start and finish: Ski-stadium. Highest point 1,156 meters. Lowest point 1,056 meters. Gradient differential 100 meters. February 13, 1968.

Results	min.		*Results*	min.
1. Toini Gustafsson, Sweden	16:45.2		4. Barbro Martinsson, Sweden	16:52.9
2. Galina Koulakova, USSR	16:48.4		5. Marjatta Kajosmaa, Finland	16:54.6
3. Alevtina Koltchina, USSR	16:51.6		6. Rita Achina, USSR	16:55.1

10 kilometers Cross-country

Statistics: 34 participants from 11 countries. Autrans. Start and finish: Ski-stadium. Highest point 1,195 meters. Lowest point 1,056 meters. Gradient differential 139 meters. February 9, 1968.

Results	5 km min.	Finish min.
1. Toini Gustafsson, Sweden	18:55.0	36:46.5
2. Berit Moerdre, Norway	19:18.4	37:54.6
3. Inger Aufles, Sweden	19:12.2	37:59.9
4. Barbro Martinsson, Sweden	19:15.6	38:07.1
5. Majatta Kajosmaa, Finland	19:09.6	38:09.0
6. Galina Koulkova, USSR	19:14.9	38:26.7

But these two Norwegian girls, plus Babben Enger Damon, took revenge on Toini Gustafsson and her team in the **3×5 kilometers relay race** by taking first place ahead of Sweden. The USSR had to be content with the bronze medal.

Statistics: 8 teams from 8 countries. Autrans. Start and finish: Ski-stadium. Held over the same course as the Ladies 5 kilometers cross-country. February 16, 1968

Results		Individual min.	Total time min.
1. Norway	Inger Aufles	19:08.8	
	Babben Enger Damon	19:19.5	
	Berit Moerdre	19:02.5	57:30.0
2. Sweden	Britt Strandberg	19:46.7	
	Toini Gustafsson	18:56.7	
	Barbro Martinsson	19:07.6	57:51.0
3. USSR	Alevtina Koltchina	19:32.8	
	Rita Achina	19:31.2	
	Galina Koulakova	19:09.6	58:13.6
4. Finland	Senja Pusula	19:32.4	
	Marjatta Oikkonen	19:51.6	
	Marjatta Kajosmaa	19:21.1	58:45.1
5. Poland	Weronika Budny	19:33.8	
	Josefa Czerniawska	19:59.1	
	Stefania Biegun	19:31.8	59:04.7
6. East Germany	Renate Kohler	20:01.9	
	Gudrun Schmidt	19:27.3	
	Christine Nestler	20:05.0	59:33.9

Nordic Combined

The **Nordic combined** consisted of three jumps from the Autrans "normal" jump platform, of which the two best jumps are counted, and a 15 kilometer cross-country race. There were 41 competitors. One expected the Scandinavians to win, for they had collected 22 medals out of a total of 27 at nine previous Olympic Games. This time, Sweden dropped out altogether, while Finland and Norway could do no better than finish in the group which occupied from 20th to 40th place. No valid explanation is available for this; one is therefore forced to the conclusion that the rest of the world has overtaken the Nordics by means of specialized up-to-date training methods of their own. Germany especially has made great strides in that respect and the victory of Franz Keller was fully justified, although it was by the closest margin imaginable. Had this event consisted only of the jump, the German would have had nothing to worry about. But over the 15 kilometer race he had to face the challenge of the Swiss, Alois Kaelin, a magnificent long-distance skier. Kaelin covered the distance faster than Keller, but not fast enough to sufficiently correct his low-point position due to indifferent jumping.

The final yards of the race became an exciting thriller, with Keller in the lead, but Kaelin—who had started three-and-a-half minutes after him—came closer and closer. Had Kaelin been able to produce a speed of only 2.3 seconds faster, he would have won the event. As it was, Keller took the gold medal. Kaelin had to be satisfied with the silver.

Statistics: 41 participants from 13 countries. Autrans. Jump from the ordinary platform. Each competitor has 3 jumps with the 2 best, on points, counting. February 10, 1968. 15 km cross-country in Autrans. Highest point 1,270 meters. Lowest point 1,056 meters. Gradient differential 214 meters. February 11, 1968.

Results	Jump	C-c.	Total points
1. Franz Keller, W. Germany	240.10	208.94	449.04
2. Alois Kaelin, Switzerland	193.20	254.79	447.99
3. Andreas Kunz, E. Germany	216.90	227.20	444.10
4. Tomas Kucera, Czechoslovakia	217.40	216.74	434.14
5. Ezio Damolin, Italy	206.00	223.54	429.54
6. Josef Gasienica, Poland	217.70	211.08	428.78

Results of Ski-jump	Distance m	Points	Total points
1. Franz Keller, W. Germany	73.0	118.1	
	77.5	122.0	
	77.0	81.3	240.1
8. Josef Gasienica, Poland	67.5	100.2	
	72.5	112.7	
	71.5	105.0	217.7
9. Tomas Kucera, Czechoslovakia	72.0	109.2	
	73.0	108.2	
	71.5	102.6	217.4
10. Andreas Kunz, E. Germany	72.5	109.3	
	72.0	105.8	
	74.0	107.6	216.9
13. Ezio Damolin, Italy	70.0	103.4	
	71.5	102.6	
	71.0	99.4	206.0
24. Alois Kaelin, Switzerland	61.0	73.1	
	71.0	97.8	
	69.5	95.4	193.2

Results of 15 km Cross-country	5 km min.	10 km min.	15 km min.	Points
1. Alois Kaelin, Switzerland	16:26.6	33:55.3	47:21.5	254.79
3. Andreas Kunz, E.Germany	17:16.8	35:28.2	49:19.8	227.20
4. Ezio Damolin, Italy	17:06.3	35:30.2	49:36.2	223.54
6. Tomas Kucera, Czechoslovakia	17:27.3	36:03.5	50:07.7	216.74
11. Josef Gasienica, Poland	17:04.2	35:40.7	50:34.5	211.08
13. Franz Keller, W.Germany	17:29.9	36:35.5	50:45.2	208.94

The **special jump** from the **70-meter** platform at Autrans was won by Czechoslovakia's Jiri Raska. His first jump of 79 meters (1,864 yards) gave him an advantage he never relinquished. Two Austrians took the silver and bronze medals.

Statistics: 58 participants from 17 nations. Ordinary Autrans platform. 2 jumps for each competitor. 5 judges eliminating highest and lowest markings. Critical point: 70 meters. February 11, 1968.

Results	Meters	Points	Total Marks
1. Jiri Raska, Czechoslovakia	79.0	115.2	
	72.5	101.3	216.5
2. Reinhold Bachler, Austria	77.5	107.8	
	76.0	106.4	214.2
3. Baldur Preiml, Austria	80.0	113.8	
	72.5	98.8	212.6
4. Bjorn Wirkola, Norway	76.5	108.7	
	72.5	103.3	212.0
5. Topi Mattila, Finland	78.0	111.1	
	72.5	100.8	211.9
6. Anatoly Jeglanov, USSR	79.5	110.0	
	74.5	101.5	211.5

The **special jump** from the **90-meter** platform at St. Nizier became an exciting duel between Raska and Vladimir Beloussov of Russia, with the Russian defeating the Czech by only half-meter on both jumps. Lars Grini of Norway collected the bronze medal. Scandinavia had only one finisher in the top group. Bjorn Wirkola of Norway finished 12th, despite having been installed as the pre-Games favorite. This represents a major decline for the Nordic countries, who took both gold medals in the special jumps at the 1964 Winter Games in Innsbruck.

Statistics: 58 participants from 17 nations. The big Saint-Nizier platform. 2 jumps for each competitor. 5 judges eliminating highest and lowest markings. Critical point: 90 meters. February 18, 1968.

Results	Meters	Points	Total Marks
1. Vladimir Beloussov, USSR	101.5	118.0	
	98.5	113.3	231.3
2. Jiri Raska, Czechoslovakia	101.0	116.3	
	98.0	113.1	229.4
3. Lars Grini, Norway	99.0	111.5	
	93.5	102.8	214.3
4. Manfred Queck, E. Germany ...	96.5	104.0	
	98.5	108.8	212.8
5. Bent Tomtum, Norway	98.5	108.3	
	95.0	103.9	212.2
6. Reinhold Bachler, Austria	98.5	107.3	
	95.0	103.4	210.7